T0329048

The Security Council

'*To sail into the future is even worse than to sail the ocean. There is nothing there. The future will be what men and circumstances make it.*'

Leo Tolstoy

Richard Hiscocks

The
Security
Council

A Study in Adolescence

THE FREE PRESS
A Division of Macmillan Publishing Co., Inc.
NEW YORK

The Free Press
A Division of Macmillan Publishing Co., Inc.
866 Third Avenue, New York, N.Y. 10022

This Edition is reprinted by arrangement with Longman Group Limited

Library of Congress Catalog Card Number: 73-18457

Printed in the United States of America

printing number

1   2   3   4   5   6   7   8   9   10

ISBN 978-1-4165-7773-7   ISBN 1-4165-7773-4

To the Memory

of

Martin Wight

Realist and Idealist

Contents

A*

Preface

In this volume I have attempted a general assessment of the United Nations Security Council during the first quarter of a century of its existence; to be precise, from its first meeting in January 1946 until April 1972. The book falls naturally into three parts. The first includes an introduction, a summary of the historical background, an account of the Council's constitution and functions, as laid down in the Charter, and of the way in which it turned out in practice, and a chapter on procedure. The second part consists of one long chapter covering most of the more important cases with which the Council has been called upon to deal. For the sake of clarity it has been divided into sections, mainly on a geographical basis, an arrangement which has certain disadvantages but, I think, nothing like so many as a purely chronological plan would involve. The last part comprises three chapters dealing with aspects of the subject which can best be handled in the light of the preceding survey and a conclusion in which I have given my personal views on the Council's future and the measures that are needed to further its satisfactory development.

My own participation in UN activities has been limited to the years 1952 to 1962, when I was the United Kingdom member of the Sub-Commission on Prevention of Discrimination and Protection of Minorities. This assignment took me to New York for about three weeks every year, enabled me to gain some acquaintance with the atmosphere and procedures at UN headquarters, and gave me opportunities to attend meetings of the Security Council as a visitor from time to time. During the period November 1970 to June 1972, most of which I spent in the United States, I was also a frequent visitor to UN headquarters, had many conversations with members of the Secretariat and the national missions, and attended meetings of the Council.

Too few of the leading figures in the UN's history have recorded their experiences in writing, and the gaps left in this respect by the premature deaths of Dag Hammarskjöld and Ralph Bunche are a

serious loss. Anyone, therefore, who is engaged in research on the
Security Council, must depend a great deal on supplementing the
information available in the documents and secondary sources, by
conversations with present and former representatives on the Council
and the members of the relevant departments of the Secretariat.

I owe much to the kindness and patience of innumerable people at
UN headquarters and of my academic colleagues. I have also been very
fortunate in having conversations with a number of those who have
played key roles in the UN's activities. I cannot mention by name all
who have been involved and to the great majority I can only express my
deep gratitude anonymously. But, at the risk of being invidious, I
wish to thank especially U Thant, Lieutenant-General E. L. M. Burns,
Lord Caradon, Professor Inis L. Claude, Sir Colin Crowe, Ambassador
A. A. Farah, Lord Gladwyn, Miss Sheila Harden, Dr Kurt Herndl,
Ambassador Max Jakobson, Judge Philip C. Jessup, Major-General
I. J. Rikhye, Mr George Ivan Smith, Dean Francis O. Wilcox, and the
following to whom I am greatly indebted for reading and commenting
on all or substantial parts of my typescript: Mr T. H. M. Baker, Lieu-
tenant-General Wolf Count von Baudissin, Dr F. Y. Chai, Dr Rosalyn
Higgins, Lady Jackson, Miss Elizabeth Monroe, Mr Anthony Parsons,
Dr W. R. Polk, Miss Ruth Russell, Colonel C. H. M. Toye, and Mr Brian
Urquhart, although the responsibility for all mistakes and deficiencies
is entirely mine. Regrettably Urquhart's fine book on Hammarskjöld
did not appear until after my typescript had gone to the publishers. I
am indebted also to the late Mr Lester Pearson for receiving me, and
I remember with affectionate gratitude the kindness of Dr Ralph
Bunche, who, by pointing out some years ago the gap in the existing
literature, first gave me the idea of writing this book.

I am most grateful to the University of Sussex for giving me two years'
leave of absence to enable me to work on the book; to the Social
Science Research Council and the Norman Angell Benefaction for
grants in support of the project; to the Center of International Studies
at Princeton University for making me a Visiting Fellow during the
winter of 1970–71 and thus providing me with an academic home near
New York and ideal conditions in which to work; and to the Board of
Directors of the Adlai Stevenson Institute of International Affairs for
appointing me to a Fellowship during the academic year 1971–72. My
close connection since its foundation with the Institute for the Study of
International Organization at the University of Sussex has also been
advantageous to my work.

Finally, I should like to thank my research assistants, Mr Richard

Coldwell and Mr Richard Stanton of the University of Sussex and Monsieur J. G. Rozenberg of the University of Brussels for their valuable help with the research for Chapter 6. I am very grateful to the staffs of all the libraries in which I have worked, in particular for the unfailing courtesy and personal interest of the Librarians and staffs at the Royal Institute of International Affairs and the Carnegie Endowment for International Peace, on whom I depended a great deal.

Sussex   RICHARD HISCOCKS
November 1972

List of Abbreviations

ECOSOC	Economic and Social Council
EEC	European Economic Community
GOC	Good Offices Committee (Indonesia)
MAC	Mixed Armistice Commission
OAS	Organization of American States
OAU	Organization of African Unity
OECD	Organization for Economic Co-operation and Development
ONUC	UN Operation in the Congo (Organisation des Nations Unis au Congo)
SCOR	Security Council Official Records
UAR	United Arab Republic
UDI	Unilateral Declaration of Independence (Rhodesia)
UNCI	UN Commission for Indonesia
UNCIP	UN Commission for India and Pakistan
UNEF	UN Emergency Force
UNFICYP	UN Force in Cyprus
UNIPOM	UN India-Pakistan Observation Mission
UNITAR	UN Institute for Training and Research
UNMOGIP	UN Military Observer Group in India and Pakistan
UNOGIL	UN Observation Group in Lebanon
UNSCOB	UN Special Committee on the Balkans
UNSCOP	UN Special Committee on Palestine
UNTEA	UN Temporary Executive Authority
UNTSO	UN Truce Supervision Organization
UNYOM	UN Yemen Observation Mission

1
Introduction

When the United Nations Organization was formed after the second World War, one of its principal organs, the Security Council, was given 'primary responsibility for the maintenance of international peace and security'. The UN is the second great organization in world history which has had the broad and noble aims of avoiding war and furthering international cooperation. The Security Council itself is the first international body which has been given the specialized task of maintaining peace and security; in fact, of doing away with war and one of its main causes, insecurity.

War has been a characteristic human activity throughout most of recorded history. The reaction against it has probably always been a concurrent phenomenon and can be observed in Greek, Roman, and medieval times. The Athenians, who raised the arts of peace to a superb level, were also brave and accomplished warriors, and their great intellectual and cultural achievements were based on naval and military, as well as political, success. But during the Peloponnesian War Aristophanes devoted three of his comedies to the human craving for peace. In her campaign to bring an end to the war, Lysistrata, the Athenian heroine of one of the plays, organized Greek women in a strike against sleeping with their husbands, until the men stopped fighting. Plato believed in humanizing warfare between Greek states and also advocated certain standards of military decency in wars against foreigners.

The Romans evolved a distinction between just and unjust wars, and this line of thought was developed by Christian writers during the Middle Ages. In his *Republic*, Cicero wrote: 'A war is never undertaken by the ideal State, except in defence of its honour or its safety . . . those wars are unjust which are undertaken without provocation.' Christian doctrine on the subject was stated with greatest authority by St Augustine in the early fifth century and by St Thomas Aquinas in the thirteenth century. They agreed that three conditions were necessary for a war to be just: first, the authorization of the ruler within whose competence it lies to declare war; secondly, a just cause, that is, that those who are attacked for some offence merit such treatment; and thirdly, a right intention on the part of the belligerents, either of achieving some good object or of avoiding some evil. This third condition laid itself open to flexible interpretation and, taken strictly, could put most wars into the unjust category. St Thomas wrote:

> So it can happen that even when war is declared by legitimate authority and there is just cause, it is, nevertheless, made unjust through evil intention. St Augustine says in *Contra Faustum* (LXXIV): 'The desire to hurt, the cruelty of vendetta, the stern and implacable spirit, arrogance in victory, the thirst for power, and all that is similar, all these are justly condemned in war.' (*Summa Theoloigca*, Qu. 40, Art. 1).

Unjust wars were condemned both by legal theorists and Church authorities.

But even the concept of the just war had the effect of accentuating the barbarity of war as well as, ultimately, the strength of the reaction against it. If the just war was God's instrument for punishing the wicked, then in waging it the same cruelty and lack of restraint was appropriate, on a larger scale, as was applied in medieval times to the punishment of criminals within a state.

By the end of the Middle Ages, separate sovereign states were emerging in Europe and the medieval ideals of a universal state and a universal Church gave way to a new secular order of society. A period followed during which interstate rivalry and religious conflict led to a series of bitter, sometimes devastating wars, and against this background a thinker fittingly appeared, who saw the need for a system of law to regulate the dealings of the new states with one another both in peace and war. Hugo Grotius's great treatise, *De jure belli ac pacis*, was written in 1623 and 1624, during the Thirty Years War, one of the most cruel conflicts in European history. In his Prologemena to this work Grotius wrote:

> Throughout the Christian world I observed a lack of restraint in relation to war, such as even barbarous races should be ashamed of; I observed that men rush to arms for slight causes, or no cause at all, and that when arms have once been taken up there is no longer any respect for law, divine or human.

Grotius concerned himself systematically with the just causes of war. Rejecting the idea that in war all laws are in abeyance, he maintained, on the contrary, that they should be carried on 'only within the bounds of law and good faith'. He considered the concept of the just war to mean that the subjects of a state might refuse to do military service in a war they thought to be unjust, thus anticipating the dilemma of some modern conscientious objectors.

During the seventeenth, eighteenth and nineteenth centuries the reaction against war took a new and more practical form, when a series of plans were put forward by statesmen and speculative thinkers for the setting up of institutions, which aimed at the more peaceful ordering of European society. Four of the most interesting were the work of the Duke of Sully, best known as the minister of Henry IV of France, the Quaker, William Penn, the Abbé de St Pierre, and the British foreign secretary, Lord Castlereagh. The plans had two characteristics in common: they were all drawn up in time of war, when the peoples of Europe were tired of conflict, and they all had features which were to recur in later European peace projects.

Sully's Grand Design, which he attributed to Henry IV and Elizabeth I of England, was made known to the world in his memoirs published in 1638 during the Thirty Years War; William Penn's *Essay towards the Present and Future Peace of Europe* appeared in 1693 during the War of the League of Augsburg; St Pierre's *Perpetual Peace* was published in 1712 towards the end of the War of the Spanish Succession; and Castlereagh's proposal for periodic meetings of the Quadruple Alliance was made when Europe was exhausted by the Napoleonic Wars.

The first three plans all provided for the setting up of a European council, senate, or parliament, representative of the different states. They aimed at peace and disarmament, under Sully's and St Pierre's proposals by curbing the right of individual rulers to make war and creating a composite international army, or in the case of Penn's scheme by the military collaboration of members of the European assembly, each providing a small force in the common cause. In every case enforcement action was envisaged against any member of the alliance or federation that was disloyal to its covenant. Castlereagh's plan for periodic but more informal meetings of the great powers set a pattern for international collaboration for peace which has influenced the British approach to the subject ever since.

In 1795, during the French Revolutionary Wars, appeared Kant's *Perpetual Peace: a philosophical sketch*, the most profound and stimulating essay on the subject ever written. To obtain a balanced view of Kant's ideas on the matter this work should be studied in conjunction with his other writings.[1] His approach differs from the plans just

[1] In particular *The Idea of a Universal History from a Cosmopolitan Point of View*, 1784, and *The Principle of Progress, considered in connection with the Relation of Theory to Practice in International Law*, 1793.

considered in that he is less concerned with specific institutional proposals and deals rather with the problem from a broadly analytical and philosophical viewpoint. His contribution can be summarized in a simplified form by describing four of his main ideas on the subject.

First, men's vanity, envy, and possessiveness lead to so much toil and suffering that, just as men organize civil constitutions regulated by law to avoid the evils of anarchy, so after many 'devastations' and 'exhaustion of their powers' the 'nations are driven forward to the goal which Reason might well have impressed upon them, even without so much sad experience.'[2] This trend is reinforced by 'the spirit of commerce', which, being incompatible with war, 'sooner or later gains the upper hand'.[3]

Secondly, the goal in question is 'the advance out of the lawless state of savages and the entering into a Federation of Nations'.[4] Kant is under no illusions about the difficulty of attaining the goal. The establishment of a continuously growing state of nations (*civitas gentium*) or world republic is desirable but men 'reject in practice what is correct in theory' and 'if all is not to be lost, there can be . . . only the negative surrogate of an alliance or federation (*Bund*) which averts war . . . and holds back the stream of those hostile passions which fear the law'.[5]

Thirdly, the only way of moving gradually towards perpetual peace is by ensuring that after every war

> the period following it shall be less and less a mere negative period . . . an interval between one war and another, and more and more a positive period in which constructive attempts are made to *establish* peace on a firmer and more lasting basis. Let, therefore, such wars as from time to time unhappily will still occur be conducted honourably and not in such a way as will further wreck confidence and respect; let the peace treaty which concludes each be, not vindictive merely, but open, generous and constructive; and above all let each succeeding period of peace be one of serious and unceasing effort on all sides towards lessening the causes of further outbreaks.[6]

Kant deals with this point mainly in his Preliminary Articles for Perpetual Peace among States, the fifth of which has a special relevance in the second half of the twentieth century: 'No state shall by force interfere with the constitution or government of another state.'

[2] *The Idea of a Universal History*, p. 15.
[3] *Perpetual Peace*, first supplement, penultimate para.
[4] *The Idea of a Universal History*, p. 15.
[5] *Perpetual Peace*, Second Definitive Article.
[6] This summary of Kant's view is quoted from the article by John Bourke, 'Kant's doctrine of perpetual peace', *Philosophy*, 1942, p. 330.

Finally, Kant's First Definitive Article for Perpetual Peace lays down that 'the civil constitution of every State should be republican'.[7] Such a constitution, he considered, gives a favourable prospect for perpetual peace because the consent of the citizens would be needed for going to war. Under a non-republican constitution the ruler may 'resolve on war as on a pleasure party for the most trivial reasons', thus infringing Kant's categorical imperative, which lays down that human beings are to be treated always as ends, never merely as means. If, however, 'the consent of the citizens is required in order to decide that war should be declared . . . nothing is more natural than that they would be very cautious in commencing such a poor game, decreeing for themselves all the calamities of war.'

Whereas lawyers, statesmen, and philosophers dealt systematically with the problems of peace and war, great creative writers and artists, though respecting and sometimes extolling the martial virtues, made some of the most powerful and influential protests against the futility and horrors of war. Shakespeare, with his intense and typically Elizabethan patriotism, painted a noble and admiring portrait of the warrior king, Henry V, but set it within the framework of the timidity, the cynicism, the grief, and the aversion to war of ordinary human beings. Goya was so bound up in his art and so non-political by nature that he could come to terms with the different political regimes in his country that resulted from Napoleon's invasion, but his humanity, his imagination, his patriotism, and his realism led him to produce the series of eighty-five engravings, known as *The Disasters of War*, which, with some of his war paintings, are perhaps the greatest artistic indictment of the injustice and savagery of war. Tolstoy, as a young man, served as a cadet and an officer in the Caucasus and the Crimea, was awarded a decoration for bravery, and was disappointed that owing to a mischance he never actually received it. He wrote one article on Sevastopol in a patriotic mood, which was received with public enthusiasm and approved by the Tsar, but, shortly afterwards, a second article on the same subject, in which he condemned war and dwelt on its meaner aspects, had to be altered before publication was allowed. Later in *War and Peace* Tolstoy produced his masterly critique of war based on personal experience, deep insight, and wide knowledge of history and human nature. His relentless exposure of the wastefulness and suffering caused by war was all the more impressive for its restraint and objectivity and for his continued appreciation of the

[7] *Perpetual Peace*, Section II.

discipline and heroism shown by the participants in the campaigns and battles of the Napoleonic period. Finally, in his old age Tolstoy strongly denounced war and maintained that the sentiment of patriotism was incompatible with Christianity, an attitude which led to his being excommunicated by the Synod of the Russian Orthodox Church and placed under police supervision.

In 1815, at the end of the Napoleonic Wars, Europe for more than twenty years had been suffering almost without a break from large-scale wars, which for most of the time had involved the greater part of the continent. Very naturally the statesmen and peoples of Europe alike reacted strongly against this experience and were hoping for a period of prolonged peace. The result was that throughout the nineteenth century, and in fact almost until the outbreak of the World War in 1914, the first serious experiments were made in semi-institutionalized international cooperation for the purpose of avoiding war. These were important as precursors of the two more formal experiments in international organization that have been made in the twentieth century and will be dealt with in the next chapter. But, as a consequence of their partial success and of the main interest of Great Britain, the dominant power at the time, being commercial and colonial, Europe was, on the whole, freer from war during the nineteenth century than at any time since the beginning of interstate rivalry at the close of the Middle Ages.

Nevertheless, two developments occurred in the nature of war at this time which held dangers for the future. In the first place, the nineteenth century was the heyday of democratic nationalism, and war came then to be looked on less as an instrument for serving the ambition of selfish rulers than as a means of furthering national liberation movements. It played an essential part in the unification of Italy and Germany and in freeing the Greeks and other Balkan peoples from Turkish rule. As a result, Bismarck's use of war was in the end approved by the great majority of German liberals, and war came to be regarded as more respectable by liberal idealists and nationalists in every country, an attitude which has been carried over to the anticolonial era in the twentieth century. Secondly, scientific and industrial progress had a decisive influence on the character and availability of weapons. The second half of the nineteenth century saw the general introduction of the breech-loading rifle and the development of the machine-gun, and by the end of the century weapon ranges were forty times greater than in the days of Napoleon. These technical improvements were made much more significant and formidable by progress in modern methods of mass production and by the introduction of conscription, first in France and Germany, and later in most countries with modern professional armies.

The first World War made clear in practice the implications of applying recent scientific inventions to methods of warfare and resulted in the strongest and most constructive popular reaction against war that the world had yet seen. The use on a vast scale of machine-guns, modern artillery, and high explosives led to immense loss of life over a long period with, on the western front, a minimum of military result. Poison gas and tanks were also employed for the first time, while aerial bombing, though on a small scale compared to later wars, brought some civilians into the front line, and the organization of blockades by both sides with the aid of submarines and surface vessels involved the whole population of some combatant countries in the war to an unprecedented degree. The consequent protest against war was reinforced by the conviction, especially of the better informed, that the whole conflict could have been avoided and that there was no logical reason why the murder of two individuals in Sarajevo should have involved most of Europe in hostilities.

In 1909 a remarkable book appeared by the English publicist, Norman Angell, entitled *The Great Illusion*. Within a few years it had been reprinted many times and had been translated into seventeen different languages. The subtitle of the book was *A Study of the Relation of Military Power to National Advantage*, and in it Angell refuted with great knowledge, clarity, and conviction the assumption that a nation's relative prosperity is broadly determined by its political power. War, he wrote, even when victorious, can no longer achieve the economic aims for which peoples strive. 'The warlike nations do not inherit the earth; they represent the decaying human element.'[8] The reception given to *The Great Illusion* throughout the world showed the widespread interest at the time in the problem of war and its avoidance, and this was revealed also by the growth of peace movements during the first World War, especially in Britain and the United States, which played a part, as will be seen, in the creation of the League of Nations. Another writer, G. Lowes Dickinson, in two books, *The European Anarchy* (1916) and *The International Anarchy, 1904–1914* (1926), made the simple point, backed by substantial historical illustration, that just as citizens require the controlling authority of the State to order their relations with one another, so states in their relations with one another need to be controlled by some international legal order. 'Modern war,'

[8] Angell's synopsis in *The Great Illusion.*

he wrote in his preface to the latter book, 'with all the resources of science at its disposal, has become incompatible with the continuance of civilization.'

The popular aversion to war in 1918, combined with the efforts of a number of statesmen, headed by President Wilson, General Smuts, and Lord Robert Cecil, led to the formation of the League of Nations, and the twenty years between the two World Wars saw the first systematic attempts to organize peace and reduce armaments on a worldwide scale. In 1928 the great majority of states signed and ratified the Briand-Kellogg Pact, by which they renounced war as an instrument of national policy. Six years later a Peace Ballot was organized in Britain by voluntary effort, and over eleven and a half million people recorded their votes, more than eleven million of them being in favour of the League of Nations. But the League failed in its main purpose, to avert a major war, because it required more of its members than they were ready to give, and because its most powerful potential supporter, the United States, did not become a member at all.

During the 1930s it was said by Stanley Baldwin, and repeated frequently by others, that one more war in the West would mean the end of European civilization. This prophecy came much nearer to fulfilment than many people now realize. In August 1941, in their joint declaration, known as the Atlantic Charter, two such hardheaded statesmen as President Roosevelt and Winston Churchill stated the need to abandon the use of force and to disarm potential aggressors 'pending the establishment of a wider and permanent system of general security'. When their implied aspiration after a system of general security was realized in the United Nations Charter, the Security Council was given unprecedented responsibility and potential power, by the provision for armed forces to maintain or restore peace and by receiving authority to act on behalf of the whole membership of the UN. The Council's 'primary responsibility for the maintenance of international peace and security' gives it a unique position in the world, and the significance of this position has become greater owing to the fundamental changes in the international setting that have taken place in recent years.

The jet engine and the self-propelling rocket have altered the meaning of distance and made the world relatively smaller and more compact, thus strengthening the possibilities for cooperation but increasing the pretexts for conflict. The contrasts in standards of living between advanced and backward countries have become greater, and improved communications have made them better known and therefore less tolerable. Improvements in medicine and social administration have accelerated the growth of population, while sources of supply are being wasted and contaminated. Causes of future tension are in this way being steadily built up. Most important of all, failure to maintain international peace and security today may mean the outbreak of nuclear war.

2
Background

The antecedents of the Security Council can be traced back to the years immediately following the Napoleonic Wars. During the wars members of the Alliance against Napoleon became exasperated by his repeated aggressions and began to see the need for some permanent arrangement to maintain peace. By the Treaty of Chaumont, which was signed in March 1814, a month before Napoleon abdicated, the four powers, Britain, Austria, Russia, and Prussia, bound themselves first to overthrow Napoleon and then to remain in alliance for twenty years to maintain the settlement to be reached as soon as Napoleon had been defeated. In the autumn of the following year, after Napoleon's escape from Elba and Waterloo, another Quadruple Alliance treaty was signed, which renewed the arrangements made at Chaumont and contained in its sixth article a plan for ordering the affairs of Europe. The essence of the plan was summed up in the statement that the four powers 'have agreed to renew their meetings at fixed periods . . . for the purpose of consulting upon their common interests, and for the consideration of measures . . . most salutary for the repose and prosperity of Nations and for the maintenance of the peace of Europe'. The article was mainly the work of Castlereagh. It formed the basis for the Concert of Europe and contained the 'germ of international government'.[1]

In accordance with the terms of the Quadruple Alliance four European Congresses were held in quick succession between 1818 and 1822. The most successful of these was the Congress of Aix-la-Chapelle in 1818. It resulted in the evacuation of France by the Allied Army of occupation—in marked contrast to French treatment of Germany after the first World War—the inclusion of France in a new Quintuple Alliance consisting of France and the four powers, and an

---

[1] A phrase used by A. J. Grant and Harold Temperley in *Europe in the Nineteenth and Twentieth Centuries (1789–1932)*.

invitation to France to take part in any further periodic meetings that might be arranged. But it soon became clear that the attitude of the Tsar Alexander and the Austrian Chancellor, Metternich, to the so-called Congress System was very different from that of Castlereagh. In the autumn of 1815 Alexander had persuaded nearly all the sovereigns of Europe to sign the Declaration of the Holy Alliance by which they bound themselves to conform to Christian principles in their relations with one another and with their subjects. The Alliance developed in effect into a league of reactionary monarchs against revolution, and at the Congresses of Troppau and Laibach in 1820 and 1821 Castlereagh became involved in controversy with Alexander and Metternich regarding the attitude that should be taken to revolutionary and constitutional movements in Spain and Italy. Alexander and Metternich on the whole favoured joint action to maintain the *status quo*, while Castlereagh laid down the principle that no state should interfere by force in the internal affairs of another, a principle that was to become a guideline of future British policy. The Congress of Verona in 1822 broke down on this issue, and the system of frequent meetings of the great powers came to an end.

But Castlereagh's plan for periodic meetings continued to exercise considerable influence on European affairs almost up to the eve of the first World War, though sometimes it had decisive results, while sometimes it was relatively in abeyance. It is convenient to confine the term 'Congress System' to the experiment that was carried out between 1815 and 1822. The tendency of the great powers to meet together to preserve peace or discuss matters of common interest has been described by historians as the Concert of Europe, the Council of Europe, or the Conference System. The Concert of Europe is perhaps the best expression of the three, because it indicates the habit of the powers to take concerted action, while leaving flexible the form the action might take.

The Concert did, in fact, take several forms. Sir Charles Webster, a leading authority on the subject, in his lecture, 'The Council of Europe in the nineteenth century'[2], makes a distinction between a *congress* which he defines as 'a meeting of the great powers, with or without other powers, at which heads of government or Foreign Ministers are present' and a *conference*, which is a meeting 'of ambassadors or men of similar position except for the representative of the power on whose territory the meeting takes place'. He then reckons that during

[2] Included in his *The Art and Practice of Diplomacy*.

the century between 1814 and 1914 there were eighteen conferences and eight congresses, the congresses being made up of the four that took place between 1818 and 1822 and four peace congresses, Vienna and Paris in 1814–15, Paris in 1856, and Berlin in 1878.

The powers acting in concert settled some disputes peacefully which might have led to war, curtailed hostilities which had already broken out, and persuaded parties to reach compromises in certain complex and dangerous situations. One of their most successful interventions was in the problem of Belgian independence during the 1830s. In the Eastern question and the Balkans the Concert again and again played a useful role. Only three powers took action in the struggle for Greek independence, which culminated in 1832, but they played a decisive part. In the Mahomet Ali affair of 1839–41, the Cretan crisis of 1896–97, and the Balkan War of 1912–13 it made valuable contributions to the settlements, while at the Congress of Berlin in 1878 it helped in the avoidance of an Anglo-Russian War. The Concert failed to prevent the Crimean War, but the Congress of Paris which drew up the resulting peace settlement was one of the most important meetings of powers during the century. Apart from deciding on the actual peace terms, the powers at Paris agreed to an important declaration dealing with the laws of maritime warfare, set up a European Commission to regulate and improve conditions of navigation on the lower Danube, and signed a remarkable protocol expressing 'the wish that States between which any serious misunderstandings may arise, should, before appealing to Arms have recourse, as far as circumstances might allow, to the Good Offices of a friendly Power'. Turkey also was admitted to 'participate in the advantages of the Public Law and System (*Concert*) of Europe', an arrangement which reminds one today of the inclusion of Turkey (and Greece) in NATO in 1952.

The Concert of Europe did not confine its activities to the continent of Europe. A convention was signed in 1880 by fourteen countries, including the United States, dealing with the status of persons and the right of protection in Morocco, and in 1906 the Conference and Act of Algeciras, the United States again participating, determined the status of Morocco after a major diplomatic conflict on the subject between France and Germany. In 1888 nine powers signed the Suez Canal Convention dealing with the free navigation of the canal, although it did not go into force until 1904. The European powers also acted together, joined by the United States and Japan, during and after the Boxer rebellion in China, 1899–1901. Furthermore, at the Berlin Conference in 1884–85 thirteen European powers, together with the

United States, came to an arrangement with the object of pursuing the further partition of Africa with as little friction as possible.

On the negative side, apart from the Congress of Paris in 1856 and the neutralization of Luxembourg in 1867, the Concert was virtually dormant from the Treaty of London in 1852, which dealt with the Schleswig-Holstein question, until after the foundation of the German Empire in 1871. In spite of various proposals for meetings, the Concert did nothing to prevent the series of wars between 1859 and 1870 connected with the unification of Italy and Germany. Bismarck and Cavour were frankly cynical about any idea of a public law of Europe, especially when working for their countries' unity, and there was so much sympathy for nationalist movements among liberal circles in England and other countries that earlier enthusiasm for peace and European cooperation temporarily wore rather thin. The final disappointment and breakdown of the Concert came in 1914. Sir Edward Grey, the British foreign secretary, suggested a four-power conference towards the end of July, but his proposal was rejected by Germany. A few days later, when the Tsar, before ordering partial mobilization of his army, telegraphed to the German Emperor suggesting that the Austro-Serbian problem should be referred 'to the Hague Conference', the latter wrote *Nonsense* on the margin of the telegram.

In addition to the Concert experiment the nineteenth century saw the growing use of peaceful settlement and arbitration to solve international disputes. Three examples of peaceful settlement were the cession of the Ionian Islands by Britain to Greece in 1864; the arrangement between Britain and Germany in 1890 by which Germany received Heligoland and a strip of Territory in West Africa in return for renouncing her protectorate over Zanzibar and claims to certain areas in East Africa in which Britain was interested; and the recognition by Sweden in 1905 of the independence of Norway after the two countries had been united under the Swedish crown since 1814. These cases of peaceful settlement, though straws in the wind, involved relatively minor controversies. But the development of arbitration as a means of solving international problems was more significant, because it was so widespread and because it involved most of the leading powers.

The two countries which most frequently resorted to arbitration were Britain and the United States, and, according to one scholar's reckoning, they were between them involved in 140 cases up to 1914.[3] The develop-

[3] N. Politis, *La Justice Internationale*, p. 35.

ment was started off by the Jay treaty of 1794[4] between these two powers, which provided for settlement by arbitration of various disputes arising out of the American Revolutionary War and the war then going on between Britain and France. This was followed by the inclusion in the Treaty of Ghent (1814) between the United States and Britain of a series of clauses providing for arbitration, the most important of which dealt with the boundary between the USA and Canada. Throughout the century from 1814 to 1914 a series of disputes concerning the United States–Canadian border were all dealt with either by arbitration or negotiation, one of the most famous agreements being the Rush-Bagot Treaty of 1817, by which each party agreed to limit its naval forces to three lightly armed vessels on the Great Lakes and one on Lake Champlain for police purposes. The existence since this time of a virtually undefended frontier 4,000 miles long is a fact which has not been sufficiently appreciated.

A further important instance of arbitration between Britain and the United States occurred in 1872, when Britain was required to pay over £3 million, in compensation for the activities during the American Civil War of the Southern warship, *Alabama*, which had been built in a British shipyard. Another great power, France, was estimated to have been involved in thirty-three arbitration cases up to 1914.[5] There were numerous cases of arbitration also involving Central and South American states, which concerned their relations with the United States and European countries, and occasionally disputes amongst themselves.

Yet attempts to regulate relations between specific states by permanent arbitration treaties proved very difficult to realize. The first Pan-American Conference, which was held in Washington in 1889 and 1890, drew up a treaty adopting arbitration as a principle of international law among American nations and making it obligatory in the settlement of disputes between them, except those which a state considered as involving its national independence. However, only eleven of the seventeen states present signed it, and Brazil alone ratified it. So it never came into force. In 1897 a permanent arbitration treaty was drawn up and signed between Britain and the United States. Subject

[4] Arbitration had been used quite frequently in ancient Greece, especially between states in the same league. Under the influence of the Church, particularly of the Papacy itself, it was also often resorted to during the Middle Ages, the most famous example of papal arbitration being at the end of the period, when Alexander VI in 1493 drew a line of demarcation between the Spanish and Portugese territories in the New World. Much less use was made of arbitration during the early centuries of the post-Renaissance era.

[5] Politis, *op. cit.*, p. 35.

to considerable qualifications, it provided for the submission to arbitration of 'all questions of difference between them which may fail to adjust themselves by diplomatic negotiation'. But the United States refused to ratify. One such treaty, however, had a better fate. Due to the improved relations between Britain and France, which resulted in the Anglo-French Alliance of 1904, an Arbitration Treaty was concluded between the two countries in 1903, by which the French and British governments bound themselves to submit to arbitration 'differences of a judicial order, which it may not be possible to settle by means of diplomacy'.[6] The Treaty was significant in itself, and it also became the model for most of the numerous arbitration treaties that were concluded during the next decade.

The one institution aiming at the peaceful settlement of disputes on a truly international scale, which came into existence before the first World War, resulted from the first Hague Conference in 1899 and was expanded in scope by the second Hague Conference in 1907. In 1898 Tsar Nicholas II proposed to the foreign powers represented at St Petersburg that a conference be held to consider the problems of limiting armaments and avoiding armed conflicts by peaceful settlement. This led to a conference at the Hague the following year. The reasons for the Tsar's action were partly financial embarrassment and the desire to economize on armaments, and partly genuine idealism. His proposal was greeted with a good deal of scepticism, but on the whole the governments invited saw certain advantages in the plan, and under strong pressure from the leaders of national and international peace movements most of them took more positive action than their convictions warranted. Even the Kaiser decided that it would be wise not to take up too negative an attitude.

The Conference of 1899, which on American and Russian initiative was followed by a second one eight years later, set out to deal with the three questions of arbitration, rules of warfare, and disarmament. On disarmament virtually nothing was accomplished at either Conference. As regards rules of warfare, three declarations were agreed on in 1899 prohibiting the use of expanding bullets, asphyxiating gases, and projectiles from balloons, and in 1907 the codification of the laws of war was extended to cover naval warfare and the status of neutrals in such warfare. The main achievement was in the field of arbitration. It was not possible to establish the principle of obligatory arbitration nor to set up an International Court, as many had hoped, with a permanent body of elected judges. But a Convention signed in 1899 by twenty-six

[6] See A. F. C. Beales, *The History of Peace*, p. 221.

states—increased in 1907 to forty-four—declared that 'with the object of facilitating an immediate recourse to arbitration for international differences, which it has not been possible to settle by diplomacy, the Signatory Powers undertake to organize a permanent Court of Arbitration, accessible at all times'. What, in fact ,was organized was an apparatus for creating a court, when required. Every signatory power had the right to nominate four qualified persons to a list of arbitrators. When two states decided to go to arbitration, each party was to name two arbitrators and the four so selected were to pick a fifth as umpire.

The so-called Permanent Court did, in practice, perform a useful function, and by 1914 fourteen cases had been settled by it. But perhaps still more important was the fact that it provided a focus point for the moral hopes of mankind in the international field. It was a modest beginning from which much might develop.

Human aspirations after peace had already found expression in the formation of a large number of peace movements during the nineteenth century. The two earliest were a Peace Society founded in 1815 in the United States and another Peace Society which came into existence in England the following year under Quaker influence. As the years went by, organizations with broadly similar aims proliferated in many countries, taking a wide variety of forms. One result was a series of Peace Congresses, the most famous of which was held in Paris in 1849, when Victor Hugo, as president, foretold European integration and looked forward to the day when 'we shall see those two immense communities, the United States of America and the United States of Europe holding hands across the sea'. While, in those early days, the main purpose of these movements were popular education, propaganda, and publicity, they employed their growing influence also to further concerted action by the European powers and the use of arbitration as a means of solving national disputes.

But when war broke out in 1914, the existing peace organizations, many of which were pacifist in character, could do very little, owing to patriotic feeling and the conviction of most people in each country that the national cause was just. Former advocates of peace rallied to the support of their governments and socialist plans in France and Germany for general strikes against war collapsed, though in Germany and England heroic minorities stood firm and suffered for their principles. Revulsion against war was, however, felt and expressed both by peoples and by their leaders. Popular feeling expressed itself in new mass movements in Britain and the United States, the purpose of which was not to protest against the immorality of war in any circumstances but to organize relations between nations in such a way that war in fact would be avoided. In May 1915 the British League of Nations Society was founded, and a month later the American League to Enforce Peace came into being.

From the beginning support to these movements was given by leading statesmen. The British foreign secretary, Sir Edward Grey, disappointed and frustrated by his failure to arrange a four-power conference during the summer of 1914, began to concern himself with peace plans in the early months of the war. He and the prime minister, H. H. Asquith, publicly supported the idea of a League of Nations and gave unofficial encouragement to the League of Nations Society. In the United States the League to Enforce Peace was headed by a former president, William Taft, and in 1916 at a great demonstration in its support in Washington the main speakers were President Wilson and Henry Cabot Lodge, the Republican leader in the Senate. A few months before the formation of this body, another ex-president, Theodore Roosevelt, supported strongly the principles for which it stood.

> My proposal is [he wrote] that the efficient civilized nations—those that are efficient in war as well as in peace—shall join a world league [and shall agree] to act with the combined military strength of all of them against any recalcitrant nation, against any nation which transgresses at the expense of any other nation the rights which it is agreed shall not be questioned, or on matters which are arbitrable refuses to submit to the decree of the arbitral court.[7]

Such a scheme, he considered, would

> mean that at last a long stride has been taken in the effort to put the collective strength of civilized mankind behind the collective purpose of mankind to secure the peace of righteousness, the peace of justice among nations of the earth.[8]

Eventually three statesmen emerged as the chief exponents of the League of Nations idea, President Wilson, General Smuts, the leading South African statesman, and Lord Robert Cecil, a member of the British Cabinet. Two of them were world figures by virtue of their positions and their personalities, and Cecil became a world figure through his wisdom, nobility of character, and years of devotion to the cause of peace. In 1941, looking back on the first World War, he wrote:

> Those four years burnt into me the insufferable conditions of international relations which made war an acknowledged method—indeed, the only

[7] 'Utopia and Hell', *The Independent*, 4 Jan. 1915.
[8] *America and the World War*, pp. 82–83.

fully authorized method—of settling international disputes. Thence-forward, the effort to abolish war seemed to me, and still seems to me, the only political object worth while.[9]

In his address to Congress in January 1918 Wilson announced the Fourteen Points which constituted the main war aims of the United States, the last of which foreshadowed the creation of the League of Nations in the following words: 'A general association of nations must be formed under specific covenants for the purpose of affording mutual guarantees of political independence and territorial integrity to great and small states alike.' The previous summer the British and French governments, realizing the need to clarify war aims, had independently appointed committees to consider the form a League might take, under the chairmanship of Lord Phillimore, a distinguished jurist, and Léon Bourgeois, a former prime minister and devoted advocate of peace. The committees presented their reports in March and June 1918, and each of them was communicated to Washington. During the summer Wilson, with the aid of his adviser, Colonel House, worked on a draft himself, making considerable use of the Phillimore Committee's report.

No public campaign advocating a League was launched in Britain and no detailed proposals were published by Wilson while the war was still in progress. Cecil and Grey wanted the United States to take the lead in creating the new institution, because they considered American participation essential for its success. Wilson for his part believed that if specific proposals were put forward officially they would invite criticism and premature controversy on a matter which needed a maximum of bipartisan support. Nevertheless a great deal of preliminary work had been done before the end of the war; so that, when a committee of the Peace Conference was appointed in January 1919 'to work out the details and functions' of a League of Nations, it was able to complete its task in less than three months.

The publication in December 1918 of General Smuts's great pamphlet, *The League of Nations; a practical suggestion,* in two ways made a vital contribution to the creation of the League. In the first place, it ensured that the League, in addition to being an organization for the prevention of war, should be an effective instrument for day-to-day international cooperation; in Smuts's words 'a great organ of the ordinary peaceful life of civilization'. Secondly, its imaginative and sometimes flamboyant language caught people's attention and made them realize the greatness of the issues that were at stake. 'To my mind,' wrote Smuts, 'the world is ripe for the greatest step forward ever made in the government of

[9] *A Great Experiment,* p. 189.

man . . . mankind is once more on the move . . . the tents have been struck, and the caravan of humanity is once more on the march.'

The League of Nations had two main aims, as laid down in the opening of the Preamble to the Covenant: 'to promote international cooperation and to achieve international peace and security.' It had two main organs through which it could act, an Assembly and a Council, which were assisted by a permanent Secretariat.

The Council owed its actual form chiefly to General Smuts, who in his pamphlet gave his views in some detail as to how it should function and be constituted. According to the Covenant it was to consist of 'Representatives of the Principal Allied and Associated Powers', by which was meant France, Great Britain, Italy, Japan, and the United States, and four other members of the League, selected by the Assembly. It was thus intended that the great powers should have a majority of one over the elected members. But the defection of the United States resulted in the Council starting off with four members in each category.

Its elective membership was raised to six in 1922. Germany became the fifth permanent member when she joined the League in 1926; at the same time the number of elected members was increased to nine, with the proviso that they were not normally eligible for immediate re-election when their terms expired, but that this rule could be relaxed by a two-thirds majority vote of the Assembly in favour of not more than three states. This arrangement was a compromise following an unsuccessful campaign by Spain, Brazil, and Poland to become permanent members. In effect, it created a new class of semi-permanent states, whose incumbents, however, required to be re-elected every three years. Finally, the number of elected members was raised to eleven in 1936.

The complicated section of the Covenant dealing with peace-keeping and security, that is Articles 10 to 17, owed its complexity largely to the different ideas in the minds of the statesmen responsible for the League's existence. On the one hand, the British, with the support of the Dominions, saw the best hope for the League in the development and elaboration of the old method of concerted action by the great powers, that is to say in peace-keeping by negotiation and conferences at appropriate times. On the other hand, the Americans, backed by France for motives of her own, were strongly influenced by the idea behind the League to Enforce Peace, that is to say, the desirability of imposing a system of collective security by sanctions, including armed force when necessary.

B

One of the main differences between the United States and Britain was over Article 10, which laid down that 'members of the League undertake to respect and preserve as against external aggression the territorial integrity and existing political independence of all Members of the League'. This amounted to an indefinite guarantee of existing territorial boundaries, in other words, to an undertaking not to promote international peace in general but to maintain the terms of the peace settlement in which the Covenant was incorporated. Cecil, backed by the British Dominions, first opposed the Article altogether and then suggested a compromise, by which the Article should be retained but a section added to it, giving the Assembly authority to advise changes in existing treaties, if they should for any reason be no longer justifiable. This proposal was turned down and a separate Article (19), which made no reference to Article 10, provided that the Assembly might 'from time to time advise the reconsideration by Members of the League of treaties which have become inapplicable'. The result was that as the years went by members felt less and less inclined to take risks in defence of a settlement, which they did not consider in every respect just, but were reluctant to take action under Article 19, which might lead to the whole settlement being reconsidered.

The main methods that were to be used to achieve international peace and security were the following:

1. In case of an infringement of Article 10, the Council was to advise as to the means by which members' obligations should be fulfilled.
2. Any war or threat of war was, under Article 11, declared a matter of concern to the whole League. In case any such emergency should arise, the Secretary-General should, on the request of any Member of the League, forthwith summon a meeting of the Council.
3. By Article 12, Members of the League agreed that if there should arise between them any dispute likely to lead to a rupture, they would submit the matter either to arbitration, or judicial settlement, or to inquiry by the Council, and they agreed in no case to resort to war until three months after the award by the arbitrators or the judicial decision or the report by the Council. Article 13 dealt in more detail with disputes suitable for arbitration or judicial settlement, and Article 14 provided for the establishment of a Permanent Court of International Justice.
4. If any dispute arose between members which was likely to lead to a rupture, and which was not submitted to arbitration or judicial settlement, they agreed, under Article 15, to submit the matter to the

Council. Should the Council's report be unanimously agreed to by members other than the representatives of one or more parties to the dispute, they undertook not to go to war with any party to the disputes which complied with the recommendations of the report.

Article 15 also contained paragraphs which revealed the so-called 'gaps in the Covenant'. Paragraph 7 stated that, if the Council failed to reach a report which was unanimously agreed to by members, the members reserve the right to take 'such action as they shall consider necessary for the maintenance of right and justice'. The provisions of the Covenant for the avoidance of war were by no means watertight, therefore, even on paper. Paragraph 8 added that, 'if the dispute between the parties is claimed by one of them, and is found by the Council, to arise out of a matter which by international law is solely within the domestic jurisdiction of that party', the Council should so report and should 'make no recommendation as to its settlement'. This reservation was necessitated by the nature of the League, whose members made no surrender of sovereignty. It was repeated more explicitly in the Charter of the United Nations and in its new form has been repeatedly invoked by UN members.

5. Article 16 dealt with economic and military sanctions. It stated that if any member resorted to war in disregard of its covenants under Articles 12, 13, or 15, it should be deemed to have committed an act of war against all other members, which undertook immediately to subject it to the severance of all trade or financial relations, the prohibition of all intercourse between their nationals and the nationals of the covenant-breaking state, and the prevention of all financial, commercial or personal intercourse between the nationals of the covenant-breaking state and the nationals of other states. It added that it was the duty of the Council in such a case to recommend to the several governments concerned what effective military, naval or air force the members should severally contribute to the armed forces to be used to protect the covenants of the League.[10]

It has been pointed out that under the Covenant, as opposed to the UN Charter, the obligation of members in certain circumstances to impose economic and financial sanctions was so formulated that each state would be 'confronted separately and individually' with the covenant-breaker or aggressor.[11] The same would apply if a member,

[10] Article 17 dealt with the problem of states which were not members of the League, but had little relevance to our subject.
[11] Andrew Martin, *Collective Security*, p. 135.

on the Council's recommendation, decided to contribute armed forces 'to protect the covenants of the League'. There was no provision by which a state could contribute to a joint force under League command, for whose action the organization itself would take responsibility. For this reason it was as well that it was left to a member's own discretion whether or not it should take part in military sanctions. But the fact remained that participation in any form of sanctions could involve considerable risks, especially if the state imposing them was weaker than the covenant-breaker or, for some reason, particularly vulnerable.

No clearcut distinction was made in the Covenant between the Council's and the Assembly's responsibilities in the major areas of League activity, though the frequent references to the Council in the Articles dealing with peacekeeping and security indicated that the drafters envisaged that the smaller body, in which great power influence was preponderant, should play the major role in this aspect of the League's work. However, Article 15 laid down that the Council might in any case under that Article refer the dispute to the Assembly and that, in any case referred to the Assembly, all the provisions of Articles 12 and 14 relating to the action and powers of the Council should apply to the action and powers of the Assembly.

Two attempts were made to close the gap in the Covenant revealed by paragraph 7 of Article 15. In September 1923 a draft Treaty of Mutual Assistance was laid before the Fourth Assembly, its purpose being to facilitate a general reduction of armaments by providing additional guarantees of security. It is of special significance, because it gave to the Council powers very similar to those later conferred on the Security Council by the United Nations Charter. It imposed on every signatory state the obligation to give military support to any signatory which was the victim of aggression, and empowered the Council to decide who was the aggressor, to impose economic sanctions, determine the military forces each signatory should provide, organize the transport of troops, and appoint a commander-in-chief of the combined operations. The arrangements were subject to two conditions. First, no state could benefit from the Treaty until it had undertaken to reduce its armaments under a plan drawn up by the Council. Secondly, a state could only be required to take part in military operations within its own continent.

The draft Treaty was submitted to non-members of the League as well as to members. Washington and Moscow rejected it outright and Berlin was strongly critical. Among member states the new British Labour government, supported by the Dominions and most neutral states, denounced it, giving as their main reason that it meant a revival of military alliances. Mussolini gave it conditional support, while France, several of her allies, and a few other states in exposed positions came out in its favour.

The second attempt was the Geneva Protocol of 1924. Its purpose was to make it impossible for any dispute to be left open. All disputes were to be settled either by judicial procedure, arbitration, or decision of the Council. Every signatory was to adhere to the Optional Clause in the Statute of the Permanent Court, which made the jurisdiction of the Court compulsory in cases of a judiciable nature. A dispute that was not submitted to the Court or to some form of arbitration was to come before the Council. If the Council was unanimous, its decision was to be binding. If the Council was divided, it was required to appoint arbitrators. The disputing parties were then bound to submit their case to the arbitrators and to abide by their decision.

Any state which went to war rather than submit its dispute to arbitration or carry out the arbitrators' award would, subject to the Council's confirmation, be considered the aggressor. It then became the duty of all signatories to cooperate in resisting the aggressor and in helping the attacked state. Article 13 of the Protocol is of special interest, because it anticipates the provisions of Article 43 of the UN Charter. The Council was authorized to receive, though not to demand, undertakings determining in advance the military, naval, and air force which members would hold ready to bring into action, when need arose, in support of the Covenant or the Protocol. Each member pledged itself 'to cooperate loyally and effectively . . . in resistance to any act of aggression', though 'only in the degree which its geographic position and its particular situation as regards armaments allow'.[12] In spite of this condition it was the arrangements for taking action against aggressors and the specific provisions for applying military sanctions that were one of the two main reasons why the Protocol never went into effect.

The second reason was the strong reluctance of some members of the League to perpetuate a territorial situation which was far from perfect and which many people considered unjust. As a result, though the League Assembly unanimously recommended acceptance of the Protocol and France and most of her Allies warmly welcomed the security offered, Britain and the Dominions, after full consideration, decided not to accept it. The British government was not prepared to commit

12 *Ibid.,* Art. 11.

itself in advance to war in defence of the *status quo*, while, in the eyes of the Dominions, the Protocol increased the danger of their becoming involved in hostilities over European frontiers that were in no way vital to their national interests. Furthermore, to Britain and the Dominions alike relations with the United States were of paramount importance, and a war arising out of the Protocol might well necessitate naval action which would conflict with the maritime rights of neutrals.

Efforts were also made at an early stage to reduce the risks involved, particularly for middle and smaller powers, by Article 10 and by the obligation to impose economic sanctions. In the first two assemblies Canada had tried to cut Article 10 out of the Covenant altogether. Then in 1923 it failed by only one vote to get a resolution passed making the Council's advice under the Article optional rather than binding and leaving the final decision as to what action should be taken with the members themselves. After coming so near to victory the Canadian point of view was henceforth accepted as valid. In 1921, mainly due to Scandinavian initiative, formal amendments to the Covenant were voted by the Assembly which had the effect, first, of modifying the automatic imposition of economic sanctions, provided for in Article 16, and leaving the decision to the Council; secondly, of making their application gradual and partial rather than immediate and complete. These amendments never acquired legal force, as France refused to ratify them. But the Assembly had laid down that, pending their ratification, the Council should be guided by their substance. So in 1935 during the Italo-Abyssinian War they were accepted as the operative directives in the application of economic sanctions.

Before the League's record in peace-keeping and security is dealt with in more detail, it would be as well to consider some of the organization's basic weaknesses.

In the first place, the League was not, and was never intended to be, an organic union with a will of its own: it was an association—*Société* was the French term—of independent states. It was for this reason that on nearly all important matters voting in the Assembly or the Council had to be unanimous;[13] majority decisions would have meant an infringement of sovereignty. As a result, the League's main task of maintaining international peace and security was from the beginning extremely difficult. Nations, as they had developed during the nineteenth century, were intensely self-conscious groups with a strong sense of group loyalty. In the long term and under ideal conditions a broader

[13] Amendments to the Covenant required ratification by all members of the Council but only by a majority of members of the Assembly (Art. 26).

group loyalty to the League itself might have developed, but conditions were far from ideal.

Members of the League could, broadly speaking, be divided into two categories, democracies and autocracies. The autocratic rulers had little sympathy with international ideals. It was thus not altogether surprising that Japan, Nazi Germany, and Fascist Italy in turn left the League, when its actions displeased them, and that the Soviet Union under Stalin attacked Finland in 1939 with such cynical self-interest that it was expelled from the organization. The democracies were more peace-loving and more international in outlook. But the League system for maintaining peace and security required them, in certain circumstances, to make war on an aggressor or impose economic sanctions, which might lead to war; and this resulted in their proving broken reeds at moments of crisis. During the first great experiment in international organization the citizens of most democracies were not yet prepared for their countries to get involved in war, with all its risks and suffering, for the sake of an ideal, however noble. For this reason Article 11 became the basis of almost all the League's peace-keeping actions, while Article 16 was only used once, and then unsuccessfully.[14]

A second weakness was the League's lack of universality. Until 1926 neither the United States, Germany, nor the Soviet Union were members. The decision of the United States in 1920 not to join was a disaster of the first order, for it deprived the League of the potential deterrent effect of American power and influence on would-be Covenant-breakers and embarrassed the great powers which did become members. In the event of economic or military sanctions being imposed, France and, still more, Britain and the Dominions would have to contend with the sensitivity of the United States as a neutral non-member. Furthermore, the failure to invite Germany to join the League until after Locarno, against the convictions of several of its wisest supporters,[15] caused some European powers, especially Germany's neighbours, to look upon the League as a somewhat one-sided group, made up of the Entente powers and their associates.

Thirdly, even from its own members including its chief protagonists, Britain and France, the League did not receive effective support on the necessary scale. In the early years those conducting the League experiment were inevitably inexperienced, owing to the pioneer character of the organization. They made mistakes through ignorance of the mecha-

[14] Against Italy in Nov. 1935: see pp. 47–48.
[15] For example, Lord Grey of Fallodon (formerly Sir Edward Grey) and Professor Gilbert Murray.

nism they were working, lack of will to work it, or because they did not fully realize the implications of what they were doing.

The League further suffered from the attitudes of two groups, the cynics and the Utopians. The opposition of cynics was, of course, to be expected, but the damage that they do, and in particular *did* to the League, tends to be underestimated in an age like the present, when cynicism is fashionable. F. P. Walters, the historian of the League and a senior member of its Secretariat, said rather sadly towards the end of his life that the sceptical, jeering attitude of critics had been a difficult experience for him during his years at Geneva.[16] The Utopians, on the other hand, often combined optimism regarding the League with only superficial knowledge about it, or even sheer ignorance. They therefore easily became disillusioned when things went wrong, joined the ranks of the cynics, and like many converts frequently became fanatics. The support the League needed most was from idealistic realists.

In addition, the leading statesmen of member states, with few exceptions, gave little positive support to the League as an institution. The French on the whole looked on it as one, but only one, means of buttressing French security, while according to Lord Cecil, when the League came into existence, British support was no more than luke-warm. Lloyd George and his foreign secretary, Lord Curzon, regarded it as no more than 'an interesting side-show', and neither they nor Baldwin, when he became prime minister, went to Geneva, because they did not think it worth their while to do so. Austen Chamberlain, Cecil adds, in spite of frequent visits to Geneva as foreign secretary after Locarno, thought of the League 'as just one cog in the diplomatic machine, to be used or not at the discretion of the Cabinet'. He says also that after the Peace Conference all or almost all members of the British House of Commons 'professed support of the League' but 'very few knew anything about it'.[17] Yet Britain's attitude towards the League was more consistently positive than that of any other permanent member of the Council.

In his book, *International Government*, published in 1916, Leonard Woolf summed up in advance the reasons for the inadequate support, which has just been described:

> History is continually getting ahead of the conceptions and belief of human beings, including diplomats and international lawyers; and the catas-

[16] During a conversation with the author in October 1970. Walters ended his career with the League Secretariat as Deputy Secretary-General.

[17] These judgments are to be found in *All the Way*, pp. 166 and 190, and in *A Great Experiment*, p. 101.

trophes and miseries of humanity are often caused by the attempts to apply these obsolete conceptions and beliefs to a world which they no longer fit ... either our conceptions must go forward and conform with an advanced world, or the world will be dragged back into line with our primitive beliefs.[18]

When the League began to carry out its peace-keeping duties, it was important that it should at once establish its authority or at least lay foundations on which it could eventually do so. This unfortunately it failed to accomplish owing partly to the attitude and ineptitude of statesmen and partly to the existence of another international body, with a traditional approach, whose activities confused the issues, embarrassing and sometimes discrediting the League Council.

This body was the Conference of Ambassadors at Paris. It was set up by the victor powers and consisted originally of the ambassadors of Britain, Italy, Japan, and the United States, under the chairmanship of the French foreign minister, its purpose being to deal with questions arising out of the execution or the interpretation of the Peace Treaties. After its decision not to ratify the Treaty of Versailles the American government was represented only by an observer.

Three cases in which the actions of the Council and the Conference were confused were the disputes between Lithuania and Poland over Vilna, the frontier quarrel between Yugoslavia and Albania, and the controversy between Mussolini and Greece which led to the Italian occupation of Corfu.

In the first of these cases, Vilna, the historic capital of Lithuania, had been seized by a Polish army in October 1920, in defiance of a demarcation line laid down by the League Council. For many months the Council wrestled with the problems of whether and how to organize a plebiscite in the disputed area. Then in 1923 the Conference of Ambassadors decided that Vilna should go to Poland, a decision which Lithuania refused to accept.

In the Yugoslav–Albanian dispute, which came to a head in the summer and autumn of 1921, Albania, a recently elected member of the League, appealed to the Council to settle its frontiers, while the great powers persuaded their colleagues in the Council to leave the matter to the Conference of Ambassadors. In the end, a just settlement was reached, largely in Albania's favour, partly as a result of Britain's suggestion that the Council should apply economic sanctions against Yugoslavia. But the formal settlement was made by the Conference of Ambassadors.

[18] *Op. cit.*, p. 180.

B*

The most serious of the three cases was the controversy between Italy and Greece. The Conference of Ambassadors had appointed a Delimitation Commission to settle the Albanian frontiers. In August 1923 the Italian general, who was a member of the Commission, was murdered with several of his colleagues on Greek territory. Mussolini, who had come into power the previous October, reacted in a heavy-handed and arbitrary manner, demanded a substantial indemnity from Greece and occupied the Greek Island of Corfu after a naval bombardment. The Conference of Ambassadors was clearly concerned, but Mussolini's action was also a blatant violation of the League Covenant. Greece appealed almost simultaneously to the Council and the Conference, while Mussolini refused to accept the Council's competence. In the end Mussolini got his way both as regards the method and terms of the settlement. The Council made certain proposals but left the final decision to the Conference. The Conference appointed a Commission of Inquiry, which largely exonerated the Greek government, but then decided that Greece should pay 50 million lire as reparation to Italy; a solution which put expediency before principle.

In spite of these missed opportunities and the harm to the League's prestige which inevitably resulted, the Council did deal with a number of disputes successfully during the 1920s and early 1930s. The first was the problem of the Aaland Islands, which was causing friction between Finland and Sweden in the summer of 1920 and might have led to war. It was brought to the attention of the Council by Britain, but Finland claimed that the problem was a purely internal one and questioned the Council's competence. The Council set up a special international commission of justice to settle the legal point, and, when the Council's competence had been established, sent a commission of inquiry to the islands. In the end Finnish sovereignty was confirmed, but a wide measure of autonomy was given to the islanders.

A second dispute concerned the Baltic port of Memel, a German town with Lithuanian hinterland. Under the terms of the Treaty of Versailles it was handed over to the Allies with a view to its eventually becoming Lithuanian. But the Poles and the French were in favour of its becoming a Free City on the Danzig model, and it remained under the Allied control for several years. Finally, in January 1923 the Lithuanian government decided to follow the Polish example in Vilna and sent in forces which took possession of the city. The Conference of Ambassadors first handled the problem. But, in the face of Polish–Lithuanian differences that it was unable to settle, it passed the matter over to the League Council, which appointed a neutral commission under an

American chairman. The solution that was finally adopted in the summer of 1925 was the work of the commission: Lithuanian sovereignty was recognized, but Polish rights as users of the port were ensured.

In 1924 and 1925 two of the Council's most effective interventions took place. A controversy between Turkey and Iraq over the province of Mosul had been referred for settlement by the Treaty of Lausanne to Turkey and Britain, as the Mandatory power acting on behalf of Iraq. Direct negotiations between the two governments were unsuccessful, and in August 1924 the Council was asked to give a decision. It appointed a commission of inquiry to investigate the matter on the spot, and in the end a frontier was accepted by the three parties in June 1926. The other case was a frontier incident between Greece and Bulgaria in October 1925, in which a Greek officer had been shot, while advancing under a white flag, and Greek forces had invaded Bulgarian territory. At Bulgaria's request the Secretary-General called a special meeting of the Council, and within a few weeks the whole matter had been settled, Greece being required to pay a small indemnity for its violation of the Covenant, while herself receiving an indemnity for the death of the officer. In both instances the Council and its Commissioners acted with impartiality, efficiency, and authority, and the League's prestige was strengthened as a result.

In Latin America the Council's record was uneven in the two main quarrels with which it concerned itself: the disputes between Bolivia and Paraguay over the Chaco territory and between Peru and Colombia over Leticia. This was due to the varying attitude of the United States towards League action in that part of the world and the uncertainty of the states immediately concerned as to whether they wanted League assistance or not. In the Chaco affair the League Council made a useful contribution at the beginning. But the lack of a generally accepted peace-making authority was responsible for much unnecessary bloodshed and for the affair dragging on over ten years. In the Letician dispute Washington supported League action. Colombia, whose territory had been invaded by Peru, appealed to the League early in 1933; the Council appointed a commission to visit Leticia; and the whole matter was settled by the withdrawal of Peruvian forces in June 1934.

The five years from 1924 to 1929 were the most successful period of the League's existence, largely owing to the Council's record and membership during that period. The Covenant laid down that the Council should consist of 'representatives of the Principal Allied and Associated Powers' and that it should meet 'from time to time as occasion may require, and at least once a year'.[19] During the summer of 1923 the Council decided that, starting the following December, it would hold four regular sessions each year in March, June, September, and December. This gave it the great advantage of regular meetings. Later, when Austen Chamberlain became British foreign secretary in November 1924 and Briand, French foreign minister in April 1925, they both made a practice of attending the Council sessions; when Germany entered the League in 1926 their example was followed by her foreign minister, Stresemann. The presence of these leading European states-men at the Council's meetings greatly increased public interest in its proceedings and added considerably to its prestige. Furthermore, they all remained in office until 1929 or longer, and as a result, after three or four years of working together, acquired a valuable personal relation-ship with one another which, at these routine meetings, they could employ to good effect without public expectation being aroused by the announcement of some special conference or official visit. Chamberlain, whose attitude towards the League was, as has been seen, realistic, was convinced by his experience during these years that the League was not merely a 'beautiful dream' but an organization of practical value.[20]

Nevertheless, the prestige built up during this period was not to endure for long. During the five years from the autumn of 1931 to the autumn of 1936 the League was subjected to two trials of strength more serious than any it had previously undergone, and in each case it failed the test. This was due not only to its basic weakness, but also to the world situation, which by then had become unfavourable to an experi-ment in international cooperation. In 1931 and 1932 the great economic depression reached its climax, affecting Europe and the Far East as well as North America, and causing most governments to become more timid and introspective. Then in January 1933 Hitler came into power and put a strain on the international aspirations of most European peoples, especially Germany's neighbours.

The first great challenge came with the action of Japan in Manchuria in September 1931, when the Japanese military authorities took the law into their hands by seizing Mukden and other areas in Manchuria. Through this arbitrary use of force the Japanese broke their engagements under the League Covenant, the Nine-Power Washington Treaty of

[19] The Covenant, Art. 4, paras 1 and 3.
[20] He expressed this view in a speech at the International Studies Conference in London on 3 June 1935; see Alfred Zimmern, *The League of Nations and the Rule of Law, 1918–1935*, 2nd edn, p. 360.

1922, and infringed, in spirit at least,[21] the Briand-Kellogg Pact. They pleaded that all they had done was to carry out 'police operations' in defence of their rights in the South Manchurian Railway Zone. But the plea became increasingly hollow as they proceeded to conquer the whole of Manchuria and set it up as the 'independent' puppet state of Manchukuo in March 1932.

China at once appealed to the League under Article 11 of the Covenant. But the League Council was so reluctant to take strong action, and initially so willing to accept Japanese assurances, that at the end of January 1932 the Chinese government demanded the application of Articles 10 and 15 and a few days later requested a special meeting of the Assembly, in which the influence of the great powers including Japan was less pronounced.

If the League's authority was to be maintained, firm collective action was required, including if need be the imposition of sanctions. But for three main reasons such action was not taken. First, the League's lack of universality was, in this case, a particularly serious weakness. Of the great powers principally interested in the Far East the United States and the Soviet Union were non-members. Secondly, the opportunity for effective cooperation between the League and the United States was missed, though at one stage the American consul-general in Geneva attended meetings of the Council. Thirdly, the four great powers who were members of the League, apart from Japan, were not prepared to take decisive action. There could be no question of an effective joint effort when two of the four were Italy under Mussolini and Germany in the death throes of the Weimar Republic. France's interest and her naval power were limited, while Britain's strategy in the Far East, with no first-class naval base east of Malta, was to keep on good terms with her old ally, Japan, and she was not willing to diverge from this course without the certainty of American support.

In November 1931 the Japanese proposed that the League should send out a Commission of Inquiry to investigate the situation in Manchuria and China. The following month the Council adopted this suggestion and appointed a strong Commission with Lord Lytton as chairman. In September 1932 the Commission presented its report, a thorough and impartial document which, while admitting that the Chinese attitude towards Japan had been provocative, vindicated the Chinese case on the basic issues and recommended the establishment of an autonomous regime in Manchuria under Chinese sovereignty, the details of which should be worked out under League auspices. The

[21] They had not actually declared war.

Assembly approved unanimously the main findings of the Commission,[22] and a month later Japan gave formal notice of her decision to withdraw from the League.

The Commission had carefully avoided describing Japan's action as a wilful violation of the Covenant or recommending that sanction should be imposed. By adopting this attitude it was reflecting the views of most supporters of the League, very few of those who believed in the theory of collective security being prepared in practice to risk involvement in war by attempting to curb Japanese aggression through sanctions. The League, in fact, by endorsing the Commission's report, was conditionally recognizing a *fait accompli*. The only penalty Japan had to pay was non-recognition by League members of Manchukuo as an independent state.

Professor Gilbert Murray found some crumbs of comfort in the situation. The League, he wrote, had succeeded in doing something that had 'never before been done in the history of the world'. It had 'got Japan and China to agree that an International Commission should be sent out to the spot to examine the facts and publish a report'. War was no longer the private affair of two nations. Further, it was 'something to have had the Assembly unanimously supporting the Lytton Report and definitely condemning the aggressive war of Japan'.[23] A more common reaction of League supporters was that the Manchurian case was an exceptionally hard one owing to the economic crisis, Japanese strength, and the remoteness of Manchuria from Europe. Under normal conditions the League would have a much better chance of asserting its authority. So far as European members were concerned, this hypothesis was soon put to the test.

By December 1934 Mussolini had for more than a year been planning and preparing a war of conquest against Ethiopia, which was situated between the Italian colonies of Somaliland and Eritrea. During that month a frontier clash between Ethiopian and Italian-Somali troops gave Mussolini the pretext which he wanted: he at once demanded a formal apology and a heavy indemnity from Ethiopia. Ethiopia appealed to the League and requested that the dispute be brought before the Council under Article 11 of the Covenant.

Italy assured the Council that she was prepared to settle the matter by arbitration, but this was mainly a device to gain time, and during the

---

[22] Siam abstained and Japan voted against the report, but, according to the Covenant, the adverse vote of any of the parties to the dispute did not affect the unanimity of the verdict.

[23] Murray, *A Survey of Recent World Affairs*, p. 11.

spring and summer of 1935 heavy reinforcements of men and materials were sent to Eritrea and Italian Somaliland. France and Britain connived at these tactics; France owing to her fear of Hitler, who had come into power in 1933, and her determination not to alienate Italy; Britain, because her main objective was to preserve peace. Peace, in fact, came before justice in the diplomatic motives of both countries.

Three proposals for a compromise solution were put forward during the summer, in each of which the main concessions were to be made by Ethiopia, though both Britain and France offered minor territorial sacrifices in Africa. Italy rejected all three proposals and it was clear that Mussolini was determined on war.

By the autumn of 1935 Japan and Germany had left the League, Mussolini was defying it, and the Soviet Union, though she had been a member for a year, was not prepared for high-principled or quixotic initiatives. It was left to Britain and France, therefore, to champion the principles on which the Covenant was based. The tragedy of the following months was that both countries gave assurances of support for these principles but lacked the conviction and courage to take the risks that supporting action would have involved. To be fair, no other country, or group of countries, was prepared to do better. The United States remained aloof, and uncertainty as to its commercial policy provided the pretext for British irresolution regarding sanctions, and, in fact, left governments in genuine doubt as to how effective an all-out sanctions policy could be. The League's basic weaknesses were coming home to roost.

In September Sir Samuel Hoare, the British foreign secretary, made a speech in the League Assembly at Geneva in support of the Covenant and collective resistance to aggression, which aroused tremendous enthusiasm in his audience and raised confidence in the League system to its highest point. Within three weeks Italy invaded Ethiopia, and within three months Hoare joined with Pierre Laval, the French foreign minister, in a plan which, had it been implemented, would have betrayed Ethiopia, by trying to buy off Mussolini with the offer of a vast area of Ethiopian territory.

In September the British government supported Hoare's line at Geneva; in November they won a general election largely on their declared support of the League Covenant; and shortly afterwards limited financial and economic sanctions went into force against Italy, although such vital materials were omitted as oil, coal, and iron and steel products, which alone might have made economic sanctions effective. In December both the British and French governments supported the Hoare-Laval plan, but British public opinion reacted against it so strongly that the government sacrificed Hoare, in order to save its own life. Hoare's conduct, however, symbolized the irresolution of British statesmen, when faced with the choice between support for the League and traditional methods of diplomacy.

The Hoare-Laval plan greatly encouraged Mussolini, led to widespread disillusionment about the League within and outside its membership, and paralysed the negotiations that had been going on, with a view to strengthening sanctions. The Italian armies continued their advance into Ethiopia, and early in May the Emperor left the country, which was formally annexed by Italy.

Excuses such as had been offered for Japanese action and the League's failure in Manchuria could not be made in this case. Mussolini's invasion of Ethiopia was a case of blatant and unprovoked aggression. Neither economic preoccupation nor geographical remoteness could explain the shortcomings of League leadership, while Ethiopia's betrayal was doubly bad, because that country had been given good reason to trust in League support. Furthermore, the dominant anxieties of France and Britain were not removed by the course they took. France's policy did not cement her friendship with Italy nor reduce the threat from Hitler, who reoccupied the Rhineland in March 1936. Britain's preoccupation with peace had merely increased the probability of war.

In the autumn of 1936 Hitler and Mussolini formed the Rome-Berlin Axis, to which Japan shortly afterwards adhered. When Hitler seized Austria and Czechoslovakia in turn, the League did not intervene. Nor, when Poland was invaded by Germany in September 1939, did any government seriously consider appealing to it.

The failure of the League to prevent a second World War was a severe disappointment at the time, but, looked at in retrospect against the background of world history, it was not surprising. The League was the first great international institution to be created with the main aim of preserving peace. Had this objective been achieved at the first attempt, it would have been uncharacteristic of human nature and the whole human story. The Covenant, as has been seen, was a complex and imperfect document; the League suffered from the start from certain serious disadvantages; and, in particular, the statesmen who were responsible for implementing the Covenant made mistakes due to lack of conviction, inexperience, or sheer misjudgment.

Leonard Woolf pointed out during the first World War (see pp. 40–1) that history, by which he meant world developments, often went ahead of man's conceptions and beliefs, and that it then became urgent that these conceptions and beliefs should catch up. Had he written on the same subject, after the foundation of the League, he might well have said that at certain periods of history, owing to the prophetic insight of influential leaders, the beliefs and conceptions of at least a human minority get ahead of men's habits and methods of conducting their affairs, and that then it becomes equally urgent that these habits and methods should adjust themselves to the ideas and beliefs that are most significant for the future. However, the process of readjustment in such cases inevitably requires a prolonged educational effort.

Both Wilson and Cecil were convinced of the key role that must be played in establishing an international system by the moral force of world public opinion; as Wilson put it in a famous speech during the summer of 1918, 'by the organized opinion of mankind'. But, apart from the difficulty of organizing public opinion, especially in such a challenging and intangible cause, neither of them appears to have faced up to the formidable problem of educating, in different countries throughout the world, at least a nucleus of political leaders and informed citizens to see the need for an international system, and of thus providing a public opinion to be organized. What was required for their purpose was not 'pie-in-the-sky' Utopians but realists who understood the need for setting up some effective world order and had some conception of the political difficulties involved in the process. The main trouble with the British peace movement during the 1930s was that its members wanted disarmament, they wanted the League system to work, but very few of them realized that, in a crisis, states could not enforce sanctions without sufficient armaments to back their collective policy. This was the basic fact behind the British government's embarrassment during the Italo-Ethiopian War and the Munich crisis.

The League, being the pioneer institutional experiment in international cooperation, needed and deserved support for its own sake and not merely as an instrument for the furtherance of national policies. But only a small group of statesmen of the first rank gave it such support: Wilson, Smuts, Balfour, Briand, and Cecil, supported by a few others of less influence but equal devotion, such as Bourgeois and Branting, by the great leader of international relief work, Nansen, and by some distinguished members of the League Secretariat like Jean Monnet, Arthur Salter, and Salvador de Madariaga. The limited extent of this support was partly due to a failure of imagination and partly to the nature of the statesman's task. It is his first duty to promote the interests of his country, and, if he is faced with the alternatives of gaining a concrete advantage for his country or furthering a noble idea, he is bound to choose the former. The taking of risks for a high ethical purpose may be admirable in an individual but is often less defensible in a statesman. Cecil complained of 'the unfamiliarity of the truth that peace is in itself the greatest of national interests'.[24] The main purpose of the educational effort that is required is to make this truth more familiar and to minimize the occasions when there is any conflict between the national advantage and the furtherance of peace.

In spite of the League's failure to preserve peace and the educational task that remains to be accomplished, it would be wrong to leave too negative an impression of the League's record. In Arnold Toynbee's view the devoted work done by supporters of the League 'was a step forward in the self-education of the human race for living together in one world as one family',[25] and William Rappard, a former member of the League Secretariat, wrote in 1938: 'Thanks to the League of Nations, war has come to be looked upon by all civilized persons as an offence in a sense that was not formerly known . . . one may without undue rashness prophesy that its dissolution, if it occurred, would merely be the prelude to its early resurrection.'[26] In this prophecy Rappard proved correct.

[24] *A Great Experiment*, p. 349.
[25] Gilbert Murray, *Autobiography*, pp. 219–20.
[26] 'What is the League of Nations?', *International Conciliation*, 1938, pp. 140 and 142.

3
The Council in theory and practice

The Council as conceived in the Charter

In spite of its inglorious later years, the League of Nations had always been, as F. P. Walters put it, 'in success or failure alike, the embodiment in constitutional form of mankind's aspirations towards peace and towards a rationally organized world'.[1] These aspirations soon found formal expression again at a meeting between President Roosevelt and Winston Churchill off Newfoundland in August 1941. In the joint declaration the two statesmen then issued, known as the Atlantic Charter, they referred to the essential need that aggressive nations should be disarmed 'pending the establishment of a wider and permanent system of general security'. The name 'United Nations' was first used in a declaration made at Washington in January 1942 by the Allied nations, in which they approved the principles of the Atlantic Charter and proclaimed their joint purposes in the war against Hitler. The first definite statement during the war of the need for an international institution was made at the Moscow Conference in October 1943, when the governments of the United States, the United Kingdom, the Soviet Union, and China recognized 'the necessity of establishing at the earliest practicable date a general international organization, based on the principle of the sovereign equality of all peace-loving States and open to membership by all such States, large or small, for the maintenance of international peace and security'.

As a result of the Moscow Conference it was arranged that the United States, the United Kingdom, and the Soviet Union should attempt to draw up more detailed and comprehensive plans for the organization. This they did, the British government having consultations with the Dominion prime ministers, and Washington exchanging views less formally with a number of Latin American governments.[2] The three

[1] *A History of the League of Nations*, p. 3.
[2] Ruth B. Russell, *A History of the United Nations Charter*, pp. 198–9.

powers then met for conversations on 21 August 1944 at Dumbarton Oaks, a private estate in Washington, the talks lasting for just over five weeks. They were followed by briefer talks between the United States, Britain, and China; the Soviet Union, as she was not at war with Japan, having refused to confer with the Chinese. Fortunately there was a substantial measure of agreement between the proposals that had been drawn up in advance, so the number of matters on which there was severe controversy was limited. The Dumbarton Oaks Proposals, published on 9 October, left some questions open but registered agreement on a wide range of subjects and provided a good foundation for the full United Nations conference that met the following spring.

Two points became clear during these early negotiations. First, the organization that was to be founded was to be a new one: there was no intention of reviving the League of Nations. The Soviet Union had been expelled from the League, and the United States had never been a member, while Roosevelt was concerned to avoid rather than follow Woodrow Wilson's example. Moreover, British and Chinese memories of the League were not, on the whole, happy. Secondly, the new organization was, like the League, to be neither a union nor a federation: it was to be based, in the words of the Moscow Declaration, on the 'sovereign equality' of states, and the phrase was incorporated in Article 2 of the United Nations Charter.

At the same time the League Covenant did have considerable influence on those who drafted the Charter. Those elements in it which had proved valuable and workable were incorporated in the new document, while its faults and omissions stimulated fresh thinking and were thus largely responsible for some of the best innovations in the Charter. C. K. Webster tells us that, when he began to work in the British Foreign Office in the autumn of 1942 on plans for a new organization, 'the model of the League of Nations was regarded as something to be avoided' but that since 'most of those who took this view knew little about it, it was possible to use its experience provided its name was not mentioned'.[3]

During the Dumbarton Oaks conversations agreement was reached on two features of the new organization which were in marked contrast to the League system. One of its principal organs was to be a Security Council which was to be given 'primary responsibility for the maintenance of international peace and security'. The name was chosen, 'because the Soviet delegation wished to insist on that aspect of the

---

[3] 'Sanctions: the use of force in an international organization', in *The Art and Practice of Diplomacy*, p. 103.

Organization'.[4] The new body was thus to concentrate on problems of security, while some of the important work carried out by the League Council was allocated, under the overall authority of the Assembly, to an Economic and Social Council. This division of functions was largely the result of the report by a committee set up in May 1939, under the chairmanship of Stanley Bruce, formerly prime minister of Australia, to inquire into the League's machinery for dealing with technical problems, which three months later recommended the setting up of a new organ to be known as the Central Committee for Economic and Social Questions. Secondly, it was agreed during the conversations that the League's unanimity rule for voting should be given up. In the case of the Assembly, which it was proposed to call the General Assembly, important decisions were to be made by a two-thirds majority of those present and voting, while other questions were to be settled by a simple majority. In the case of the Security Council, owing to differences of opinion, the detailed voting procedure was left open. But it was agreed that decisions should be made by a qualified majority and that they would require the assent of all the great powers, who were permanent members, in matters to which they were not a party.

The United Nations Conference on International Organization, which was called to prepare the Charter for the new world organization on the basis of the Dumbarton Oaks Proposals, met at San Francisco from 25 April to 26 June 1945. In his last address, which was to have been delivered on 13 April (he died on 12 April), President Roosevelt had written:

> Today we are faced with the pre-eminent fact that, if civilization is to survive, we must cultivate the science of human relationships—the ability of all peoples of all kinds to live together and work together in the same world at peace.
>
> Let me assure you that my hand is steadier for the work that is to be done, that I move more firmly into the task, knowing that you—millions and millions of you—are joined with me in the resolve to make this work endure.
>
> The work, my friends, is peace; more than an end of this war—an end to the beginning of all wars; yes, an end, forever, to this impractical unrealistic settlement of the differences between governments by the mass killing of peoples.

The first decision that President Truman made after taking up office was that the San Francisco Conference should go ahead as planned, and he made the decision with a deep sense of its importance.[5]

---

[4] Webster: 'The making of the Charter of the United Nations', *ibid.*, p. 79; Webster was a British delegate at Dumbarton Oaks and San Francisco.
[5] Harry S. Truman, *Memoirs*, vol. I, 9.

The Conference was a success largely owing to the valuable spade-work that had been done before and during the Dumbarton Oaks meetings. In all essentials the Proposals drawn up at the meetings were accepted. A number of alterations and additions were made which, taken together, were of considerable importance, but none of them greatly affected the basic features of the Proposals. Some of the toughest discussions took place on matters which involved a conflict of interest between the great powers and the smaller states. The smaller states, for example, objected to the provision that decisions in the Security Council should require the assent of all the great powers, on the grounds that it conflicted with the principle of the sovereign equality of states. But on this point they had to yield, because it was clear that the provision was a *sine qua non* of membership for the great powers and that without it there would be no international organization at all.

The early sections of the Charter contain features which are broadly relevant to the Security Council, although the sections in question are not specifically concerned with the Council. The Preamble begins with the striking phrase, 'We the peoples of the United Nations determined to save succeeding generations from the scourge of war', in contrast to the more formal and legal opening of the Preamble to the Covenant, 'The High Contracting Parties'. The phrase was suggested by the United States delegation, the intention being to strike a democratic note and to emphasize the role of peoples as well as of governments in the organization. The Preamble and Article I also both make references to human rights, an innovation arising out of recent experiences, especially in Nazi Germany, and in future frequently to be made the basis of fears for international peace and security by members of the Security Council. Again the Preamble and Article 2 condemned the use of force except in the common interest, whereas the Covenant had forbidden resort to war. The new term was an improvement, because the use of force between the wars had frequently been excused on the grounds that its purpose was to restore order and that it did not involve an act of war.

On 26 June the fifty states represented at San Francisco signed the Charter without reservations. The Committee on Foreign Relations of the United States Senate, which had recommended ratification of the League Covenant only after putting forward a whole series of amendments and reservations, approved the Charter without qualification by 20 votes to 1; the Senate itself voted to join the United Nations by 89 votes to 2. On 24 October, with the addition of Poland, the United Nations formally came into being with fifty-one original members.

The previous April the League Assembly had held a final meeting at which it transferred its powers and functions to the United Nations and voted itself out of existence.

At the last plenary session of the San Francisco Conference President Truman made a speech, in which he said:

> You have created a great instrument for peace and security and human progress in the world.
>
> The world must now use it.
>
> If we fail to use it, we shall betray all those who have died in order that we might meet here in freedom and safety to create it.
>
> If we seek to use it selfishly—for the advantage of any one nation or any small group of nations—we shall be equally guilty of that betrayal.
>
> The successful use of this instrument will require the united will and firm determination of the free peoples who have created it. The job will tax the moral strength and fibre of us all.
>
> We have all to recognize—no matter how great our strength—that we must deny ourselves the licence to do always as we please.[6]

The fresh and imaginative statements that have been quoted, which were made by two presidents of the United States at a time when the United Nations was coming to birth, have special significance today owing to the irrational fluctuations that have taken place in the American people's attitudes toward the UN, and the general tendency of member states to use the organization as an instrument for promoting national interests rather than as an urgently needed institution for furthering international aims.

The arrangements in the Charter, as it was finally approved, for maintaining international peace and security incorporated four improvements over the League Covenant. First, not only was the Security Council given the special task of maintaining peace and security, but its authority in this area of the UN's work was recognized as binding. Article 24 lays down that UN Members 'confer on the Security Council primary responsibility for the maintenance of international peace and security, and agree that in carrying out its duties under this responsibility the Security Council acts on their behalf'. Article 25 adds that Members 'agree to accept and carry out the decisions of the Security Council in accordance with the present Charter'. An authority on international law has stated that the powers thus conferred on the Council by Article 25 are 'greater than have ever before been exercised by any international body' and 'constitute the most far reaching of the innovations which the Charter has introduced into international

---

[6] *Memoirs*, i, 291.

organization'.[7] The powers involved, in fact, a limitation of sovereignty for all Members except the permanent members of the Security Council.

A British argument, which was put forward by scholars and members of the Dumbarton Oaks delegation, was that the division of labour between the Security Council and the Economic and Social Council (ECOSOC) made it difficult to develop the corporate spirit which had proved so valuable in the League Council. Security questions led to tension and suspicion, whereas cooperation in solving technical problems favoured the development of a positive attitude and a sense of common purpose. The argument has some force. But the advantages of specialization were considerable. The matters handled by ECOSOC were varied and highly complex, covering the financial, economic, social, cultural, and human rights fields, requiring expert representatives, whereas security problems needed a more political approach. Furthermore, as the Charter recognized, it was desirable that the Security Council should be a smaller body with higher status.

Secondly, the abandonment of the League's principle of unanimity was a big step forward, in spite of the privileged position for the five great powers which it involved. Article 27 stated that decisions of the Security Council on procedural matters should be made by an affirmative vote of seven of its eleven members, and decisions on all other matters by an affirmative vote of seven members including the concurring votes of the five permanent members; that is, each of the permanent members was given a veto. The veto provision was inevitable owing to Articles 24 and 25, which made the council's decisions binding, the great powers not being willing to be bound by decisions in which they had not concurred.

It has been argued that the veto was too high a price to pay for limiting national sovereignty; that the Articles in question actually extended the sovereignty of the permanent members of the Council, while limiting that of all other UN Members, who were less likely to abuse it. But the Charter did reflect the facts of power politics, and, so far as the two super-powers are concerned, still does so, and no international system would have a chance of success which did not reflect these facts. The voluntary reduction of state sovereignty which is embodied in Articles 24 and 25 was a historic act and may turn out to be the modest nucleus from which some system of world government gradually develops.

A third improvement on the League Covenant was the provision in the Charter for organizing armed forces to give effect to the Security

[7] J. L. Brierly, *The Law of Nations*, p. 111.

Council's decisions; for organizing, in General Smuts's words 'a peace with teeth'. The forces were to be made available by the Member states but coordinated under the Council's control. Chapter VII of the Charter dealt with 'Action with respect to threats to the peace, breaches of the peace, and acts of aggression'. If the Council should determine the existence of any such threat, breach, or act, it was its duty under Article 39 to recommend or decide what measures should be taken to maintain or restore international peace and security. As in the case of the Covenant, the measures to be used against the delinquent parties could take the form of either financial and economic or military sanctions. But, whereas under the League system it was left to the Member states to decide what armed forces they should contribute on the Council's recommendation, under the Charter, the Security Council could decide what action by armed forces should be taken. It was necessary, therefore, that the Council should have at its disposal such forces as were required to implement its decisions.

Articles 41 and 42 dealt respectively with the use of financial and economic sanctions and the use of military sanctions. Article 43 laid down that Members should make available to the Security Council armed forces on its call in accordance with a special agreement or agreements, governing the number and types of forces and other relevant matters, which should be negotiated as soon as possible. Article 45 made the very practical provision, arising out of a Soviet suggestion at Dumbarton Oaks, that Members should 'hold immediately available national air-force contingents for combined international enforcement action'. Articles 46 and 47 provide for the establishment of a Military Staff Committee which was 'to advise and assist the Security Council on all questions relating to' its 'military requirements for the maintenance of international peace and security, the employment and command of forces placed at its disposal, the regulation of armaments, and possible disarmament'. It was to consist of the chiefs of staff of the permanent members of the Security Council or their representatives.

Fourthly, Article 28 laid down that the Security Council should be 'so organized as to be able to function continuously'. Each member of the Council was for this purpose to be 'represented at all times at the seat of the Organization'. The purpose of this arrangement was to ensure that the Council could act promptly in an emergency. Its usefulness and the vital need for it, have been proved on many occasions. In at least two instances the President of the Council, who for his own reasons did not wish the Council to meet promptly, had to use his ingenuity to postpone an immediate meeting, and clearly infringed the spirit of the Charter in so doing.[8]

Chapters v to viii of the Charter, which contain Articles 23 to 54, are mainly concerned with the Security Council and its activities, while other Articles before and after this section also deal with the Council and the maintenance of international peace and security. The more important Charter provisions which relate to the Security Council and have not already been dealt with will now be considered.

Article 4 provides that the admission of a new Member to the United Nations will be effected by a decision of the General Assembly upon the recommendation of the Security Council.

Article 7 states that the Security Council is one of the principal organs of the United Nations; the others being the General Assembly, the Economic and Social Council, the Trusteeship Council,[9] the International Court of Justice, and the Secretariat. It adds that 'such subsidiary organs as may be found necessary may be established in accordance with the present Charter'; that is to say, no amendments to the Charter are necessary to bring them into existence.

In Chapter iv, dealing with the General Assembly, Articles 11, 12, 14 and 15 refer to the Assembly's responsibilities relating to peace and security. The most important passages are the following:

Article 11
1. The General Assembly may consider the general principles of cooperation in the maintenance of international peace and security, including the principles governing disarmament and the regulation of armaments, and may make recommendations with regard to such principles to the Members or to the Security Council or to both.
2. The General Assembly may discuss any questions relating to the maintenance of international peace and security brought before it by any Member of the United Nations, or by the Security Council, or by a state which is not a Member of the United Nations . . . and . . . may make recommendations with regard to any such question to the state or states concerned or to the Security Council or to both. Any such question on which action is necessary shall be referred to the Security Council by the General Assembly either before or after discussion.
3. The General Assembly may call the attention of the Security Council to situations which are likely to endanger international peace and security.

---

[8] The representative of the United States in connection with the Guatemalan question, June 1954, and the representative of Mali in the case of Rhodesia, April 1966.
[9] The body responsible, under the General Assembly, for dealing with the non-self-governing trust territories, the successors of the League's mandated territories.

Article 12

1. While the Security Council is exercising in respect of any dispute or situation the functions assigned to it in the present Charter, the General Assembly shall not make any recommendations with regard to that dispute or situation unless the Security Council so requests.

Article 14

Subject to the provisions of Article 12, the General Assembly may recommend measures for the peaceful adjustment of any situation, regardless of origin, which it deems likely to impair the general welfare or friendly relations among nations . . .

Article 15

1. The General Assembly shall receive and consider annual and special reports from the Security Council; . . .

Chapter v. *The Security Council*

This chapter deals with the Council's constitution, duties, and methods of working in general terms.[10]

Article 23 lays down that the Council shall consist of eleven members of the United Nations.[11] Five of them are to be permanent members; namely, China, France, the Soviet Union, the United Kingdom, and the United States. The remaining six are to be non-permanent members, elected by the General Assembly, 'due regard being specially paid, in the first instance, to the contribution of Members of the United Nations to the maintenance of international peace and security and to the other purposes of the Organization, and also to equitable geographical distribution'. The non-permanent members are to be elected for a term of two years and are not to be eligible for immediate re-election.

Article 26 provides that 'the Security Council shall be responsible for formulating with the assistance of the Military Staff Committee . . . plans to be sumitted to the Members of the United Nations for the establishment of a system for the regulation of armaments'. This contrasts with the General Assembly's duty under Article 11 to consider and make recommendations regarding the *principles* governing disarmament and the regulation of armaments.

Article 27 has already been dealt with, but certain implications of its provisions are of great importance. The veto means that the system of

[10] Articles 24, 25, 27, and 28, para. 1, have already been considered: see pp. 55–58.
[11] This Article was amended in 1965 and the Council's membership increased to fifteen: see pp. 97–99.

collective security established under the Charter cannot be used against either a permanent member or any state which has the full support of a permanent member. Nor can it be used against any state at all, unless the permanent members all agree on the desirability of this being done. As Inis Claude has put it: 'The Charter endorsed the *ideal* of collective security in unqualified terms, but envisaged its application in severely limited terms.'[12]

The provision in Article 28 for the continuous functioning of the Council was accompanied by another stating that it should 'hold periodic meetings at which each of its members may, if it so desires, be represented by a member of the government or by some other specially designated representative'. This was inserted at British suggestion in order to continue a valuable tradition of the League Council by which foreign ministers met together regularly and considered matters of common concern. The Article also provided that the Council could hold meetings 'at such places other than the seat of the Organization as in its judgment will best facilitate its work', an arrangement of which it has on several occasions taken advantage.[13]

Articles 29 and 30 state that the Council may 'establish such subsidiary organs as it deems necessary for the performance of its functions' and shall 'adopt its own rules of procedure'.

Article 31 provides that any UN Member, 'which is not a member of the Security Council may participate, without vote in the discussion of any question brought before the Security Council whenever the latter considers that the interests of that Member are specially affected'. Article 32 adds that any Member which is not a member of the Council or any state which is not a Member of the UN, 'if it is a party to a dispute under consideration by the Security Council, shall be invited to participate, without vote, in the discussion relating to the dispute'.

Chapter VI. *Pacific settlement of disputes*

Since the San Francisco Conference, leading authorities have agreed that Chapter VI is one of the worst drafted sections of the Charter.[14] The original provisions of the Dumbarton Oaks Proposals concerning

[12] 'Management of power in UN', *International Organization*, vol. xv, 1961, 229.
[13] From Oct. to Dec. 1948 and during the winter of 1951–52, in Paris, and in Jan. and Feb., 1972, in Addis Ababa.
[14] See C. K. Webster, *The Making of the Charter of the United Nations*, p. 35; L. M. Goodrich, *The United Nations: Pacific Settlement of Disputes*, p. 968; R. B. Russell, *A History of the United Nations Charter*, p. 657; and L. M. Goodrich, E. Hambro, and A. P. Simons, *Charter of the United Nations*, pp. 257–9.

pacific settlement were strongly criticized, but, although some improvements were made at San Francisco, the wording and the procedure envisaged were not always clear.

The Charter makes the useful distinction between Threats to the peace, Breaches of the peace, and Acts of aggression, which are dealt with in Chapter VII, and Peaceful settlement of disputes, which is the subject of Chapter VI. But apart from the imprecise wording in Chapter VI there are two more sources of confusion. First, the draftsmen do not appear to have made up their minds whether the peaceful settlement of disputes was really the responsibility of the parties to the dispute or of the Council. Secondly, two different causes of danger to peace are recognized: 'disputes' and 'situations which might lead to international friction or give rise to a dispute'. The distinction was valuable in much the same way as was the Charter's condemnation of the use of force as compared with the League Covenant's condemnation of resort to war. It implied that it was the United Nations' business to deal with any dangerous or disturbing trend, as well as any acknowledged dispute. But the power of the Security Council in relation to 'situations' is not made clear.[15]

However, to a large extent the wording of Chapter VI made up in flexibility for what it lacked in precision. There have been few specific references in Council resolutions to the actual articles in the chapter,[16] and the Council has taken a broad, positive view of its part in peaceful settlement. Its approach has been 'pragmatic, and essentially political rather than legal', and members have in general favoured a generous interpretation of the Council's proper role.[17]

The responsibility of the disputing parties for peaceful settlement is emphasized by making it the subject of Article 33, with which the chapter opens. It runs as follows:

1. The parties to any dispute, the continuance of which is likely to endanger the maintenance of international peace and security, shall, first of all, seek a solution by negotiation, enquiry, mediation, conciliation, arbitration, judicial settlement, resort to regional agencies or arrangements, or other peaceful means of their own choice.
2. The Security Council shall, when it deems necessary, call upon the parties to settle their dispute by such means.

[15] The impression left by Articles 35, 36, and 37 is that the Council may make decisions about disputes but only recommendations about situations; a rather illogical state of affairs, in view of the fine distinction between disputes and situations.
[16] See Goodrich, Hambro and Simons, chap. VI, for details.
[17] *Ibid.*, pp. 259 and 268.

Articles 34, 35, and 36 deal with the Security Council's responsibilities, though the General Assembly is also mentioned, subject to the limitations on its competence referred to in Articles 11 and 12. The main provisions are:

Article 34
The Security Council may investigate any dispute, or any situation which might lead to international friction or give rise to a dispute, in order to determine whether the continuance of the dispute or situation is likely to endanger the maintenance of international peace and security.

Article 35
1. Any Member of the United Nations may bring any dispute, or any situation of the nature referred to in Article 34, to the attention of the Security Council or of the General Assembly.

Article 36
1. The Security Council may, at any stage of a dispute of the nature referred to in Article 33 or of a situation of like nature, recommend appropriate procedures or methods of adjustment.

The last two Articles of the chapter concern procedures, when the parties fail to settle disputes, and run as follows:

Article 37
1. Should the parties to a dispute of the nature referred to in Article 33 fail to settle it by the means indicated in that Article, they shall refer it to the Security Council.
2. If the Security Council deems that the continuance of the dispute is in fact likely to endanger the maintenance of international peace and security, it shall decide whether to take action under Article 36 or to recommend such terms of settlement as it may consider appropriate.

Article 38
Without prejudice to the provisions of Articles 33 to 37, the Security Council may, if all the parties to any dispute so request, make recommendations to the parties with a view to a pacific settlement of the dispute.

There has so far been no case in which all parties to a dispute have requested Council action under Article 38.

In Chapters VI and VII provision is made for three main methods of action by the Council: it can 'decide', it can 'recommend', and it can 'call upon'. Only the decisions are binding under Article 25; the recommendations are clearly not enforceable; while in forcefulness the procedure of 'calling upon' comes somewhere between the other two. But a wide variety of methods and expressions for Council action has been envisaged and used in the Council's own resolutions. For example,

Article 52 requires the Council to 'encourage' the settlement of disputes through regional arrangements, while on one or two important occasions the Council has actually 'ordered' parties engaged in hostilities to stop fighting. No provision is made for 'decisions' in Chapter VI; that is to say, the Council is not empowered to enforce settlements on its own terms, though the Dumbarton Oaks Proposals envisaged that collective measures might be used for this purpose.[18]

Chapter VII. *Action with respect to Threats to the peace, Breaches of the peace, and Acts of aggression*

The main provisions of this chapter have already been considered (see pp. 56–57), but two of the Articles that have not been mentioned deserve attention in this summary.

Article 40 states that the Security Council, after determining the existence of a threat to the peace, breach of the peace, or act of aggression, and before deciding or recommending what measures shall be taken, as provided for in Article 39, may call on the parties concerned, in order to prevent an aggravation of the situation, 'to comply with such provisional measures as it deems necessary or desirable'.

Article 51 provides that:

> Nothing in the present Charter shall impair the inherent right of individual or collective self-defence if an armed attack occurs against a Member of the United Nations, until the Security Council has taken measures necessary to maintain international peace and security. Measures taken by Members in the exercise of this right of self-defence shall be immediately reported to the Security Council and shall not in any way affect the authority and responsibility of the Security Council under the present Charter to take at any time such action as it deems necessary in order to maintain or restore international peace and security.

The first sentence was made necessary by the incomplete nature of the UN's collective security system, while the second sentence was added to preserve the authority of the Security Council and to prevent the self-help measures allowed to UN Members from interfering with the limited collective system that was being set up. The Article amounts to an admission that the UN cannot guarantee the safety of its members in all circumstances and to the recognition of their right to resort to collective self-defence, that is, military alliances, in a world in which consideration of the balance of power will still be necessary so far as the relationship between great powers is concerned.[19] Article 51, has,

[18] See *Dumbarton Oaks Proposals*, Ch. VIII, section B, para. 1.
[19] See Inis L. Claude, *Power and International Relations*, p. 280.

in fact, provided the basis for the conclusion by UN Members of a whole series of collective security and mutual defence treaties, starting with the Inter-American Treaty of Reciprocal Assistance, which was signed at Rio in 1947.

Chapter VIII. *Regional arrangements*

Chapter VIII contains three articles of which the following are the essential passages:

Article 52
1. Nothing in the present Charter precludes the existence of regional arrangements or agencies for dealing with such matters relating to the maintenance of international peace and security as are appropriate for regional action . . .
2. The Members of the United Nations entering into such arrangements or constituting such agencies shall make every effort to achieve pacific settlement of local disputes through such regional arrangements . . . before referring them to the Security Council.

Article 53
1. The Security Council shall, where appropriate, utilize such regional arrangements or agencies for enforcement action under its authority. But no enforcement action shall be taken under regional arrangements or by regional agencies without the authorization of the Security Council . . .[20]

Article 54
The Security Council shall at all times be kept fully informed of activities undertaken or in contemplation under regional arrangements . . . for the maintenance of international peace and security.

These Articles amounted to a further admission that the UN system of collective security was incomplete and that it was desirable that it should be supplemented by security arrangements on a regional basis. The climate of opinion at Dumbarton Oaks and San Francisco had been favourable to such arrangements. In the course of conversations at Washington during the war Churchill, with League of Nations experience in mind, had expressed the view that a world organization should be built up on a basis of regional councils.[21] He was probably thinking mainly of the Manchurian crisis and of the British Dominions' attitude towards European involvements. But delegates to the preparatory conferences, who were influenced by the League's example, no

[20] An exception is then made in the case of states that during the second World War have been enemies of UN Members.
[21] The occasion was a visit to Washington in May 1943. See *The Hinge of Fate*, pp. 717–19.

doubt remembered that the Locarno Treaties had ushered in the most harmonious period in intra-European relations between the wars. Furthermore, the Latin American states were anxious that the Charter should not invalidate the regional security arrangements that they had been developing during recent years,[22] while the Arab states and even Australia and New Zealand showed an interest in the possibilities for regional organization in their parts of the world.

Nevertheless, great care was taken, both in Chapter VIII and in the 'Miscellaneous provisions' of Chapter XVI, to prevent the general security system from being infringed by regional arrangements. Article 52 stated that regional arrangements or agencies and their activities must be 'consistent with the Purposes and Principles of the United Nations' and that the Article in no way impaired the application of Articles 34 and 35. In Chapter XVI, Articles 102 and 103 provided respectively that every treaty and every international agreement entered into by any UN Member must be 'registered with the Secretariat and published by it', and that in the event of a conflict between obligations under the Charter and obligations under any other agreement 'the Charter shall prevail'. Articles 53 and 54, as can be seen in the extracts given, also jealously safeguarded the authority of the Security Council in relation to regional organizations.

In Chapter XII, which concerns the International Trusteeship System, Articles 82, 83, and 84 deal with the so-called 'strategic areas'. Articles 82 and 83 state that in any trusteeship agreement[23] there may be designated a strategic area or areas; that all functions of the UN relating to the strategic areas shall be exercised by the Security Council; but that the Security Council shall 'avail itself of the assistance of the Trusteeship Council to perform those functions of the United Nations under the trusteeship system relating to political, economic, social and educational matters in the strategic areas'. The only area that has been designated as 'strategic' is the Trust Territory of the Pacific Islands—the Marianas, Marshalls, and Carolines—which was taken from Japan by the Americans during the second World War and placed under UN trusteeship, with the United States as the administering authority. In March 1949 the Security Council and the Trusteeship Council agreed, the United States concurring, that the non-strategic

---

[22] Through a series of Conventions and Declarations starting with the Inter-American Conference for the Maintenance of Peace in 1936 and culminating in the Act of Chapultepec, which was drawn up at Mexico City in 1945.

[23] i.e. the terms of trusteeship for each territory to be placed under the trusteeship system, to be agreed upon by the states directly concerned and approved by the General Assembly: see Articles 79 and 85.

functions listed above, in relation to the area, should in fact be exercised by the Trusteeship Council.

Article 96, in a chapter dealing with the International Court of Justice, states that the Security Council may request the Court to give an advisory opinion on any legal question.

Chapter xv is concerned with the Secretariat and contains three articles which relate to the Security Council. Article 97 lays down that 'the Secretary-General shall be appointed by the General Assembly upon the recommendation of the Security Council'; Article 98, that the Secretary-General shall act in his capacity as 'chief administrative officer of the Organization in all meetings of the Security Council; and Article 99, that the 'Secretary-General may bring to the attention of the Security Council any matter which in his opinion may threaten the maintenance of international peace and security'.

In a short chapter entitled 'Transitional security arrangements' Article 106 provides that joint action for the maintenance of international peace and security shall not be held up because the special agreements provided for in Article 43 have not come into force.

Chapter xviii deals with amendments. Article 108 lays down that amendments to the Charter shall come into force when they have been adopted by a vote of two-thirds of the members of the General Assembly including all the permanent members of the Security Council, and ratified in accordance with their respective constitutional processes. Article 109 provides that a

> General Conference of the Members of the United Nations for the purpose of reviewing the present Charter may be held at a date and place to be fixed by a two-thirds vote of the members of the General Assembly and by a vote of any seven members of the Security Council. . . . If such a Conference has not been held before the tenth annual session of the General Assembly following the coming into force of the present Charter, the proposal to call such a conference shall be placed on the agenda of that session of the General Assembly, and the conference shall be held if so decided by a majority vote of the members of the General Assembly and by a vote of any seven members of the Security Council.

The purpose of this specific provision was to mollify the opponents of the veto by facilitating the reconsideration of the Charter within a fixed time.

The Council in practice up to 1965

As has been seen, the United Nations' plans for maintaining peace and security, as incorporated in the Charter, were in a number of ways an improvement on the League of Nations. But the system of collective security they included was restricted by the veto, and the limited system that was envisaged was dependent for its success on the cooperation of the permanent members of the Security Council. The biggest blow to the Charter's prospects was that in the postwar years this cooperation was not forthcoming. The world situation, in fact, was dominated by the Cold War, that is, by the deeplying distrust and rivalry between the Soviet Union and the West under the leadership of the United States.

Hopes of great power cooperation had been largely based on Allied unity during the war, which left the misleading impression that international collaboration was easy to achieve. But actually Allied unity, so far as the Soviet Union was concerned, was a remarkable and exceptional achievement, due mainly to the intense opposition that Hitler had aroused but partly also to Churchill's magnanimous and decisive leadership. Within a few hours of the Nazi invasion of Russia, Churchill, after mentioning in a broadcast his longstanding opposition to Communism, promised that Britain would give whatever help it could to Russia and would appeal to all its allies to do the same. But, as the war drew to a close, the two great realists amongst the Allied leaders both saw trouble ahead. Churchill revealed his misgivings through his strategic proposals relating to the war in Europe, which the United States rejected, while Stalin at the Yalta Conference remarked to Roosevelt and Churchill, in a discussion on the UN voting system, that 'the danger in the future' would be 'the possibility of conflicts among ourselves'.[24]

Roosevelt was for a time almost naïvely optimistic about the chances of coming to a working arrangement with Stalin. But before his death he began to have doubts. In his last annual message to Congress he wrote: 'The nearer we come to vanquish our enemies the more we inevitably become conscious of differences among the victors.'[25] A moderate and conditional hopefulness appears to have been the prevailing attitude at the San Francisco Conference, influenced partly, no doubt, by the American president's example. Varied viewpoints were, of course, represented in that great assembly, and many of the delegates were international optimists chosen to participate in an act of collective faith.

As regards the Security Council, where relations between the great powers would most clearly and frequently be put to the test, it was hoped that in the early stages major problems could be avoided, so

---

[24] James F. Byrnes, *Speaking Frankly*, pp. 36–37.
[25] Message on the State of the Union, 6 Jan. 1945.

that members could settle down to working out satisfactory methods of procedure and a harmonious relationship to one another. This hope was quickly disappointed. Within two days of the Council's first meeting on 17 January 1946 Iran complained of Soviet interference in its internal affairs. The question was put on the Council's agenda at it second meeting on 25 January. This led to a bitter controversy, with the United States supporting and encouraging Iranian protests, and towards the end of March the Soviet representative withdrew from the Council for several weeks. Two days after the Iranian complaint the Soviet Union and the Ukraine had made counter-complaints about the presence and activities of British forces in Greece and Indonesia. During the following years relations between the Soviet Union and the West rapidly deteriorated, with the Soviet rejection of Marshall Aid in the summer of 1947, the Soviet-supported Communist coup in Czechoslovakia in February 1948, and the Berlin blockade of 1948–1949.

The military situation during the period greatly increased the tension and suspicion between the two sides. Anxious to return its men to civilian life as soon as possible and confident in its monopoly of atomic weapons, the United States government reduced its armed forces from approximately 12 million in the summer of 1945 to about 1·5 million by the end of 1946. The British forces fell from over 5 million to under 1.5 million during the same period, and to 750,000 by 1949. The exact figures for the Soviet army were not known, but it is most improbable that they ever fell much below 3 or 4 million men. The dangers of this imbalance of conventional forces became clear as the implications of Soviet policy in Poland, Germany, and Czechoslovakia were realized. As early as March 1946 Churchill had spoken in his Fulton speech of an 'iron curtain' descending across the European continent and had added that in the Eastern states of Europe 'police government' was 'prevailing in nearly every case'. The purges carried out by Stalin in Eastern Europe, following Tito's defiance of him in the summer of 1948, brought home the harsh realities of the situation. The first Western measures to correct the imbalance, which took the form of the Brussels Treaty in 1948 and the North Atlantic Treaty in 1949, were soon followed by the explosion of the first Soviet atomic bomb in September 1949.

The Cold War culminated in the United States' refusal in the autumn of 1949 to recognize the new Communist government of China and to admit its representatives to the United Nations. As a result the Soviet member walked out of the Security Council on 13 January 1950, and the whole Communist bloc, except Yugoslavia, decided to boycott all UN organs in which Nationalist China was represented. This made possible the condemnation of North Korean aggression in the Security Council on 25 June and the decision two days later to repel the attack. On this one occasion, therefore, collective action was taken against a state which had the full support of a permanent member of the Council. Throughout the spring of 1950 the Secretary-General of the United Nations, Trygve Lie, tried very hard to get Communist China admitted to the UN and to persuade members of the Council to hold the periodic meetings provided for in Article 28 of the Charter in order to give opportunities at least for progress towards agreement. In his memoirs Lie wrote that he had always believed that the isolation of Russia after the 1917 revolution had been a great mistake and that the repetition of this error in the case of Communist China should have been avoided.[26] Had his aims been achieved before June 1950, it seems quite probable that the North Korean attack and the subsequent war would have been avoided,[27] a sobering thought for practitioners in foreign policy. As it was, the Korean conflict raised the temperature of East–West rivalry, while it lasted, and increased tension within the Security Council, where the West had taken up the Communist challenge.

A number of people with close experience of the United Nations have compared it to a mirror reflecting the world situation and the changing relationship between the powers.[28] The UN certainly functioned in this way during the early years of its life. It came into existence during a period in world history of rapid change and extreme difficulty: when ideological conflict was comparable in bitterness to religious wars; when technological development was taking the form of nuclear weapons and automation; and when decolonization with its immense political and social implications, which reached its height a few years later, was being stimulated by the emergence of India and Pakistan as independent states, and by the Indonesian conflict between Holland and the former Dutch East Indies. With the UN the main impact of these developments, from the point of view of power politics, was on the Security Council, where the situation was complicated in addition by

[26] *In the Cause of Peace*, p. 254.

[27] A suggestion put forward by Andrew W. Cordier and Wilder Foote in their introduction to the *Public Papers of the Secretary-General of the United Nations*, vol. I: *Trygve Lie, 1946–53*, p. 19.

[28] For example, U Thant, Lester Pearson, Sir Gladwyn Jebb (now Lord Gladwyn), permanent representative of the UK to the UN, 1950–54, and George Ignatiev, permanent representative of Canada, 1966–68. The common element in their description was the UN's 'reflecting' function.

the decline of Britain and France to middle power status, the temporary eclipse of China, and the concentration of influence in the two super-powers, whose experience of diplomacy on a world scale had been relatively limited.

The strains placed in consequence on the new organization were great. Its most powerful members devoted most of their attention to the long-term, and even more to the short-term, problems of the Cold War instead of taking the initiative in the joint constructive effort in concilia-tion and cooperation that a great international venture required. So the UN's most consistent progress during its early years was in the econ-omic and social fields, where American generosity set an example, and power, on the whole, counted for less. On the political side the disillu-sionment and sense of frustration were for a time so strong that there was serious apprehension that the UN would go the same way as the League. (The disillusionment of the Nixon era is not a unique pheno-menon, though the reasons for it are different.) But the worst fears were allayed, when, five weeks after the outbreak of the Korean war, the Soviet representative returned to the Security Council to take his turn as chairman and prevent the recurrence of actions of which his govern-ment disapproved.

It had been hoped by many that the Security Council, like a cabinet or any good committee, would work by a process of consultation, dis-cussion, and conciliation to reach conclusions agreeable to all or at least to an effective majority. Unfortunately this turned out as a rule not to be the case. Consultation between the permanent members was rare and, owing to the clash of interests, representatives in their state-ments were usually making a case rather than seeking a settlement. As a result debates ended normally not in an agreed consensus but in a formal vote.

The practice of taking formal votes led to an unfortunate and notorious development in the Security Council. From the voting point of view the position of the West under United States' leadership, during the early years of the United Nations, was much stronger than that of the Soviet Union and the Communist states. In the original General Assembly the United States could normally count on the support of at least thirty-six of the fifty members, excluding itself, and this guaranteed it more than a two-thirds majority.[29] Its position in the Security Council was still more favourable.

In 1946 an oral agreement, known as a 'gentleman's agreement', was

[29] The 36 were made up as follows: Latin American Group, 20; Western Europe 8; Commonwealth, 6; China and the Phillippines.

reached in London, where the Security Council was meeting, by which the permanent members undertook to support the election of the non-permanent members in accordance with a fixed plan of regional distribution: two of the elective seats were to go to Latin America, one to the British Commonwealth, one to the Middle East, one to Western Europe, and one to Eastern Europe.[30] This meant that the United States could normally depend on the voting support of three of the other four permanent members, Britain, France, and China:[31] of the representatives of Latin America, Western Europe, and the Commonwealth, and sometimes of the Middle East as well: that is, upon at least eight out of the eleven votes, including its own. The Soviet Union, on the other hand, could count on the support of the East European representative only. There were differences of opinion as to the duration and binding nature of the agreement, although it exercised the main influence on the Council's composition until the increase in membership in 1966. But from 1950 onwards the East European seat was rather unfairly allotted to Yugoslavia, Turkey, or Greece, countries that were eastern in a geographical, but not in a political sense, and later to Asian countries, such as the Philippines and Japan, as the easiest way of giving representation to a region whose claims had been neglected. The Soviet Union then stood virtually alone.

As a result, when it came to a vote in the Security Council, the Soviet Union was almost invariably in a losing position. The only weapon it could use to prevent decisions or recommendations, which would be against its interests, was the veto, and it used this weapon frequently. As Vishinski said in a UN Committee in November 1948, 'the veto balances power'.[32] In Alexander Rudzinski's words, in Soviet eyes the UN 'became "a branch of the State Department" an "American voting machine" isolating the USSR and its satellites and reducing them to hopeless minority'.[33] At the end of 1955 the veto had been used altogether seventy-nine times, on seventy-seven of those occasions by the Soviet Union. On 22 June 1962 it cast its hundredth veto. As will be seen in the next chapter, the Soviet representatives used their vetoing power without restraint and sometimes with little wisdom, but their action was hardly more culpable than the obvious satisfaction of the

[30] *Repertory of Practice of United Nations Organs*, vol: II, p. 88, para. 16.

[31] After de Gaulle's return to power in 1958 France could no longer be depended upon.

[32] See Joseph E. Johnson's article 'The Soviet Union, the United States, and international security', *International Conciliation*, Feb. 1949.

[33] See his article, 'The influence of the UN on Soviet policy', *International Organization*, May 1951.

United States in using the UN as an instrument of Western policy, tending, as two American authorities have put it, 'to rub the Soviet Union's nose in the fact of its minority status'.[34]

The veto accurately reflected the divided world in which it was so often used. It reflected also the deliberate choice of the great powers to pursue methods of diplomacy based on national power rather than to cultivate the high principles of international cooperation and tolerance on which the United Nation's Charter is based. And the term 'veto' in this connection is used to include the Soviet vetoes, the vetoes cast by Britain and France during the Suez crisis of 1956, and the ready use made by the United States of the 'veto' it possessed through its built-in majority in a UN body to score points off its chief rival. The cynical *Realpolitik* of Stalin, it is true, made the furtherance of these high principles very difficult, so long as he lived, but the other main actors on the world stage were not entirely blameless, especially when Stalin's background is compared with their own backgrounds of democratic political life and social and intellectual enlightenment.

The extensive use of the veto had a disheartening effect on supporters of the United Nations, especially in the West and the United States, who were not aware of the limitations of the Charter and had expected too much of the organization. It led people in many countries, quite illogically, to blame the UN as an institution for results which were due to the world situation, the policies of the member states, and, in the case of the democratic members, to the attitudes of the people themselves, who did not realize the amount of faith, patience, and sustained effort that would be needed on the part of their governments to make the great experiment work successfully. On the Communist side the Soviet Union's minority position during the UN's early years increased its sense of isolation, made it resentful of the organization itself and determined to keep its power under control.

A major casualty resulting from East–West suspicion and conflict during the immediate postwar years was the plan drawn up in the Charter for organizing armed forces under UN control to implement the Security Council's decisions. The Military Staff Committee was set up in February 1946 and proceeded at once to deal with the problem of implementing Article 43. It submitted its report to the Council during the spring of 1947 and was asked to continue its work while its report

[34] Wilcox and Haviland, *The United States and the United Nations*, p. 123. Francis Wilcox, in addition to his distinguished academic career, was a member of the United States delegation to the San Francisco Conference and Assistant Secretary of State for International Organization Affairs, 1955–61.

was examined by the Council, the examination taking place during June and July.

The report contained forty-one draft articles, twenty-five of which had been accepted unanimously. The sixteen articles on which it had failed to agree involved a number of basic issues on which it asked for guidance. The articles that had been accepted included some important points; for example, that the permanent members of the Security Council should, in the first instance, contribute the greater part of the armed forces; that national forces, when carrying out enforcement measures, should be based as directed by the Council but under the Military Staff Committee's strategic direction; and that contingents should retain their national character and be commanded by officers appointed by their own governments, while the Council might appoint an overall or supreme commander.

The main differences reflected the division between the Soviet Union and the West, although on one major point the United States stood alone. The Soviet Union wanted strict equality both in size and composition for the contributions made by all the permanent members, with the only exceptions made dependent on the Council's decision. The others were in favour of 'comparable' contributions made up of those elements which each member was able and willing to contribute and which would best serve the purposes for which the force was required. The Soviet principle, if consistently enforced, would have meant that China's capacity in ships and aircraft would have set the standard for the whole force. The second difference concerned the location of forces in peace time: the United States, China, and the United Kingdom wanted them stationed where the Security Council thought fit, so that they could take prompt action in any part of the world, while the Soviet Union insisted that they should remain in their own countries until they were actually required. As regards the size of the forces, the United States wanted 20 divisions, 3,800 aircraft, 3 battleships, 6 carriers, 15 cruisers, 84 destroyers, and 90 submarines, while the Soviet Union had in mind 12 divisions, 900 aircraft, no battleships or carriers, 5 or 6 cruisers, 24 destroyers, and 12 submarines.[35] It was here that the United States was isolated, the estimates of the other permanent members being much closer to, or even less than that of the Soviet Union. As enforcement action against a great power was not contemplated, the American attitude was illogical, and during the preparatory work on the UN Charter in 1945 John Foster Dulles had testified that, because

[35] The figures are taken from *Yearbook of the United Nations, 1947–48*, p. 495.

C*

no such action was envisaged, the forces to be made available to the United Nations should be quite small.[36]

In fact, the differences were due not to strategic or technical reasons but to deeplying political distrust. As Inis Claude has written:

> In the final analysis, it would appear that the failure to create the mechanism for enforcement action envisaged in the United Nations Charter is attributable not to the unilateral opposition of the Soviet Union, but to the bilateral mistrust of the Soviet Union and of the Western bloc, led by the United States.[37]

The Soviet Union was difficult, even intractable, in the negotiations, but it was understandably concerned at the prospect of large forces being organized and stationed in different parts of the world under the control of a body in which it appeared to be in a permanent minority, with four-fifths of the forces provided by other powers. The United States did offer some concessions regarding the size of the forces, but its proposals remained excessive and it showed little sensitivity about the Soviet Union's understandable fears and the fact that the proposals of all four of the other permanent members were much more modest than its own.

The Military Staff Committee was given the task of implementing the United Nations' system of *limited* collective security; and collective security, if it is to work, demands detachment and, to quote Claude again, 'fundamental flexibility of policy and sentiment'; it 'recognizes no traditional friendships and no inveterate enmities, and permits no alliances *with* or against'.[38] All these must give way to a determination to establish some kind of international order, just as a good citizen must support the police force, because its purpose is to maintain an ordered society, even if individual policemen may seem unpleasant characters compared with misguided and culpable friends. It was not surprising that the major powers did not establish a satisfactory international order in the early postwar years. What was disappointing, and not entirely excusable, was their failure to make sustained efforts to achieve limited progress in the right direction.

In its examination of the Military Staff Committee's report during the summer of 1947 the Security Council made no substantial progress. Since then the attempt to implement Article 43 has virtually been abandoned. In July 1948 the Committee informed the Council that it could make no further progress until the Council had reached agreement on the general principles already reported on. The Military Staff Com-

[36] See Claude, *Power and International Relations*, p. 180.
[37] *Ibid.*, p. 190.
[38] *Swords into Plowshares*, p. 262.

mittee has continued ever since to hold fortnightly meetings of a purely formal nature, which last on an average from four to nine minutes and at which nothing substantive is discussed. There are two main reasons for continuing the regular meetings. The Committee was established by the Charter and its draft rules of procedure lay down that fortnightly meetings should take place. The permanent members of the Council, who provide the members of the Committee, consider that it should remain in existence in case the need for it should arise. Furthermore, the Committee is one of the symbols of the special responsibility of the permanent members for peace-keeping. Any attempt to abolish it, which a cessation of its activities might provoke, would provide an opportunity for calling in question the privileges of the permanent members, including the veto. One small advantage of these perfunctory meetings is that they provide regular opportunities for the permanent members to maintain contact with one another without making any special or noticeable efforts to do so.

In 1948, therefore, it was clear that the United Nations could not provide the security that was needed by great and small powers alike. The limited collective security system provided for by the Charter was not working for two reasons. It was dependent for its success on the readiness of the great powers to take common action, and the great powers were deeply divided. Secondly, owing to this division, it had not proved possible to implement the arrangements made in Article 43 for enforcing the Security Council's decision. So, on the rare occasions on which the permanent members might agree, the system could not work in the way that was intended. As regards the security of the great powers against attack from one another, it was known that the Charter made no provision for this eventuality. But it had been hoped that a measure at least of the good relations that had existed between them as wartime allies would survive during the peace. By this time, however, the tension between them was, for ideological, diplomatic, and military reasons, acute.

Many member states resorted, in consequence, to self-help, and this they did, without breach of their obligations to the United Nations, by taking advantage of their rights under Chapter VIII of the Charter and Article 51 to enter into collective security and mutual defence treaties with one another. It was laid down in Chapter VIII, Article 53, that no enforcement action should be taken, under regional agreements, without the authorization of the Security Council. This had an inhibiting effect on the states concerned, because it made action under such regional arrangements subject to the veto. As a result, virtually all the treaties that were concluded were based explicitly or by implication on UN members' inherent right of individual or collective self-defence under Article 51, should they be subject to armed attack, although some of the treaties also contained features envisaged in the regional arrangements provided for in Chapter VIII.

The Inter-American Treaty had already been signed at Rio in 1947 by the twenty-one American republics. There followed the Brussels Treaty in 1948 between Belgium, France, Luxembourg, the Netherlands, and the United Kingdom, to which Western Germany and Italy adhered in 1954; the North Atlantic Treaty of 1949, to which Canada, the United States and ten West European countries were parties and which three other states had signed by 1955; the Joint Defence and Economic Co-operation Treaty between the Arab League States in 1950; the South-East Asia Collective Defence Treaty of 1954; and the Baghdad and Warsaw Pacts, which were both signed in 1955. In addition, the United States signed mutual Defence or Security Treaties with the Philippines and with Japan in 1951, with Korea in 1953, and with China in 1954, and the Security Treaty, known as the ANZUS Pact, with Australia and New Zealand in 1951. All these treaties made some reference to the obligations of the parties under the UN Charter, and six of them, the Rio, Brussels, North Atlantic, and Arab League Treaties, and the Warsaw and Baghdad Pacts, together with a revised version of the Treaty between the United States and Japan, which was signed in 1960, made specific reference to Article 51.

These developments amounted to a return to the old system of military alliances, to an international society in which consideration of the balance of power counted for more than reliance upon collective security. But it was a conditional return in circumstances quite different from those which prevailed before 1914 and even before 1939. The alliances that were made were all within the acknowledged framework of the United Nations Organization. Under Article 51 the parties to treaties undertook to report immediately to the Security Council the measures that they took in exercise of their right of self-defence and recognized that they should 'not in any way affect the authority and responsibility of the Security Council' under the Charter. In the North Atlantic Treaty the preamble and five of its fourteen articles contained deferential references to the United Nations and, when the United States Senate considered the Treaty, its committee on Foreign Relations stated that the treaty was 'expressly subordinated to the purposes, principles, and provisions of the UN Charter' and was 'designed to foster those conditions of peace and stability in the world which are essential if the United Nations' was to 'function successfully'.[39] This was no empty form of words. Collective security at the time was not working, as had been intended, but the *idea* of collective security and its desirability nevertheless exerted an influence. Members of the United Nations believed, on the whole, that the maintenance of peace was the concern of international society. When South Korea was attacked, no organized international forces were available as envisaged in Article 43, but sixteen member states, in addition to the United States and South Korea, provided combatant forces to resist the aggression. When wars broke out in the Middle East and Kashmir, members were determined, and effectively determined, that they should not be allowed to continue. In the case of the Suez crisis in 1956, the determination involved the temporary cooperation of the United States and the Soviet Union against Britain and France. Strange and unnatural as this collaboration was, it was the most striking and dramatic example of the United Nations system asserting itself, in spite of all the handicaps under which it was suffering.

In the case of three further Articles the intentions of the Charter were very different from what happened in practice. Two concerned the Security Council specifically, while the third was of more general application.

Article 23 lays down that in electing the non-permanent members of the Council due regard should be 'specially paid, in the first instance to the contribution of Members of the United Nations to the maintenance of international peace and security and to the other purposes of the Organization, also to equitable geographical distribution'. The wording is not particularly clear, but it appears to give priority to the first of the two considerations.[40] In fact, greater weight has been given in practice to 'geographical distribution', though it cannot accurately be said to have been equitable. The first consideration has been largely disregarded, especially since the Council's enlargement in 1966. Elections, which have led to Canada having three two-year spells as a non-permanent member during the twenty-one years from 1948 to 1968, and to Norway and Denmark having four such spells between them during the twenty-year period from 1949 to 1968, have clearly not entirely neglected the contributions of the members chosen to the UN's main purposes. But the fact remains that greater weight was given to 'geo-

---

[39] Francis O. Wilcox, 'Regionalism and the United Nations' *International Organization*, summer, 1965, p. 793.

[40] The first consideration is introduced by the words 'in the first instance', while the second, after a comma, is preceded by the words 'and also'.

graphical distribution', and this was shown by the steady adherence to the 'gentleman's agreement', with the one exception of the East European seat.

The second case related to the provision in Article 28 for holding periodic meetings. It had been suggested by the British at Dumbarton Oaks for two reasons. It was feared that the arrangement by which the Council was to function continually would result in states being represented by men of secondary rank, that is, by diplomatists rather than by decision makers, and it was felt that they should sometimes be represented by members of their governments. Secondly, it was considered desirable that the higher level meetings should take place regularly rather than occasionally, so that, without attracting undue attention or arousing unwarranted expectations, the foreign ministers concerned could establish positive and fruitful personal relations with one another, as had the League foreign ministers during the second half of the 1920s. The Council adopted provisional rules of procedure, at its first meeting in January 1946, and the fourth of them provided that periodic meetings, as called for in Article 28 should 'be held twice a year, at such time as the Security Council may decide'. In spite of this, no periodic meeting had been held up to the end of 1965.

Amongst those concerned about the future of the UN and the effectiveness of the Security Council as an international body there was a widespread feeling that the concept of periodic meetings was a good one. All three Secretaries-General in turn urged that the relevant provision should be implemented. The first point in Trygve Lie's Twenty-Year Programme for Peace, which he drew up in 1950, ran as follows:

> Inauguration of periodic meetings of the Security Council, attended by foreign ministers, or heads or other members of governments . . . together with further development and use of other United Nations machinery for negotiation, mediation, and conciliation of international disputes.

He considered that such meetings should not as a rule be held at UN Headquarters but 'in Geneva, the capitals of the Permanent Members, and in other regions of the world' and 'should be devoted to a periodic review of outstanding issues before the United Nations, accompanied by quiet and private consultations on these issues among the foreign ministers'.[41]

In his report to the 1955 session of the General Assembly Dag Hammarskjöld raised the question of periodic meetings and the possibility of developing procedures in the Council 'which would give

---

[41] See Andrew W. Cordier and Wilder Foote, *Public Papers of the Secretaries-General of the United Nations*. Vol. I. *Trygve Lie 1946–1953*, pp. 299, 300, and 277.

increased continuity and intensified contact in the treatment of certain questions of world concern'.[42] Three years later, in an address to both Houses of Parliament in London, he referred to the 'unused paragraph' in the Charter and reminded his audience that, at the time the Charter was being drawn up, Anthony Eden, as foreign secretary, had told the House of Commons that it was by the proposed periodic meetings that governments would be able to carry out the fourth purpose of the UN, 'to be a centre for harmonizing the actions of nations' in the attainment of their common ends. In 1958 also Britain, Canada, and the United States actually proposed that there should be a periodic meeting at the time of the Lebanon crisis. The proposal was tentatively approved, but the idea was finally given up in favour of an emergency session of the General Assembly.

There were several reasons why no periodic meeting was held during the UN's first twenty years. In the first place, at the Potsdam Conference in the summer of 1945 a Council of Foreign Ministers was set up to deal with outstanding matters arising out of the war. It consisted of the five permanent members of the Security Council, although France and China were only to attend the meetings which concerned them. This gave the foreign ministers opportunities to meet one another from time to time. Secondly, the East–West dispute made it unlikely that periodic meetings would be fruitful, the Americans and British alike believing that, in the circumstances, there was no real basis for profitable negotiations with the Russians. Thirdly, the absolute dependence of the Soviet Minister on instructions from Moscow made it impossible to revive the cordial and constructive meetings of the post-Locarno period.

One innovation was made in the early years of the Hammarskjöld regime, which was of some value, though it was no real substitute for the ministerial meetings that had been intended. It had become customary for parties to be given each month for members of the Council by the retiring president. They had become formal and rather tedious social functions. But the British and French representatives now set the precedent of making them partly working lunches, which the Secretary-General attended and at which he kept members in touch with his own ideas on current questions in the field of peace and security.[43] They at least provided opportunities at a diplomatic level for positive personal contacts in a favourable social setting.

The third case in which the intentions of the Charter were not carried

[42] *Secretary General's Report to the 10th Session of the General Assembly*, p. xii.
[43] This custom was discontinued after Hammarskjöld's death, though U Thant continued to attend.

out as envisaged related to Article 109, concerning Charter revision. The Article provided in para 3 that if a general conference for the purpose of reviewing the Charter had not been held before the Assembly's tenth annual session, the proposal to call such a conference should be placed on the agenda of that session, and that the conference should be held, if so decided by a majority vote of Assembly members and by a vote of any seven members of the Security Council. During each of the General Assembly's first two sessions review conferences were proposed in order to eliminate, or at least study the 'veto privileges'. But when the tenth annual session convened in 1955, no review conference had actually met. So the proposal to call one was placed on the agenda. Useful preparatory work on Charter revision had been done in individual member states, but the Soviet attitude towards revision was negative. As Charter amendments were subject to the veto there was, therefore, a general feeling that a conference would be unproductive and might exacerbate relations between the Soviet Union and the West, which had recently been improving.

As a result the tenth session resolved that a general review conference should be held 'at an appropriate time' and that a committee of the whole Assembly should be set up to consider 'in consultation with the Secretary-General the question of fixing a time and place for the Conference, and its organization and procedure'. The Security Council later concurred with the Assembly's decision. The propriety of this postponement procedure was questionable. It was doubtful if a future session of the Assembly would have the right, on the committee's advice, to call a conference by the special voting system laid down in Article 109, para. 3. If it had not, then a procedure for calling a conference by a two-thirds Assembly majority was provided for in para. 1 of the same article.[44] The course adopted had the effect of evading the reconsideration of the Charter, which the permanent members had agreed to in order to reassure the opponents of the veto (see p. 66). In fact, no general review conference has yet been held.

In spite of the shortcomings of the plan for collective security contained in the Charter, the failure of the limited system it did set up, and the disappointment and frustration that resulted, the Security Council took a broad and pragmatic view of its responsibilities both for peaceful settlement and for dealing with breaches of the peace. Its effectiveness was limited by the hard facts of international power politics and by the

[44] For this whole question see Goodrich, Hambro and Simmons, *op. cit.*, pp. 645–47.

idealogical conflict of the postwar years. Nevertheless, stimulated by the leadership of successive Secretaries-General and supported by the determination that the UN's main purposes must not be allowed to fail, it managed by a mixture of persistence and improvisation to achieve much. Its achievements and its failures can best be appreciated by considering its record in the many cases with which it was called upon to deal, after first examining the developments that took place in its procedure and method of working.

4
Procedure

The problems connected with the Security Council's procedure are complex and have been the subject of several specialized investigations.[1] No attempt will be made, therefore, in this study to treat the subject exhaustively for its own intrinsic interest: it will be dealt with selectively and only in so far as is necessary for a clear understanding of the chapters that follow.

There are three main documentary foundations for Security Council procedure: the Charter itself, the Council's Provisional Rules of Procedure, and the San Francisco Statement of 8 June 1945 on Voting Procedure in the Security Council. Chapter v of the Charter, after dealing in its first four Articles with the Council's constitution and duties, proceeds in Articles 27 to 32 to lay down the broad lines of its method of working and procedure. The provision in Article 30 that the Council should adopt its own rules of procedure was implemented at the Council's first meeting on 17 January 1946, when the Provisional Rules of Procedure were approved. They have been amended at nine subsequent meetings but remain provisional.[2] At Dumbarton Oaks, as has been seen, the practice of the Council's detailed voting procedure was, owing to differences of opinion, left open. At the Yalta Conference a formula was agreed on by the United Kingdom, the United States, and the Soviet Union, which was the subject of discussion and consideration in committee at San Francisco. In the end the procedure now laid down in Chapter v was accepted and the three powers, together with China, agreed on an explanatory Statement on Voting Procedure in the Security Council, with which France later associated herself, which has come to be known as the San Francisco Statement.

The Statement, which supplemented and interpreted the broader

[1] See bibliography; especially Sydney D. Bailey's, *Voting in the Security Council*, which has been of great value in the preparation of this chapter.

[2] At the Council's first meeting a Committee of Experts was set up, composed of representatives of all members of the Council, to consider the rules further. In addition to recommending minor modifications in the original rules that have been adopted by the Council, the Committee has had referred to it a number of specific procedural questions from time to time. A thorough rediscussion of the rules, with a view to making them definitive, appears to have been avoided, because members, especially the permanent members, did not want to be put in a straitjacket of rules nor risk opening up every controversial subject again.

provisions of the Charter, became a subject of controversy and requires some preliminary consideration. It was a declaration of intention by the four powers and was not formally endorsed by the Conference. It is not, therefore, legally binding. But the Soviet Union, though often diverging from the spirit of the Statement, has rigidly insisted on the validity of its main provisions concerning the veto, and the other permanent members, having adhered to it, are in no position to challenge the Soviet attitude on this basic issue. The Statement deals with three main points.

It includes a number of general comments on the power of veto. The veto, it explains, gives no new right to the permanent members, because it was a right which the great powers, in fact, all members of the League Council always had. 'In view of the primary responsibilities of the permanent members, they could not be expected, in the present condition of the world, to assume the obligation to act in so serious a matter as the maintenance of international peace and security in consequence of a decision in which they had not concurred.' The Statement adds that it would also be possible for five non-permanent members as a group to exercise a veto, and that it was not to be assumed 'that the permanent members, any more than the non-permanent members, would use their "veto" power wilfully to obstruct the operation of the Council'. It was in connection with this last sentence that the Soviet Union was later considered to have infringed frequently the spirit of the Statement.

Secondly, it distinguishes between those Council decisions which are subject to the veto and those which are not. Decisions of the Council which involve its taking direct measures under Chapters VI, VII, and VIII of the Charter,[3] are subject to the veto, though in those made under Chapter VI and Article 52 (3) parties to a dispute must abstain from voting. Decisions, which do not involve the taking of such measures, will be governed by a procedural vote, that is, not be subject to the veto, and in this category come all decisions made under Articles 28–32. The Statement enumerates seven subjects which are procedural[4] and

[3] The references in the Statement are to the Dumbarton Oaks proposals but, for the sake of clarity, these are being altered to relate to the corresponding Articles of the Charter.

[4] The passage runs as follows: 'This means that the Council will, by a vote of any seven of its members, adopt or alter its rules of procedure; determine the method of selecting its President; organize itself in such a way as to be able to function continuously; select the times and places of its regular and special meetings; establish such bodies or agencies as it may deem necessary for the performance of its functions; invite a member of the Organization not represented on the Council to participate in its discussions when that Member's interests are specially affected; and invite any State when it is a party to a dispute being considered by the Council to participate in the discussion relating to that dispute.' The text of the San Francisco Statement can be found in Bailey, Appendix I, and Goodrich, Hambro, and Simons, pp. 217–20.

then adds that 'further no individual member of the Council can alone prevent consideration and discussion by the Council of a dispute or situation brought to its attention under Article 35. Nor can parties to such dispute be prevented by these means from being heard by the Council'.

The third point dealt with in the Statement is the most significant: the question of the marginal cases, where the decisions and actions of the Council may or may not be considered procedural. The enumeration of procedural subjects makes no claim to completeness, and the Statement makes two contributions to solving the resultant problem. First, it points out that decisions and actions of the Council, which at first sight appear procedural,

> may well have major political consequences and may even initiate a *chain of events*[5] which might, in the end, require the Council under its responsibilities to invoke measures of enforcement under Chapter VII. This chain of events begins when the Council decides to make an investigation, or determines that the time has come to call upon States to settle their difference, or makes recommendations to the parties.

To such decisions and actions the veto applies. Secondly, when a decision has to be taken as to whether a certain point is a procedural matter or not, the problem arises whether the preliminary question is itself to be considered a procedural matter or whether the veto applies. In answering the question the Statement starts with the evasive or naïvely optimistic remark that 'it will be unlikely that there will arise in the future any matters of great importance on which a decision will have to be made as to whether a procedural vote would apply'. It then goes on to say that 'should, however, such a matter arise, the decision regarding the preliminary question as to whether or not such a matter is procedural' must be subject to the veto. The procedure that this ruling involved came to be known as the 'double veto'.

The increase in the size of the Security Council, which was approved in 1965 and went into effect in 1966, was an important milestone and dividing line in the Council's life. For the sake of simplicity and clarity, therefore, the procedural problems during the periods which preceded and followed the change will be considered separately.

1946 to 1965

Procedural and other matters

According to Article 18 decisions of the General Assembly on 'important questions' shall be made by a two-thirds majority of the members

[5] Author's italics, due to the words having given their name to the theory involved.

present and voting, while decisions on 'other questions' shall be made by a simple majority. In the case of the Security Council, unfortunately, Article 27 provides that decisions on 'procedural matters' shall be made by an affirmative vote of seven members, while decisions on 'all other matters', that is, the more important substantive matters, shall be made by an affirmative vote of seven members including the concurrent votes of the permanent members, in fact, they shall be subject to the veto. It would have been more logical and would have saved a good deal of doubt and controversy, if a definition had been given of the important questions to which the veto would apply, and if every other question had been placed in the category of 'all other matters'. The formula used in Article 27, which was approved at San Francisco, originated at Yalta and was no doubt due to the great powers' jealousy of their rights.

There were three reasons for the controversies that arose about whether matters before the Security Council were procedural or not. In the first place the Charter itself makes no clear distinction. Secondly, the San Francisco Statement, which supplements the Charter is, in some respects, difficult or even impossible to interpret. It gives a list of subjects which are considered procedural and two paragraphs later modifies it by the chain of events theory, which is obscure and almost bound to give rise to differences. Further, under the double veto procedure, it gives the main power to the permanent members in deciding the preliminary question as to whether a matter is procedural or not, after saying previously that in matters of great importance such questions will rarely, if ever, arise. Thirdly, the Statement is not legally binding and has been criticized frequently by the small and middle-sized member states.

The main controversies, in fact, centred round the double veto. It was used successfully three times up to 1948. The first occasion was in June 1946 and related to a resolution on the Spanish question. The second occasion, in September 1947, concerned a resolution to refer the Greek frontier question to the General Assembly. The third occasion was in May 1948 and was the most important in its actual result, as it prevented the Security Council from setting up a subcommittee to investigate the Communist *coup* in Czechoslovakia. In each case it was the Soviet Union which exercised the vetoing power.

There was, however, a growing feeling amongst the permanent, as well as the non-permanent members of the Council that the double veto was an undesirable device, by which a single power could, by a subjective and arbitrary decision, further its own interests and prevent the Council from performing its legitimate and intended duties, such, for example, as referring a problem to the General Assembly or instituting an impartial investigation in the Czech case. A procedure was indeed evolved by which the double veto could, in certain circumstances, be evaded. In a case of doubt, instead of voting on the preliminary question of whether the matter was procedural or not, which the San Francisco Statement said was subject to the veto, the problem of the category into which the matter fell could be postponed until after the main debate on the matter or even until after any resolution arising out of the debate had been voted on. The President of the Council could then give his ruling on the question and, if the ruling was challenged, its validity would depend on a vote which did not involve the veto. The use of this procedure in the end undermined the double veto.

The test case came in September 1950, when the Council was considering a complaint of armed invasion of Taiwan (Formosa). It was proposed that a representative of the People's Republic of China should participate in the Council's discussion. Nationalist China voted against the proposal and then, after the President had declared it adopted, against a second resolution stating that the first had been procedural. The President thereupon ruled that for 'patently valid reasons' the first resolution had been procedural. Nationalist China challenged this ruling, but, when it was put to the vote, 'there having been no votes in favour, none against and no abstentions, the President declared that his ruling stood'.[6]

This amounted to a *reductio ad absurdum* of the double veto. According to the San Francisco Statement, Nationalist China had some justification for attempting a double veto. On the other hand, the Statement also spelt out, as a procedural matter, inviting 'any State when it is a party to a dispute being considered by the Council to participate in the discussion'; and, as the President put in his ruling, if a situation was allowed to stand in which one permanent member was permitted to pronounce as substantive a vote which is regarded as procedural by no less than nine members of the Council, it might well impede the whole functioning of the United Nations in the future. The President's hand was also strengthened by the fact that in this case Nationalist China was endeavouring to assert itself against the actual government of China.

The Soviet Union naturally voted against Nationalist China on this occasion. This greatly weakened its case in September 1959, when it tried to use the double vote against a Western proposal to establish a subcommittee to conduct inquiries relating to Laos. The case was similar to that of Taiwan in 1950 in that both the President and the permanent member concerned could appeal to the San Franciscan

[6] SCOR 507th meeting, pp. 7–8.

Statement, because one of the procedural matters set out in it was establishing 'such bodies or agencies as it may deem necessary for the performance of its functions'. Actually, in declaring the resolution procedural in spite of the Soviet Union's contrary vote, the President chose to take his stand on the Charter and the Council's rules of procedure, but the representative of the United States, in the course of a statement supporting the President's stand, made the following important points: 'I happen to think that the San Francisco declaration is significant largely as a matter of attitude. . . . The United States has consistently taken the view that the so-called double veto cannot be used to make substantive a matter declared by the four-Power statement to be procedural.'

The veto

Up to the end of 1965 the veto had been used altogether on 108 occasions, in which were included 103 times by the Soviet Union.[7] France joined with the Soviet Union in one of its three vetoes relating to the Spanish question in June 1946; she vetoed a Soviet proposal to set up a Security Council Commission, as opposed to a Consular Commission, on Indonesia in August 1947; while France and Britain together twice used the veto during the Suez Crisis of 1956. Britain also vetoed a resolution on Southern Rhodesia in September 1963; and China vetoed the application for Membership of the Mongolian People's Republic in December 1955. The United States cast no veto during this period, due very largely to the fact that it could normally count on a majority in the Security Council without doing so. On many occasions no doubt the knowledge or the fear that the veto would be used also exercised an influence on the Council's actions.

The veto, as has been seen, was often the only weapon the Soviet Union could use to assert its rights and its influence, in view of its minority position in the Security Council. It is unfair, therefore, to blame it for the use of the veto *per se*. But the indiscriminate way in which it often chose to employ the weapon was certainly open to criticism: it by no means confined itself to using it when its vital interests were endangered or its rights seriously affected. For example, the unwise and 'light-hearted' way in which it first used the veto in February 1946 aroused the justified misgivings of the Secretary-General.[8] The Syrian and Lebanese governments had brought to the

[7] See the very useful table in Bailey, pp. 28–31.
[8] Trygve Lie, *In the Cause of Peace*, p. 34.

Council's attention the continued presence of British and French troops in their countries; the Council had before it a draft resolution expressing its confidence that the troops would be withdrawn as soon as practicable; and the Syrian and Lebanese delegates had said that the resolution was acceptable to their governments. In spite of this, the Soviet representative, Vishinski, vetoed the resolution on the ground that it did not go far enough. The Council's work on the dispute would thus have come to nothing, had the British and French representatives not stated immediately that their governments would voluntarily regard themselves as bound by the terms of the resolution.

Two of the Soviet government's worst habits were to use the veto, in Charles Yost's words, to 'curry favour' with other states[9] and to prevent a question being referred to another body or a subsidiary organ being established such as an investigating committee or an observation team, which could have served a useful purpose. Examples of the first were a veto cast in June 1962 on an Irish proposal regarding Kashmir, in which India and Pakistan were called on to reopen negotiations and refrain from any statements or actions which might aggravate the situation, and another used in September 1964 against a Norwegian draft resolution calling for restraint and resumption of talks in the dispute between Malaysia and Indonesia, the Soviet Union's aim in these two cases being to please India and Indonesia respectively.[10] Examples of the second were vetoes on proposals to refer two matters to the International Committee of the Red Cross: the Soviet accusation in July 1952 that the United Nations forces had used bacteriological warfare in Korea, and the welfare of the surviving members of the RB-47 crew, shot down by Soviet fighters in July 1960. In the Czechoslovak case of 1948 a Soviet veto followed the double veto that has been described. But the Soviet failure to prevent the setting up of a subcommittee for Laos in 1959 appears to have brought an end to this series of negative actions.

The repeated use of the veto in the case of applications for admission to the United Nations rightly came under strong criticism, especially from the Secretary-General, Trygve Lie, who was a strong advocate of universality of membership. Applications were vetoed by Nationalist China once, in the case cited, and by the Soviet Union fifty-one times in relation to seventeen applications, Italy's being turned down on no less than six occasions. Between September 1950 and December 1955 no new Member was admitted, the Soviet Union vetoing every Western-

[9] See his article, 'The United Nations: crisis of confidence and will', *Foreign Affairs*, Oct. 1966, p. 21.
[10] See Bailey, pp. 42–43, for details and other examples.

sponsored applicant and the Western *bloc* voting against the admission of Communist states. Then on 14 December 1955 came the so-called 'package deal', by which six West European countries, four Communist countries, and six Afro-Asian countries were all admitted together. Since that time only seven applications have been vetoed, four of them being made up of two applications each from the Republics of Korea and Vietnam.

The effect of the veto has been considerably modified by practices which have developed and been generally accepted relating to abstention from voting and absence from meetings of the Council. Paragraph 3 of Article 27 lays down that decisions of the Council on all non-procedural matters shall be made by an affirmative vote of seven members including 'the concurring votes of the permanent members'. A strict interpretation of this passage would mean that for a decision of the Council to be valid the positive concurrence of all five permanent members is needed. The passage, however, has been interpreted quite differently in practice. The only reference to abstention in this Article on voting is in the last clause of paragraph 3, which provides that 'in decisions under Chapter vi, and under paragraph 3 of Article 52, a party to a dispute shall abstain from voting'.[11]

Strangely enough it was the Soviet representative in the Council who set the example of a very free interpretation of the phrase 'concurring votes'. In April 1946, on a resolution relating to the Spanish question, he abstained from voting and explained that he did not like the resolution but did not want to prevent its being passed by casting a negative vote. Although he added that his abstention was not to be taken as a precedent, it almost inevitably has been treated as such. Every other permanent member has used the same procedure, which has become common practice in the Council. In fact, on a high proportion of the 244 resolutions adopted by the Council from 1946 to 1967 there was at least one of the permanent members who abstained.[12] In August 1947 the Syrian President of the Council summed up the position in the following statement, which was not questioned:

> I think it is now jurisprudence in the Security Council—and the interpretation accepted for a long time—that an abstention is not considered a veto,

[11] This reference is, in the opinion of some legal authorities, 'quite inadequate for the protection of the great principle that nobody would be a judge in his own cause', because it refers only to 'disputes', not to 'situations', and does not cover the Council's actions under Chapter vii. See Bentwich and Martin. pp. 69–70, and Andrew Martin, *Collective Security*, pp. 103–4.

[12] See Bailey, pp. 70–71: the author gives his own estimate of the number of abstentions and the estimates of two other authorities as well.

and the concurrent votes of the permanent members mean the votes of the permanent members who participate in the voting. Those who abstain intentionally are not considered to have cast a veto. That is quite clear.[13]

In the case of a permanent member absenting himself from Council meetings, clarity was not so easy to achieve. In the spring of 1946 the Soviet representative twice withdrew from the Council during its consideration of the Iranian question. The decisions taken in his absence were not clearly substantive—they were mainly to defer proceedings—but he maintained that they were incorrect and illegal. The Council rejected his contention, two members arguing with a good deal of force that absence amounted to intentional abstention. In January 1950 the Soviet representative withdrew for nearly seven months as a protest against the Council's attitude on Chinese representation. During this period decisions of far reaching importance were taken regarding the aggression against South Korea. On his return the Soviet representative strongly protested that they were illegal, but the Council rejected his standpoint and the matter was allowed to drop. This result was facilitated by the Soviet Union's own attitude on abstention and by Article 28 of the Charter, which provides that the Security Council should 'function continuously'. This provision would be impossible to implement, if any permanent member could stop the Council's work by staying away from its meetings.

As Martin and Edwards have pointed out, the result of deliberate practice over the years has been a virtual amendment of the Security Council's voting procedure under Article 27, paragraph 3, and 'decisions of non-procedural matters are now validly passed by an affirmative vote of seven Members, including the concurring vote of the permanent Members *present and voting*'.[14]

Actual as opposed to virtual amendments to the Charter are subject to the veto. So, in view of the Soviet attitude, no formal modification of the permanent members' power of veto has been possible. But the attempts of the General Assembly to bring about a change during the UN's early years are of interest, because they produced some valuable suggestions and drew widespread attention to the problem. The attempts were in some measure a renewal of the efforts made by the middle and smaller states at San Francisco. But, now that it had become clear where the main danger of abusing the veto lay, they were supported to a limited extent by the United States and by other Western powers.

[13] SCOR, 2nd year, 173rd meeting, 1 Aug. 1947, p. 1711.
[14] Andrew Martin and John B. S. Edwards, *The Changing Charter*, p. 32.

The General Assembly during its first session passed a resolution on 13 December 1946 requesting the permanent members of the Security Council 'to make every effort, in consultation with one another and with fellow members of the Security Council, to ensure that the special voting privilege of its permanent members does not impede the Security Council in reaching decisions promptly'. The Council passed the matter to its Committee of Experts (see p. 82, n. 2) in the summer of 1946 and no further action was taken. But it was significant that, in his report to Congress on the United Nations for 1946, the American President wrote that the United States considered 'that the "veto" should be employed sparingly and only when there is a clearcut justification for its use' and then referred to the practice that had been growing up of voluntary abstention by permanent members.[15]

During its second session the General Assembly asked its Interim Committee (see pp. 289–90) to undertake a study of Security Council voting procedure. In April 1947 it adopted a resolution, introduced by China, France, the United Kingdom, and the United States and based on the Committee's report, which recommended the Security Council to consider as procedural a listed series of decisions, and recommended the permanent members to seek agreement amongst themselves about forbearance in the use of the veto, in particular to consult together wherever feasible on important decisions to be taken by the Council and to exercise the veto only when they consider the question of vital importance, taking into account the interests of the United Nations as a whole. The permanent members met to consider the resolution the following October but could agree on only one point: the principle and practice of consultation before important decisions are to be made. They announced in a formal statement that they had agreed 'to meet again as soon as convenient to arrange for the calling and holding of such consultations'.[16] Two weeks later the General Assembly passed another resolution requesting the permanent members not to use the veto in connection with admissions to the United Nations.

The October statement about a further meeting on consultations does not seem to have been followed up. But the General Assembly's attempts to limit the veto were worth while, because they emphasized the strong feeling among UN members that restraint and responsibility should be exercised in using it, and because they led to the formal suggestions about consultations between permanent members and the need to take into account the interests of the United Nations as a whole.

---

[15] President's *Annual Report to Congress* on the United Nations, 1946, p. 31.
[16] SCOR, 4th year, 452nd meeting, 18 Oct. 1949, p. 2.

These suggestions may already have influenced the attitudes of permanent members, for example, towards negotiations on the Middle East,
and may well prove fruitful in the future, provided the governments and
representatives concerned give the necessary lead.

A number of authorities have pointed out that the vetoes, in spite of
their frequency, had in the end a limited effect on the policies supported
by a majority of the Security Council.[17] For example, there were fifty-
two vetoes on admissions to the UN, yet nearly all the applicants have
since become members. Britain and France nullified the Soviet's first
veto in the case of Syria and Lebanon. Soviet vetoes on the Spanish
question, on the Greek frontier incidents, and on the re-election of
Trygve Lie, and British and French vetoes during the Suez crisis, were
all circumvented by the General Assembly. The use of the veto, of
course, seriously reduced the effectiveness of the Security Council and
accentuated the division between the permanent members which their
basic differences caused. But Sydney Bailey has estimated that, when
every method of evasion and modifying circumstances has been taken
into account, there remains, out of the 109 vetoes that were cast up to
the end of 1967, only 'a hard core of 25 vetoes and one double veto . . .
which wholly prevented the action, recommendation, or expression of
opinion proposed'.[18]

Participation of non-member states and individuals

Under Article 32 of the Charter it is rightly obligatory that a state which
is not a member of the Council, or not a member of the UN but is a
party to a dispute being considered by the Council, should be invited
to participate, without vote, in the discussion relating to the dispute.
But the provision under Article 31, by which a UN Member which is
not a member of the Council may participate in a discussion when the
Council considers its interests are specially affected, is permissive only.
It has, however, been very liberally interpreted in practice. During the
UN's first nine years, thirty-seven such invitations were extended and
only four denied. Furthermore, the phrase 'specially affected' was not
taken very seriously. In February 1968 Colombia was allowed to participate in a session on South West Africa, and in December 1969 Bulgaria
and Mauritius were permitted to take part in a session concerned with
an alleged act of aggression by Portugal against Guinea.

---

[17] See, for example, Norman J. Padelford, 'The use of the veto', *Internationa
Organization*, June 1948, p. 246; Inis L. Claude, *Swords into Plowshares*, pp.
155–6; Martin and Edwards, p. 91; Bailey, pp. 54–62.

[18] Bailey, p. 61.

Three of the four invitations that were denied were refused on the very reasonable ground that invitations to discuss a matter could not be given until the matter was put on the agenda. The fourth concerned the request of the Philippines in August 1949 to participate in discussions on the Indonesian question. It was turned down owing to members' doubts as to whether the Philippines' interests were in reality 'specially affected'. But within a fortnight the Council had revised its decision.[19] In September and October 1956, during the discussion of the Suez problem, an Egyptian representative was allowed to take part, but requests from seven other Arab states and Israel for permission to participate were twice postponed, although on the second occasion they were invited to present their views to the president of the Council for circulation to members. In December 1971, when the question of the Indo-Pakistani War came before the Council, Tunisia asked to participate, but the Italian representative maintained that owing to the urgency of the crisis the deliberations should be restricted to members of the Council and the main parties concerned. He won his point, but only briefly, because the following day the Tunisian representative was invited to attend.

This openhanded interpretation of Article 31 has great disadvantages. The members who are invited to participate are not disposed to miss their opportunities, and the length of their contributions to the discussions is often in inverse proportion to the value of what they have to say. During the Congo debates in February 1961 representatives of twenty-three UN members were invited to the Security Council. At the meeting in Addis Ababa early in 1972 again twenty-three states, which were not members of the Council, participated in its discussions.

Under Rule 39 of the Council's provisional rules of procedure the Council 'may invite members of the Secretariat or other persons, whom it considers competent for the purpose, to supply it with information or to give other assistance in examining matters within its competence'. At the Addis Ababa meeting this rule was also interpreted liberally, a dozen persons being allowed to address the Council. It was emphasized that they spoke as individuals and not as representatives of organizations, but they were mostly individuals playing leading roles in African liberation movements.

As the United Kingdom representative suggested, when the Philippines had asked to participate in the discussions on Indonesia, the Council should be careful of the manner in which it applies Article 31,

---

[19] See *Repertory of Practice of United Nations Organs*, vol. II, p. 156.

and the same care should be applied to the application of Rule 39. A systematic effort is required to tighten up the Council's procedure and raise the level of its sessions; the chief obstacles to be overcome being the woolly-minded benevolence of some of its members, especially of its non-permanent members, and the reluctance of its permanent and non-permanent members alike to offend the susceptibilities of would-be additional participants.

Annual reports to the General Assembly

Paragraph 3 of Article 24 lays down that the Security Council shall submit annual and, when necessary, special reports to the General Assembly for its consideration, and Article 15, paragraph 1, provides that the General Assembly shall receive and consider these reports. The Council has dutifully prepared and submitted annual reports and a number of special reports on the admission of new members. But the General Assembly has given the annual reports a minimum of attention; in fact, by its third session it appeared to have become recognized practice for the Assembly to confine itself to taking note of the Council's reports. One rather formal point was given brief consideration during the fifth session, and on several occasions the Council's special reports on the admission of new members were discussed.[20]

Paul Martin, a former Canadian minister of external affairs, has explained that Canada was responsible for Article 24 (3) which requires the Security Council to report to the General Assembly, the purpose being 'to give the Assembly some sense of supervision of the Council's acts', but found it necessary to add rather sadly, 'it has not turned out that way'.[21] It did not so turn out for several reasons. The Assembly's agenda was always very full. If the reports had been discussed, there would have been a danger of reopening matters of substance, which had already been dealt with in detail by the Council. Furthermore, consideration which involved disapproval might have infringed upon the Council's 'primary responsibility for maintaining peace and security'. Nevertheless, used occasionally and with discretion, the Assembly's right to consider the Council's reports could have a stimulating effect. As it is, the Charter has given all UN members in the Assembly the opportunity each year to challenge the Security Council to live up to its responsibilities, and they have not taken advantage of it.

[20] See *Repertory of Practice of United Nations Organs*, vol. I, 488–9.
[21] *Canada and the Quest for Peace*, p. 7.

The rules of procedure

The Council's rules of procedure have not been subject to a thorough revision, and remain provisional (see p. 82, n. 2). Some of them have been disregarded, some have been modified in practice for the sake of convenience, and some of the permissive ones have not been implemented. There are sixty-one altogether, of which only a limited number are of general interest and importance. They are arranged in eleven chapters.

Chapter I, which deals with meetings, provides in Rule 1 that, apart from 'periodic' meetings, they shall be held 'at the call of the President at any time he deems necessary, but the intervals shall not exceed fourteen days'. This rule was adhered to fairly consistently during the Council's first three years, when there were only three cases when the intervals between meetings exceeded fourteen days.[22] But later such intervals became more frequent, and it became the custom for the President to consult with members to find out whether there was any objection to waiving the rule.[23] During 1959 there were only five meetings of the Council, two of them on one day, though this was exceptional.

Chapter III, on representation and credentials, lays down in Rule 13 that 'each member of the Security Council shall be represented at the meetings of the Security Council by an accredited representative' but adds that 'the Head of Government or Minister of Foreign Affairs of each member of the Security Council shall be entitled to sit on the Security Council without submitting credentials'.

Chapter IV, concerning the presidency, provides under Rule 18 that the presidency 'shall be held in turn by members of the Security Council in the English alphabetical order of their names' and that 'each President shall hold office for one calendar month'. This system has enabled the representative of every member to become President, even since the enlargement of the Council, but it has the disadvantage of not allowing Presidents, particularly the weaker personalities, to gain the experience and authority which a longer tenure of office would make possible.

Chapter VI, on the conduct of business, is concerned mainly with procedural details, but it includes two rules which have a wider importance.

[22] See L. M. Goodrich, 'The UN Security Council', *International Organization*, summer, 1958.
[23] For details see *Repertory of Practice of United Nations Organs*, vol. II, 110, para. 4.

Rule 28 relates to Article 29 of the Charter, dealing with subsidiary organs, and states that 'the Security Council may appoint a commission or committee or a rapporteur for a specific question'. The use of rapporteurs, though successful in the case of committees of the General Assembly, has not been adopted by the Security Council, because, where the issues are political, it would not normally be possible for members to agree on anyone for the appointment.[24] But the Council has used *ad hoc* commissions and committees effectively. They have fallen into two categories: those dealing with particular questions in the field, as, for example, the Greek Frontier and Indonesian questions, Palestine, and the Indo-Pakistani dispute; and those drafting and other committees, meeting at the Council's meeting-place and dealing with specific questions, such, for example, as the Spanish and Corfu Channel questions, Palestine, and Iran.[25]

Rule 38 states that any Member of the UN invited to participate in the Security Council's discussions, in accordance with Articles 31 and 32 of the Charter, may submit proposals and draft resolutions, though these may be put to a vote only at the request of a representative on the Security Council. The Ukrainian SSR took advantage of this rule in January 1946, when it was invited to participate in the Council's discussion on Indonesia and then permitted to submit a formal resolution for setting up a Commission of Inquiry.[26]

An unfortunate omission in the chapter is that there is no statement, as there is in the relevant section of the General Assembly's Rules of Procedure (Rule 17), empowering the President to call a speaker to order if his remarks are not relevant.[27]

Chapter VIII deals with the question of languages. The rules of procedure laid down originally that there should be five official languages, Chinese, English, French, Russian and Spanish, and two working languages, English and French. Speeches made in one of the working languages were to be translated only into the other working language, while speeches made in an official language were to be interpreted into

[24] In December 1949 the Canadian President of the Council, General McNaughton, came near to being appointed a rapporteur, when he was asked by the Council to meet informally with the two parties to the Kashmir dispute, 'to examine the possibility of finding a mutually satisfactory basis for dealing with the problems at issue'. But suggestions put forward in the Council that he should be made a rapporteur with a carefully defined function were not taken up. After he ceased to be President he confined himself to acting as a channel of communication between the parties and gave up even this role after a few weeks.
[25] For details see *Repertory of Practice of United Nations Organs*, vol. II, 115–31.
[26] Bentwich and Martin, p. 74.
[27] Rule 39 has already been dealt with: see pp. 93–94 above.

both the working languages. In practice the normal procedure was for the translations into English and French to be consecutive and the translations into the official languages to be simultaneous with the aid of earphones. Even this procedure took up a lot of time and made the atmosphere more formal and stilted than, for example, in the Council of the League of Nations, where translation was into English and French only. In 1969 the rules were amended to make Russian and Spanish working languages as well, and this involved the danger of the great waste of time that would have resulted from three or four consecutive translations. Since then, fortunately, it has become the normal practice for speakers to waive the right to consecutive translation. So the change has brought about an overdue speeding up in the Council's procedure.

In Chapter IX, on the publicity of meetings, Rule 48 states that 'unless it decides otherwise, the Security Council shall meet in public' and adds that 'any recommendation to the General Assembly regarding the appointment of the Secretary-General shall be discussed and decided at a private meeting'. Rule 55 provides that at the close of each private meeting the Security Council shall issue a *communiqué* through the Secretary-General.

The last Chapter (XI) concerns 'relations with other UN organs' and refers specifically to the International Court of Justice. Articles 4 and 10 of the Court's Statue provide that 'the members of the Court shall be elected by the General Assembly and by the Security Council', that the election should be by absolute majority, and that the vote in the Council 'shall be taken without any distinction between permanent and non-permanent members'. Rule 61 reflects these provisions of the Statute and lays down that the election of members of the Court shall be by an absolute majority of votes.

From 1966 onward

Under the gentleman's agreement of 1946 about the geographical distribution of non-permanent seats, the only provision made for the representation of Asian and African seats in the Security Council was under the restrictive headings 'British Commonwealth' and 'Middle East'. This involved no great injustice at the time, because only twelve[28] of the UN's fifty-one original members came from Asia or Africa, and of these China was a permanent member of the Council, India was in the Commonwealth, and seven states were in the Middle East, leaving

[28] Not including the Union of South Africa, a member of the Commonwealth.

D

only Ethiopia, Liberia, and the Philippines with no chance of representation. But, by 1955, UN membership had risen by twenty-five to seventy-six, and of the new members thirteen were from Asia or Africa. By 1962 the total membership was 110, of which fifty-six were Asian or African states.

The first formal proposal to enlarge the Security Council was made by eighteen Latin American states in 1956, when at their request the matter was put on the agenda of the eleventh session of the General Assembly. It was on the agenda again the following year and was considered by the Conference of Non-Aligned Countries at Belgrade in 1961 and the Conference of Independent African States at Addis Ababa in 1963. It won increasing support, as more and more African and Asian states were admitted to UN membership. Finally, it was agreed to increase the number of elected members from six to ten and the number of votes required for decisions from seven to nine, the necessary resolution being passed by the General Assembly in December 1963. The changes, which involved amendments to the Charter, went into force in August 1965, when they had been ratified by two-thirds of the UN members, including all the permanent members of the Security Council.

The proportion of elected Council members to the total UN membership fell from 1 to 8·5 in 1945 to approximately 1 to 19 in December 1963. But, apart from the quantitative argument for an increase in Council membership, the unfairness of the gentleman's agreement in 1963 could be put right neither by such a makeshift arrangement as the allocation of the East European seat to an Asian member (see p. 71), nor by a more radical reallocation of only six elective seats. The problem was satisfactorily solved by the inclusion in the General Assembly resolution of December 1963 of an agreed distribution of elective seats as follows:

5 for African and Asian states.
1 for East Europeans.
2 for Latin Americans.
2 for West Europeans and others.

This meant that Asian and African members had one representative per eleven states, as compared with one per ten for Latin America and West Europe and Others, and one per nine for East Europe,[29] a reasonable arrangement in view of the small size or small population of many

[29] See Jaskaran S. Teja, 'Expansion of the Security Council and its consensus procedure,' *Netherlands International Law Review*, vol. XVI, no. 4.

of the new African members. No definite allocation of the five Afro-Asian seats was made between the two continents, but as the African states are more numerous[30] there have in fact always been three African and two Asian elected representatives on the Council, while, apart from the year 1967, one of the African or Asian seats has always been held by an Arab state.

The new composition of the Security Council gave it a much more balanced representation. At the first meeting of the expanded body in February 1966 the Japanese president pointed out that, as a result of the increased membership, for the first time in the UN's history all regions of the world were represented in the Council directly and proportionately. Up to 1965, apart from the Chinese and Middle East representatives and an occasional Asian member replacing an East European state or representing the Commonwealth, all members of the Council were either European or strongly influenced by the European cultural tradition. Now the UN had given the new African and Asian states, nearly all of them developing countries, the opportunity for the first time to play an important role in international affairs. They took advantage of it to air their problems and anxieties, especially their economic problems and their racial anxieties, and to develop the diplomatic contacts which UN headquarters offered on a, for them, unprecedented scale.

The weakness of Africa's contribution to the Security Council so far has been due chiefly to lack of trained and experienced personnel. The emancipation of African countries from colonial rule took place so quickly in 1960 and the following years that everyone was surprised: in 1960 alone sixteen new African members were admitted to the United Nations. The standard of education left by the colonial powers was, on the whole, low, and the new states had not time to prepare themselves adequately for their responsibilities. As a result the African missions in New York were in most cases understaffed and inexperienced, though good men were sometimes found to be leaders. Furthermore, the governments to which they were responsible usually knew little or nothing of UN affairs, so that the advice and servicing they obtained from home was much less than was available to most of the existing UN missions.

The situation was aggravated by the desire of the new African members to exert the maximum influence as a group rather than as individual states in a world organization, and this led to their becoming the most

[30] The figures were: at the end of 1965, Africa, 37, and Asia, 27; and at the end of 1971, Africa, 41, and Asia, 32; excluding the Union of South Africa and China.

tightly knit bloc within the United Nations, strongly influenced by the Organization of African Unity (OAU) with its headquarters in Addis Ababa. The OAU placed a doctrinaire emphasis on the sovereign equality of states and, in influencing the selection of African candidates for the Security Council, attached more importance to a member's willingness to support an orthodox OAU viewpoint than to its size, diplomatic experience, and influence in world affairs. In defiance of the Charter, a member's contribution to the maintenance of international peace and security appears to have carried little weight with the Organization. This attitude has minimized the operation of the principle of natural selection on the major African powers as regards membership of the Council, and brought about the absurd situation in 1970 of Africa being represented on the Council by three states with a total population of only about ten million.

Nevertheless the attainment of independent nationhood by so many African countries within a few years, their immediate reception into a great world organization, and the admission of three African states into the Security Council, as the largest elected group, constituted together a remarkable development in world history. That it was treated incidentally and not always given the significance it deserved was due to a myopia which seems often to affect statesmen when faced with great international issues; a myopia which afflicted British and French statesmen in the 1930s when faced with the rise of Hitler, and successive American governments after 1949 in face of the Communist success in China. In human terms the new arrivals in the Security Council were not always treated with the patience and understanding which their inexperience and the phenomenon which brought them there demanded.

The effect of enlargement on voting

The enlargement of the Council led to a radical change in the voting power of individual members and groups of members. The dominant position of the United States came to an end. Whereas, up to 1965, it was difficult for an opposition group to master the five votes necessary to defeat an American or Western resolution on an important issue, since 1966 the Afro-Asian group, together with the Soviet Union and the East European member, has had the seven votes necessary to prevent any resolution from passing, whether they vote against it or only abstain. In the past the support of at least one permanent member was necessary to obtain the seven votes needed to pass any resolution, while under the new order the non-permanent members can pass procedural and non-procedural resolutions, with one vote to spare, provided the veto is not used. The veto is, in fact, employed much less frequently than before. The Western powers remain reluctant to use an unpopular weapon, and the Soviet Union can usually defeat a resolution it dislikes without resorting to it.

It is, however, much more difficult for any group to manage the Council in a positive sense, except in the case of resolutions on racial or anticolonial issues, when the Afro-Asians can usually count on the support of Latin American as well as Communist members. On other matters, a good deal of negotiation, diplomatic skill, and readiness to compromise has normally been necessary to produce the nine votes required to pass a resolution, and this has led to important changes in the method of working and atmosphere within the Council.

The new style of the Afro-Asian group

It may well be asked whether the use of the term 'Afro-Asian group' is justified. The interests and problems of Japan, for example, come much closer to those of the great industrial powers of the West than to those of the newly emancipated African states. Such large and relatively experienced states as India, Pakistan, and the Phillippines also cannot reasonably be lumped together with the Maldives and Gambia, neither of whom maintain missions in New York. On the other hand, comparable anomalies can be found within the Latin American group. The General Assembly resolution of December 1963 allocated five seats in the Security Council without distinction to 'African and Asian states', and the great majority of these states have at least two characteristics in common: they have recently been freed from colonial status, and they are economically underdeveloped. The expression 'Afro-Asian group', therefore, may be usefully employed, in spite of its imperfection.

In 1966 the African and Asian states were, on the whole, inexperienced in diplomacy and the broad consideration of international issues and absorbed in their own pressing political and economic problems. Such diplomatic experience as their leaders had had was in association with the former colonial powers and strongly influenced by European example, which in most cases they were anxious to repudiate. Politically their main aim was to assert their newly won freedom and their right to play a part in world affairs. Economically they combined planning for the future with resentment about their previous exploitation, and it was this second preoccupation which revealed itself most frequently in the

Security Council. Resentment of largely out-of-date colonialism was, in fact, the bugbear which caused them to lose a sense of proportion as members of a world body. Moved by emotion rather than reason they attached an importance to the surviving evil of Portuguese colonialism, which was out of proportion to its real significance in world affairs, while remaining relatively unmoved at the ruthless suppression of the Czechoslovakian people's liberal aspirations in 1968.

This subjective approach to their new responsibilities has led the African and Asian representatives to use the Security Council too often as a propaganda platform rather than as the great organ it was intended to be for furthering international cooperation and maintaining peace and security. Furthermore, many of them have adopted in it a deliberately contentious and flamboyant style. Their purpose in so doing has sometimes been partly personal; to attract the attention of their home governments and others to their performances on an important international stage, and press correspondents at the UN have sometimes been badgered, because their papers have not reported the performances more fully. Their motives have more often been to further regional or group causes, to which they pay more attention than to such great international issues as the control and non-proliferation of nuclear weapons, peace in the Indian subcontinent, and a Middle East settlement.[31]

These tendencies towards propaganda and a flamboyant style were due partially, in the first place, to the recent arrival of the Asian and African states in the Security Council. They brought with them habits acquired in the General Assembly, and this has had the effect of turning the Council, during many of its sessions, into something like a small version of the Assembly. They were due quite as much, and perhaps even more, to the bad example set by the super-powers, who for years have used the Council as an arena for debating and dramatizing the issues of the Cold War. It was they rather than the African and Asian members, who, through their rivalry, had given unreality to the term, 'United Nations', and had made it difficult for the Security Council to become the instrument for international cooperation that was envisaged at San Francisco. A third reason was the encouragement given by the Soviet Union and Communist members of the Council to a contentious attitude on the part of the African and Asian states. For example, during the debate in December 1970 on the alleged invasion

---

[31] The African Mediation Mission to the Middle East in 1971 was a welcome but not very successful exception.

of the Republic of Guinea by Portuguese forces, the experienced and relatively moderate Polish representative used terms more extreme than those employed by most of the African speakers and referred to the action under discussion as 'the spearhead of the colonialist reconquest of Africa, supported and supplied with arms by NATO'.

The most harmful consequence of the new Afro-Asian style was to debase the value of Security Council resolutions. Too often African and Asian states made extreme declarations and impractical proposals which had no chance of producing useful results, such, for example, as repeated exhortations to the British government to use force in Rhodesia. This method of procedure was damaging to the causes they intended to serve and to the United Nations itself. Resolutions that are not implemented undermine the UN's authority, while more moderate recommendations would have had more chance of being effective. The Afro-Asian group has also used the Council as a place in which to discuss minor matters, not really related to the maintenance of peace and security in the broad sense; in fact, for purposes it was never intended to serve. The reaction of the permanent members has been a greater reluctance to bring big international issues before the Council, and this form of resentment, from the UN's point of view, has made matters still worse.

The veto

During the years immediately preceding the enlargement of the Council, the veto was used much less frequently than it had been before. From 1962 to 1964 it was used only five times: four times by the Soviet Union and once by the United Kingdom. In 1965 it was not used at all. There were three main reasons for the change. Relations between the Soviet Union and the United States had improved noticeably as a result of Khrushchev's more flexible policy, Sino-Soviet rivalry, and the settlement of the Cuban missile crisis. The Soviet government also realized increasingly that indiscriminate use of the weapon was frowned on by UN members. Furthermore the veto tended to result in the matter under consideration being transferred to the General Assembly, where it was more difficult for a great power to exert its influence.

After the Council's enlargement it was relatively easy, as has been seen, for a permanent member to defeat resolutions, except those concerned with racial and colonial issues, without employing the veto. So the restraint on its use has continued. The Soviet Union has used it from time to time, notably on three occasions during the Indo-

Pakistani War in 1971; the United Kingdom has resorted to it several times on the Rhodesian question, the British government considering the veto a more honest reaction than abstention to a resolution it had no intention of implementing, and in March 1970 the United States vetoed with Britain a resolution on Rhodesia, partly as a protest against Afro-Asian methods, and partly to make clear that the veto was a weapon it was quite prepared to use, although it had not hitherto done so.

An important result of the relative ease with which any group of states has been able since 1965 to block positive action in the Security Council has been to make members realize, at an early stage, the need for an attitude and method of working quite different from those which had prevailed during the Cold War period. The basis of any successful democracy is a substantial measure of unity or at least social cohesion in the state or organization where it is practised, so that the various elements can differ without losing a sense of common purpose. But unrestrained majority voting of any kind is not so well suited to an organization like the UN or a body like the Security Council, in which there are deeplying political, economic, and cultural divisions. This was the basic reason for the new attitude of Council members which emerged after 1965.

The method of consensus

The new method of working, which resulted from the changed attitude, took the form of the frequent use of the so-called consensus procedure. A consensus in the Security Council may be defined as a unanimous decision of the Council, taken with or without a vote, as a result of a process of negotiation and compromise.

It might be objected that this method of working was not new and that before 1966 many decisions of the Council had been reached without voting and therefore by common consent. Most of the decisions then taken, however, were different, both in character and in the way by which they were reached from the consensus decisions agreed on by the new method after 1965. According to the *Repertory of Practice of United Nations Organs* the Council took about 1,206 decisions during the period 1946 to August 1959, of which 835 were by voting.[32] But the great majority of those taken without vote were of a routine or procedural nature and required little or no previous negotiation or com-

[32] See the General Surveys relating to Article 27 of the UN Charter in vol. II, p. 66; in Supplement no. 1, vol. I, p. 270, and in Supplement no. 2, vol. II, p. 308.

promise to obtain unanimous support. Between 1946 and 1970 the Council adopted 179 resolutions relating to the maintenance of international peace and security, which covered most of its more important decisions, and fifty of them were passed by consensus. Of these consensual resolutions only seven were adopted during the first eighteen years of the Council's existence, whereas during the five years from 1966 to 1970 the average was more than six a year.[33]

There are three main kinds of consensus procedure in the Security Council: consensual resolutions, consensual decisions, and statements of consensus by the President. Before dealing with each of those categories in turn, it will be as well to consider the key role played by the President of the Council in all consensual practices.

Every international body with a clearly defined purpose, like the Security Council, tends to develop at least a limited amount of *esprit de corps*. The members, whatever the differences that may divide them from one another, like to feel that the body from time to time is fulfilling the purpose it was intended to serve. The general support for the consensus procedure after 1965 reflected the increased difficulty of agreeing on positive action by the Council and the desire of members that the Council should nevertheless from time to time take such action and pass useful resolutions. It has been the custom of most UN bodies to decide on short adjournments, when necessary, to enable members or a group of members to discuss and, if possible, reach agreement on, the terms of a draft resolution, and on such occasions a good President has often played an important lubricant role. The development of a consensus method has given Presidents greater opportunities and greater responsibility in this respect.

When a matter on the Security Council's agenda appears to be suitable for the consensus approach, the President will usually have preliminary consultations with a few members, who are either most closely concerned or most likely to contribute to a solution of difficulties, in order to agree on a plan of action. A series of meetings follows, more often with groups of members but sometimes with all members, drafts are prepared and discussed, and modifications made with a view to making unanimity possible. Before 1966, when the procedure of consultation was less fully developed, the President consulted occasionally, mostly on procedural points, with deputies or representatives delegated for the purpose by the heads of missions. But after 1965 a more formal informality was evolved. Questions of

[33] See F. Y. Chai, *Consultative and Consensual Practices in the Working of the Security Council*, Annex, Table i.

D*

substance as well as of procedure were considered; the heads of missions usually attended themselves; and some useful customs were adopted; for example, no records of the meetings were kept, there was no voting, and a strong convention grew up that no reference should be made in subsequent public debates to the points made at private meetings. The privacy of the meetings, in fact, gave them their special value, because it was often easier in private to persuade members, especially permanent members, to make concessions than in the public sessions, where national prestige might be involved and the reactions of governments and world opinion had to be considered.

The limited space available for these private meetings has been criticized. The President has a private office adjacent to the Security Council Chamber and a small oblong conference room, which will only just accommodate all members of the Council. But the very inadequacy of the accommodation has its advantages, because it helps to preserve the informality and intimacy of the consultations.

The restraint and sense of responsibility usually shown by Presidents in carrying out the consensus procedure is well illustrated by the action of the Soviet representative on 29 September 1966, when he was President of the Council. Having just read out the formulation of a consensus agreement reached by the Council on the Dominican question, he added in his capacity as representative of the USSR a very moderate statement to the effect that the Soviet Union considered that, in spite of their usefulness, two previous Council resolutions and the agreement just reached 'do not eliminate those most important problems on which depend the fundamental solution of the Dominican question'.[34]

Consensual resolutions have covered most of the important examples of the consensus method, because the formal resolution is the most appropriate way by which the Security Council can make decisions on the big issues that come before it. An outstanding example from this category was Resolution 242 on the Middle East which the Council approved unanimously on 22 November 1967. It has provided the framework for the negotiations that have since taken place to bring about a settlement and has contributed to the maintenance of an uneasy peace. Lord Caradon, who sponsored the resolution, described it, before the vote, in the following terms, which throw light on the whole consensual process:

> The draft resolution which we have prepared is not a British text. It is the result of close and prolonged consultations with both sides and with all

[34] See Bailey, p. 82.

members of the Council. As I have repeatedly said, every member of this Council has made a contribution in the search for common ground on which we can go forward.

The adoption of a consensual resolution may or may not be accompanied by a debate, and, if there is a debate, it may take place either before or after the vote. The discussion is sometimes waived, if it is felt likely that it might break up the consensus over some contentious but not fundamental point. An example of this procedure occurred in the very difficult and urgent case of the resolution concerning the hijacking of commercial aircraft in September 1970, when the lives of several hundred people were endangered. After a series of consultations by the President and modifications and concessions made by the Soviet and United States representatives, a draft resolution was approved by all members, and it was agreed that a debate should be avoided. However, the special envoy of the non-member state, Algeria, insisted on his right to speak before the resolution was adopted. The Council's generous attitude towards the participation of non-member states in its discussions, under Article 31 of the Charter, had been continued after 1965. But on this occasion, the Council asserted its right to restrict its meetings to members only; the consensus was adopted immediately; and the meeting adjourned without a debate.[35]

When debates do take place, as is more usual, it is more usual also for debates to precede the vote, but the practice has been growing, especially, though not exclusively, in the case of consensual resolutions, for the discussion to follow the voting. This eliminates the possibility of different interpretations of the consensus inhibiting members from casting a positive vote.

Consensual decisions are made without a vote and often without discussion. They have usually been procedural in character and have not required previous consultations. But, on a number of occasions, their content has been substantive, and they have been preceded by consultations. For example, on 9 June 1967, during the Six-Day War between the Arabs and Israel, the Council agreed, without a vote and after consultations, to ask the parties concerned to re-establish freedom of movement for UN observers in the war area and to restore the use of Government House, Jerusalem, to General Odd Bull, the head of the UN Truce Supervision Organization.

As regards the third kind of consensus procedure, the statement of consensus by the President, F. Y. Chai distinguishes between three

[35] See Chai, pp. 35–36.

varieties of presidential statement.[36] The first is the straightforward statement, which the President uses to express the attitude of the Council when there is some objection to adopting a resolution and yet a formal statement is considered appropriate. It is usually preceded by consultations among members. A good example is the statement made by Ambassador Goldberg of the United States on 22 September 1965, regarding the fighting between India and Pakistan over Kashmir. He said that, having consulted his colleagues, he had been authorized to make a statement on behalf of the entire Council, the essence of the statement being that the Council expressed its satisfaction that the cease-fire demanded by it, in a recent resolution, had been accepted by the two parties and called upon the governments concerned to implement the cease-fire by a fixed time.

An interesting variation of this form of presidential statement occurred on 8 December 1967. Chief Adebo of Nigeria issued, as a Council document, an important statement on the Middle East 'reflecting the views of members of the Council', without, however, holding a formal meeting of the Council to approve it. It said that members recognized 'the necessity of the enlargement by the Secretary-General of the number of observers in the Suez Canal Zone and the provision of additional material and means of transportation'. The advantage of this procedure was that members did not have to express their reservations, which they could not have avoided doing, had a meeting been held. It has been used since on less important matters.[37]

Secondly, a presidential statement may take the form of a summary, in which the President sums up the views expressed in a debate, as a means of closing a discussion, when it appears unlikely that a formal draft resolution would be accepted. The importance of the President having adequate consultations in such a case was shown in June 1965, when the President attempted to summarize a debate on the situation in the Dominican Republic. The Soviet representative at once pointed out that it was a strict rule that, before the President does any summing-up on behalf of the members of the Council or the Council as a whole, consultations should be held with all the members of the Council, and that such consultations had not been held. The complaint got some support, and the President agreed to try again.[38]

The third variety of presidential statement is an appeal to parties on

[36] Chai was for many years Director of the Security Council and Political Division of the UN Secretariat.

[37] See Bailey, pp. 83 and 221 and Chai, pp. 25–26.

[38] See Chai, pp. 22–23, and Bailey, pp. 211–17.

behalf of the Council to comply with a previous resolution, exercise restraint, or cooperate in the maintenance of peace. A good example of such an appeal occurred on 10 January 1964, in connection with the question of the Panama Canal zone. The Council decided without voting to authorize the President to appeal to the governments of the United States and Panama to bring to an immediate end the exchange of fire and bloodshed and to request them to impose restraint on their military forces and the civilian population.

Opinions are divided as to whether or not the development of consensus procedure since 1965 represents an improvement in the Security Council's practice. When it is agreed to aim at a consensus, every member of the Council is virtually given a veto, and, although in the circumstances members tend to use their power to say 'no' with responsibility and sensitivity to other members' views, the search for agreement may well lead to watering down the resolution, decision, or statement, until, in some cases, they become ineffective or even meaningless. On the other hand, the positive attitude and sense of common purpose, which the consensual approach implies, is an improvement on the negative, bitter, and frustrating atmosphere that so often prevailed in the Council during the cold war period. Furthermore, in relation to the bigger international issues, the consensual procedure is a comparatively new technique, and there is no reason why Council members, with more experience and a higher sense of responsibility, on which the whole future of the United Nations depends, should not overcome the procedure's main weaknesses, while retaining its advantages. Already consensual resolutions on such subjects as the Middle East, Cyprus, and Bahrein have been constructive and valuable.

A periodic meeting

U Thant raised the question of periodic meetings in his Annual Reports for 1966–67 and 1967–68, suggesting that a 'modest beginning' might be made by holding one such meeting to test their values. Although no action was taken on this suggestion, the Finnish representative on the Council, Max Jakobson, took up the matter vigorously in 1970, and his efforts culminated in a Presidential statement on 12 June, expressing the consensus of the Council on the subject. Its key passages were the following:

> The members of the Security Council . . . consider that the holding of periodic meetings, at which each member of the Council would be repre-

sented by a member of the government or by some other specially designated representative, could enhance the authority of the Security Council
and make it a more effective instrument for the maintenance of international peace and security . . .

. . . periodic meetings . . . would provide members with an opportunity
for a general exchange of views on the international situation, rather than
for dealing with any particular question, and . . . would normally be held
in private, unless it is otherwise decided.

As a result the first periodic meeting was, in fact, held the following
October during the meeting of the General Assembly.

As the meeting was private, no record of its proceedings is available,
though some interesting statements were made, which might not have
been made in a public session.[39] In accordance with the rules of procedure a formal *communiqué* was issued afterwards in place of a verbatim
record. It stated amongst other things that representatives of member
states had had a general exchange of views on current issues affecting
international peace and security and mentioned in particular the problems of the Middle East and southern Africa. It added that members of
the Council had emphasized the importance of reaching early agreement
on guidelines for future peace-keeping operations and had agreed to
examine possibilities for further improvements in the Council's methods
of work. They had agreed also that the holding of periodic meetings was
an important step in the direction of strengthening the Council's
capability to perform its main task, and that the date of the next
periodic meeting would be determined through consultations among
members.[40] However, largely through the lack of interest of the
permanent members, no periodic meeting was held during 1971.

There were several reasons for the indifference or hostility of the
permanent members, varying, of course, with the members. Two of the
three reasons which had prevented the holding of periodic meetings up
to 1965 still held good and had in some ways been strengthened by the
arrival of Communist China (see p. 79). In addition the major powers
in the Council considered it of more value for their foreign ministers to
meet together alone, as their representatives at the UN had often done
since 1967 to discuss the Middle East, than to try to establish rapport
with the foreign ministers of very small states, of which unfortunately
there was an unusually high proportion in the Council at the time of the
periodic meeting in 1970.

The meeting in October 1970 was prepared neither well nor long

[39] This information was given to the author by U Thant.
[40] The full text of the *communiqué* is given in the *Report of the Security Council to the General Assembly, 1970–71*, p. 3.

enough in advance. It occurred at a time when an important session of the General Assembly was taking place, was attended by only eleven foreign ministers, and lasted for only two and a half hours, which gave no time for a discussion. After an hour and a half no more than four ministers were left, three of those representing permanent members having gone off to social engagements. In these circumstances, the meeting can hardly be considered a serious experiment; not even the 'modest beginning' U Thant had in mind to test the value of periodic meetings.

On the other hand, under reasonably favourable conditions, the potential value of periodic meetings remains considerable. A *sine qua non* of their success would be a real will among the permanent members to further international peace and security through the United Nations and the Security Council. Such a will has only occasionally been manifest, for example, at the beginning of the Congo crisis and when the permanent members voted unanimously to establish a peace-keeping force in Cyprus. But, in the present state of the world, it is latent, if dependent on the fortuitous nature of political leadership. Given careful nurturing it may well become strong and evident enough for an experiment in periodic meetings to succeed. One condition favouring success would be a strengthening of the Council's membership, the foreign ministers of the permanent members naturally considering it more worth while to meet their colleagues from India and Japan, the Asian members in 1972, than ministers from much less influential states. Other favourable conditions would be planning meetings far in advance, thorough preparation, and careful choice of the agenda.

At least until the holding of periodic meetings has become established practice it would probably be as well for particular issues not to be put on their agendas. This point was made by Dag Hammarskjöld in his annual report for 1958–59, as well as in the Presidential statement of June 1970. Apart from general aspects of the international situation which may be of concern to the Council, suitable subjects for the agenda would be two of those mentioned in the *communiqué* issued after the periodic meeting in 1970: guidelines for future peace-keeping operations and the Council's methods of work. Another appropriate subject would be the interesting suggestion put forward by the Brazilian representative in May 1970 for setting up *ad hoc* committees, responsible to the Council, for the pacific settlement of particular disputes, in which the parties to a conflict or threatening situation would take part together with a small number of other member states and have a continuing responsibility to endeavour to reach a solution.

In addition to the progress such meetings might lead to in the solution of international problems, the establishment of a routine of periodic meetings, say twice a year, would bring ministers of the major powers into more frequent contact with one another within the UN framework and with a constructive purpose. It would also give them opportunities to become acquainted, in similar circumstances, with some ministers of smaller powers, their problems, and their points of view. Goodwill without scepticism on both sides would be a precondition of success, a relationship which is difficult but not impossible to achieve.

5
The Council's record[1]

The main casualties, which resulted from the Cold War situation, so far as the UN Charter was concerned, were the provisions made in Chapter VII for a limited system of collective security and for organizing armed forces to implement the Security Council's decisions. But the Charter still left the Council considerable scope for action.

Within the terms of Chapter VII the Council's influence in favour of peace was negligible in cases which involved conflicts between the superpowers or the main issues dividing East and West. But it remained possible that the permanent members might agree on decisions or recommendations relating to other questions. Furthermore, they could take action, under Articles 39, 40, and 41, to maintain or restore international peace and security, which did not necessitate recourse to armed forces.

The opportunities for positive action provided by Chapter VI were still wider. It was more likely that the permanent members would agree on joint action, or at least refrain from vetoing such action, in relation to disputes or situations which might lead to friction or a dispute than in the case of the eventualities which are the subject of Chapter VII, that is, threats to the peace, breaches of the peace, and acts of aggression. What is more, as has been suggested, the very imprecision of the chapter makes easier a flexible interpretation of its provisions. Chapter VI, in contrast to Chapter VII, is also rather permissive than mandatory in its working: while the articles in Chapter VII usually lay down what 'shall' be done, the more frequent terms in Chapter VI are 'may' or 'should'. The Security Council under Chapter VI cannot impose a settlement: it can only call on parties to settle their dispute themselves or recommend a settlement.[2] But these powers enable it to exercise considerable

[1] The treatment of the Council's record in this chapter is not intended to be exhaustive: some cases have been deferred to the next chapter, while others of small importance have been omitted altogether.

[2] This distinction has been widely accepted in practice. In an article on the International Court's Advisory Opinion on Namibia (*International and Comparative Law Quarterly*, April 1972), Dr Rosalyn Higgins calls its validity in question, but if her argument is accepted, the Council's influence will be increased.

influence in a variety of ways for the peaceful solution of international problems.

In addition, Chapter xv, dealing with the Secretariat, contains provisions which have turned out to have important implications for peaceful settlement. Article 99 empowers the Secretary-General to bring to the Security Council's attention any matter which in his view threatens international peace and security. Article 98 lays down that the Secretary-General, in addition to acting as the UN's chief administrative officer at all meetings of the Council and the General Assembly, 'shall perform such other functions as are entrusted to him by these organs', and shall 'make an annual report to the General Assembly on the work of the Organization'. These powers and duties, as interpreted by successive Secretaries-General, have had considerable influence on the Council's record and methods of work. In particular, Dag Hammarskjöld's personal introductions to his annual reports, with their thoughtful and constructive suggestions, have made a major contribution to what may become, in his own phrase, 'a common law of organized international cooperation'.[3]

The first three Secretaries-General all did their best to support the authority and extend the usefulness of the Security Council in spite of great power rivalry. The support they received from the great powers themselves, of course, varied considerably. But their efforts had the backing and goodwill of the great majority of the smaller and middle powers, though the attitudes of these powers towards the Council as an institution often left something to be desired.

Hammarskjöld, who held office from 1953 to 1961, did more than anyone else to develop the role of the UN in general and the Security Council in particular, within the field of peaceful settlement. He was, in his philosophic way, less concerned with the failure to create an effective system of collective security, which he considered an ultimate rather than an immediate objective, than with the need, in the existing international situation, to minimize the dangers to peace and to improvise methods for furthering this end. Having accepted the fact that it was extremely difficult for the UN to exercise an influence on problems that were clearly 'within the orbit of presentday conflicts between power blocs', he was particularly anxious that the UN should keep 'newly arising conflicts outside the sphere of the bloc differences', and, 'in the case of conflicts on the margin of, or inside, the sphere of bloc differences', that it should bring such conflicts out of this sphere by

[3] *Introduction to the Report of the Secretary-General on the Work of the Organization*, Aug. 1959.

aiming at their strict localization. Hammarskjöld himself described his policy as 'preventive diplomacy'.[4]

During the emergence of the UN's new role or roles in the field of peaceful settlement, a useful distinction came to be made between peace-making and peace-keeping. As a chapter of this book deals with problems of peace-keeping, it would be as well to define the distinction as it will subsequently be employed. It would be confusing to use either term to describe the enforcement action envisaged in Chapter VII of the Charter. The one occasion on which enforcement was undertaken on a large scale, against North Korea in 1950, can best be considered an unusual attempt at collective security, while the instance in 1966, when the Security Council authorized Britain to use force to prevent oil from reaching Rhodesia, may be classed as a case of limited enforcement action. 'Peace-making' may be taken to cover the settlement and attempts to settle disputes and threatening situations, before they lead to hostilities, and bringing an end to hostilities, when they have broken out. 'Peace-keeping' is action to restore peaceful conditions and maintain peace in troubled areas with the aid of military, para-military, or police personnel made available by the United Nations.[5]

The Security Council has carried out its primary responsibility for maintaining peace and security in five main ways. The first two of these are in the category of peace-making and the third and fourth in that of peace-keeping. First, in a few cases the Council has solved or helped to solve problems before they have resulted in hostilities. Secondly, and rather more often, it has brought an end to fighting that has broken out. In this work of peace-making it has produced results by exerting its inherent moral authority as a UN organ. This has usually been rein-forced by the strength of world opinion, and sometimes a major power, in most cases the United States, has exerted pressure in its own way to back up the Council's influence. On some occasions the Council has helped to produce the wanted result by the mere act of providing a UN framework, through which member states can make their influence felt, thus facilitating acquiescence by the party or parties from whom concessions are required. Thirdly and fourthly, it has sought to stabilize conditions after a cease fire and prevent the recurrence of fighting, either by setting up a peace-keeping force or by the organization of an

[4] He develops his ideas on the subject in his *Introduction to the Report of the Secretary-General on the Work of the Organization*, August 1960.

[5] Both terms can, of course, be used in other ways. Words should be our tools, rather than our masters. The concept of 'peace-keeping' is discussed by Rosalyn Higgins in the preface to her *United Nations Peacekeeping 1946–1967*, vol. I, and by Alan James in *The Politics of Peace-Keeping*, ch. 1.

observer group. Such a peace-keeping force is not specifically provided for in the Charter, which envisages only the establishment of armed forces for implementing Security Council decisions under Chapter VII. Peace-keeping forces, in fact, have been set up on the authority of either the Security Council or the General Assembly. They have consisted of armed forces, but the forces, apart from exceptional occasions in the Congo, have been allowed to use their weapons only in self-defence. The observer groups have usually been unarmed and have been made up mostly of commissioned officers. Their duties, as their title implies, have been to provide information, to observe and report about conditions on disputed or troubled frontiers.

The Council's fifth method of working was the appointment of a Commission, a mediator, or a UN representative. This method does not fall exclusively into the category of either peace-making or peace-keeping. It might be the duty of such an agent to carry out preparatory work in either field.

THE COLD WAR: THE EARLY STAGES

Iran

The first case to come before the Security Council during its opening meetings in January 1946 led to a serious clash between the United States and Britain on the one hand, and the Soviet Union on the other. In 1941 Soviet and British troops had occupied north and south Iran respectively, in order to facilitate the sending of supplies to the Soviet Union by the Western allies along the only available land route, Iran. By a tripartite treaty signed in January 1942, Iran had recognized the arrangement, but it was not to constitute a military occupation and all forces were to be withdrawn not later than six months after the end of the war. Later some American troops had joined the Russians and the British in Iran.

Iran now accused the Soviet Union of supporting a separatist movement in the Iranian province of Azerbaijan and of preventing Iranian troops from entering the province. The Soviet Union denied the allegations. On 30 January the Security Council dealt with the matter as diplomatically as possible by unanimously passing a resolution in which, the parties having agreed to seek a solution by negotiation, it requested them to inform it of any results achieved by the negotiations.

This first attempt brought no progress towards a solution. All the

Allied forces were to be withdrawn by 2 March, and the withdrawal of American and British troops was in fact completed by that date. But the Soviet forces remained and were actually reinforced, in spite of British and American protests. In their negotiations with Iran, Soviet officials had proposed the recognition by Iran of the internal autonomy of Azerbaijan and the setting up of a Soviet-Iranian joint stock oil company.

During March the situation deteriorated, and on the 18th Iran, influenced by the resolute attitude of the United States, again referred the matter to the Security Council, this time adding a complaint that the Soviet troops had not withdrawn by the prearranged date. The Council considered it on the 26th, and the American secretary of state, James Byrnes, showed the importance he attached to it by attending the meeting himself. But meanwhile President Truman had sent a strong message to Stalin reminding him of the 1942 Treaty and threatening counter-action, unless the Soviet troops were withdrawn. When the Council met on 26 March, the Soviet representative stated that negotiations between his government and the Iranian government had resulted in an understanding,[6] and that the evacuation of Soviet troops had already begun and would probably be completed within five or six weeks.

Negotiations and discussions continued during the next two months. The Security Council kept up its pressure on the Soviet Union, and on two occasions the Soviet representative refused to participate in the Iranian meetings for periods of several weeks, on the grounds that the Council ought not to be considering the question. On 15 April the Iranian Ambassador in Washington informed the Council that, as a result of an agreement between Iran and the Soviet Union, the Soviet government had agreed to evacuate all Iranian territory by 6 May and that the Iranian government had no doubt that the agreement would be carried out. It therefore withdrew its complaint from the Security Council. The Council, however, retained the matter on its Agenda,[7] and it was not until 21 May that Iran was able to report to the Council

[6] Qavam al Saltana, the Iranian prime minister, promised to bring in a Bill establishing a Soviet-Iranian oil company, with the Soviet government having 51 per cent of the shares. But he knew that the Majlis (parliament) would never approve it, and the following year the Majlis turned it down by an overwhelming majority. Without Security Council action and American pressure the Soviet Union would clearly have preferred retaining the troops in north Iran to such an uncertain arrangement.

[7] This was against the formal, well-intended, but probably unwise advice of Secretary-General Trygve Lie.

that it had at last been able to investigate conditions in Azerbaijan and that Soviet troops had in fact evacuated the province on 6 May.

The Iranian case was a real success for the Security Council in the field of peace-making. The Soviet Union had to withdraw its forces; it did not achieve its aim of establishing autonomous Azerbaijan; and ultimately it obtained neither an oil concession nor a jointly controlled Soviet-Iranian oil company. Strong American diplomacy, to a lesser extent British diplomacy, and Iranian ingenuity had contributed to the result, but steady and sustained pressure was exerted by the Council as well. Truman had wisely refrained from publicizing his note to Stalin and it was much easier for the Soviet Union to yield publicly to the firm but velvet-glove influence of moderate Council resolutions than it would have been to an open bilateral ultimatum. A senior Soviet diplomatist, in conversation with a colleague from the West, quoted the Iranian case as an instance when the Soviet Union carried out a Security Council ruling.[8]

A British newspaper wrote in January 1946 that Persia's decision to bring her controversy with Russia before the Security Council presented the UN 'with a test case right at the beginning of its career'.[9] Two months later another British paper suggested two reasons why the Persian question was so important: because it related to a strategically key position, and because it was 'such a direct challenge to the UNO'.[10] The UN, as has been seen, survived both test and challenge creditably. But, because its chances of survival have been called in question from time to time, and especially during the era of Nixonian negativism, it is perhaps interesting to note the comments of two American papers during the height of the Iranian crisis. On 17 March *The New York Herald Tribune* wrote: 'The Iranian crisis may seriously endanger the existence of the UNO', and two days later *The Christian Science Monitor* asked: 'Is the UNO going to break on the rock of Iran?' Thus from its earliest infancy the vitality of the UN has been called in question.

On 21 January 1946, within two days of the Iranian complaint against the Soviet Union, counter-allegations were made from the Communist side. The Soviet representative complained to the Council of the presence of British troops in Greece, which, he said, constituted inter-ference in the internal affairs of that country and was causing 'extreme

---

[8] This was told me by the Western diplomatist concerned, though the source cannot be revealed.

[9] *The Scotsman*, 27 Jan. 1946.

[10] *The Sunday Times*, 24 Mar. 1946.

tension fraught with the possibility of serious consequences . . . for the maintenance of international peace and security'. On the same day the representative of the Ukranian SSR drew the Council's attention to military operations which had been directed against the local population in Indonesia, in which regular British troops had been taking part, and which in the opinion of his government constituted 'a threat to the maintenance of international peace and security'. These complaints were generally considered to be a riposte to the Iranian charge against the Soviet Union. Both cases were considered by the Council during the first half of February, and they led to such acrimonious exchanges between Britain and the Soviet Union that Trygve Lie personally suggested to the two chief protagonists, Bevin and Vishinski, that the should moderate their speech.[11]

Bevin had good reason to feel indignant. In the Iranian case the government of Iran had itself complained of Soviet interference, while in the case of Greece the representative of that country made clear to the Council that the presence of British troops was due to 'a request made by the Greek government' and that 'neither the civil nor the military authorities of Great Britain had at any time sought to intervene in any manner whatsoever in the internal affairs of Greece'.[12] In Indonesia the British forces had taken over from the Japanese after Japan's surrender and had incurred Dutch criticism for being too favourable towards the newly proclaimed Republic of Indonesia. Nevertheless, the Soviet Union's counter-moves were tactically skilful and directed attention away from its own actions in Iran.

In general these three cases, which reflected the contentious relations between the Soviet Union and the Western powers, gave the Security Council a thoroughly bad start. During its early meetings the Council provided a platform for bitter mutual reproaches between the rival sides. Had it started its proceedings with some joint cooperative effort of the former wartime allies, as the Council's handling of the Indonesian question in the end almost turned out to be, the United Nations might have developed on different, perhaps on very different lines.

Greece

The Security Council's discussion of the Soviet complaint against Britain revealed wide support for the Greek and British points of view

[11] See *In the Cause of Peace*, p. 33.
[12] *Report of the Security Council to the General Assembly, 17 Jan.–15 July 1946*, pp. 31–32.

and was brought to an end by the acceptance of a presidential suggestion on 6 February to take note of the views and declarations of
members and consider the matter as closed. But there remained the basic
problem, which was the support being given to Communist guerrillas
in Greece by that country's Communist neighbours, Albania, Bulgaria,
and Yugoslavia. So the Greek question was considered again by the
Council repeatedly during the remainder of the year.

In August the Ukrainian SSR complained that the policy of the Greek
government constituted a threat to peace, and at a series of meetings in
September four resolutions in turn were considered and rejected. In the
end the question was removed from the list of matters of which the
Council was seized. Towards the end of the year, however, Greece
herself asked the Council to consider a situation which was leading to
friction between her and her neighbours owing to the latter giving 'their
support to the violent guerrilla warfare that was waged in northern
Greece against public order and the territorial integrity' of the
country.[13] The Council then unanimously adopted a resolution setting
up a Commission of Investigation, which was to ascertain the facts
relating to the alleged border violations and to make any proposals
that it might deem wise for averting a repetition of them.

Between December 1946 and September 1947 the Security Council
considered the Greek question at no less than forty-eight meetings. In
June 1947 the Commission of Investigation submitted its report, but a
draft resolution submitted by the United States, proposing that the
Commission's recommendations should be adopted, though supported
by nine members, was vetoed by the Soviet Union. After numerous
attempts to agree on some course of action had failed, the Council on
15 September 1947 again removed the question from the list of matters
of which the Council was seized. The following month the General
Assembly took up the question and soon appointed a Special Committee on the Balkans, known as UNSCOB, which was followed four
years later by a Balkan Sub-Commission of the Peace Observation
Commission (see p. 291).

On the Greek question the Soviet Union used its veto six times. It
was a clear example of an East-West dispute, which the Security
Council could not settle owing to the veto, being handed over to the
General Assembly. The United Nations cannot be given sole credit for
the Greek government's surviving the intervention of its Communist
neighbours. This result was due partly to the government's own efforts,

[13] *Repertoire of Practice of the Security Council 1946–51*, p. 309. The Council's
handling of the Greek question is dealt with on pp. 301–2 and 308–12 of this volume.

partly to the substantial support given it in turn by Britain and the United States, and partly to the Soviet–Yugoslav split in 1948, after which Yugoslavia soon ceased to be a menacing neighbour. But the United Nations, through the Security Council and the General Assembly, did play a considerable part in preserving the independence and territorial integrity of Greece. It provided a channel for publicizing frontier violations, and the presence in Greece over a number of years of UNSCOB and the Balkan Sub-Commission in turn made it difficult, if not impossible, for intervention to take place unnoticed.

Syria and Lebanon

The story of the Security Council's action in this case has already been briefly told (pp. 87–88). The matter was not brought to the Council by the Soviet Union. The initiative was taken by the Syrian and Lebanese governments with the encouragement of the Secretary-General.[14] But it did provide another occasion for an East-West encounter, though the Soviet Union threw away the advantage of a favourable deal by overplaying its hand, thus giving its opponents a chance to reveal themselves in a good light. It is probable that the French, and certain that the British, did not intend to stay long in either country, as their subsequent conduct indicated. But the Council's action ensured that there was no undue delay in their withdrawal. 'It is certainly a historic event,' the Lebanese representative said later, 'when two small states can, through the action of the Security Council, obtain satisfaction for their claims, because they have a right to it.'[15]

The Corfu Channel case, 1946–49

In October 1946 two British destroyers were damaged by mines, with the loss of forty-four lives, while passing through the channel between Albania and Corfu. Having failed to settle the matter by diplomatic correspondence, Britain submitted the question to the Council as a dispute under Article 35. The Council appointed a subcommittee to investigate the matter, consisting of representatives of Australia, Colombia, and Poland. But this body could not come to an agreement, because the Polish member would not acknowledge Albania's responsibility. A

[14] Trygve Lie, p. 33.
[15] *Ibid.*

draft resolution proposed by Britain, finding that the minefield could not have been laid without the knowledge of the Albanian authorities and recommending the two parties to settle the dispute on this basis, was approved by seven members but vetoed by the Soviet Union. The Council thereupon adopted a second British draft recommending the parties to refer the dispute to the International Court of Justice.

This is the only instance in which the Council recommended that a dispute should be referred to the Court.[16] Albania and Britain both complied with the recommendation, although Albania at first objected to the Court hearing the case on the unilateral application of Britain. The Court delivered its judgments on the substance of the dispute in 1949. It held that a mine-sweeping operation carried out by the British navy in November 1946 was a violation of Albanian sovereignty, but that Albania was responsible under international law for the explosions that had taken place in Albanian waters and for the damage and loss of life which they had caused. Albania was ordered to pay the United Kingdom a sum of £844,000 as reparations. But it did not do so.

The Corfu Channel Case was the kind of small-scale dispute which an international body with the Security Council's authority might have been expected to settle without difficulty. Its failure to do so was the result of the cold war element in the situation: if Britain had again had recourse to the Council, in accordance with Article 94 (2), with a view to having the Court's judgment enforced, the Soviet Union would almost certainly have vetoed any effective action.

Indonesia

The Indonesian question, as has been seen, was first brought to the Security Council's attention by the Ukrainian SSR as a countermove to Iran's complaint against the Soviet Union. But it continued off and on to be one of the Council's main concerns for the next four years, and that body's handling of the problem turned out in the end to be one of its most valuable achievements in peacemaking.

The Council's consideration of the matter during February 1946 reflected the artificial way in which it had been raised. The Ukrainian representative had drawn attention critically to the action of British troops in an unpleasant and thankless postwar task, and there was a good deal of underlying irritation that the matter had been raised in the

---

[16] That is, for juridical settlement: the Council has also requested Advisory Opinions.

Council at all. It was scarcely surprising, therefore, that no agreement could be reached on either of the resolutions that were proposed, and after a few days the matter was dropped. But the situation in Indonesia was very difficult and had both far-reaching and very topical implications. So it came before the Security Council again in its full seriousness repeatedly.

The Dutch colonial empire in the East Indies had lasted for nearly three and a half centuries at the outbreak of the second World War, and the Dutch had a reputation for being relatively good and conscientious colonizers. Indonesia, therefore, was a heritage with which they were very loath to part. But the war had irretrievably undermined their authority. Japan's conquest of the colonies in 1942, her encouragement of Indonesian aspirations, the Declaration of Independence by the Indonesian Republic in August 1945, and the strong anticolonial trend of the time made it impossible for the Dutch to put the clock back permanently, in spite of temporary military successes. They could not indeed expect to regain the East Indies, which they had lost, at a time when Britain was preparing to give up India, which it still controlled.

In December 1942, some months after the Japanese victory in Indonesia, Queen Wilhelmina made a speech in which she called for the reconstruction of the Kingdom of the Netherlands 'on the solid foundation of complete partnership'. But the kind of commonwealth relationship which this statement suggested was only possible between peoples with many traditions and interests in common, whose partnership was a voluntary act and not based on the assertion of force. The Dutch threw away the possibility of such a solution by repeated resort to force during the early postwar years.

Between the autumn of 1945 and spring 1947 negotiations went on between the Dutch government and the Indonesian Republic, with the two main participants, the lieutenant governor-general, van Mook, and the Indonesian prime minister, Sjahrir, assisted from time to time in turn by two senior British diplomatists, Lord Inverchapel and Lord Killearn, acting as intermediaries in the Chair. During the Security Council's discussions in February 1946 the sovereignty of the Netherlands over Indonesia had not been called in question even by the Soviet representative. But throughout the Dutch–Indonesian dispute the distinction was always very important between the legal and political approaches, between the *de jure* and the *de facto* situation in the islands. Realist appraisals of the problem by the Dutch themselves also frequently differed from their emotional reaction based on sentiment and tradition.

Among the main subjects dealt with in the negotiations were: the ultimate and transitional status of the Republic; its relationship with the Dutch government and other states; whether the Republic's *de facto* authority in Java, which the Dutch were willing to recognize, should be extended to Sumatra; and the position in the areas outside Java and Sumatra, where the Dutch authorities had re-established civil control with little opposition. The proceedings were complicated by the existence of extremist elements in Indonesia, which during the summer of 1946 kidnapped Sjahrir and other officials in an attempt to carry out a *coup d'état* and thus provided some justification for a strong Dutch line.

In November 1946 the two sides initialled the Linggadjati Agreement, which was signed by their governments the following March. Its most important provisions were that the Netherlands recognized the *de facto* authority of the Republic of Indonesia over Java, Madura and Sumatra; that the two governments should 'cooperate in the rapid formation of a sovereign democratic state on a federal basis, to be called the United States of Indonesia'; that the United States of Indonesia should consist of the Republic of Indonesia, Borneo, and the Great East (East Indonesia); and that the two governments should cooperate in establishing a Netherlands-Indonesian Union, consisting on the one hand of the Kingdom of the Netherlands, including Surinam and Curaçao, and on the other hand of the United States of Indonesia. Of this Union the King (Queen) of the Netherlands was to be the head. For two reasons the circumstances in which the Agreement was reached were unfavourable and unpromising for the future. In the first place, no common interpretation of its complicated terms had been decided on. Secondly, at the time of its initialling there were 55,000 well-armed and well-trained Dutch troops in Java alone.

After weeks of friction during the late spring and early summer of 1947 and accusations that the Republic had violated the terms of Linggadjati, the Dutch, on 20 July, started a 'police action' which brought them rapid gains. But within ten days two UN members had drawn the Security Council's attention to the matter. India cited Article 35 of the Charter. Australia went further, by referring to the hostilities in progress in Java and Sumatra between armed forces of the Netherlands and the Republic of Indonesia, which in its view constituted a breach of the peace under Article 39. It proposed also, as a provisional measure under Article 40, that the Council should call upon the two governments to cease hostilities forthwith and to commence arbitration in accordance with a provision of the Linggadjati Agreement.

In its handling of the Indonesian question from then on the Security

Council provided a channel through which members of the United Nations with different points of view on the subject could act together to produce a solution of the problem by peaceful means, though the points of view of the most interested and influential members were indeed very varied.

Among the permanent members of the Council Britain and France, as colonial powers, had most sympathy with the Dutch in their dilemma. They supported the Dutch claim to sovereignty in Indonesia, favoured a solution by bilateral negotiations, if possible, and, when it proved impossible, sought to minimize UN intervention. But there was a limit to the support they would give to the Dutch. The British, who were engaged in emancipating their own Empire, were not prepared to aid the Dutch in efforts to reassert their control by force, while the French realized that a bitter colonial conflict in Indonesia would weaken their own position in Indo-China.

The United States was torn by conflicting considerations. On the whole, her traditional anticolonialism was sharpened by the desire not to be outdone by the Soviet Union in championing colonial self-determination. But her attitude was modified in the early stages of the dispute by regard for the colonial powers, who were her European allies, and later by the fact that in 1949 Holland became a co-member of NATO.

The Soviet Union, in its ardent opposition to colonialism, seemed to have no difficulty in reconciling its objection to UN intervention in Iran with support for such intervention in Indonesia. India, due to her size and newly won sovereignty, was, among Asian states, the natural leader of anticolonialism. She strongly supported Indonesia, opposed the use of armed force in Asia by any European country, and favoured a solution through the United Nations. Australia's attitude was to some people rather surprising. It can be explained by her exposed geographical position, by her proximity to Indonesia, and by the natural interest of a smaller power in strengthening the UN's authority. She came down strongly on the side of Indonesia; so much so that she was Indonesia's nominee on the Security Council's Good Offices Committee and loyally fulfilled her trust. She also strongly supported UN intervention.

In these circumstances, it was hardly surprising that members of the Security Council, when handling the Indonesian problem, were often unable to agree. But, in spite of their different viewpoints, the Council, in the course of sixty-nine meetings between 31 July 1947 and 13 December 1949, during which it considered the Indonesian question, moved steadily towards a sound objective, which was a solution that did not result from the successful use of force. On 1 August 1947, within two days of the Indian and Australian appeals, the Council called on the two parties to cease hostilities forthwith and settle their disputes by arbitration or other peaceful means. On 25 August, following a request from the Republic of Indonesia that a Commission of observers should be appointed, the Council asked those of its members who had career consuls in Batavia[17] to set up a Consular Commission to report on the situation in Indonesia, in particular, on the observance of the cease-fire order of 1 August. At their first meeting the Consuls asked the powers represented on the Commission to make officers available to observe any possible violations of the ceasefire. As a result twenty-five officers were attached to the Commission, and the UN thus obtained its first group of military observers.

On 25 August also the Council agreed to tender its good offices to the parties in order to assist in the pacific settlement of this dispute and to set up 'a committee of the Council, consisting of three members of the Council, each party selecting one, and the third to be designated by the two so selected'. This body was called the Security Council Committee of Good Offices for Indonesia (known as the GOC). The Netherlands designated Belgium to represent it; Indonesia nominated Australia; and the foreign ministers of Belgium and Australia chose the United States as the third member. Dr Frank Graham, as the United States' representative, became chairman.

Two interim reports and one full report of the Consular Commission, which were issued in September and October, made clear that the two parties were interpreting the cease-fire order differently, the Dutch acting on the assumption that it did not preclude mopping-up operations against pockets of Republican troops behind their own advance positions. On 3 October, therefore, the Security Council adopted an Australian proposal requesting the Committee of Three, that is, the GOC, 'to proceed to exercise its functions with the utmost dispatch'. The GOC, in fact, started work towards the end of the month, and on 1 November the Security Council passed a resolution requesting it to assist the parties in reaching an agreement, which would ensure the observance of the cease-fire resolution, and requesting the Consular Commission, together with its military assistants, to make its services available to the GOC.

The Committee's task was difficult owing to conflicting interpretations of the terms 'cease-fire' and 'good offices', the strong military

[17] This automatically excluded any Communist member.

position of the Dutch following their 'police action', and the very conciliatory attitude of the permanent members of the Council, all of whom, except for the Soviet Union, were hoping for a bilateral settlement. But the unyielding line taken by the Dutch, together with fears of a second 'police action', finally led to a series of discussions, starting on 8 December and sponsored by the GOC, on board the USS *Renville*. The Dutch delegation after issuing, early in the New Year, twelve political principles in the form of an ultimatum, suddenly agreed to six additional principles put forward by Dr Graham, which contained substantial concessions to the Republic. This unexpected change was the result of American pressure at governmental level and made possible the signature of two agreements on 17 and 19 January 1948.[18]

The Renville Agreements comprised a truce, the twelve Dutch principles, and the six additional principles. The truce established as the boundary for the cease-fire the so-called 'van Mook line', which was very favourable to the Dutch. The Dutch principles included four taken from the Linggadjati Agreement, concerning Indonesian independence, the United States of Indonesia and its relations with the Kingdom and King of the Netherlands, and they provided for a United Nations presence up to the time when sovereignty was transferred to the government of the United States of Indonesia. The additional principles provided that sovereignty throughout the Netherlands Indies should remain with the Kingdom of the Netherlands until transferred to the United States of Indonesia; that the United States of Indonesia, when created, would be a sovereign and independent state in equal partnership with the Kingdom of the Netherlands; that in any provisional federal government all states would be offered fair representation; and that within a period of from six to twelve months a plebiscite would be held to determine whether the populations of the various territories of Java, Madura, or Sumatra wished their territory to form part of the Republic of Indonesia or not. They also underlined the point relating to the United States of Indonesia by arranging that the existence of the GOC could be continued at the request of either party.

The Agreements provided neither a complete nor a fully integrated basis for settling the Indonesian problem. The two parties also, as at Linggadjati, had not agreed on a common interpretation.[19] But they did avert the threatened resort to force by the Dutch at the time, and,

[18] See Alastair M. Taylor, *Indonesian Independence and the United Nations*, p. 316, n. 16. Taylor quotes Dr Graham as saying that had Secretary of State Marshall not prodded the Dutch from Washington, there would have been no Renville Agreement.
[19] *Ibid*, p. 96.

as regards the future, they had, in contrast to the Linggadjati Agreement, been negotiated under UN auspices and had from an international standpoint, therefore, an added moral authority.

Virtually no progress was made during the next eleven months. The Dutch were in a strong position; the Indonesians were not prepared to accept their various demands; the GOC, by its terms of reference, was meant to assist in a settlement, not impose one. While the Security Council repeatedly called on it to provide information and continued its efforts, the majority of Council members were not prepared to strengthen its hand.

Finally, on 18 December 1948 the Dutch repudiated the Renville Truce and two days later launched their second 'police action'. They advanced rapidly into Republican territory, occupied the capital, Jogjakarta, and captured many Republican leaders, including the president and prime minister. But they had at last overreached themselves.

The reactions were immediate both in the United Nations and throughout the world. On 19 December the United States requested an emergency meeting of the Security Council. On the 24th the Council passed a resolution calling upon the parties 'to cease hostilities forthwith' and 'immediately to release the President and other political prisoners arrested since 18 December'. A second resolution, four days later, noted that the Netherlands government had not so far released the president and other political prisoners and called on it 'to set free these political prisoners forthwith and report to the Security Council within twenty-four hours'.

The spontaneous and widespread protests against Dutch actions were even more significant. The American attitude of forbearance changed completely. On 22 December it was announced that Marshall Aid to the Dutch East Indies, amounting to about $14 million, was to be suspended, and early in the New Year a resolution was introduced into the American Senate calling for an end to all financial aid to the Netherlands until it had complied with the Security Council's resolutions. A special Conference of nineteen Asian nations was held at New Delhi in January to consider the Indonesian question. In the opening address Nehru said that the attempt to suppress Indonesian nationalism must fail and that there could be no acceptance or reimposition of colonial control. The Conference concluded with passing a resolution which took the form of recommendations to the Security Council, providing for the restoration of the Republic in Jogjakarta, a transfer of sovereignty by 1 January 1950, and the use of UN machinery in

Indonesia as the best instrument for achieving the programme. Some American and Australian trade unions came out strongly against the Dutch, and the Australian Waterside Workers forbade the shipment of goods to Indonesia. Ceylon, India, Pakistan, and Burma imposed bans on overflights of their territory by Dutch KLM aircraft. In spite of Britain's earlier sympathy with the Dutch position, the United Kingdom representative said in the Security Council on 24 December that the state of the world was 'too serious for a conflict of the nature of that now going on in Indonesia to be allowed to continue with all its incalculable consequences'. Western countries, indeed, in the face of increasing Communist success in China, were becoming worried that the Indonesian conflict might seriously weaken the anti-Communist front in Asia.

The new attitude of the Security Council towards the Netherlands was summed up in the resolution it passed on 28 January 1949, without a dissenting vote, though France abstained on the whole resolution and there were other abstentions on individual paragraphs. Its main provisions were the following. The parties were called upon to stop all hostilities and to cooperate in the restoration of peace and the maintenance of law and order. The Government of the Netherlands was called on to release immediately all political prisoners arrested since 17 December 1948 and to facilitate the restoration of a republican administration in Jogjakarta. It was recommended that an interim federal government should be established not later than 15 March 1949; that elections should be held for an Indonesian constituent assembly by 1 October 1949; and that transfer of sovereignty over Indonesia by the Netherlands to the United States of Indonesia should take place at the earliest possible date and not later than 1 July 1950.

The Committee of Good Offices was henceforth to be known as the United Nations Commission for Indonesia (UNCI). The Commission was to act as the representative of the Security Council in Indonesia, to have all the functions assigned to the GOC by the Security Council since 18 December 1948 and the functions now conferred on it by the resolution. For example, it was to assist the parties in the implementation of the resolution and in the negotiations leading up to the transfer of sovereignty; it was to have authority to consult with representatives of areas in Indonesia other than the Republic and to invite representatives of such areas to participate in the negotiations; it was to observe on behalf of the United Nations the elections to be held throughout Indonesia and make recommendations regarding the conditions necessary (*a*) to ensure that the elections are free and democratic, and (*b*) to

E

guarantee freedom of assembly, speech and publication at all times. The Commission was also to assist in achieving the earliest possible restoration of the civil administration of the Republic, and to render periodic reports to the Council and special reports, whenever the Commission deemed necessary. The Consular Commission was requested to facilitate the work of the United Nations Commission for Indonesia by providing military observers and other staff and facilities and was temporarily to suspend other activities.

Shortly before the resolution was approved by the Security Council the representative of the Netherlands explained to the Council the fundamental objections of his government to certain elements in the draft. He summed them up by saying that the resolution would 'put the Netherlands under the guardianship of the United Nations'. After months of moderation and tolerance towards Dutch policy in Indonesia this was precisely what the Council intended to do.

The resolution of 28 January, in fact, provided the programme according to which Indonesia moved forward towards independence during the course of 1949. The Dutch government at first dragged its feet and tried to prevent the restoration of the Republic in Jogjakarta. But it could not resist the combination of the Security Council in a determined mood and the American threat to withhold aid. On 10 March the Council considered the first report of the UNCI, in which the Commission reported that the Dutch government had not complied with the basic requirements of the resolution of 28 January but had proposed to convene a round table conference on Indonesia at The Hague, which the Commission viewed as a 'counter-proposal or substitute' for the resolution. The Council responded by approving a directive on 23 March in which it stated that UNCI should assist the parties in reaching agreement as to (*a*) the implementation of the Council's resolution of 28 January, and (*b*) the time and conditions for holding the proposed conference at The Hague.

From then on the negotiations went relatively smoothly, first in Batavia from April until August, and later at The Hague Round Table Conference from August until November, with UNCI playing an important role. The Commission had a far stronger position than either the Consular Commission or the GOC, because it was 'the representative of the Security Council in Indonesia' and had clear terms of reference. Its most important achievement was the part it played in restoring the government of the Republic to Jogjakarta. After this event it issued the following statement: 'This event has established an important precedent. For the first time, a Government has been restored and returned to its constitutional position and its capital through the assistance of an international Organization which has made use not of armed force but of its pacific offices.'[20]

At The Hague a Charter of Transfer of Sovereignty was agreed on by which the Netherlands 'unconditionally and irrevocably' transferred complete sovereignty over Indonesia except New Guinea, to the Republic of the United States of Indonesia and recognized it as 'an independent and sovereign state'.[21] New Guinea was to continue under the Netherlands, but its political status was to be determined within one year by negotiations between the Republic and the Netherlands. On 27 December 1949, at a ceremony in the royal palace in Amsterdam, Queen Juliana signed the Act of the transfer of sovereignty. The following September Indonesia became a member of the United Nations.

At the Security Council's meeting on 12 December 1949 the Indonesian representative said: 'We realize that without the intervention of the Security Council the Indonesian Question would have been solved on the battlefield by force of arms.' When the solution that was reached is compared with the long-drawn-out struggles in Indo-China and Algeria, two dependencies towards which French feelings were as strong as Holland's towards the East Indies, the extent of the achievement in Indonesia becomes clear. American pressure had played an important part in the result, and it is difficult to assess the relative significance of the different factors which were involved. But the most powerful factor of all was the worldwide anticolonial trend, as revealed by the extent and intensity of the reaction which the second 'police action' provoked. As has been seen, the critics among UN members of Dutch policy in Indonesia had very different attitudes towards the problem. It was the great merit of the Security Council in this case that it enabled members to work together, if not always in harmony, to produce a lasting and relatively peaceful solution.

The unfortunate epilogue to the Indonesian question, the problem of West Irian (West New Guinea), was never formally considered by the Security Council. It was a source of considerable friction and minor hostilities between the Netherlands and Indonesia, until they signed an Agreement on the subject in August 1962, and it came before the General Assembly on a number of occasions. After hostilities broke out in West Irian during the winter of 1961–62, the resulting communica-

[20] A. M. Taylor, p. 410.
[21] The two states remained linked in a Netherlands–Indonesian Union, but, due to differences over New Guinea and the question of debts, it came to an end in 1956.

tions between the Acting Secretary-General and the two governments were, on several occasions, brought to the attention of the Council in writing but not discussed by it.

The Agreement arranged for the transfer of the administration of West Irian from the Netherlands to Indonesia, provisions being made to safeguard the rights of the inhabitants to self-determination.[22] A United Nations Temporary Executive Authority (UNTEA) was to take over the administration for an interim period, in order to facilitate the transfer. The Authority was to be assisted by a UN Security Force provided by the Secretary-General and under his authority, and, pending the establishment of UNTEA, a military observer group was to be sent to the country. These arrangements were approved by a resolution of the General Assembly.

The Spanish question, 1946

The Council's handling of the Spanish question fell within the early cold war period but only reflected cold war tension in a mild degree, because both sides in the East–West conflict were opposed to Franco. The Spanish question was, in fact, a case on its own and of limited significance. What it did show up was the Soviet Union's jealous support of the Council's rights and the uncertainty of UN members about the eligibility of such a country as Franco's Spain for UN membership. It was also the first occasion on which a member of the Council invoked Chapter VII of the Charter.

The question was brought before the Council by Poland in April 1946, on the ground that the activities of the Franco government endangered international peace and security. Poland submitted a draft resolution proposing that the Council, in accordance with its authority under Articles 39 and 41, should call on UN members to sever diplomatic relations with that government. The Council could not agree on this course. But finally, after it had appointed a subcommittee to look into the matter, nine Council members favoured the subcommittee's proposal that, unless political conditions in Spain improved, the

[22] In fact, the concept of self-determination was meaningless in this case, as the majority of Papuans were illiterate, and many had not even heard of the Netherlands or Indonesia. Only in a few coastal villages, inhabited by people of Malayan stock would a real plebiscite have been possible. It would have been better for the UN's integrity had this fact been acknowledged. But the Dutch aim by then was to leave West Irian without losing face, and Dutch honour required that provision for 'self-determination' should be made.

General Assembly should recommend members to sever diplomatic relations with that country. The relevant resolution was vetoed by the Soviet Union, because it did not go far enough and because the Soviet Union considered the Council rather than the Assembly the appropriate body to take action.

The following December, the deadlocked Council having dropped the matter, the Assembly did recommend that members should recall immediately their diplomatic representatives from Madrid. But four years later it revoked this recommendation, declaring that the establishment of diplomatic relations with a government did not imply any judgment on that government's domestic policy. In December 1955 Spain was admitted to UN membership.

THE MIDDLE EAST

There is no part of the world in which the Security Council has been so frequently involved as the Middle East. It has achieved much, and its sustained concern has, on the whole, exerted a beneficial influence on one of the most serious international disputes of the age. But it has failed to realize its main aim, which was to bring about a real *modus vivendi* between Israel and the Arab states.

The Anglo-Egyptian question, 1947

In July 1947 Egypt complained to the Security Council that British troops were maintained on Egyptian territory against the will of the people, contrary to the principle of the sovereign equality of the members of the United Nations, and that the United Kingdom had occupied the Sudan and endeavoured to impair the unity of the Nile Valley. The resulting dispute, she maintained, was likely, if continued, to endanger the maintenance of international peace and security. Egypt therefore requested the Council to direct:

1. The total and immediate evacuation of British troops from Egypt, including the Sudan.
2. The termination of the present administrative regime in the Sudan.

The representative of the United Kingdom replied that no proof had been offered that international peace and security had been under any threat, unless the Egyptian government contemplated creating it; that, since both Egyptian demands concerned the Treaty of 1936, the one real issue before the Council was the legal issue of the validity of the Treaty; and that the Treaty had been freely concluded, that it was in no way inconsistent with the Charter, and that the Security Council was not entitled to override treaty rights.[23] He denied also that the United Kingdom had designed to sever the Sudan from Egypt.

The Egyptian representative maintained that the Council was not called on to pass judgment on the legal rights of the parties to the 1936 Treaty but to take account of the 'bald political facts' with a view to the maintenance of international peace and security. The dispute, in fact, raised the question of the Council's right to decide on the validity of treaties and the whole complex problem of the distinction between the legal and political approaches to international disputes. The reluctance of members to get involved in this problem was revealed by their failure to approve any of the three draft resolutions that were submitted, and particularly by the voting on the last draft, which was put forward by China and recommended the resumption of negotiations and the submission by the parties of a report to the Council: it was rejected by two votes in favour, none against, eight abstentions, with one member not participating.[24]

The matter was dropped, though the President ruled that it remained on the agenda, because the Council had not decided to remove it.

The Palestine question: Israel and the Arab states

The problem of Palestine's future, which was referred to the United Nations in April 1947, became the problem of Israel and the Arab states, when the state of Israel came into existence in May 1948. The first UN body to deal with it was the General Assembly, and the Security Council did not take part in the proceedings until it was requested to do so by the Assembly in November 1947, nor assume the leading role until war broke out the following May.

[23] By the terms of the 1936 Treaty the British military occupation of Egypt was replaced by an Anglo-Egyptian alliance; British forces in Egypt were to be reduced and withdrawn to the Suez Canal zone; and the joint Anglo-Egyptian administration of the Sudan was to continue. But the Treaty was signed under the shadow of Italy's annexation of Ethiopia and did not reflect the views of the younger generation of politically active Egyptians.

[24] For this whole question see *Repertoire of Practice, 1946–1951*, pp. 314–15, and p. 96.

The emergence of Israel and the Arab-Israel War

After the second World War, Britain, as holder of the mandate over Palestine, failed to work out any settlement of the country's future which was acceptable to both Jews and Arabs. On 2 April 1947, therefore, she turned to the UN for a settlement, requested the Secretary-General to put the question of Palestine on the agenda at the next regular session of the General Assembly, and asked that a special session of the Assembly be convened as soon as possible for the purpose of appointing a committee to study the question in preparation for the regular session. The special session took place soon afterwards and appointed a UN Special Committee on Palestine, consisting of eleven members. The Assembly during its regular session the following October adopted, with minor amendments, the committee's majority report.

The plan thus accepted provided for the termination of the mandate, the partition of Palestine into separate Arab and Jewish states, bound together in an economic union, and the establishment of an international regime in Jerusalem. A UN Palestine Commission was established to carry out these recommendations. The Security Council was asked to assist in implementing them, to consider whether the situation in Palestine constituted a threat to peace, and to take the necessary measures to preserve the peace.

There were two main obstacles to enforcing the partition proposals. First, the Arabs were strongly opposed to them and the proposals themselves led to fighting between Arabs and Jews in Palestine. Secondly, the Security Council was uncertain about its enforcement powers. It could not enforce a settlement under Chapter VI, and it was reluctant to resort to Chapter VII, with Article 43 still not implemented. Trygve Lie's view was that, in the exceptional circumstances, enforcement action was justified under the general provisions of Article 24 but this could only have been acted on, had the permanent members been prepared to collaborate in so doing.[25] As it was, Britain, as mandatory power, would not use troops to enforce any settlement that was unacceptable to both parties; the United States was not prepared to take enforcement action, which might alienate the Arab oil states and American Jewish votes in an election year;[26] while the Western powers

[25] See Trygve Lie, *In the Cause of Peace*, pp. 167–8. The exceptional circumstances were that, in the case of Palestine, the mandatory power was handing over the mandated territory to the UN for disposition.

[26] In making decisions on the Middle East American political leaders are highly sensitive about Jewish votes and also about the substantial contributions made by Jews to party funds. See the article by Kermit Roosevelt, 'The partition of Palestine: a lesson in pressure politics', *The Middle East Journal*, Jan. 1948.

were all most reluctant to see Soviet troops move into the Middle East at the UN's invitation.

In February 1948 the UN Palestine Commission reported that it could not carry out its functions under the Assembly resolution, unless adequate military forces were made available to it. On 1 April the Security Council requested the Secretary-General to convene another special session of the General Assembly on Palestine and on the same day called upon Arabs and Jews in Palestine to cease acts of violence immediately. On 23 April the Council also established a Truce Commission for Palestine, which was to be composed of representatives of those members of the Council which had career consular offices in Jerusalem, that is Belgium, France, Syria and the United States, although Syria chose not to participate. Meanwhile Britain announced that it would lay down its mandate on 15 May.

The special session of the General Assembly lasted from 16 April until 14 May, and on its last day the Assembly decided to bring an end to the Palestine Commission and appoint a UN Mediator in Palestine. The same day the Jewish State of Israel was proclaimed in Tel Aviv, with the boundaries recommended by the partition plan, and was immediately recognized by the United States and three days later by the Soviet Union. War broke out between Israel and the Arab states, whose forces crossed the old frontiers of Palestine the following day.

The United Nations had failed to solve the complex and highly emotive problem of the relationship between Arabs and Jews in Palestine. But it was a problem, soluble only by the use of force, which Britain had been reluctant to use for a generation. It had been exacerbated by the curse of Hitler's racism. An Anglo-American Committee of Enquiry, set up in 1945 at the invitation of the British foreign secretary, to consider the plight of Jewry as a whole, had also failed to find a solution. Now the Security Council was faced with a straightforward breach of the peace.

The Council was helped in its immediate peace-making task by two developments. Count Folke Bernadotte, president of the Swedish Red Cross was appointed mediator on 20 May, and the relatively modest Truce Commission, set up in April, was provided with a team of military observers, though they could do nothing but observe and report.

On 22 May the Security Council passed a resolution calling for a cease-fire in Palestine and directing the Truce Commission to report on the result. As this action did not have the required effect, the Council passed a stronger resolution a week later calling for a four-weeks' truce, instructing the mediator in conjunction with the Truce Commission to supervise the observance of the resolution, and threatening that, if the parties did not accept it, the Council would reconsider the situation with a view to taking action under Chapter VII of the Charter. This stronger line, reinforced by the efforts of the mediator and the need of both sides for a respite from fighting, was successful. Both sides accepted the truce, and it went into effect on 11 June, though the provisions for a standstill on armaments could not be implemented.

Shortly before the truce expired on 9 July the Council passed a resolution appealing urgently to the parties to accept a prolongation of the truce. The Israeli government agreed to do so, but the Arab states refused, complaining that the truce enabled the Jews to consolidate their position. Then an unexpected development took place, which revealed the respect of one Arab ruler for the UN's authority. King Abdullah of Jordan, who wanted the truce prolonged, suggested to Count Bernadotte that the Security Council should pass a resolution *ordering*, not *calling upon* the parties to cease fire.[27] This, with the cooperation of Council members, was duly done, and the resulting resolution of 15 July specifically mentioned Articles 39 and 40 of the Charter and declared that failure to comply with the order would be considered a breach of the peace, which would require immediate consideration of further action under Chapter VII. The order was accepted by both parties though not fully respected.

During the next twelve months, under the impact of Count Bernadotte's assassination by Israeli extremists in September and aided by the patient and resourceful efforts of his successor, Dr Ralph Bunche, who was appointed acting mediator, there was some progress towards a more lasting settlement. Further outbreaks of fighting in the Negev during October resulted in a series of Council resolutions, which were adopted between 19 October and 29 December. But in the end armistice agreements were signed during the period February to July 1949 between Egypt, Jordan, Lebanon, and Syria, on the one hand, and Israel, on the other. On 11 August the Security Council paid special tribute to the qualities of Count Bernadotte and expressed deep appreciation of the services of Ralph Bunche, while the office of mediator, having fulfilled its purpose, was brought to an end. Bunche was appropriately rewarded for his achievement by the Nobel Prize for Peace.

[27] I was told this by Dr Ralph Bunche, who was with Bernadotte, when the King made the suggestion. The resulting Council resolution was proposed by the Canadian representative, General McNaughton, acting on the suggestion of Bunche.

E*

The aftermath of the war, 1949–56

The basic problem in the Middle East remained unsolved, because hostilities had been brought to an end by a series of armistices, not by a peace settlement, and the Arab states continued to regard themselves as legally speaking in a state of war. However, the UN, mainly through the Security Council, had limited to weeks what might have been a prolonged conflict, and the area was to be spared a renewal of major hostilities for over seven years. The work of mediation had been greatly facilitated by the fact that both super-powers had actively supported it, while stability in the Middle East was furthered during the next few years by the Tripartite Declaration of May 1950. In this declaration Britain, France, and the United States proclaimed their interest in promoting the establishment and maintenance of peace and stability in the area and their opposition to the use or threat of force between any of the states. They affirmed their opposition to the development of an arms race between Israel and the Arab states and declared that they would take action, both within and outside the United Nations, to prevent a violation of frontiers or armistice lines.[28]

Maintenance of the Armistice agreements was facilitated by the development of the Truce Commission for Palestine. During the summer of 1948 the Commission had at its disposal an efficient body of military observers, numbering at the height of its truce supervision activity about 500. Finally, under the authority of the mediator, who was acting on a Security Council decision, it became, with the new name of the UN Truce Supervision Organization (UNTSO), an important subsidiary organ of the Council. Under the armistice agreements UNTSO and its Chief of Staff were assigned specific duties, and its numbers finally stabilized at about 130.[29]

The UNTSO observers performed a useful, if limited role, though they were seriously hampered by Israel's refusal to allow them on her territory. The three signatories of the Tripartite Declaration each exercised some influence in the area; in particular, Britain over Jordan, France over Syria and Lebanon, and the United States over Israel and, to some extent over Egypt. So they could back up the moderating effects of UNTSO's presence.

[28] The declaration in the end was more honoured in the breach than in the observance. France, furious with the Egyptian attitude towards Algeria, broke it in spirit towards the end of 1954 and in fact the following year (see Michel Bar Zohar, *The Prophet Armed*, pp. 201–10); Britain disregarded it in 1955, when she agreed to arm Iraq against the Soviet Union under the Baghdad Pact; and the Soviet Union and Czechoslovakia started selling arms to Egypt in the autumn of 1955.

[29] See Rosalyn Higgins, *United Nations Peacekeeping 1946–67*, pp. 66–71.

Another innovation arising out of the armistice agreements was less successful. Each agreement provided for the setting up of a Mixed Armistice Commission (MAC) to supervise its implementation. The main tasks of the Commissions were to help avoid any resumption of hostilities, facilitate the transition to a permanent peace, establish permanent armistice demarcation lines, arrange for the exchange of prisoners of war, and hear claims and complaints relating to the application of the agreement. Each Commission was to be composed of two or three representatives from each of the two parties, the chairman being the chief of staff of UNTSO or a senior officer of its observer personnel designated by him.

The composition of the Commissions presupposed a willingness to cooperate between the parties which was, for the most part, lacking. There were numerous frontier infringements during the period and two successive UNTSO chiefs of staff[30] complained that at a MAC meeting one party acted as a prosecuting attorney, the other as the defence, and the chairman had to act as judge without the support of a jury. In these circumstances the chairman's decision either way might be considered partisan. In fact, on one occasion a chairman's abstention was considered partisan and caused Israel to sever all connection with the Israel-Jordan MAC.[31] There was, in consequence, increasing reluctance to appeal to the Commissions, and by December 1955 there were 568 Syrian and 401 Israel complaints awaiting the next formal meeting of the Israel–Syrian MAC, although no formal meetings had been held for more than four years.

In the background during these years, and tending too often to be taken for granted, were the shocking tragedy of over a million Arab refugees, who were the victims of the Arab-Israel war, and the harsh decision of Egypt to refuse passage through the Suez Canal to Israeli shipping and the shipping of other nations carrying strategic good to Israel. The decision was based on her contention that a state of war with Israel still prevailed, and she persisted in it despite a strongly worded Security Council resolution of September 1951 calling on her to end the restrictions. Furthermore, in spite of the assertions in the Tripartite Declaration, from 1955 onwards arms were being sent to both sides by Britain, France, the United States, Czechoslovakia, and the Soviet Union, on the morally thin pretext of preserving a balance and with no serious attempt by the major powers to agree on some form of control over this very dangerous procedure (see p. 138, n. 28). There was a

[30] General Riley and General Bennike.
[31] Higgins, p. 123.

growing and sinister divergence also between American and Soviet attitudes towards the Middle East: from 1954 the Soviet Union began openly to back the Arab side and its new position was reflected in March of that year in its veto of a second Security Council resolution calling on Egypt to lift its restrictions on Israel shipping.

The Suez crisis and its consequences

On 26 July 1956 President Nasser nationalized the Suez Canal. This resulted in the centre of gravity in the Middle East moving for a time from Israel and its neighbouring states to the Suez Canal, in which Britain and France had close and long-standing interests. Nasser's action was touched off by a piece of rough diplomacy on the part of the American secretary of state, John Foster Dulles. After an Egyptian arms deal with the Soviet bloc in September 1955 the United States had offered, with Britain and the World Bank, to finance the Aswan High Dam, a project of great economic importance to Egypt. But, following anti-Arab lobbying in Washington and Egypt's recognition of Communist China, Dulles changed his mind in the summer of 1956, and the nationalization of the Canal was Nasser's way of retaliating.

The reaction of Britain and France to such a move would have been strong at any time, owing to their political, economic, and financial concern with the Suez Canal and the Suez Canal Company. But at the time when it was made they were particularly sensitive; due partly to their touchiness as colonial powers, whose empires were in process of dissolution; partly to Nasser's support for the Algerian revolt; and partly to the fact that Sir Anthony Eden was then British prime minister. Eden had a special interest in the Middle East. He had been responsible on the British side for negotiations leading to two conciliatory treaties with Egypt in 1936 and 1954. And he felt personally let down by Nasser's unilateral action. Moreover, he was haunted by ghosts from his own early career, in the form of Mussolini and Hitler—he had been a sick man for several years—and he misjudged Nasser by comparing him to Hitler, so that any major concession to him would have had the flavour of Munich. In these circumstances negotiations were made difficult because France and Britain were thinking in terms of force from the beginning.

As far as the UN was concerned the Suez crisis fell into two phases. There was first the period before the outbreak of war, when the Security Council took a limited but significant part in the efforts to reach a settlement. Secondly came the war itself and its result, when the UN was faced with the task of restoring and maintaining peace. During this second phase matters were quickly taken out of the hands of the Security Council through the use of the veto, and the key role at this important stage was played by the General Assembly. But it would be pedantic to interrupt the story for this reason. The UN's whole Suez operation was carried out in the fields of peace-making and peace-keeping, the Council's own sphere of activity. The decisions made by the Assembly at the time affected the Council's future actions and methods, and the Council resumed its responsibilities in the area when the immediate emergency was over.

Time was provided for negotiations after Nasser's action, because Britain's lack of preparedness made military action impossible for some weeks. A conference of the Canal's principal users, which was held in London during the third week in August, produced a plan, but it was turned down by Nasser. Next Dulles suggested the setting up of a Suez Canal Users' Association, which might cooperate with Egypt in running the Canal. But the main powers concerned differed as to what its functions should be, and Dulles himself turned against the idea. In fact, a tragic element in the situation during this period was the lack of understanding and trust between the American and British governments. Relations between Dulles and Eden had been bad for some time, and both were in poor health.[32] In his policies towards Egypt and Britain Dulles was opinionated and inconsistent. Eden resented this attitude towards a problem which was of major concern to Britain, and was himself far from frank in his relations with the American government. This state of affairs, together with French and British partiality to the use of force, reduced the chances of a peaceful settlement to a minimum.

Nevertheless on 23 September Britain and France referred the question to the Security Council, which considered it at nine meetings between 5 and 13 October. Their main purposes in doing so were to propitiate public opinion in Britain and other countries and to make a good impression on uncommitted UN members. The Council meetings were attended by the foreign ministers of the major powers, three of the meetings were held in private to facilitate an agreement, and the Secretary-General, Dag Hammarskjöld, arranged a series of private consultations in his own office with the foreign ministers of Britain, Egypt, and France, in which during intensive discussions considerable

[32] Eden had had a very serious operation in 1953, from which he had not fully recovered and Dulles underwent surgery for cancer on 3 November 1956, at the height of the Suez crisis.

progress was made. As a result of Hammarskjöld's good offices and compromises by both sides, six 'requirements' or principles were agreed upon as the basis for a settlement.

But regrettably Eden and the French government did not want a settlement through the UN and considered the whole procedure in New York primarily as a prelude to military action. A draft resolution, therefore, which Britain and France submitted to the Security Council on 13 October, not only contained the six principles but provocatively stated that they corresponded to the plan put forward by the London conference, which Nasser had rejected, and curtly invited the Egyptian government to submit alternative proposals for implementing the principles 'not less effective' than the rejected plan. The resolution, therefore, was vetoed by the Soviet Union, apart from the section containing the six principles, which was approved unanimously.

The six principles belong unfortunately in the category of historical might-have-beens. But they were a striking example of what could be achieved within the Security Council framework with the help of a determined and resourceful Secretary-General and some flexibility on both sides. Nasser was sensitive to the implications of his actions from the point of view of international law;[33] his foreign minister, Mahmoud Fawzi, was a good and straightforward negotiator; the British foreign secretary, Selwyn Lloyd, favoured a peaceful settlement, provided it 'offered an adequate measure of international, or users' control' over the Canal; and he and his minister of state, Anthony Nutting, both considered that the New York discussions had given Britain substantially what was required to guarantee the efficient running of the Canal.[34] Implementation of the six principles should have presented no unsuperable problem, had the attitudes of Eden and the French government towards a peaceful solution been positive.

Meanwhile France and Israel were planning joint action in the Middle East, by which an Israeli attack on Egypt was to provide a pretext for French intervention over Suez. Britain's cooperation was required, because Israel was vulnerable to Egyptian bombing attacks and Britain alone had, in Cyprus, a base for bombers which could put Egyptian airfields out of action. The plan was presented to Eden by two French emissaries on 14 October, while Selwyn Lloyd was still in New York. Two days later the French and British prime ministers with their foreign ministers met in Paris, and on 22 October the Israeli prime

[33] See Louis Henkin, *How Nations Behave: law and foreign policy*, pp. 188, 189, and 194.
[34] See Anthony Nutting, *No End of a Lesson*, pp. 71–78.

minister, Ben Gurion, met French ministers and Selwyn Lloyd at Sèvres outside Paris, where a secret three-power treaty was signed. The treaty was necessarily secret because it was calculated to deceive, because it plotted rather than prevented the violation of the Arab–Israel frontiers in defiance of the Tripartite Declaration, and because Britain did not want to alienate the whole Arab world. Eden himself was so receptive to the French proposals that the British government did not seriously consider the results of the UN discussions, nor the possibility or the probability that a peaceful solution might emerge from them.

Israel attacked Egypt on 29 October and received British and French air support. The next day Britain and France sent an ultimatum to the Israeli and Egyptian governments, calling on both sides to stop fighting and to withdraw their forces to a distance of ten miles from the Suez Canal on each side. Egypt was also required to accept temporary occupation by Anglo-French forces of Port Said, Ismailia, and Suez. On 31 October, Egypt having rejected the ultimatum, British and French air attacks began on military targets in Egypt. Meanwhile the Israeli campaign had been successful, and by 2 November Israel had achieved her main objectives by occupying virtually the whole of the Sinai peninsula and opening the straits of Tiran, which controlled the Gulf of Aqaba. Egypt replied by sinking ships to block the Suez Canal. Anglo-French forces landed in Egypt on 5 November.

On 29 October the United States requested an immediate meeting of the Security Council. The following day two draft resolutions in turn proposed by the United States and the Soviet Union called on Israel to withdraw its forces behind the established armistice lines and called respectively for restraint by all UN members from the use of force in the area and for an immediate ceasefire by Israel and Egypt. Both were vetoed by Britain and France. Whereupon, on 31 October, Yugoslavia submitted a draft resolution, in accordance with the Uniting for Peace resolution of November 1950 (see pp. 290–91), by which the Council decided, as it was prevented from exercising its primary responsibility for the maintenance of international peace and security, to call an emergency special session of the General Assembly. This draft, as it was procedural, was passed, in spite of the opposition of Britain and France.

On 2 November, the second day of the emergency session, the Assembly approved by sixty-four to five votes with six abstentions a resolution, introduced by the United States, which noted that military operations were being conducted by French and British forces against Egyptian territory, and urged all parties involved to agree to an immediate cease-fire and withdraw their forces behind the armistice lines. On this resolution the United States voted with the Soviet Union against Britain and France. But the United States and influential members of the Commonwealth did not like this new alignment and wanted to facilitate a retreat by Britain and France without too much loss of face. So, with the Canadian foreign minister, Lester Pearson, taking the lead, and with the full backing of Hammarskjöld, a plan was evolved for the organization of a UN force to move into Egypt, Eden announcing in the House of Commons that British forces would be withdrawn if UN troops would replace them. On 4 and 5 November two resolutions were approved by the General Assembly, both by fifty-seven to nil with nineteen abstentions, the first requesting the Secretary-General to submit to it within forty-eight hours a plan for setting up an emergency international United Nations Force to secure and supervise the cessation of hostilities, and the second establishing a UN Command for the Force and appointing as chief of the command the Canadian chief-of-staff of UNTSO, Major-General E. L. M. Burns. On 6 November Eden announced that a cease-fire would take effect for the British forces from midnight, and France had no alternative but to follow suit.

There were three main reasons for the British decision. First, the country was seriously divided about the government's policy. Secondly, there was strong opposition to it within the Commonwealth, led by Canada and India. Thirdly, Britain was faced by a financial crisis, due to a flight from the pound, which the United States and the International Monetary Fund would help to check only if the adventure were called off; an attitude which was hardly surprising in view of the fact that Washington had not been informed of the British and French ultimatum until shortly after it was issued. This third reason was probably decisive in determining the abruptness of the change.

The danger of the situation was emphasized on 5 November, when the Soviet Union asked the President of the Security Council for immediate consideration by the Council of the question: 'Non-compliance by the United Kingdom, France and Israel with the decision . . . of the General Assembly of 2 November 1956', and went on to propose that all members of the UN, especially the United States and the Soviet Union, should give military assistance to Egypt 'by sending naval and air forces, military units . . . and other forms of assistance'. The Council met the same day but would not accept the item for its agenda, the American representative stating that the Soviet proposal, 'which, in the context of events in Hungary (see pp. 256–58), set a sombre record of cynicism, embodied an unthinkable suggestion'.

The United Nations Emergency Force (UNEF), which was now set up, was the creation of the General Assembly, and it was organized according to the plan drawn up by the Secretary-General at the Assembly's request. By a resolution of 7 November the Assembly approved the guiding principles laid down in the plan and invited the Secretary-General to take all appropriate administrative measures for its execution. It established also an Advisory Committee to help him, of which he was to be the Chairman, composed of one representative from each of seven countries, five of which[35] provided contingents for the Force. He was to be assisted also by a group of military representatives of the contributing countries, chaired by a major-general who was to be his personal adviser. It was laid down that the Force should not contain any nationals of the permanent members of the Security Council; a reasonable provision, considering that the permanent members included Britain, France, and the two main protagonists in the Cold War. UNEF's Commander was to be responsible to the Secretary-General.

Due to Hammarskjöld's drive and resourcefulness the first UNEF unit arrived in Egypt on 15 November, and by March 1957 the Force had reached its peak size of 6,073 men. The Anglo-French forces had completed their withdrawal by 22 December. In January and February the Assembly noted in two resolutions Israel's failure to comply with its requirements. But on 1 March Israel announced that it was prepared to withdraw all its forces from Egypt, including those stationed on the Gulf of Aqaba and the Straits of Tiran.

The reputation of the United Nations stood very high after the Suez crisis. It had brought an end to the military intervention of two major powers within a few days and induced Israel to withdraw all her troops from Egypt after a successful invasion. Furthermore, the effective cooperation of the super-powers had shown that East–West differences could take second place to the cause of peace, while President Eisenhower had courageously called Israel to order, in spite of the possible consequences in American domestic politics during an election year. There were also long-term consequences of importance. The submission of Britain and France to UN pressure made it easier for India and Pakistan to yield to the Security Council's demand for a cease fire in 1965, and UNEF, as the pioneer peace-keeping force, had great influence on the whole future of UN peace-keeping.

[35] Brazil, Canada, Colombia, India and Norway: there were five other contributors.

The UN's achievements had been made possible by an imaginative improvisation, and UNEF not only solved the crisis of November 1956, a task which it had accomplished by the end of February 1957, but stayed on to stabilize the situation on the frontier between Egypt and Israel for the next ten and a half years. In carrying out this second duty, it cooperated closely with UNTSO. But, while UNTSO remained in existence to implement, observe, and supervise the armistice agreements of 1949, UNEF's task was heavier, as it had 'to secure and supervise the cessation of hostilities', and the task was made more difficult by Israel's refusal to allow its troops to be stationed on her side of the frontier. UNEF was, however, large enough to interpose itself between the forces of the two sides, and, although it could not enforce its authority, it could prevent incidents by its very presence and as an impressive peace-keeping symbol. As a result, on this section of Israel's frontier, the situation was much better than before 1956, and incidents were reduced to a minimum. In particular, the presence of UNEF troops on the Gulf of Aqaba and at Sharm el Sheikh on the Straits of Tiran ensured that the Straits would remain open for all shipping, whereas before the crisis Egypt had been refusing passage to Israeli ships.

Elsewhere along Israel's frontier, apart from the Lebanon section, where UNTSO and MAC worked effectively, conditions became increasingly serious. There were numerous incidents and complaints to the Security Council, and Israel's reluctance or outright refusal to participate in the Mixed Armistice Commissions restricted UNTSO's usefulness severely. Along the Jordan Border, matters were made worse in 1962 by an Israeli scheme for diverting waters from the Jordan river. In the case of Syria, the number of outstanding complaints rose from hundreds in 1955 to tens of thousands in 1966,[36] and in April 1967 there was a short battle on the frontier, in which Syria lost a substantial part of its small air force.

In November 1966 a defence pact was signed between Syria and the UAR, and relations between the UAR and Israel rapidly became as bad as those between Israel and Syria. In fact, each side came to believe that an attack or serious provocation from the other was likely. Towards the middle of May 1967 Nasser sent his chief-of-staff to Damascus, and large numbers of Egyptian troops were moved up to the Sinai border. On 16 May a state of emergency was declared for the Egyptian armed

[36] For the 1955 figures see p. 139. According to a report by the Secretary-General (S/7572) of 1 Nov. 1966, 'the total number of accumulated and outstanding complaints as of 14 October 1966 was as follows: Israel 35,485; Syria, 30,600'.

forces, and the same day a senior Egyptian general sent a request to General Rikhye, the UNEF Commander, that his troops be withdrawn from the eastern border.

Rikhye replied that he had no authority to withdraw UNEF troops, except on instructions from the Secretary-General, and at once informed New York. U Thant asked the Egyptian ambassador to the UN for a clarification from Cairo and held an informal meeting with representatives of the countries contributing contingents to UNEF the next day. On 18 May confirmation was received from the Egyptian foreign minister that his government had 'decided to terminate the presence' of UNEF on Egyptian territory. U Thant then called a formal meeting of his Advisory Committee. At both meetings opinion was divided. India, Pakistan, and Yugoslavia were in favour of immediate withdrawal. Canada, Denmark, Norway, Sweden, and Brazil believed that an appeal should be made to the UAR not to request the withdrawal and that such a request, if made, should be considered by the General Assembly. On the morning of the 19th the Secretary-General informed Cairo that its request would be complied with, but that he had serious misgivings about it.

This decision was the most controversial action of U Thant's Secretary-Generalship, and opinions about it are still sharply divided. No final judgment on its wisdom will be possible until more is known about the balance of power and opinion within Egypt and Nasser's contact with the Soviet Union at the time, because these two factors would have determined Nasser's reaction to a stronger UN line. The situation was extremely complex and in some respects obscure. U Thant's motives and complete integrity are beyond doubt. He had serious fears that UNEF might disintegrate, owing to India's and Yugoslavia's determination to withdraw their contingents.[37] And his decision was based on the sound legal principle that a UN peace-keeping force could only remain in a country with the government's consent and on a specific arrangement made by Hammarskjöld with Egypt by which this principle was effective in the case of UNEF,[38] Yet his tactics in response to Egyptian demands are open to criticism.[39]

[37] India and Yugoslavia were two of the largest contributors.

[38] See Higgins, *United Nations Peacekeeping*, vol. I, 335–67, and 480–811, which includes the relevant documents and comments.

[39] However, Michael Howard and Robert Hunter (see *Israel and the Arab World: the crisis of 1967*, p. 19) have written: 'Dag Hammarskjöld might have played a lone and perhaps successful hand. But U Thant had been appointed to his post, and held it successfully for six years, precisely because he was not a Hammarskjöld. His actions were correct, if unimaginative.'

Dag Hammarskjöld had gone to great pains to persuade Nasser to agree that consent to UNEF's presence would not be withdrawn without negotiation with the UN, so long as its task was not completed, and Hammarskjöld believed that he had succeeded, though the agreement was through implication rather than by an express statement.[40]

In the spring of 1967 it was crystal clear that UNEF's task of securing the cessation of hostilities was incomplete. It seems unlikely also that Nasser himself, as opposed to the more extreme elements in the UAR, really wanted war at that time. About a third of the regular Egyptian army was tied up in Yemen. The withdrawal of UNEF implied the movement of Egyptian troops to the Gulf of Aqaba and Sharm el Sheikh. Once they were there it was difficult in the highly emotional Arab mood of that time to resist closing the straits to Israeli shipping again, and the Israeli premier had made clear on 13 May that this government would react strongly to any such action.

There were good reasons, therefore, why U Thant should have played for time and provided an opportunity for moderate counsels to prevail. He could have done so in at least three different ways: the Advisory Committee had not exercised its right of appeal to the General Assembly,[41] but he could have recommended it to do so; he could have made a strong public statement against the wisdom of the UAR's decision without questioning its right to make it; and he could have gone to Cairo to see Nasser before rather than after he answered the Egyptian note. It is possible that none of these methods would have succeeded. But any one of them would have had the definite advantage of preventing, or at least modifying the disillusionment felt by some of the UN's strongest supporters at the withdrawal from a dangerous area of its first peace-keeping force, with a fine record behind it, at a time when its physical and symbolic presence was needed more than ever.

In U Thant's defence it should be added that no member state requested a meeting of either the General Assembly or the Security Council while the issue was still in doubt. Furthermore, some of his strongest critics among UN Members failed to give him the necessary support at the time or to exercise the requisite diplomatic restraint. The reactions of Western powers to Egypt's request for the withdrawal of UNEF infuriated Cairo and made U Thant's efforts to negotiate much more difficult.

[40] Higgins, *loc. cit.*

[41] It had the right under para. 9 of the General Assembly resolution of 7 Nov. 1956 referred to on p. 145. The Arabs had strong support in the Assembly, but, whatever the result of the appeal, it would have gained time and emphasized in the eyes of all UN members the seriousness of the situation.

The six-day war

The withdrawal of UNEF was a severe blow to the UN's prestige, and a bad impression was made worse by the Security Council's failure to prevent the war, which was soon to break out.

The failure was a clear case of the Council's near impotence to act as a peace-maker, when the permanent members or the East–West conflict are involved. East–West tension in the Middle East was greater than it had been at the time of Suez, and during the two and a half weeks that followed the withdrawal of UNEF neither side was sure what the other's attitude would be. But the super-powers had put peace first in 1956, and once war had started in June 1967 they showed that they did not want it to continue, and cooperated to bring it to an end. It was only tragic that the war itself was required to bring them to this more reasonable state of mind.

The responsible parties in this tragedy, apart from the Middle East states themselves, were the major powers, and especially the Soviet Union and the United States. Each side in the Arab-Israel conflict knew that it had the backing of a super-power, and, although Moscow and Washington showed restraint when hostilities started, their support over the years had provided the weapons and the confidence, which had enabled the Arabs and the Jews to defy compromise. France and Britain were also to blame. In spite of the Tripartite Declaration of 1950, in which the three Western powers had asserted their opposition to the use of force and the development of an arms race in the area, all of them together with the Soviet Union, owing to power politics, sheer commercialism, misguided sentiment, or internal political considerations had been giving other peoples more efficient means of killing one another than they could have provided for themselves.

On 22 May Nasser declared a blockade of the Straits of Tiran and said that in no circumstances would the UAR allow the Israeli flag to pass through the Gulf of Aqaba. On 24 May the Security Council met at the request of Canada and Denmark. It had before it a report from the Secretary-General, in which he described the situation in the Middle East as more menacing than at any time since the autumn of 1956. But U Thant was in Cairo at the time, and at the suggestion of several members further consideration of the question was postponed until he had reported on his visit.

Between 29 May and 3 June the Council met again four times to consider the situation in the Middle East, a further report from the Secretary-General, and an item submitted by the UAR on Israel's 'aggression'. In his report U Thant stressed the seriousness of the decision to restrict shipping in the Straits of Tiran and pointed out that the government of Israel had declared that the closing of the straits to Israeli ships would be regarded as a *casus belli*. In March 1957 the United States, Britain, and France had undertaken to ensure free passage through the straits into the Gulf of Aqaba. In the Council discussions, therefore, Britain and the United States had stressed the importance of this matter. But American preoccupation with Vietnam, Britain's economic problems, and the intensely strong feeling of the Arab states on the subject had prevented the Western powers from agreeing on any definite plan of action. War broke out on 5 June.

Hostilities started with an Israeli air attack on Egyptian airfields, in which nearly 300 planes were destroyed and the Egyptian air force was virtually eliminated. By the morning of 10 June Israeli forces had occupied the Sinai peninsula, including the western shores of the Tiran straits and the eastern bank of the Suez Canal. They had conquered Western Jordan, including the whole city of Jerusalem, and captured the formidable heights which dominated Israel's northern borders on the Syrian side. They had completely defeated the Egyptian and Jordanian armies, and the destruction of the Syrian army had only been cut short by a cease-fire.

During the six days that the war lasted the Security Council met ten times. Effective action was first held up by Soviet insistence that a cease-fire should be accompanied by Israeli withdrawal from Arab territory. The desperate military situation of the Arabs, however, led Moscow to change its attitude. The Council unanimously passed resolutions on 6 and 7 June, the first *calling for* a cease-fire, the second *demanding* one, and Israel, Jordan, and the UAR accepted the cease-fire on the 7th. A further resolution on the 9th, demanding 'that hostilities should cease forthwith', was needed before a cease-fire followed between Israel and Syria. This was arranged by the UNTSO Chief of Staff on 10 June, and the following day UN observers were deployed on both sides to supervise the cessation of hostilities.

There were soon rumours that the 'hot line' between Washington and Moscow had been used during the war, and the publication of President Johnson's memoirs in the autumn of 1971 made clear that the hot line had indeed been employed repeatedly and to very good effect.[42] Kosygin took the initiative within a few hours of war breaking out. He told Johnson that 'the Russians intended to work for a cease-fire' and expressed the hope that the United States 'would exert influence on

[42] Lyndon B. Johnson, *The Vantage Point*, pp. 287 and 298–303.

Israel'. Johnson replied positively. The most dangerous moment was on the morning of 10 June, after Israeli forces had dislodged the Syrians from their strongpoint on Israeli's northern border, because the way was then clear for an advance into Syria and the capture of Damascus. In Johnson's words 'the Soviet Union was obviously extremely sensitive about Syria', and Kosygin told him that morning that unless Israel unconditionally stopped operations within a few hours the Soviet Union would take 'necessary actions, including military'. Johnson at once ordered the American Sixth Fleet to move towards the Syrian coast, while pressing Israel to make the cease-fire completely effective, and the crisis was surmounted.[43]

Had the Security Council resolutions demanded Israeli withdrawal as well as a cease-fire, the aftermath might have been less burdensome but the war would certainly have lasted longer, and with incalculable consequences, including the risk that the super-powers might become actively involved. The war was brief, partly because Israel attained its essential objectives so quickly, partly owing to the personal contact between Johnson and Kosygin, and partly also owing to the essential role played by the Security Council. Neither super-power was prepared to make public concessions nor to let its protégés know that it was negotiating with the enemy's protector, and the Security Council was the essential channel through which the results of the hot-line conversations were implemented. Throughout the war the Council was also the focal point of world opinion in favour of peace and exerted continuous pressure to bring an end to hostilities.

Subsequent negotiations

The cease-fire in June 1967, in contrast to the settlement after the Suez crisis, left Israel in possession of its territorial gains. Territorial expansion by means of armed force was in clear conflict with the principles of the UN Charter, so the Security Council was faced with two problems; how and under what conditions to bring about Israel's withdrawal from the occupied area, and how to maintain peace along the temporary frontiers pending a permanent settlement.

During the five years that followed the war both problems defied a satisfactory solution. But the Security Council quickly made a substantial contribution towards dealing with the second. During the actual war UNTSO had played a valuable role by providing information about hostilities. Also, as has been seen, this subsidiary organ of the

[43] *Ibid.*, pp. 301–303.

Security Council helped, through its Chief-of-Staff, to bring about the ceasefire between Israel and Syria and then, through its observer teams, supervised it. Furthermore, in July, at the Secretary-General's suggestion, the Security Council approved a statement of consensus, drawn up by its President, which provided that UNTSO should extend its activities to the Suez Canal sector of the cease-fire line. In December, following a sharp outbreak of hostilities between Israel and Egypt in October, the Council approved an increase of the observers on the Canal from about fifty to ninety, again by means of a consensus statement, but this time without a meeting of the Council (see p. 108). This solution to the problem of maintaining peace on the frontiers was not entirely satisfactory, because there were repeated infringements of the cease-fire by both sides. But the UNTSO observers at least exercised a restraining influence and kept the Security Council fully informed of what was happening.

The problem of arranging for Israel's withdrawal from the occupied territories was more stubborn and fundamental. On the one side, Israel was not prepared to withdraw unless she was assured that such action would result in a peace settlement and Arab recognition of her existence as a state. On the other side, the Arab countries considered withdrawal to be a necessary precondition for negotiations. On 17 June the General Assembly met in an emergency special session, which the Soviet Union had requested, in the belief that the Assembly provided the best hope of giving UN support to the kind of solution it favoured. None of the draft resolutions submitted to the Assembly obtained the two-thirds majority necessary for adoption. But a draft sponsored by the Latin American states received the largest vote and, by winning support for a number of basic principles, contributed greatly to the resolution finally adopted by the Security Council.

This was resolution 242, which the Council approved unanimously on 22 November 1967. A unanimous vote on such a difficult and controversial subject was a remarkable achievement. The result owed much to the tact, the goodwill, and the popular and persuasive personality of Lord Caradon, the British representative, who sponsored the resolution. But the Assembly debates had laid a good foundation, and, as Caradon emphasized, the resolution was the culmination of a joint effort and was based on a general desire to find common ground on which to progress toward a solution (see pp. 106–107).

As with most consensual resolutions a price had to be paid for unanimity, and the price in this case was convenient ambiguity, without which agreement would hardly have been possible. Resolution 242 provided a good basis for negotiation and narrowed the gap that remained to be bridged. But it was an uncertain formula for an actual settlement and left much to the determination, the ingenuity, the readiness for compromise, and the breadth of mind on both sides. It was magnanimity, however, that on both sides was conspicuously lacking.

The essence of the resolution was contained in two affirmations and one request, and it started with a preamble 'emphasizing the inadmissibility of the acquisition of territory by war'. The first affirmation laid down that 'the fulfilment of Charter principles requires the establishment of a just and lasting peace in the Middle East' in accordance with the following principles:

(i) Withdrawal of Israel armed forces from territories occupied in the recent conflict.

(ii) . . . respect for and acknowledgment of the sovereignty, territorial integrity and political independence of every State in the area and their right to live in peace within secure and recognized boundaries free from threats or acts of force.

The second affirmation stated the necessity:

(a) For guaranteeing freedom of navigation through international waterways in the area.

(b) For achieving a just settlement of the refugee problem.

The Secretary-General was then requested to designate a special representative to proceed to the Middle East 'in order to promote agreement and assist efforts to achieve a peaceful and accepted settlement'.

The two main ambiguities related to the phrases 'territories occupied' and 'secure boundaries'. Did the first mean 'all occupied territories' or just some of them?[44] Did the second mean the boundaries of 1948 or those boundaries modified to provide greater security? The different interpretations of the phrases by the two sides made it difficult for their protecting powers to cooperate in working for a settlement, as they had cooperated in supporting resolution 242.

The Secretary-General responded to the request by appointing as his special representative Dr Gunnar Jarring, who was at the time Swedish ambassador to the Soviet Union and who had considerable UN experience in a variety of roles. During the next few years negotiations to reach a settlement within the framework of resolution 242 were in fact carried out in three different ways: by Dr Jarring himself; by the four

[44] There is no ambiguity in the French text.

powers, that is, the two super-powers plus Britain and France; and bilaterally by the two super-powers alone. Dr Jarring's role as a mediator was hampered from the first by Israel's insistence on direct negotiation between the parties and the Arab refusal to accept this method. Early in 1969 France suggested four-power discussions, and they took place over a period of two years, this approach having the advantage that both France and Britain were aiming at a compromise solution. Bilateral negotiations between the super-powers had the strength and weakness of all such encounters: they brought the two protagonists into direct contact, but their basically different points of view were less likely to be modified by world opinion or mediatory influence.

By the end of April 1972 no solution had been reached, and no real progress had been made towards one. In fact, the situation had worsened in two respects. First, Israel's attitude had hardened as a result of nearly five years of successful occupation, American support, and the restraining influence of the Soviet Union on Egyptian militarism. Secondly, the prestige of the Security Council and the United Nations as a whole had suffered as a result of the Council passing numerous resolutions with little effect, rebuking one side or the other for aggressive or provocative acts, two particularly blatant examples being the insistence of Israel, the victor in the Six-Day War, on holding a military parade in the Arab part of Jerusalem in May 1968, and on making fundamental changes in the section of Jerusalem which she had occupied as a result of the Six-Day War.

The Arab–Israel conflict provides a clear illustration of the Security Council's limited effectiveness in cases where super-power rivalry is involved. It raises the whole question of the right and wisdom of intervention by major powers, especially nuclear powers, in the conflicts of other countries, either by supplying arms and war material or by sustained diplomatic support, except when their vital interests make intervention virtually inevitable. It brings home furthermore the tragic implications for international relations and world peace, when domestic considerations, such as concern for electoral support, are allowed to influence major diplomatic decisions.[45]

[45] In this connection the following four facts are relevant: President Nixon had a majority of only 336,000 votes out of a total of over 72 million in the 1968 elections; the Jews in the United States have a strong influence on the Press and radio as well as several million votes; after Mrs Meir's visit to Washington in December 1971, Nixon agreed to resume the shipment of modern Phantom aircraft to Israel; and yet the Soviet Union was, on the whole, exercising a restraining influence on the UAR government during the winter of 1971–72.

In the Middle East dispute each of the two super-powers had taken up the posture of a champion of one side. But their interests were not vitally involved. The best proof of this was their cooperation to bring about peace in the wars of 1956 and 1967. Having both helped to end hostilities during the Six-Day War on the basis of a cease-fire without a withdrawal, they were under a strong moral and diplomatic obligation to cooperate in finding terms for a settlement. The fact that they failed to do so and showed no sense of urgency in the matter revealed weaknesses in their claims to world leadership. They had both used the UN machinery effectively, while bringing an end to the fighting. But they were reluctant to continue doing so when the emergencies were past. The Security Council itself could not achieve a settlement without the goodwill and full backing of its most powerful members.

Inter-Arab disputes

Sudan–Egypt border, 1958

By a letter dated 20 February 1958 the permanent representative of the Sudan at the UN requested an urgent meeting of the Security Council 'to discuss the grave situation existing on the Sudan–Egyptian border, resulting from the massed concentrations of Egyptian troops moving towards the Sudanese frontiers'. In an accompanying communication the Prime Minister of the Sudan stated that at the beginning of the month the Egyptian Government had sent a note to the Sudan Government, demanding the handing over of two areas of Sudanese territory which it claimed, and demanding further that the inhabitants of these regions should participate in an Egyptian plebiscite within three weeks. In spite of a visit by the Sudanese foreign minister to Cairo, no amicable settlement had been reached and large numbers of Egyptian troops were reported on the border.

The Council considered the matter the following day. The Egyptian representative deplored Sudan's hasty decision to appeal to the Council, denied the presence of Egyptian forces, apart from border guards, near the Egyptian frontier, and agreed to postpone settlement of the question until after the Sudanese elections, which were due within a week. Members of the Council expressed the hope that the two parties would be able to settle the question peacefully by negotiation and that meanwhile neither party would do anything to aggravate the situation. The President summed up the Council's views by noting the assurances of the Egyptian representative and adding that the question put forward by the Sudan, of course, remained before the Council.

The incident was an example of the way in which the Security Council, by the very act of taking up a matter, can, without passing a formal resolution, exercise a salutary restraining influence.

Lebanon, Jordan, and the UAR, 1958

On 22 May 1958 President Chamoun of Lebanon complained to the Security Council about 'the intervention of the United Arab Republic in the internal affairs of Lebanon, the continuance of which is likely to endanger the maintenance of international peace and security'. Lebanon complained to the Arab League at the same time. The Council postponed dealing with the matter in order to give the regional organization an opportunity of solving the problem, but the League failed to do so, and the Council acted.

On 11 June it decided to dispatch urgently an observation group to Lebanon in order to ensure that there was no illegal infiltration of personnel or supply of arms or other material across the Lebanese borders, and authorized the Secretary-General to take the necessary steps to that end. Hammarskjöld, as usual, acted with great speed. He appointed the United Nations Observation Group in Lebanon (UNOGIL) the next day, composed of three highly qualified and experienced men, and provided them with a staff of observers, the nucleus of which was drawn from UNTSO.

The background to the Lebanese complaint was complex. In February 1958 Egypt and Syria had joined to form the United Arab Republic, a development which alarmed President Chamoun, who found himself, as the ruler of a semi-Christian country, between the two parts of an unfriendly and formidable Arab state. The internal situation in Lebanon was also dangerous. The creation of the UAR had aggravated Muslim–Christian rivalry, President Chamoun had managed to alienate many even of the Christian leaders, and there were widespread rumours that he was planning to alter the constitution to enable himself to be re-elected for a second term as president. It was in these circumstances and in face of growing internal opposition to his regime, amounting in some cases to civil war, that Chamoun appealed to the Security Council.

The difficult conditions in which UNOGIL had to work were made worse by unexpected developments in Iraq. Jordan and Iraq had responded to the formation of the UAR by themselves forming a federation, thus bringing into the open a latent rivalry within the Arab world.

On 14 July, in the course of a military *coup*, King Faisal and his prime minister, Nuri es Said, who were both pro-Western, were murdered and a republic was established. The Lebanese and Jordanian governments, believing the hand of Nasser to be behind the events in Iraq and fearing that their countries were threatened by the UAR, appealed respectively to the United States and Britain for military aid, and American and British troops were landed in Lebanon and Jordan within three days. Both Western powers informed the Security Council that their forces would be withdrawn, if the UN could arrange to replace them. But, as a result of their action, the Middle East had again become a focus-point of East–West rivalry.

As things turned out the Soviet Union was content to use the UN as a forum for arraigning the United States and Britain for their interven-tion, though for a time the situation was critical. The Security Council failed to agree on any course of action. Proposals were put forward in turn for a summit meeting and for a periodic meeting of the Council to be attended by heads of governments (see p. 79), but both were turned down. In the end the Council decided to call an emergency special session of the General Assembly. During this session, owing largely to some patient and highly skilful diplomacy by Hammarskjöld, the Ass-embly adopted unanimously on 21 August a resolution which was actu-ally sponsored by ten Arab states, including all those which had been involved in the recent disputes. It called on all UN members not to interfere in each other's internal affairs and requested the Secretary-General to make such 'arrangements as would adequately help uphold-ing the purpose and principles of the Charter in relation to Lebanon and Jordan ... and thereby facilitate the early withdrawal of the foreign troops'.

UNOGIL's task during this eventful summer was challenging in the extreme and for a time impossible to fulfil. In its early days the greater part of the frontier between Lebanon and the UAR was controlled by the rebel opponents of the government, and the country through which it ran was difficult and sometimes inaccessible. The observers' first report, therefore, was based on inadequate evidence but gave the im-pression that 'the vast majority' of the armed rebels were Lebanese rather than infiltrators from outside. Conditions improved after the election of General Chehab as the new president at the end of July and after Hammarskjöld had been given almost a free hand by the General Assembly's resolution. UNOGIL at its height comprised nearly 600 military observers, who were equipped with about 300 vehicles, some light aircraft and helicopters. This subsidiary organ of the Security

Council performed three useful tasks. It exercised a restraining influence on the internal conflict in Lebanon; it helped to prevent any dangerous development of intervention from the UAR and three weeks before it ceased operation on 9 December 1958 had been able to report to the Security Council resumption of cordial relations between Lebanon and the UAR; and it facilitated the withdrawal of American and British troops from Lebanon and Jordan in October and November. In the words of its final report UNOGIL had been 'a symbol of the concern of the international community for the welfare and security of Lebanon'.

In further fulfilment of his charge from the General Assembly Hammarskjöld in September 1958 established a UN 'presence' in Jordan, which consisted of the Director of the UN's European Office in Geneva and a small staff and had a stabilizing influence in Jordan.

Kuwait–Iraq, 1961

In June 1961 the sheikdom of Kuwait, which had been a British protectorate since 1899, signed a treaty with Britain by which it became a fully independent state. Iraq at once laid claim to Kuwait as 'part of the [Iraqi] province of Basra'. Within two weeks Kuwait appealed to Britain for help, and a small British force was landed. On 1 July Kuwait requested an urgent meeting of the Security Council to consider 'the situation arising from threats by Iraq to the territorial independence of Kuwait'. Britain supported the request, and the following day Iraq responded by asking for a Council meeting to consider 'the situation arising out of the armed threat by the United Kingdom to the independence and security of Iraq'.

The Council met on 2 July to deal with the two complaints. The circumstances were unusual in that Arab suspicion of any British intervention in the Middle East was offset by resentment at Iraq's claiming the right to absorb a newly independent, small, though very wealthy state. A British draft resolution calling on all states to respect the independence and territorial integrity of Kuwait was vetoed by the Soviet Union. A draft submitted by the UAR calling on the United Kingdom to withdraw its forces from Kuwait immediately was supported by only three votes. Before adjourning the meeting the President stated that members of the Council would remain vigilant with regard to the dangerous situation that unfortunately still existed, and that he was prepared to convene the Council whenever circumstances made it necessary.

The threat from Iraq did not materialize. The British forces were withdrawn in October and were replaced for a short time by forces from the Arab League. Iraq's change of attitude was the result largely of pressure from other Arab states, but it was facilitated by Kuwait's reference of the matter to the Council.

Yemen, 1963–64

In September 1962 the Iman of Yemen died and was succeeded by his son. Within a few days, with the autocratic hand of the previous ruler removed, latent discontent revealed itself. A military revolt broke out, and a republic was proclaimed. The republican government appealed to the UAR for help, and the new Iman, to Saudi Arabia. Both countries responded, and a civil war followed with dangerous international implications. In December the UN General Assembly recognized the republican government.

On his own initiative the Secretary-General held consultations with the representatives of Yemen, Saudi Arabia, and the UAR at the UN; sent Ralph Bunche on a fact-finding mission to Yemen in February and March 1963; and received information also from Ellsworth Bunker, whom the United States government had sent on an independent but similar mission. As a result, Saudi Arabia and the UAR agreed to withdraw their support from the two sides, a demilitarized zone was to be established along the border between Saudi Arabia and Yemen, and impartial observers were to check on the observance of the terms of disengagement. In order to decide on the nature and functions of any UN observer group that might be employed, the UNTSO chief-of-staff visited the three countries concerned. After he had reported, the Secretary-General estimated that the personnel required would not exceed 200 and that the observers would not be needed for more than four months. Saudi Arabia and Yemen agreed to share the cost of the operation. The Secretary-General kept the Security Council informed of these developments in a series of reports.

U Thant had received no directives from the Security Council but had acted on a very liberal interpretation of his powers under Article 99 of the Charter. While it is arguable, however, that the Secretary-General may need to establish facts before he can form an opinion on a threat to international peace and security, Article 99 hardly envisaged his entering into negotiations with governments while doing so. The Soviet Union, therefore, ever jealous of the Security Council's authority, requested a meeting of the Council to consider U Thant's reports, since they 'contained proposals concerning possible measures . . . on which, under the Charter, decisions are taken by the Security Council'.

The Security Council met on 10 June 1963 and agreed to a resolution requesting the Secretary-General 'to establish the observation operation defined by him'. It was adopted without opposition, though the Soviet Union abstained. The UN Observation Mission in Yemen (UNYOM) was set up originally for two months. In the end its life was extended by two-month periods until September 1964. From June 1963 until September 1964 the Security Council did not give formal consideration to its work on a single occasion, although U Thant obtained the informal approval of Council members to each extension. UNYOM's mandate was limited to 'observing, certifying, and reporting' whether the parties to the Saudi–UAR disengagement agreement were in fact upholding it. Its task was extremely difficult owing to its inadequate size and equipment, the wild mountainous nature of the area in which it was operating and the fact that neither Saudi Arabia nor the UAR were carrying out the agreement—substantial UAR forces were still in Yemen at the time of the Six-Day War.

During its early months UNYOM comprised nearly 200 observers, but towards the end of 1963 the number was reduced to about twenty-five, and the Secretary-General's civilian Special Representative for Yemen replaced a general as its head. It was finally withdrawn on U Thant's own recommendation after consultation with Saudi Arabia and the UAR. In U Thant's final report on UNYOM to the Security Council he regretted that the Mission had been able to observe only limited progress towards the implementation of the disengagement agreement but added that 'during the fourteen months of its presence in Yemen, the UN Mission exercised an important restraining influence on hostile activities in that area'. UNYOM was, on the whole, one of the least successful of the UN's peace-keeping or observation missions.

The Anglo-Iranian Oil Company, 1951–52

In March 1951 the Iranian parliament decided that the country's oil industry should be nationalized, and a few weeks later the Iranian government promulgated a law setting out how the decision was to be implemented. It rejected the Company's request for arbitration in accordance with the 1933 agreement between the Company and itself, and on 26 May Britain submitted the matter to the International Court. Iran denied the Court's competence to deal with the dispute, which, it said, was exclusively within its domestic jurisdiction, and the Iranian government interfered increasingly with the Company's installations and personnel. The International Court, therefore, in July ordered the Iranian government and the Company to do nothing which might prejudice the rights of either party or aggravate the dispute. The Iranian government rejected this order, announced that the Company's British staff must leave Iran by 4 October, and on 27 September seized the Company's main refinery at Abadan. The following day Britain requested that the failure of the Iranian government to comply with the Court's provisional measures should be put on the Security Council's agenda.

The proposed item was included in the agenda, in face of Soviet and Yugoslav opposition, and the Council considered the question at six meetings between 1 and 19 October. Britain submitted two draft resolutions in turn; the first calling on Iran to comply with the Court's provisional measures, and the second calling for the early resumption of negotiations and the avoidance of any action which would further aggravate the situation. But the opposition of Communist countries and the sympathy of undeveloped countries with the Iranian point of view led to so many doubts as to the Council's competence being expressed that the Council finally approved a French proposal, in which Britain acquiesced, that the debate should be adjourned until the Court had ruled on its own competence in the matter. The following summer the Court decided that it had no jurisdiction to deal with the dispute. But reference of the case to the Council had acted as a safety valve for British public indignation and made it easier for the British government to avoid the use of force.

Bahrein

The British government's announcement early in 1968 that it intended to withdraw from the Persian Gulf by the end of 1971 raised the question of Iran's ancient claim to Bahrein. A strong assertion of this claim would have seriously affected Iran's relations with the Arab states, and the Shah was prepared to waive the claim, provided that Iranian honour and public opinion could be satisfied by a clear indication that the people of Bahrein wanted independence. An obvious way of establishing this point would have been through a plebiscite. But the Bahrein government was not prepared to contemplate this method, because it would amount to calling in question its right to sovereign independence.

After preliminary negotiations between Britain and Iran during 1968 and 1969 it was agreed that the best procedure would be for the Secretary-General to appoint a special representative, who would ascertain the wishes of the people of Bahrein by means acceptable to all parties. This method was facilitated in January 1969 by the Shah's statement to the Press in New Delhi that he would not use force to reclaim Bahrein and that he would accept the will of the people of Bahrein, if it were expressed in an internationally acceptable manner. At the end of the year the British and Iranian heads of missions at the UN made a joint approach to the Secretary-General who agreed to use his good offices and appointed Ralph Bunche to act for him in the matter. Soon afterwards Bunche had a meeting in Geneva with representatives of the Bahreinian government.

On 28 March 1970 the Secretary-General sent a note to members of the Security Council informing them that, at the request of the British and Iranian governments, he had agreed 'to exercise his good offices in a matter pertaining to Bahrein', and that he had appointed as his personal representative Winspeare Guicciardi, the director-general of the UN office at Geneva, who would be going to Bahrein to ascertain the wishes of the people, the costs of the mission being borne by the parties. The personal representative visited Bahrein from 30 March to 18 April, and the Secretary-General sent the resulting report to the Security Council on 30 April. The report was based on numerous consultations with organizations, societies, institutions, and groups as well as individuals, and in it Winspeare Guicciardi expressed his conviction that 'the overwhelming majority of the people of Bahrein wished to gain recognition of their identity in a fully independent and sovereign State free to decide for itself its relations with other States'.

At the beginning of April the Soviet representative had complained to the Secretary-General that he had communicated information to members of the Security Council concerning the adoption of measures connected with the problem of Bahrein, without consulting them beforehand and that decisions relating to the maintenance of peace and security should be taken by the Security Council. U Thant replied that differences between states might be solved amicably 'if dealt with at an early stage quietly and diplomatically', and that, when members approached the Secretary-General to use his good offices to such an end, he felt obligated to respond positively. In this case the mission in Bahrein entailed only fact-finding, and any substantive action would be taken by the Security-Council. In fact, at the request of Iran and Britain, the Council met to consider the matter on 11 May. It approved unanimously a resolution endorsing the report of the Secretary-General's personal representative and welcomed particularly the wish expressed by the people of Bahrein. Following the Council's endorsement, both Iran and Britain accepted the findings and conclusions of the personal representative, and the problem was thus solved.

The Bahrein case is not well known, because it was so unobtrusively successful. Handled differently, it might have led to protracted bitterness and even hostilities. As it turned out, it was a model of what can be accomplished, within the UN framework, by foresight, goodwill and intelligent diplomacy.

KOREA

During the second World War Korea was promised independence by the Allies at the Cairo Conference in 1943. But in 1945 the Japanese in Korea surrendered both to the Americans and the Russians and, as a result, Korea was divided along the 38th parallel into two parts under American and Russian occupation, much as Germany was divided between the Soviet Union and the Western Allies.

Failure to agree on Korea's future led the United States to refer the problem to the UN. In November 1947 the General Assembly appointed a UN Temporary Commission on Korea to supervise elections for a National Assembly and the withdrawal of the occupation forces. The Communist authorities in North Korea would neither cooperate with the Temporary Commission nor allow it to cross the 38th parallel. So it confined itself to supervising elections in the South which resulted in the establishment of the Republic of Korea. At the end of 1948 the General Assembly approved the Temporary Commission's reports and replaced it by a rather smaller body called the Commission on Korea, which was given the tasks of bringing about the unification of the country, observing and verifying the withdrawal of the occupying forces, and observing and reporting any developments which might lead to military conflict. The American and Russian forces were withdrawn before the end of 1949.

On 25 June 1950 the Commission reported that North Korean forces had invaded the Republic of Korea. The Security Council met the same day at the United States' request and, in response to an appeal from the Republic of Korea, passed a resolution by nine votes to nil, with one abstention (Yugoslavia) and one member absent (the Soviet Union), determining that the North Korean action constituted a breach of the peace, calling for immediate cessation of hostilities and the withdrawal of North Korean forces to the 38th parallel, and calling also on all members to render every assistance to the UN in the execution of the resolution and to refrain from giving assistance to the North Korean authorities. Two days later President Truman, basing his action on a broad interpretation of the Council's resolution, ordered United States air and sea forces to give cover and support to the South Korean troops and instructed the American Seventh Fleet to prevent any attack on Taiwan.[46] A few hours later the Security Council met again and approved a United States draft resolution, which noted that the authorities in North Korea had not responded to the previous resolution and *recommended* that UN Members should furnish such assistance to the Republic of Korea as might be necessary to repel the armed attack and to restore international peace and security in the area.

On 7 July the Council passed a third resolution which recommended that all members providing military forces and other assistance pursuant to the two previous resolutions should make such forces and assistance available to a unified command under the United States; requested the United States to designate the commander of such forces; and authorized the unified command to use the UN flag in the course of operations against North Korean forces concurrently with the flags of the various nations participating.

The situation facing the Security Council at this time was in two respects unique. In the first place, as has been seen, the Soviet Union had chosen to absent itself from Council meetings and was not therefore in a position to use its veto. Secondly, the United States had substantial forces available in Japan, so that the Council's past failure to implement Article 43 of the Charter was not an insuperable obstacle to enforcement action, though the action would not be what was envisaged in the Charter.

There has been much controversy as to the constitutional basis of the UN action in this case; in particular as to whether or not it fell within the framework of Chapter VII of the Charter. In none of its three resolutions did the Security Council make *decisions*, the term used in Article 41. It confined itself rather to exhortations (*calling upon*) and

---

[46] The Seventh Fleet was also ordered to prevent attacks on the mainland by Chiang Kai-shek's forces. The question of Taiwan was considered by the Security Council on a number of occasions between August and November 1950 as a result of a complaint by China of armed invasion by the United States. But with the United States in effective naval control of the area, the complaint was little more than a formal protest within the framework of the Korean War. The question was raised again in the Council during January 1955, both by New Zealand and the Soviet Union, when hostilities were taking place between Communist China and Taiwan over certain islands near the Chinese coast, but with no significant result, except that, in contrast to November 1950, Communist China refused to send a representative to the Council meeting.

recommendations. But recommendations is the term used in Article 39, which is also in Chapter VII, and in all three resolutions the Council determined that the North Korean attack constituted 'a breach of the peace', which is one of the eventualities dealt with in the Article. It is therefore reasonable to regard with D. W. Bowett 'the Korean action as enforcement action authorized by recommendations under Article 39',[47] and to agree with another authority, Rosalyn Higgins, that, 'while the action in Korea was undoubtedly *sui generis*, it may properly be described as enforcement action recommended by the Security Council under Articles 39 and 42, the command of which was delegated to the United States as agent of the UN'.[48]

The dominant contributor to the United Nations forces was the United States, due mainly to its great strength, but partly also to the proximity of its forces in Japan and partly to the fact that the attack on South Korea, from which it had only recently withdrawn, was a direct challenge to its authority. It provided about 50 per cent of the ground forces, 86 per cent of the naval forces, and 93 per cent of the air forces. The Republic of Korea was the next largest contributor and provided over 40 per cent of the ground forces. But about fifteen other nations made military contributions amounting to approximately 36,000 troops out of a grand total of nearly three-quarters of a million at the forces' maximum strength. From a historical point of view, a significant contributor was Ethiopia, which sent over a thousand troops.

The United States appointed General MacArthur Commander-in-Chief of the UN forces in Korea. An attempt to establish a Korea Command Structure with a broadly based UN staff drawn from the contributing countries, in which Lester Pearson and Andrew Cordier played a leading part, was unsuccessful, due partly to the personality of MacArthur and partly to the desire of every powerful military bureaucracy to run its own show. All that was set up was a Committee of Sixteen in Washington, consisting of diplomatic representatives of the contributing countries, who were used to send information to their governments rather than for decision-making or prior consultation. An advantage of this centralized system was that the Soviet Union could not interfere with the conduct of the war, when it returned to the Security Council. Two disadvantages, however, were that the contributing countries could not exercise a restraining influence on General MacArthur and that an opportunity was missed for establishing a precedent for the cooperative direction of UN operations.

[47] *United Nations Forces*, p. 34.
[48] *United Nations Peace Keeping*, vol. II, 178.

In August 1950 it was the Soviet Union's turn to provide the President of the Security Council, and the Soviet representative took this opportunity to resume his seat. From then on the Soviet veto prevented any further action by the Council, and all further UN action relating to the conduct of the war and the negotiations for peace was taken by the General Assembly. It was in these circumstances that the American secretary of state, in November 1950, sponsored a General Assembly resolution, entitled 'Uniting for Peace', which has facilitated consideration by the Assembly of cases involving a threat to the peace, breach of the peace or act of aggression, when the Security Council has been prevented through deadlock from exercising its responsibility. The procedure provided for in this resolution was not resorted to during the Korean War. In fact, the fundamental decisions which determined the original UN and US response in Korea had been taken by the Security Council in June and July, and subsequent problems relating to the Chinese intervention went straight to the Assembly. In January 1951 the Korean item was formally removed from the Council's agenda.

In the summer of 1950 the decision to resist the North Korean offensive was greeted with some euphoria as an example at long last of collective security being put into practice successfully. Since then there has been a growing tendency to look upon it as an example of United States power politics, in which the UN became an instrument of American policy. Both these attitudes are oversimplified.

The Korean action can only be understood in the light of the world situation at the time. Three aspects of the situation are specially relevant. First, in the months before the North Korean attack a number of influential Americans had expressed the view that the defence of Korea was not a vital interest of the United States: too local a view, therefore, of American *Realpolitik* is of debatable validity. Secondly, in the summer of 1950 the Cold War was at its height: the Berlin blockade had ended only just over a year before, and the true nature of Stalin's policy in Eastern and Central Europe had become clear, as the Communist parties took control of one government after another and as Tito's defection in 1948 was followed by a series of drastic and widespread purges. Thirdly, the United Nations was still very much on trial: it had commendable achievements to its credit in Iran, Indonesia, Kashmir, and the Middle East, but it had yet to meet the challenge of major and deliberate aggression.

It was not unreasonable in 1950 to link the challenge of Communism with the challenge to the United Nations, because Stalin had shown complete disdain for the Charter principle of 'equal rights and self-determination of peoples'. And that is precisely what President Truman and the UN Secretary-General, with rather different emphasis, actually did.

Trygve Lie made very clear that he believed the UN to be fully involved. At the Council's first meeting on Korea he made a statement, before the debate began, in which he said that the actions of the North Korean forces were a violation of the principles of the Charter and that it was the clear duty of the Council to take the steps necessary to re-establish peace in the area. Within the following three weeks he sent out two letters; one to all member governments calling their attention to the Council's second resolution and recommending them to furnish assistance to the Republic of Korea, and the other to the members, which had supported the Council's stand, asking them to consider the possibility of giving such assistance. Actually fifty-one states supported the Council's action, a clear indication of the widespread feeling that more was at stake than the national interests of the United States.

President Truman, in his *Report to Congress for 1950 on the United States and the United Nations*, expressed the conviction that to have ignored the appeal of Korea for aid would have meant the end of the UN as a shield against aggression. In his report the following year he stated that, in spite of all difficulties and discouragements, the UN remained the best means available to the present generation for achieving peace for the community of nations. Many Americans shared their President's appreciation of the UN's role in a defensive action against Communist aggression. In Leland M. Goodrich's opinion 'the invocation of the Charter . . . paid heavy dividends in terms of national security' and 'placed US resistance to the North Korean attack on a higher plane than the defense of a purely national interest'.[49] The Korean action administered both a decisive check to Communist aggression and a boost to the UN's prestige.

However, it was not a triumph for collective security as envisaged in the Charter. It was rather an unusual and mainly successful exercise in modified collective security, made possible by exceptional circumstances and never likely to recur. It in no way reduced the restrictions on collective security, which were inherent in the Charter or had resulted from the failure to implement Article 43. On the contrary, the Korean experiment underlined the significance of the veto and the need for powerful armed forces, if any enforcement action were to be undertaken with success.

[49] See his *Korea: a study of U.S. policy in the United Nations*, p. 211.

INDIA AND PAKISTAN

Junagadh and Hyderabad

On the eve of Indian independence in 1943 the greater part of the sub-continent comprised the provinces of British India, while the remainder was made up of 562 Indian states, which covered over two-fifths of the total area, included nearly a quarter of the total population of nearly 400 million, and acknowledged the paramountcy of the British crown. The principle of paramountcy left internal administration to the Indian rulers but gave the British government control over foreign relations and defence and the right to intervene in the event of flagrant mis-government. When power in British India was transferred to the two newly independent governments of India and Pakistan, British para-mountcy lapsed, and the Indian states were left free to accede to either India or Pakistan or, in theory at least, to remain independent.

The British were reluctant to annul their often long-standing treaties with the Indian princes, but their experts on India on the whole agreed that there was no practicable alternative and that accession of the states to either India or Pakistan was almost inevitable, especially when they were surrounded by the territory of one or other of the two new countries. As a result of practical considerations, therefore, together with the pressure exerted by the forceful Indian minister in charge of the States Department, all the states within the boundaries of the new India had acceded to the Indian Union by the time power was trans-ferred in August 1947, with the exception of Hyderabad, Junagadh, and Kashmir. Of these Hyderabad and Junagadh had Muslim rulers with predominantly Hindu populations, while Kashmir had a Hindu Maharajah and a population over three-quarters of which were Muslim.

Junagadh was a small state on the north-west coast of the sub-continent, about 300 miles from Karachi by sea but bordered by Indian territory on the land side. Soon after the transfer of power its ruler announced his accession to Pakistan; some of his Hindu subjects revolted; Indian troops invaded the state; a plebiscite was held, in which an overwhelming majority favoured joining India; and the Indian government annexed the state.

Pakistan naturally resented this procedure, and it referred the matter to the Security Council in January 1948. The Council considered it at a number of meetings in February, March and May. But many Pakistanis realized that the Hindu majority in Junagadh favoured accession to India, and the problem was already overshadowed by the question of Kashmir. In the end, early in June, the Council handed the matter over rather halfheartedly to a Commission it had set up in January primarily to investigate the situation in Kashmir, and the Council's consideration of the problem in fact lapsed.

Hyderabad was, in area, one of the largest Indian states and in population it was much the largest, with about 17 million inhabitants. Over 85 per cent of its people were Hindu; it was surrounded by Indian territory; and as a separate state, therefore, it would have been an awkward and illogical enclave. On the other hand, it had great traditions; its university was a centre of Urdu culture; its ruler, the Nizam, was a moderate and impressive personality; his administration, though not democratic, was in many respects well run and progressive; and it had been free from communal strife between Hindus and Muslims. It was quite capable of existing as an independent state, and the Nizam had every legal right to choose this course.

When the transfer of power took place the Nizam was uncertain what he should do. His real wish seemed to be for independence, but he realized the difficulty of his relationship with India. While the Indian government brought great pressure on him to accede to the Indian Union, his more extreme Muslim advisers urged him to take a strong line for independence, and thus prevented any compromise settlement with India, by which, for example, India might have assumed the rights of paramountcy only. In November 1947 the Nizam and the Indian government made a standstill agreement for a period of one year, while the main problem was being settled. But before the year had come to an end a mass civil disobedience movement by the Hindus, organized largely from across the border, was followed by an economic blockade by India and an invasion by the Indian army in September 1948. As a result of *force majeure*, Hyderabad was absorbed into India.

On 21 August 1948 Hyderabad informed the Security Council by letter, under Article 35 (2) of the Charter, that a grave dispute had arisen between Hyderabad and India, which, unless settled in accordance with international law and justice, was likely to endanger the maintenance of international peace and security. The letter stated that Hyderabad had recently been exposed to violent intimidation, to threats of invasion and to economic blockade, which were intended to coerce it into a renunciation of its independence. On 13 September Hyderabad informed the Council that the State was being invaded. The

F*

Council dealt with the question on 16 September and at seven subsequent meetings between then and 24 May 1949.

At the first two meetings, during which the Council considered the Hyderabad question, the representative of Hyderabad urged that the situation demanded immediate action by the Council, under Article 35 of the Charter and under Chapter VII as well. The representative of India maintained that Hyderabad was not a state and was not competent to bring any question before the Security Council. He then went on rather unfortunately to say that his government's patience was exhausted[50] and that it had used force only to maintain law and order, which had completely broken down in parts of Hyderabad, without making any convincing defence of India's right to invade Hyderabad in order to do so. The Dutch had used the same argument to defend their 'police action' in Indonesia in 1947, which India had strongly criticized, also calling upon the Security Council to take action under Article 35 of the Charter.

On 22 September the Nizam informed the Secretary-General that he had withdrawn his complaint from the Security Council and that the Hyderabad delegation to the Council, which had been sent at the instance of his former ministry, had ceased to have any authority to represent him or his state. During the Council discussions that followed the main points at issue were whether the Nizam's withdrawal had been voluntary or under duress and whether the credentials of the Hyderabad delegation were still valid or not. Having made its case, the delegation stated in October that it did not propose to seek representation at the Council's next meeting. The Indian representative maintained that the Hyderabad question had been withdrawn, while the case against India was left in the hands of the representative of Pakistan.

On 24 May 1949, during the last meeting at which the Hyderabad question was discussed, the representative of Pakistan suggested that an advisory opinion as to the Council's competence in the matter should be obtained from the International Court of Justice and that a plebiscite be held under the guidance and supervision of the Security Council to settle the question of accession or independence. But in face of a *fait accompli*, the Nizam's acquiescence, and the substantial Hindu majority in the Hyderabad population, the Council took no further action, though formally it remained seized of the question.

[50] Hitler had made this phrase notorious, while engaged in his aggressive actions during the 1930s.

Kashmir

The question of Kashmir[51] was first referred to the Security Council by India on 1 January 1948, and it has occupied the Council's attention on and off ever since. With its large Muslim majority and a long section of its frontier contiguous to Pakistan, Kashmir's natural destiny was to join its Muslim neighbour. But, whereas the Indian government had shown great concern for the Hindu majorities in Junagadh and Hyderabad and had not recognized their rulers' legal rights to determine the future of their states, they were little concerned about the wishes of the Muslim majority in Kashmir and readily recognized the Maharajah's right to accede to India. This inconsistency greatly weakened India's case in the eyes of its fellow UN members, especially Britain and the United States with their concern for democratic proprieties.

Four other aspects of the Kashmir question were important. India is much the largest and most populous of Asian countries with a democratic form of government in the Western sense, and this fact has to some extent offset the point just mentioned in the case of the Western democracies, and especially in the case of Britain, owing to India's membership of the Commonwealth. Secondly, the northernmost tip of Kashmir is very near the most southerly meeting point of the Soviet and Chinese frontiers, and this actually has increased Kashmir's interest for the two great Communist powers. Thirdly, the tribesmen of the North-West Frontier Province are notoriously independent and unruly, and their role in the Kashmir dispute has both created additional problems and given a pretext for provocative action to both sides. Finally, Nehru was by birth a Kashmiri Brahmin, and this fact made him highly sensitive about Kashmir's future.

At the transfer of power the Maharajah of Kashmir was in a difficult position. As a ruler, he was self-indulgent, corrupt, and autocratic, and could expect little from the Indian or Pakistani governments if he joined fortune with either of them. On the other hand, Kashmir had common frontiers with both India and Pakistan, and he could hardly expect to resist the pressures that his two neighbours could put on him.

Early in the autumn of 1947 the Muslims of Poonch in the west of the state, who favoured accession to Pakistan, revolted against the Maharajah's unpopular rule and were soon afterwards joined by Muslim tribesmen from the north-west, who crossed the border from Pakistan

[51] 'Kashmir' has been used throughout as an abbreviation for the fuller and more correct term 'Jammu and Kashmir'.

and Afghanistan and advanced so rapidly that the capital, Srinagar, was threatened. The attitude of the Pakistani government to the invaders is obscure, but it is unlikely that it gave them planned support, though probable that some Pakistani officials connived at least at their action. In this emergency the Maharajah, many of whose troops had deserted, appealed to India for help, signed an instrument of accession to India, and appointed as head of his administration a popular leader, Sheikh Abdullah, who was on good terms with Nehru and was head of the political party, known as the National Conference, which included Hindus as well as Muslims. Lord Mountbatten, whom the Indians had chosen as their first Governor-General, accepted the accession but made clear that he considered it should be referred to the people of Kashmir, after order had been restored. Indian troops were flown in to save Srinagar, and soon afterwards the Indian government appealed to the Security Council.

India complained that Pakistan was assisting in the invasion of Kashmir. Pakistan denied the charge and countered with complaints about India's actions in Hyderabad and Junagadh. The Council considered the question at several meetings during January 1948, and decided to set up a three-member UN Commission for India and Pakistan (UNCIP) to investigate and mediate. One member was to be selected by India, one by Pakistan, and the third was to be designated by the two so selected. India and Pakistan chose Czechoslovakia and Argentina respectively, and, when these two states failed to agreed on a third, the President of the Council nominated the United States. In an important resolution passed on 21 April the Council increased the membership to five, instructed the Commission to proceed at once to the subcontinent and place its good offices and mediation at the disposal of the Indian and Pakistani governments, with a view to facilitating the restoration of peace and order and the holding of a plebiscite. It also provided for the establishment in Kashmir of such observers as the Commission might require in carrying out its tasks. Meanwhile, early in the year, units of the Pakistan regular army had entered Kashmir and won back some of the ground that the tribesmen had lost to the Indian army.

The Commission arrived in the subcontinent on 7 July, and during the twelve months that followed the Council confined itself, so far as Kashmir was concerned, to endorsing and supporting its work. In August UNCIP submitted proposals to India and Pakistan for a ceasefire, a truce agreement, and plebiscite to determine the future status of Kashmir. It also requested the Secretary-General to take steps to appoint, at short notice, military observers to supervise the cease-fire. India and Pakistan both accepted the proposals, though Pakistan expressed certain reservations concerning the organization of the plebiscite. The two parties subsequently agreed to order a cease-fire, which went into effect on 1 January 1949.

On 5 January the Commission embodied its plebiscite proposals in a formal resolution, which provided for the appointment of a Plebiscite Administrator, who was to organize and ensure the freedom and impartiality of the plebiscite. This time India expressed reservations. But in January the first UN observers arrived in Kashmir to report on the cease-fire; in April an American, Admiral Nimitz, was appointed Plebiscite Administrator by the Secretary-General, in consultation with the Indian and Pakistani governments and with UNCIP; and in July the cease-fire became a truce, when the two parties finally agreed upon a demarcation line.

Although India and Pakistan had both agreed to a plebiscite in principle, it was never held, because they could never agree as to the conditions under which it was to be carried out or on who was to control the country while it was taking place. The fundamental difficulty was that India was claiming a state, a large majority of whose inhabitants were Muslim. As a result Pakistan was at first unwilling to compromise in a case in which it had strong inherent rights, whereas India, while reluctant openly to defy the principle of self-determination, really feared the outcome of a plebiscite and preferred to accept such advantages as she could gain from the Maharajah's accession and the subsequent use of force. In addition, it was arguable that conditions in the greater part of the state were so wild and primitive that the only area where a meaningful plebiscite could be organized was the much-prized Vale of Kashmir itself.

The Security Council used many methods in its efforts to bring about a settlement. The Plebiscite Administrator was never called on to carry out his main tasks, but many attempts were made to prepare the way for him. During the winter of 1949–50 the Canadian President of the Council was asked to mediate between the two sides (see p. 96, n. 24). At about the same time UNCIP reported that it had made considerable progress with the truce, but that, so far as mediation was concerned, it believed it had exhausted all the possibilities, and that it thought any further attempt at negotiations would be better carried out by an individual UN representative. As a result, in April 1950, the Council appointed Sir Owen Dixon, an Australian judge, as UN Representative for India and Pakistan. He resigned the following September and was succeeded in April 1951 by an American, Dr Frank Graham, who made a series of six reports to the Council, the last in 1958, without solving the basic problem. In the spring of 1957 the Council again asked its President, this time Dr Jarring of Sweden, to examine with India and Pakistan the possibilities of a settlement, although Dr Graham was still in office. But he reported within five weeks his failure to make any real progress. Sir Owen Dixon's report of September 1950 was revealing. He made clear that he had been able to reach no agreement on means, including demilitarization, for ensuring the freedom and fairness of a plebiscite and believed that the only hope of reaching a settlement by agreement was partition and some (unspecified) means of allocating the Vale of Kashmir. He concluded by suggesting that it might be better to leave the parties to themselves in negotiating terms for a settlement.

In fact, India and Pakistan did resume direct negotiations during August 1953, and the matter was removed from the UN for the first time since the beginning of 1948. Encouraged by Dr Graham, the two prime ministers held discussions in New Delhi for three days and at the end of them issued a communiqué stating that they had agreed to appoint a Plebiscite Administrator by April 1954, although Nehru made clear that Admiral Nimitz was no longer acceptable to India and that he wanted the Administrator to be from a smaller country. Towards the end of the year further meetings took place between Indian and Pakistani experts to discuss the preliminaries to holding a plebiscite, and the results appeared to have been satisfactory. But in this dispute time had not proved a healer. The deep and emotional rivalry which had led to partition in 1947 still existed; developments since then had increased mutual suspicion; and attitudes on both sides had hardened. India had poured money into Kashmir and increased the number of its forces stationed there. In 1951 it had convened a constitutional assembly for Kashmir, which had been chosen by nominal elections, in which seventy-three out of seventy-five candidates were returned unopposed, and which had then voted overwhelmingly for permanent accession to India and was later, in 1956, to approve a new constitution integrating the State into India. Pakistan, on the other hand, made a fateful decision when in the spring of 1954 it entered into an agreement to receive military aid from the United States, thus nullifying the good effects of the bilateral talks and provoking Nehru into finally going back on his word to hold a plebiscite in Kashmir: henceforth he spoke rather in terms of partition.

Since the Delhi talks the United Nations has never again made such a sustained attempt to reach a settlement of the Kashmir problem as it had made during the previous six years, has resigned itself to the need for a direct agreement between the parties, and has concentrated on the more limited but useful task of keeping the peace. From 1953 to 1956 the dispute did not appear on the Security Council's agenda, though the work of its observers and its Representative continued.

UN military observers first went to Kashmir early in 1949, but it was not until July of the same year, when a truce was agreed upon, that the UN Military Observer Group in India and Pakistan (UNMOGIP) went fully into action. By the terms of the agreement between India and Pakistan it was provided that UNCIP 'will station Observers where it deems necessary',[52] and henceforth observers were stationed each side of the cease-fire line, where they have been ever since. The number of UNMOGIP observers has usually been between thirty and fifty, though it rose to over ninety during the hostilities in 1965. According to the Secretary-General they serve along a cease-fire line nearly 500 miles long

> about half of which is in high mountains and very difficult of access UNMOGIP exercises the quite limited function of observing and reporting, investigating complaints from either party of violations of the cease-fire line and the cease-fire and submitting the resultant findings . . . to each party and to the Secretary-General, and keeping the Secretary-General informed in general on the way in which the cease-fire agreement is being kept . . . the operation has no authority, or function entitling it to enforce or prevent anything or to try to ensure that the cease-fire is respected.[53]

Nevertheless over a period of twenty-three years UNMOGIP has performed a steady and useful function, which has received little publicity and recognition, largely because it has become a matter of successful routine. By its very presence it has helped to keep a difficult situation from deteriorating and to prevent the recurrence of hostilities.

During the last three months of 1963 a series of complaints relating to Kashmir were made to the Security Council by India and Pakistan. These culminated in a request from Pakistan on 16 January 1964 for an early meeting of the Security Council to consider the grave situation that had arisen owing to the 'unlawful steps' being taken by India to destroy the special status of Kashmir. As a result the Council considered the question at fifteen meetings between 3 February and 18 May. During these meetings Pakistan complained of the lack of progress in the solution of the Kashmir question and of Indian attempts to integrate Kashmir into the Indian Union. India maintained that the whole of Kashmir had become an integral part of India and that under no

[52] See Higgins, *United Nations Peacekeeping*, vol. II, 336.
[53] *Report of Secretary-General on Situation in Kashmir*, quoted in *ibid.*, p. 246.

circumstances could India agree to the holding of a plebiscite. The reactions of Council members differed, and at the last meeting the President confessed that he had been unable to work out any agreed conclusions. Some believed that the Secretary-General might give useful assistance in facilitating the resumption of negotiations, while others felt that the intervention of any outside elements might complicate negotiations between the parties.

These attitudes were the background to the events that followed in 1965. India had become more inflexible after consolidating her hold on the greater part of Kashmir; Pakistan had now little hope of arriving at a settlement either through direct negotiation or UN mediation; and members of the Security Council were becoming increasingly doubtful about the Council's ability to contribute effectively to the solution of the problem.

The bad relations between India and Pakistan were exacerbated during the early part of 1965 by a dispute involving hostilities over the Rann of Kutch, a small frontier territory of little real value or importance, and the matter was the subject of a series of written complaints to the Council. Following a British offer of mediation the two governments agreed on a cease-fire at the end of June and agreed also either to settle the border-line themselves or to refer the matter to an impartial tribunal.[54]

More serious was an excessive number of incidents along the cease-fire line in Kashmir. On 3 September the Secretary-General submitted a report to the Security Council, which was based on information he had received from UNMOGIP. In it he stated that the cease-fire agreement of July 1949 had collapsed, that from the beginning of the year until mid-June 2,231 complaints had been made to UNMOGIP, and that the investigations of the Observers had confirmed 377 violations of the line, 218 of which had been committed by Pakistan and 159 by India. He mentioned as specially serious an incursion by an Indian battalion into Pakistan during May and a series of violations beginning early in August, which had usually taken the form of armed men, generally not in uniform, crossing the line from Pakistan for the purpose of armed action on the Indian side.

The Council met to consider the report on 4 September and dealt with the Kashmir question at twelve meetings between then and November. The situation that confronted it amounted to an undeclared war, which had started seriously in August and was to drag on for several

---

[54] The matter was finally settled by the award of a tribunal of three, with a Swedish chairman, in Feb. 1968.

months. The bitterness of the dispute was revealed by the sustained and increasing pressure which the Council had to exert in order to restore peace. At the first meeting the Council unanimously passed a resolution calling upon the two governments to cease fire immediately and to withdraw to their own sides of the cease-fire line. Two days later the Secretary-General reported that no official response to the resolution had been received and that reports from the Chief Observer indicated that the conflict was broadening and intensifying. The Council renewed its call to the two governments, requested the Secretary-General to exert every possible effort to give effect to the resolutions, and decided to keep the issue under urgent and continuous review. The Secretary-General spent the following week in India and Pakistan but on 16 September had to report that he had not yet succeeded in securing from the two sides an effective measure of compliance with the Council's resolution and suggested that the Council might *order* a cease-fire 'pursuant to Article 40 of the Charter'.[55] On 20 September, therefore, the Council passed a resolution which demanded that both governments should issue orders for a cease-fire, which was to take effect two days later, and requested the Secretary-General 'to provide the necessary assistance to ensure supervision of the cease-fire and the withdrawal of all armed personnel'. Both India and Pakistan responded to the demand for a cease-fire, and it went into effect on 22 September.

Further action by the Council was needed before hostilities finally came to an end, including *demands* that the parties honour their commitments to observe the cease-fire and that they formulate a plan for the withdrawal of all armed personnel.[56] But military action gradually decreased, and by the end of the year there was a general relaxation of tension along the front line. A remarkable feature of all the Council resolutions to bring about and enforce a cease-fire was that they were passed either unanimously or with only one or two abstentions. In fact, the Soviet Union and the United States were acting together as guardians of the peace.

Early in January 1966 the prime minister of India and the president of Pakistan met in Tashkent, at the invitation of the Soviet Union, with Kosygin as mediator. The meeting ended with the two statesmen declaring their firm resolve to restore normal and peaceful relations between their countries and reaffirming their obligation under the Charter not to have recourse to force but to settle their disputes through peaceful means. They further agreed that all armed personnel of the

[55] Article 40 does not contain the verb 'order'.
[56] These were included in Council resolutions of 27 Sept. and 5 Nov.

two countries should be withdrawn not later than 25 February 1966 to the positions they held prior to 5 August 1965.

The Secretary-General responded to the Council's request to him on 20 September 1965 'to ensure supervision of the cease-fire and the withdrawal' by increasing the size of UNMOGIP and by organizing a new group of observers, known as the UN India-Pakistan Observation Mission (UNIPOM), with a total strength of eighty to ninety. The reason for this was that UNMOGIP's duties were related to the 1949 truce agreement and its authority was limited to Kashmir, while hostilities in 1965 had taken place along the international frontier between India and Pakistan as well as across the Kashmir cease-fire line. An advantage of this apparently awkward arrangement was that, when the troop withdrawals were completed on 25 February 1966, UNIPOM could be dissolved. The work of the two bodies was, of course, coordinated.

The Kashmir question was extremely complex. As with other cases handled by the United Nations, the legal, the political, and the ethical approaches to the problem were likely to lead members to different conclusions. It is most improbable that members of the Security Council could have come to any agreement on applying Chapter VII of the Charter, and they never seriously thought of doing so, although the Council's three *demands* during the 1965 war can be considered as having been made in the spirit of Chapter VII. Moreover, after Pakistan's military aid agreement with the United States in 1954, the Soviet Union could have been counted on to veto any action under Chapter VII against India. On the other hand, Council recommendations under Chapter VI were not binding and could only be implemented through the cooperation and the agreement of the two sides. In the circumstances, the failure of the UN to solve the problem, though disappointing, was not surprising. It was a considerable achievement that the Council brought about two cease-fires during the wars of 1948 and 1965, thus limiting the most serious hostilities to which the dispute gave rise. In addition, UN observers have kept watch on the cease-fire line since the summer of 1949 with beneficial results, though the amount of violence they have prevented must remain a matter of speculation.

The Bangladesh War

Another cause for dispute between India and Pakistan came to a head in 1971. Relations between the peoples of West Pakistan and the Bengalis of East Pakistan had been strained since the creation of their country in 1947. They were further embittered in November 1970, when a disastrous cyclone did great damage in East Pakistan, and the people complained with good reason of the dilatory relief measures taken by the government, whose seat was in the West.

In December the first national elections took place in the twenty-three years of Pakistan's existence. They resulted in a clear majority being won by the party known as the Awami League, whose centre of power was East Pakistan and whose leader was Sheikh Mujibur Rahman. One of the main points in its programme was that there should be a federal government with far-reaching autonomy for East Pakistan and the federal government controlling only defence and foreign policy. The leader of the second largest party, Zulfikar Ali Bhutto, reacted by refusing to attend the meeting of the National Constitutuent Assembly, which had been arranged for early March. The President of Pakistan, General Yahya Kahn, therefore postponed the meeting. The Awami League replied first with a non-violent non-participation movement, then with violence, and finally by proclaiming East Pakistan the independent Republic of Bangladesh. Civil War followed. The President outlawed the League, arrested the Sheikh and accused him of treason, and banned political activity throughout Pakistan. The civil war was virtually over by the third week in April, but more than a quarter of a million refugees had already crossed the frontier into India.

It was the arrival of the refugees that first involved India directly, and the repressive regime that was established greatly increased their numbers. A governor and martial law administrator were appointed for the province. The Bengali language was suppressed for official purposes and Bengalis were replaced by West Pakistanis in responsible government positions. Early in August Sheikh Mujibur Rahman, who had been imprisoned in West Pakistan, was put on trial for treason before a military court *in camera*. The Pakistani army was ordered to crush the rebellion and save the unity of Pakistan, and several hundred thousand East Pakistanis are estimated to have lost their lives during the process. By mid-June the number of refugees in India was said to be 5.5 million, and by October 7 million, though some estimates were still higher. This imposed an immense strain on India's economy and administrative resources and greatly embittered relations between the two countries.

Military oppression in East Pakistan led to the organization of guerrilla freedom fighters, who received aid and support from India. There were numerous frontier incidents, and on 3 December India launched an all-out offensive on the Pakistani forces in East Pakistan. A few days later she recognized Bangladesh as an independent state, and on 16 December the Pakistani army surrendered.

The human elements in this tragic story; the desire of the Bengalis of East Pakistan to control their own affairs, the harsh measures taken to suppress their autonomy movement, and the sufferings of the victims and of the millions of refugees, drew the world's attention to the Indian subcontinent, and there was great disappointment that the United Nations failed to avert war. Had the relationship between India and Pakistan been friendly, it would have been a clear case for settlement within the framework of Chapter VI of the Charter, but the individual virtues of their two peoples were unfortunately not reflected in the attitudes of the governments. During the nine months from March to December 1971 either one or other of the two states did not want the problem referred to the Security Council on terms acceptable to the other, and each of them had the support of a super-power.

As the Secretary-General pointed out in July in a memorandum to the President of the Security Council, the problem involved a conflict between the two principles of the territorial integrity of states and of self-determination, both of which were recognized by the Charter.[57] Pakistan was prepared to accept reference to the Council on the purely international aspects of the problem but took its stand on Article 2 (7) in refusing to have its internal affairs discussed. India, on the other hand, insisted that the domestic aspect also should be considered, as it was the cause of the whole refugee problem. In a desperate internal situation the president of Pakistan was strengthened in his rigid attitude by the belief that he had the support of China and the United States, who, he hoped, would somehow come to his rescue. American policy was both unimaginative and ambiguous. As the United States government was preparing a *détente* with Communist China, it raised hopes in China's ally, Pakistan, but without deciding how they could be fulfilled. It announced an embargo on arms to Pakistan in March and then continued to send arms shipments to that country.[58] India, as it moved towards a solution by force, became increasingly opposed to Council action and was supported in its attitude by the Soviet Union, with whom it signed a twenty-year friendship treaty in August.

The attitude of the Council's two other permanent members, Britain

[57] S/10410 of 3 Dec. 1971, p. 3.
[58] See the article by Sydney H. Scharnberg, 'Pakistan dividend', *Foreign Affairs*, Oct. 1971.

and France, was more detached. They did not favour reference to the Council, partly because they saw no point in having a meeting at which nothing was likely to be achieved, and partly because they would be in a better position to play a conciliatory and constructive role later, if they refrained from taking sides. But this policy, though wise by national standards, was overcautious from an international point of view. A further clue to the Council's inaction is provided by the list of Council Presidents during the crucial months. The representatives of Burundi (May), Nationalist China (June), France (July), and Nicaragua (October) took no serious initiatives. Italy and Japan, who were in the Chair in August and September, were genuinely anxious to do something, but by this time the reasons against reference to the Council, which have been mentioned, were reinforced by a mood of inertia and resignation, and no member was prepared to request a meeting.

When war broke out on 3 December it was felt that the Security Council must take some action, and a meeting was held the following day at the request of nine members, including Britain and the United States though not the other permanent members. Fears that, in face of the existing diplomatic groupings, it could achieve little were unfortunately confirmed. Between 4 and 12 December three draft resolutions, calling for an immediate cease-fire and the withdrawal of forces to their own side of the frontier, were all vetoed by the Soviet Union in order to prevent interference with the Indian campaign. In each case Britain and France abstained. On 6 December the Council invoked the Uniting for Peace resolution and referred the question to the Assembly. So the UN's one achievement during the actual hostilities was an Assembly resolution of 7 December, also calling for an immediate cease-fire and withdrawal of forces, which was approved by a vote of 104 to 11, with 10 abstentions.

Even after Pakistan's capitulation on 16 December a considerable amount of discussion took place in the Council on several draft resolutions before one of them was approved on 21 December. It was couched in rather general terms, but the main provisions were a demand for the cessation of all hostilities, until all armed forces had withdrawn to their respective territories and to positions which fully respected the Kashmir cease-fire line of 1949, a call for international assistance in the relief of suffering, and authorization of the appointment by the Secretary-General, if necessary, of a special representative to lend his good offices for the solution of humanitarian problems.

The United Nations' record throughout the whole dispute was not only negative. On the humanitarian side, since April 1971 it had carried out a vast relief programme involving contributions and pledges of over a quarter of a billion dollars on behalf of the refugees in India and the population of East Pakistan. The Secretary-General, in his memorandum of July, drew the attention of the President of the Security Council to the Council's responsibility in the situation and on 20 October offered his good offices to the Prime Minister of India and the President of Pakistan. There is no doubt also that, in addition to the Council's resolution of 21 December, the three draft resolutions aiming at a cease-fire and the withdrawal of troops, in spite of being vetoed, contributed to a complete withdrawal of Indian troops from East Pakistan within three months of Pakistan's defeat. Had the UN not been acting as a channel for world opinion India might well have exploited her victory to improve her position in Kashmir.

On the other hand, if nine members of the Security Council decided *after* the outbreak of war that the Council must take some action, it seems unfortunate that they did not come to the same conclusion during the previous spring or summer. A meeting of the Council then could have resulted in a conference or some other form of high-level negotiations, however limited their chances of success. At least it might have forced the Soviet Union to declare its position; it might have led President Yahya Khan to modify his oppressive and provocative policy in East Pakistan; and it might have induced President Nixon to clarify his mind and his intentions.

Goa

On 8 December 1961 Portugal complained to the President of the Security Council about the build-up of Indian forces on the frontier of the small Portuguese territory of Goa, on the west coast of India. Ten days later it made a further complaint, this time about a full-scale Indian armed attack on Goa. The same day the Council decided to put the matter on its agenda in spite of Soviet opposition. But a draft resolution calling for an immediate cessation of hostilities and a peaceful solution, while receiving the seven affirmative votes necessary for adoption, was vetoed by the Soviet Union, three Afro-Asian members also voting against it. Goa was thus incorporated into the Indian Union by force of arms, in defiance of the UN charter.

In the Council discussion the Indian argument was expressed in emotional as well as rational terms, C. S. Jha, the Indian representative, saying the question was 'a matter of faith for us. Whatever anyone else may think, Charter or no Charter, Council or no Council.'[59] The essence of India's case was better put by the representative of Ceylon when he stated that Portugal's retention of Goa was 'in complete indifference to the historic facts which led to the emergence and growth of a free India'. The essential case against India's methods, on the other hand, was expressed by the United States representative, Adlai Stevenson, when he quoted Nehru as saying that 'no right end can be served by wrong means' and added that India's action was 'a blow to international institutions . . . which are available to assist in the adjustment of disputes'.

The main importance of the Goan episode was that it brought an end to hopes that the country of Gandhi and Nehru might give the world an example of peaceful and tolerant behaviour in international relations.[60] In the cases of Junagadh and Hyderabad, India has used force, also in defiance of the Charter, though in favour of solutions the two peoples approved. In Goa neither party was prepared to resort to a plebiscite, but the majority of the people no doubt favoured India too. Yet in Kashmir the Indian government had cynically disregarded the wishes of the Muslim majority. The representative of China well summed up Indian policy in Goa during the Council's debate on the question. The people of his country, he said, while not unsympathetic to Indian aspirations, deplored India's use of force. His delegation was shocked by what had happened, because they believed, first, that India was 'dedicated to the philosophy of non-violence preached so eloquently and passionately by the great man of India, Gandhi', and because in more recent years Indian leaders had spoken for peace and for upholding the ideals of the United Nations, and secondly, because the material interests involved in Goa did not appear to be of such magnitude as to tempt India to sacrifice its principles to attain them.

VIETNAM AND ITS NEIGHBOURS

The War in Vietnam

The Vietnam War has been one of the great international tragedies of the time, and it has, therefore, been a major disappointment that the

---

[59] Indian public opinion had been incensed by events in Angola earlier in the year, when riots had been fiercely suppressed by the Portuguese government.

[60] It is noteworthy that Arthur Lall, a former Indian Head of Mission at the UN has criticized his country's handling of the Goan problem: see his *Modern International Negotiations: principles and practice*, p. 124.

United Nations could neither prevent nor stop it. There were three main reasons for its inability to do so, or even attempt to do so. First, of the four principal parties involved in the conflict from the start, three were not members of the UN—at least until November 1971—North and South Vietnam and Communist China. So, if the whole problem had been seriously considered by the UN, the one party which was a member, and indeed a permanent member of the Council, the United States, would have had an unfair advantage. Secondly, the Vietnam War was a clear case of American–Communist confrontation, and, had the UN taken up the question, it would have been virtually paralysed by the veto, which could have been used either by the United States or the Soviet Union, another interested and increasingly involved party. Thirdly, the last occasion on which Vietnam had been considered on a broad international basis was at the Geneva Conference of 1954, which was called to discuss Korea and Indo-China and therefore met against a background of the East–West conflict. Four of its original participants, including the two protagonists in that conflict, were permanent members of the Security Council with the power of veto, and the other five, Communist China, the two Vietnams, Laos and Cambodia, were not at the time members of the UN. It was not altogether surprising, therefore, that the UN was not asked to take part in the settlement which was arranged. Nor was it surprising that some participants subsequently favoured a reconvening of the Geneva Conference rather than transferring the problem to the UN.

These three reasons have frequently been cited when international handling of the Vietnam question has been suggested. In particular, the Communist powers have never forgotten that the United States and South Vietnam refused to adhere to the declarations providing for Vietnamese elections, which concluded the Geneva Conference, and were mainly responsible for the elections not taking place.[61]

The two occasions when Vietnam reached the Security Council's agenda confirmed the futility of referring to the United Nations matters connected with a basically ideological conflict, in which the two super-powers were either militarily or diplomatically fully involved.

Early in 1964 the United States requested an urgent meeting of the Council to consider the serious situation that had arisen, as a result of North Vietnamese attacks on United States naval vessels in international waters in the Gulf of Tonkin. The Council met twice to consider the matter. The American representative stated that two United

---

[61] The United States, of course, maintained that under the existing conditions free and fair elections could not be held.

States vessels had on two separate occasions been subject to torpedo and machine-gun attacks by North Vietnamese torpedo boats and that his government had subsequently taken limited action in the form of aerial strikes in self-defence. At the suggestion of the Soviet representative the President arranged to invite the North Vietnamese government to give information relating to the complaint either in the Council or in some other form. In fact, the Council did not discuss the matter again but received written statements both from North and South Vietnam. The North Vietnamese foreign ministry maintained that the American accusation was based on a myth and was a pretext for extending the war. Furthermore, the Security Council had no right to examine the problem: only the chairman and participants in the 1954 Geneva Conference had full competence in the matter.

Towards the end of 1965 the United States suspended the bombing of North Vietnam for five weeks in an effort to facilitate negotiations. In this connection, on 31 January 1966, the American representative, Arthur Goldberg, requested an urgent meeting of the Security Council to consider the Vietnam question, in order to bring the matter to the world's attention and get things moving again. On the same day he submitted a draft resolution whereby the Council would call for immediate discussions among the interested governments to arrange a conference looking towards the application of the Geneva Agreements of 1954 and the establishment of a durable peace in South-East Asia. On 1 and 2 February the Council held two meetings to discuss the United States' request. During the discussion the Soviet representative both opposed the inclusion of the question in the agenda and mentioned a statement by the Vietcong[62] to the effect that the Security Council had no right to take any decisions on questions involving South Vietnam and that it would regard as null and void all Council resolutions on the subject. In the end the Council voted to include the question by a bare majority of nine but then decided at the President's suggestion that informal and private consultations would be held to decide on the most effective and appropriate ways of continuing the debate. The matter was, in fact, not discussed further, the President informing members by letter towards the end of February that unsolved differences among representatives were so serious that a further debate at the time would be inopportune. He attempted to summarize the common feeling of many members on the question, but his conclusions were challenged by several states.

In spite of the virtual impotence of the Security Council in face of

[62] The National Liberation Front of South Vietnam.

ideological conflict, super-power rivalry, and the other special difficulties of the situation in Vietnam, the Secretary-General made repeated efforts by public statements and still more by quiet diplomacy to get the parties involved to stop fighting and start discussions. In so doing he helped to keep the question before the conscience of mankind. A sad comparison may be made between the Vietnam War and the Korean War, another largely ideological struggle, which was, however, fought within a UN context and was brought to a comparatively early end. The UN had favoured the Geneva discussions on Vietnam in 1954, and the possibility of a UN conciliation and observer mission had been raised during the Conference.[63] Had the UN been allotted a positive role in Vietnam at that early stage,[64] the developments that followed might have been very different, and the United States might have been saved from its involvement in a war of which so many of its people disapproved.

Vietnam's neighbours

A series of cases involving the Security Council, which were related to Vietnam's neighbours, were of no major importance, but they are of interest because they illustrate the part played by the ideological conflict in events throughout the area, and in one case owing to the procedural implications.

In May 1954 Thailand complained to the Security Council about a threat to its security owing to the activity of Viet Minh forces near its borders. The Council considered the question at three meetings. Thailand submitted a draft resolution requesting the Peace Observation Commission (see p. 291) to appoint a subcommission to look into the matter, and the draft received nine votes in its favour but was vetoed by the Soviet Union.

In September 1959 the foreign minister of Laos in a cablegram to the Secretary-General requested the dispatch of an emergency force to halt aggression along his country's north-eastern frontier, which he attributed to 'elements' from North Vietnam. The Secretary-General asked for an urgent meeting of the Security Council, and, when the

---

[63] See Lincoln P. Bloomfield, 'The United States, the Soviet Union, and the prospects for peacekeeping', *International Organization*, Summer, 1970.

[64] This could only have been done if the United States itself had played a more positive part in the general negotiations and if Communist China had already been a member of the UN and prepared, therefore, to accept a UN role: the reasons why the UN did not in fact take part in the settlement have been given on p. 184.

Council met, the question was included in the agenda against the isolated opposition of the Soviet Union. The Council then proceeded to appoint a four-man subcommittee to look into the Laotian complaint, this being the occasion when the Soviet Union's attempt to use the double veto was thwarted by the President (see pp. 86–87). After visiting Laos the subcommittee reported that there had been military action against Laos of a guerrilla character but with evidence of centralized coordination from North Vietnam. Any Council action arising out of this report would clearly have been vetoed by the Soviet Union. So Hammarskjöld, in spite of a Soviet protest, accepted an invitation to visit Laos himself and later appointed a senior UN official as Special Consultant to the Secretary-General in that country, diplomatically emphasizing the economic aspect of his task. Hammarskjöld's aim appears to have been, in a difficult cold war situation, to keep Laos on the path of neutrality: neither to allow the Veit Minh's actions to pass unnoticed nor to encourage the right-wing elements in the country which were favoured by the United States. He defended what amounted to the establishment of a small UN presence in Laos in face of Soviet criticism, by describing it as a form of modest but useful UN assistance which avoided 'the stormy weather of a major international political debate'.

In May and June of 1964 the Security Council considered at eight meetings a complaint from the neutralist government of Cambodia that armed forces of the United States and South Vietnam had committed repeated acts of aggression against its territory. The two accused parties denied most of the charges, accepted responsibility for two or three, and called attention to the absence of well-marked frontiers between Cambodia and South Vietnam. The Cambodian government suggested that the Geneva Conference be reconvened and that the small International Control Commission set up by the Conference should be used to supervise the frontier. However, the Council decided to send three of its members to the places where the most recent incidents had occurred, in order to consider measures to prevent any recurrence. In its report the three-man mission recommended, amongst other things, sending a group of UN observers to Cambodia, entrusting the Secretary-General with the implementation of this decision in consultation with Council members, and the appointment by the Council of a person of high international standing, approved by both parties, to arrange for the resumption of talks on the dispute. The recommendations were not carried out. The Cambodian government, considering the report unfavourable, requested that its complaint to the

Council 'should simply be placed on file'. It nevertheless continued to send complaints about frontier incidents to the Council.

The Federation of Malaysia, consisting of the Federation of Malaya, North Borneo, Sarawak, and Singapore, was proclaimed on 16 September 1963, after a UN Malaysian Mission had satisfied itself that a majority of the peoples of North Borneo and Sarawak wished to join the Federation. The following day Indonesia took exception to the representative of the new Federation occupying Malaya's seat in the UN General Assembly. Both Indonesia and the Philippines also expressed reservations about the findings of the UN Malaysian Mission and refused recognition to the new state. There followed a period of confrontation during which Indonesia instituted an economic blockade against Malaysia and guerrilla raids took place across the frontiers of North Borneo and Sarawak, resulting in British, Australian, and New Zealand forces coming to the aid of Malaysia.

In September 1964 the Security Council met to consider a specific Malaysian complaint about an Indonesian paratroop attack on South Malaya. The Council discussed the matter at five meetings, in the course of which Norway submitted a conciliatory draft resolution, which regretted the incidents that had occurred, called upon the parties to refrain from all threat or use of force and to respect the territorial integrity and political independence of each other, and recommended the governments concerned to resume their talks. Nine votes were cast in favour of the draft, but it was vetoed by the Soviet Union, which thus emphasized once again the strength of the ideological element at the time in the international relations of South-East Asia. The confrontation ended, when General Suharto succeeded Sukarno as effective ruler of Indonesia in the summer of 1966,

AFRICA

Africa has, in several respects, an unusual relationship to the United Nations: as regards the nature of the UN's African membership, the way African members have organized themselves within the world body, and the character of the African problems with which the Security Council has been called upon to deal.

When the UN was founded in 1945 nearly the whole of Africa was in colonial status, and, apart from the Union of South Africa, there were only three African states among the original members. At the beginning of 1972, African membership in the UN was forty-two. This meant that during the UN's early years most African members had had little experience of participation in a world organization or even of the responsibilities of statehood. Most European and Latin American states, on the other hand, had been members of the League of Nations. Asia was in some respects similar to Africa, but in others quite different. A sizeable number of Asian states, mostly small states, won their independence and became UN members after the second World War, yet much the greater part of Asia, in terms of area and population, was made up of former members of the League; China, Japan, India,[65] and the Soviet Union. The inexperience of African members has been considered in the last chapter: that aspect of the Security Council's record, which is indicated in the subtitle of this book, has a special, though by no means exclusive relevance to them.

Among the continental groups within the United Nations the African members have the tightest and most demanding group organization. The Organization of African Unity was set up at a conference of African states at Addis Ababa in 1963. It was created partly as a result of events in the Congo during the previous three years, when a coordinated approach to the Congo problem was desirable, but when in fact various different viewpoints had emerged. A more fundamental reason was the sense of common purpose of former colonial peoples, who wished to establish their security and their identity in a great international organization of which they had high hopes.

One of the OAU's main functions is the coordination, and sometimes the initiation of the African group's policies and activities at the UN. As regards the choice of African representatives on the Security Council, the group nominates candidates in the first instance, taking care to pick those who can be relied upon to be good Africans. Their choice is then referred to the OAU's Council of Ministers, which so far has always confirmed it. But the last word rests with them, subject, of course, to the final approval of the General Assembly. The OAU has a representative of ambassadorial rank in New York, who acts as a liaison officer between the group and Addis Ababa. The African group works together as a team on all specifically African issues, with the OAU acting as a harmonizing influence in the background and occasionally putting forward suggestions of its own.

Such a system has one serious disadvantage, in that the Security Council was intended to act, in matters relating to peace and security,

[65] After the first World War India, which then comprised the present India, Pakistan, and Bangladesh, was on the way to self-government, under the Constitution of 1919, and was given separate membership of the League.

not as a kind of federation of geographical areas but for the United Nations as a whole with a broad international loyalty. But it has compensating advantages. The weaknesses, as well as the achievements, of the United Nations during the first twenty-seven years of its existence must be attributed primarily to the two super-powers, who have been the main influences on its development. But the forty-one African members, with their quite different traditions and their different concepts of international politics, have undoubtedly a contribution to make, and they can only make it if they act together in a common spirit and from time to time speak with one voice, so that their more powerful fellow members in the UN, including even the super-powers, cannot ignore what they have to say. As the international loyalties of all UN members develop and the specifically African problems are solved, it may be hoped that bloc solidarity will give way progressively to a broader approach to international institutions.

The OAU has also had another role. It has provided a rival, though more limited international authority to which the parties to a dispute, or African states as a group, can refer a problem, when they wish to avoid recourse to the United Nations. For example, the Algeria–Morocco border dispute in 1963 and the Nigeria–Biafra problem in 1967 were both referred to the OAU, while the Organization persuaded the Somali government to withdraw an appeal to the Security Council relating to its border dispute with Ethiopia and also helped to bring about President Kaunda's mediation in 1967, in the case of Somalia's dispute with Kenya. In this aspect of its activities the OAU may be compared to the Organization of American States (OAS), which the United States and most Latin American states have preferred to the UN as a mediatory authority.

The questions which the African members repeatedly referred to the Security Council all related to the legacy of colonialism: the situation in the Portuguese African colonies, racial discrimination in the Republic of South Africa and Southern Rhodesia, and the status of South-West Africa. For the handling of these questions they are well organized with a special committee to deal with each, and with a standing committee which concerns itself solely with colonial and racial problems pertaining to Africa, consisting of the chairmen of the special committees, the African representatives on the Security Council, and the current chairman of the African group.

The African case on these questions is often put forward in the name of human rights, but mainly as an effective means of appealing to the Western members concerned, rather than from any deep interest in the broad problem of human rights.[66] as revealed in the Universal Declaration, which is a document largely European, or at least Western in origin. African members have not referred to the United Nations the cases of tribal and racial intolerance between 1960 and 1972, when tens of thousands lost their lives in the Congo and Burundi and hundreds of thousands in the Sudan and Nigeria. Nor have they shown readiness to jeopardize existing frontiers in Africa through any great sensitivity to the principle of national self-determination. This group subjectivity has damaged their effectiveness in championing the great cause of non-discrimination in southern Africa.

France and North Africa

The cases under this heading, which were considered by the Security Council or referred to it, were all within the context of decolonization, and the issue in every instance was France's claim that under Article 2 (7) of the Charter the Council had no competence in the matter. On those occasions, when the countries concerned were Morocco and Algeria, the discussion was, in fact, confined to this issue, though it was sometimes also argued that there was no threat to international peace and security. In the case of Tunisia, other points of some significance were also involved.

In 1956 France recognized Morocco as an independent state after exercising a protectorate over it for forty-four years. During the last five years of its dependent status the question of French activities in Morocco was raised in the General Assembly, and in August 1953 a group of Asian and African states requested an urgent meeting of the Security Council to investigate the danger to international peace and security arising out of France's deposition of the Sultan. Following discussions at several meetings, the Council decided not to include the item in its agenda. The record was similar in the case of Algeria. The situation in that country was discussed in the General Assembly every year from 1955 to 1961, before Algeria became independent in 1962, but on the three occasions when it was brought to the Council's attention, in 1955, 1956, and 1959, it was not included on the agenda. A complaint by France, regarding Egyptian military assistance to the

[66] This conclusion is based on a statement made by Africans, at a conference in Africa, to a highly respected Scandanavian expert on the United Nations to the effect that the African peoples, on the whole, do not know the meaning of the term, 'human rights'. The statement obviously does not apply to an educated and expanding elite.

Algerian rebels, was included at a meeting on 29 October 1956, but it was overtaken by the Suez crisis and was never actually considered.

The record in the case of Tunisia during the years preceding its independence was similar. The situation in Tunisia was discussed several times in the General Assembly but failed to be adopted as an item on the Security Council's agenda. After the country became independent in 1956, however, the position was complicated by the fact that Algerian rebels were using bases on Tunisian territory from which to operate in Algeria. This led early in February 1958 to Tunisian complaints to the Security Council that French armed forces had violated Tunisian territory and to French countercharges that the rebels were using bases in Tunisia and the Tunisians were giving them aid. At a meeting in February the Security Council considered the complaints but decided to adjourn when the representatives of the United Kingdon and the United States informed the Council that their governments had made an offer of good offices to France and Tunisia, which had been accepted. At the end of May further complaints were made by each side, which were considered by the Council early in June. But on the 18th of that month the representatives of France and Tunisia informed the Council that they had reached an agreement by which all French troops were to be evacuated from Tunisia within four months, except for those stationed at Bizerta.[67] The case was a good example of the Council, while not solving a problem directly, acting as a channel for mediatory offers, which led to a satisfactory result.

The final episode occurred in July 1961, when the Security Council's action was less effective. Tunisia complained to the Council of aggressive acts by French naval and air forces against Bizerta. The French action had been due to a sudden demand from the Tunisian President that France should begin to withdraw from the base immediately, at a time when France's relations with Algeria precluded any sign of weakness. France therefore made a counter-complaint; the Council met and passed an interim resolution calling for an immediate cease-fire; but it failed to agree on further action. Hammarskjöld himself then attempted mediation by visiting Tunisia at President Bourguiba's invitation, but the French refused to receive him either in Africa or Paris. In the end the matter was referred to a special session of the General Assembly, which passed a resolution reaffirming the Council's interim resolution and calling upon the parties to enter into immediate

[67] At the time of Tunisian independence negotiations for a new defence treaty had broken down, but the Tunisians were soon pressing for the withdrawal of French troops from all Tunisian territory apart from the base at Bizerta.

negotiations to devise measures 'for the withdrawal of all French armed forces from Tunisian territory'. After two years of negotiations, during which Algeria became independent, France and Tunisia reached an agreement, and French troops were withdrawn. The UN's role was, in fact, limited to giving the dispute a full airing, both in the Council and the Assembly, and making it difficult for France to delay withdrawal for too long.

The Congo

The United Nations' involvement in the Congo in the summer of 1960 resulted in the most formidable and complicated operation which the organization has ever undertaken. Without the ability, courage, patience, and resourcefulness of Dag Hammarskjöld, who was Secretary-General at the time, it is unlikely that it would have been undertaken on an appropriate scale or carried through with the considerable measure of success that it actually achieved.[68]

Until a few years before the Belgian Congo became independent in June 1960, the Belgian government thought in terms of the colony's slow paternally controlled evolution towards maturity and did little to prepare the Congolese, either through education or practical experience, for running their own affairs. But Belgium could not insulate the Congo indefinitely from the outside world, and in particular from the example of British and French decolonization. In 1958 de Gaulle's offer of autonomy to the neighbouring French Congo and a Pan-African Conference in Accra between them acted as an irresistible stimulus and, after riots in the capital, Leopoldville, in 1959, the Belgium government agreed in January 1960 to give the country independence within six months. This inconsistency of intention had disastrous results. The Congo was the second largest country in Africa, its peoples were very diverse, their natural leaders were ill-prepared for the task which faced them and quite inadequately educated for it. In 1960 only about two dozen Congolese had received higher education, most of them having recently graduated from two local and quite new universities.

The Congo became independent on 30 June 1960 and within a week the army mutinied against its Belgian officers. This action was followed by other outbreaks of violence, a breakdown of essential services, and

---

[68] The criticisms and strain to which Hammarskjöld was subjected during the Congo crisis are made vividly clear in B. Urquhart's *Hammarskjöld*; but see reference to this book in the preface.

G

the interruption of major economic activities in different parts of the country. Without the Congolese government's permission Belgium proceeded to land paratroops to protect its nationals, and shortly afterwards the independence of the wealthy province of Katanga was proclaimed by its President, Moïse Tshombe. Three leading Congolese ministers then appealed to the United States for aid. Eisenhower wisely referred them to the United Nations, and President Kasavubu and the prime minister, Lumumba, thereupon cabled to the Secretary-General requesting the urgent despatch by the UN of military assistance to protect their country against Belgian aggression.

On 13 July Hammarskjöld requested an urgent meeting of the Security Council. The same day he explained at a meeting of the Council that he was bringing the Congo situation to its attention under Article 99 of the Charter[69] and strongly recommended that it should authorize him to take the necessary steps, in consultation with the Government of the Congo, to provide the government with the military assistance for which it had asked. On 14 July, the Council adopted a resolution without opposition, calling upon Belgium to withdraw its troops from the Congo and authorizing the Secretary-General to take the steps he had suggested. This resolution was supplemented by another on 22 July, adding little to the first, but inviting the UN specialized agencies to give the Secretary-General such assistance as he might require, and a third on 9 August, which was more significant though not entirely clear. It called upon the Belgian government to withdraw its troops from Katanga immediately and then continued with two further clauses, declaring the entry of the UN Force into Katanga to be necessary, and yet reaffirming that the UN Force in the Congo will 'not be a party to or in any way intervene in or be used to influence the outcome of any internal conflict, constitutional or otherwise'.

The emergency Hammarskjöld now faced was the kind of situation with which he was supremely qualified to deal: he enjoyed vigorous action in a crisis, whatever demands it made upon him. He saw at once the importance of what was at stake and the need for immediate action. His first task had been to pilot the resolution through the Security Council on 13 and 14 July. This he had done with the help of the able Mongi Slim of Tunisia, the only African member of the Council, in face of the danger of a French veto and Soviet hesitation, which had only been overcome by strong African pressure. The resolution had authorized him to take 'the neccesary steps', and he had explained in his first statement to the Council that, if it adopted his proposal, he would be guided by his experience in the Middle East and base his actions on the principles set out in his detailed report on UNEF.[70] He added that the personnel of the UN Force should be 'such as to avoid complications'; and that it should not exclude African units, though it should exclude the use of troops from any permanent members of the Council.

The Council meeting ended at about 3·30 a.m. on 14 July. Hammarskjöld returned to his office and made telephone calls to different parts of the world, arranging for troops to be made available, aircraft to transport them, and the use of the necessary airports. The first troops reache d the Congo the next day. Within four days a UN Force of 3,500 had arrived, made up of contingents from Ghana, Ethiopia, Morocco, and Tunisia. By the end of the month it numbered about 11,000, drawn from seven different states.

The first positive result of the Council resolution and the arrival of the UN Force in the Congo was the withdrawal of the Belgian troops. Ralph Bunche, who was appointed the Secretary-General's first special representative in the Congo, at once started negotiations with the Belgian representatives in Leopoldville, and it was agreed that the Belgian troops should withdraw from the positions they occupied as soon as these had been taken over by the UN Force. By the end of July a substantial proportion of them had already left, and by the beginning of September there were no Belgian troops remaining in the Congo, although two to three hundred Belgians were employed by the government of Katanga in the police and gendarmerie. Secondly, the UN Force made a useful contribution to restoring law and order. The very presence of international troops induced confidence, and they could have achieved still more had they been allowed to proceed with their original policy of disarming the mutinous Congolese army. Unfortunately Lumumba insisted that this process should stop, and the Congolese forces, commanded by promoted NCOs and warrant officers, added to the country's difficulties during the next few years. Matters were made worse by dissension among the political leaders. On 5 September President Kasavubu dismissed Lumumba from the post of prime minister, and the latter replied by declaring Kasavubu no longer chief of state. After eight days of confusion power was seized by Colonel Joseph Mobutu, the Army's chief-of-staff, who introduced a new constitution of his own devising and, in association with Kasavubu,

[70] A/3943 of 9 Oct. 1958.

remained in control of the government until the following February. But his authority was disputed in parts of the country, and political instability made the UN's task still more difficult.

The most intractable problem it faced was the secession of Katanga. At the time of the mutiny and his declaration of Katangan independence Tshombe had asked for Belgian help, and the response which followed made possible the *de facto* existence of Katanga as a separate state for two and a half years. While not recognizing Katanga's secession, the Belgian government sent to Elizabethville, the provincial capital, senior advisers on political, economic, military, and security problems, and in July 1960 set up a Belgian Technical Mission. It committed itself therefore, in fact if not in theory, to an independent Katanga. Most important of all, the great mining and commercial enterprises, with their headquarters in Brussels, led by the Union Minière du Haut-Katanga, recognized that Katanga, since its proclamation of independence, had become 'the collector of taxes and mining royalties and of all obligations due to the State'.[71] So the sums in question were all paid over to the Katanga government, the revenues from the Union Minière alone amounting to about £14 million a year.

Lumumba, as prime minister, demanded that UN forces should be used to 'subdue the rebel government of Katanga', and, when Hammarskjöld refused to allow them to be so used, declared that the Secretary-General had lost the confidence of the Congolese government. Ralph Bunche visited Katanga during the first week in August and reported that even the arrival of UN forces in the province might result in serious incidents with which they could not cope within the framework of their first Security Council mandate. So Hammarskjöld, in order to comply with the Council's new resolution of 9 August, and after negotiations with Katanga through the Belgian authorities, took the difficult and courageous step of personally leading the first UN contingent into Katanga by air on 12 August, with the result that the withdrawal of Belgian troops began the following day.

Hammarskjöld also requested a meeting of the Council in order to obtain a clarification of his mandate on the point at issue between himself and Lumumba. During the meetings which followed nine members of the Council supported the Secretary-General in his contention that, once the Belgian troops had withdrawn from Katanga, the conflict was an internal matter between the central government and the province, and that the UN had no right to intervene. The Soviet Union and Poland, on the other hand, supported Lumumba's criticisms. In the

[71] See Jules Gérard-Libois, *Katanga Secession*, pp. 102–6 and 115.

circumstances, therefore, no formal decision of the Council was possible. But the President concluded the meeting by stating his conviction that the Secretary-General would have found in the debate the clarification which he desired, and that it would assist him in the pursuit of his mission.

During the four years of its intervention in the Congo the UN performed two quite distinct roles, one military and one administrative and technical. The first appeal of the Leopoldville government to the UN in July 1960 had been for technical assistance "in the field of security administration". Belgium, when it decided to grant the Congo independence unexpectedly soon, had left behind at the Republic's disposal all the Belgian magistrates, teachers, and officials who were in the colony's service. At the time of the mutiny many of these people left the country hurriedly, thus precipating a crisis in the civil administration and welfare services comparable in severity to the crisis in order and security. A good number of them soon returned, and the Belgian population of Leopoldville rose from 4,800 in July 1960 to 6,000 in October. But the unsettled conditions and the resulting administrative and economic dislocation made necessary an extensive international technical assistance and relief programme, which soon became the largest which the UN and its specialized agencies were providing anywhere in the world. It constituted the civil operations side of the UN Operation in the Congo (ONUC[72]).

ONUC was set up as a result of the Security Council resolution of 14 July 1960, and the main directives governing its activities came from subsequent Council resolutions. However, differences of opinion among the permanent members reduced the Council to inaction or ineffectiveness over long periods. From September 1960 to February 1961 it was virtually deadlocked. After the Soviet Union had vetoed a draft resolution reaffirming the three Council resolutions on the Congo of July and August and the mandate of the UN Force, the Council on 17 September, invoking the Uniting for Peace resolution, referred the question to the General Assembly. Three days later the Assembly adopted, by seventy votes to nil, with eleven abstentions, a resolution sponsored by seventeen Afro-Asian states, which fully supported the three Council resolutions, requested the Secretary-General to continue to take vigorous action in accordance with the resolutions, thus virtually giving him a vote of confidence, and calling on all states to refrain from providing military assistance in the Congo, except at the Secretary-General's

---

[72] Derived for convenience from the French title, Organisation des Nations Unis au Congo: "Organisation" was later changed to "Opération".

request. During 1962 the Security Council did not meet once to discuss the Congo, and during 1963 it merely received two reports on the subject from the Secretary-General. The master-mind of the whole Congo operation was Dag Hammarskjöld,[73] and after his death in September 1961 U Thant followed his strong lead.

Like the Dutch in the case of Indonesia, the Belgians were emotionally involved in the Congo problem, and their rational appraisal of the trends and ideas of the time was offset by sentiment, pride in past achievements, and over-sensitivity about their own considerable mistakes and the sometimes ill-informed criticisms of others. They were impatient, when they were invited to do useful and essential jobs by the central government and were then condemned as interlopers by newcomers, who knew much less about local conditions than they did, but they sometimes failed to realize the great damage done to their cause by the self-seeking mercenaries and ultras who were backing Tshombe in Katanga. In the circumstances rivalry between the UN and Belgians in the Congo was inevitable. As regards the government in Brussels, so long as the Liberal-Social Christian administration of Eyskens and Wigny was in power, it played a double game, backing Tshombe without formally recognizing his secession and at the same time supporting the moderates in Leopoldville. When it was succeeded in April 1961 by the more left-wing Lefèvre–Spaak coalition, formed from the Social Christian and Socialist parties, the Belgian government set out to improve relations with the UN in the Congo, favoured increasingly the central government in its conflict with Katanga, and believed that the future of the Congo depended on the return of Katanga to the Republic.

The differences among the Council's permanent members were based on ideology, past experience, and present interests. Britain and France, as colonial powers, sympathized with Belgium in its dilemma, and they wanted to prevent Africa from becoming involved in super-power rivalry. But there the similarity of viewpoints ended. France, as has been seen, had been arraigned repeatedly before the Security Council in connection with its North African dependencies. Under de Gaulle's leadership she was hostile to the UN and opposed to its intervention in the Congo. She therefore abstained on all the Security Council's resolutions except that of 22 July 1960, which Belgium asked her to support, and after February 1961, following the Soviet Union, refused to pay her financial assessment for the Congo operation. Britain, on the other hand, although abstaining on the Council's first resolution, voted for three of its four subsequent resolutions and abstained on the other, and,

[73] His judgment was not faultless but, in the very difficult circumstances, nearly so.

while critical of some UN actions, on the whole supported its Congo operation, with increasing confidence in Hammarskjöld's leadership. She had, like Belgium, to contend with a small minority of ultras with commercial interests in Katanga. But the main lines of her policy were determined by much broader considerations; for example, her relations with African national leaders in her colonies or former colonies and her experiment in federation between Nyasaland and the Rhodesias, which would not have been helped by the success of Katangan secession. She paid her assessment, waived the cost of the air transport she had provided for UN forces, and made a voluntary contribution towards the cost of the civilian operation.

The United States was aware of the great dangers inherent in the Congo situation. Eisenhower was anxious to prevent the ideological conflict from spreading to Africa, and he was vulnerable to the Congolese threats to appeal to the Soviet Union or the Bandung powers, if the UN did not come to the rescue. He sympathized with the views of his NATO allies but appreciated also the standpoint of the newly independent African states. The United States bore the main burden of transporting troops and supplies to the Congo; it defrayed 41·5 per cent of the total cost of the operation, which amounted to about $400 million; and it was much the largest purchaser of the UN bonds issued to meet the organization's peace-keeping debts, which were largely incurred in the Congo.

The Soviet Union's original aim in the Congo was to appear as the champion of African nationalism by supporting the UN action against Belgium, and it voted in favour of the Security Council's first three Congo resolutions. Then, finding itself rather surprisingly in association with the United States, Britain, and the UN Command in the Congo, it gave its separate support to Lumumba at the time when he broke with Hammarskjöld over Katanga, and his government was provided with 100 Soviet military trucks and some transport planes. This move was followed by the fall of Lumumba, the closing of the Soviet Embassy in Leopoldville by Colonel Mobutu, and the removal of the transport planes. When Khrushchev joined Lumumba's followers in violent attacks on the Secretary-General, he alienated moderate African opinion, outside as well as inside the Congo, and the General Assembly's overwhelming vote in September in favour of continuing the UN operation was a measure of Soviet isolation. While Khrushchev gained some favour with African extremists by his championship of Lumumba, he realized that the Soviet Union's attitude must be modified, because the last thing it wanted was to alienate the new African states. It therefore abstained on or supported the two important Security Council resolutions in 1961. In this change it was influenced by its dispute with Communist China, which had just come to a head, China having recently shown a growing interest in Africa.

The attitude of the UN membership, on the whole, towards the Congo operation was revealed by the vote in the General Assembly. The Latin American members and the great majority of the non-aligned states from Asia and Africa supported it. But amongst the Africans there were differences in attitude, which caused difficulties for the Secretary-General. On the one hand, there was the Casablanca group, consisting of Morocco, the UAR, Ghana, Guinea, Mali, and originally Libya, with whom were associated the Algerian revolutionaries and Ceylon. They supported Lumumba, and during the winter of 1960–61, as a protest against the UN attitude towards Katanga, three of them, Morocco, the UAR and Guinea, together with Yugoslavia and Indonesia, withdrew their contingents from ONUC. On the other hand there was the more moderate Brazzaville group, made up of all the former French colonies except Guinea, which developed during the summer of 1961, through the addition of Libya and most of the former British territories, into the Monrovia group twenty states strong.[74] They supported the UN's mediatory role in the Congo, as well as a looser conception of Pan-Africanism than the Casablanca group. These developments provided the background to the formation of the OAU in 1963.

The United Nations Force in the Congo was much the largest of the UN's peace-keeping forces: at its maximum it numbered about 20,000, thirty states altogether contributing to it, although not all of them at the same time.[75] It was also naturally the most costly and involved the UN in the main financial problem in its history, when France and the Soviet Union refused to pay their assessed shares of the expense. The Congo force differed from UNEF in that the latter had been set up by the General Assembly and its Commander had been appointed by the Assembly, whereas ONUC was established by the Secretary-General under the Security Council's authority and was a subsidiary organ of the Council within the terms of Article 29 of the Charter. As agent of the Council the Secretary-General was really commander-in-chief of the force and was in control of the whole operation in both its military and civilian aspects. He was also responsible to the General Assembly

[74] The three group names were taken from the cities where they conferred in 1960 and 1961.
[75] See Bowett, *United Nations Forces*, p. 206.

under the terms of its resolution of September 1960. Opinions differ as to the precise constitutional basis of ONUC. But the judicious conclusion of D. W. Bowett may be accepted that the Security Council set the Organization up within the terms of Articles 39 and 40 of the Charter, to achieve the general purpose of the UN as set out in Article 1 (1), and in so doing acted in accordance with Article 24, making use also of the Secretary-General's services under Article 98.[76]

In view of the differences among the Council's permanent members and the consequent incompleteness and obscurity of the Council's directives, the Congo operation could hardly have been attempted without the Secretary-General's leadership and the experience, efficiency, and loyal cooperation of certain key members of the Secretariat. Hammarskjöld wisely strengthened his position soon after the breach with Lumumba, by setting up a Congo Advisory Committee in August 1960, consisting of representatives of the states contributing to the UN Force. But in another respect he was less wise. He selected within the Secretariat a small group of close advisers for the Congo operation, nicknamed the Congo Club, which included three high-ranking Americans, Ralph Bunche, Andrew Cordier, and Heinz Wieschhoff, and no representative of a Communist country. All three were very able and loyal, but, however difficult it might have been to work with an international team on such an exacting task, it was an error of judgment not to make the attempt. The choice of a onesided group in the long term injured the UN by aggravating Soviet suspicion of the Secretariat, and increased ideological tension over the Congo, which it was one of Hammarskjöld's main aims to lessen. The position improved under U Thant, who asked the advice of Soviet members of the Secretariat on some matters and kept them better informed.

Hammarskjöld complained on several occasions that he had not received clear directives from the responsible UN organs, and on 26 September 1960 he stated before the General Assembly that, if they were not forthcoming, he would have no choice but to follow his own conviction. At a meeting of the Security Council in August the President, as has been seen (p. 196), expressed the conviction, although the Council had reached no formal decision, that the Secretary-General would have found the clarification he desired in the debate. No doubt encouraged by this suggestion, Hammarskjöld in December and again in February 1961, said he felt entitled to be guided by the moral validity of operative paragraphs in vetoed draft resolutions of the Council, when there had been no difference of opinion about them. On 21 February

[76] *Ibid.*, pp. 177–80.

G*

1961, however, the Council, influenced by the murder of Lumumba in Katanga a few days before, authorized an important extension of ONUC's powers. Hammarskjöld had, from the beginning, always maintained that UN troops could use force 'only in self-defence'. Now the Council urged that the UN 'take immediately all appropriate measures to prevent the occurrence of civil war in the Congo, including . . . the use of force, if necessary, in the last resort'.

The two tasks still facing ONUC after the withdrawal of Belgium troops in 1960, and alongside its aid and relief programme, were the problems of law and order, and the secession of Katanga. It is not normally the United Nations' duty to ensure the internal security of a state. But the situation in the Congo was exceptional. The UN had been called upon in an emergency to help an inexperienced government, and one of the results of the emergency and of the UN's own action was to weaken the government by the withdrawal of many experienced administrators. In order to carry out its main duties of preserving the Congo's territorial integrity and political independence, therefore, it was necessary for ONUC to prevent the country sliding into anarchy. But the Secretary-General was convinced also that the principle of non-intervention in its internal affairs must also be respected, in accordance with the Security Council's resolution of 9 August 1960. To combine respect for this principle with helping to restore law and order would be difficult, but the attempt had to be made. If the UN were forced out of the Congo, Hammarskjöld believed, the result would be civil war and disintegration, and the world would again be confronted with 'a confused Spanish War situation'.[77]

ONUC's task in relation to law and order was made more complicated by the lack of a legally constituted government in the Congo for eleven months from September 1960 to August 1961. Such a situation encouraged disorder and defiance of Leopoldville's authority, and, in addition to a number of tribal outbreaks in different parts of the country, Antoine Gizenga, the left-wing follower of Lumumba, set up a secessionist regime in Stanleyville, capital of the northern province of Orientale. This for a time received Soviet support, until the Russians discovered that when they intervened in Congolese politics they were no more popular than the Belgians, and those of them who had gone to Stanleyville withdrew.

ONUC's efforts were aimed at preventing foreign intervention, whether government-sponsored or mercenary; discouraging civil strife; and establishing a legally constituted and acceptable central govern-

[77] See Joseph P. Lash, *Dag Hammarskjöld*, pp. 250–1.

ment. Its hands were, of course, strengthened in February 1961 by the authority it received from the Council to use force in the last resort in its endeavours to prevent civil war. During that month also the Mobutu government gave way to one headed by Joseph Ileo, who, however, was soon discredited by drawing too close to Tshombe. But the Council resolution, which extended ONUC's powers, also expressed concern at the serious conditions in the Congo, and urged the convening of parliament and the disciplined reorganization of the Congolese army. In May President Kasavubu announced his intention of reconvening parliament. ONUC played a major role in making the necessary arrangements and persuading the main political groups to come to an understanding. As a result, at the beginning of August, with the unanimous approval of parliament, a government of national unity was formed by the honest and conciliatory Cyrille Adoula, who remained prime minister until 1964.

The UN's attitude to Katanga changed as Tshombe showed no readiness to compromise, the Security Council's directives became stronger, and it became progressively clear that the secession of that key province was the main obstacle to the settlement of the Congo problem. Katanga's *de facto* independence was dependent on Belgian support, and Hammarskjöld's original aim was to induce the Brussels government to withdraw all military and civil support which it had placed at the disposal of the authorities in the Congo, except that furnished through the UN to the central government. In this he failed. But during the six months from mid-February to mid-August 1961 ONUC's position was greatly strengthened by three developments. The Council resolution of 21 February, in addition to the other provisions already mentioned, urged that 'measures be taken for the immediate withdrawal . . . from the Congo of all Belgian and other foreign military and paramilitary personnel and political advisers not under the UN Command and mercenaries'; in April the new Belgian government came into power with its different Congo policy; and in August Adoula's national unity government was formed in Leopoldville.

Tshombe's financial and military position was strong, and his confidence was buttressed by royal favour in Brussels,[78] by support from the Union of South Africa and the Central African Federation, and by some moral backing from Britain, France, and various groups in the United States. It consequently took another eighteen months for the Katanga problem to be settled. But the UN troops in Elisabethville, the Katangan capital, used force three times during 1961. On the first two occasions in

[78] He was received by the King in December 1960 and given a decoration.

August and September they had officially the limited objective of rounding up mercenaries for deportation,[79] and during the second Hammarskjöld was killed in an air crash on the way to confer with Tshombe in Northern Rhodesia. The third, in December, was a more serious confrontation and resulted in Tshombe's agreeing on certain conditions to bring an end to secession. It had been preceded by the Security Council's most forceful directive to ONUC, when a resolution was passed on 24 November, strongly deprecating secessionist activities and authorizing the Secretary-General to take vigorous action, including the use of force, for the immediate apprehension, detention or deportation of all foreign mercenaries and other hostile elements including military and civil advisers.

Further negotiations followed, which were accompanied by a good deal of prevarication by Tshombe. But in August 1962 detailed proposals were drawn up for the reintegration of Katanga, known as the Thant Plan for National Reconciliation, which were reinforced by separate arrangements for an economic boycott, if Katanga failed to accept it. After further use of force in December by the UN troops in Katanga, which was provoked by Tshombe's gendarmerie, secession really ended the following month, and Ileo arrived in Elisabethville as Minister Resident of the central government to supervise reintegration. The UN force, which had been reduced to under 6,000 by December 1963, was withdrawn completely before the end of June 1964.

The Congo operation was the most complex the UN has undertaken. The instrument it used was one of the most miscellaneous forces that has been assembled in modern times. Some of the best-qualified armies were excluded from it, while its nine largest contributors were, with one exception, developing countries in Africa and Asia.[80] It had to carry out its task in a country more than a quarter the size of the United States, with poor communications and little or no effective administration. The troops served under trying and frustrating conditions, always liable to be attacked, but not allowed for the most part to use their weapons except in self-defence.

ONUC leadership was not faultless, but it was imaginative, courageous, and devoted, and it has considerable achievements to its credit. It brought an end to foreign intervention in the Congo, prevented the country from becoming a cold war area, preserved its unity, and helped

[79] Conor Cruise O'Brien, the UN representative in Katanga, interpreted his instructions differently and probably with some justification, though the subject is highly controversial.

[80] The states which contributed contingents over 1,000 strong were: Ethiopia, Guinea, India, Indonesia, Malaya, Morocco, Nigeria, Sweden, and Tunisia.

the Congolese people to develop a greater consciousness of their national identity, in addition to its remarkable though less advertised record in public administration, technical assistance, health services, and education. U Thant and Ralph Bunche both considered the UN's Congo operation to be one of its most successful accomplishments.

A short but highly controversial aftermath of the Congo operation occurred, which deserves mention, because it was considered at no less than seventeen meetings of the Security Council during December 1964. After the withdrawal of the UN Force, the situation in the Congo quickly deteriorated, and in July 1964 Tshombe succeeded Adoula as prime minister. A rebellion followed with its centre in Stanleyville, and Tshombe recruited mercenaries, mostly Belgian and South African, to help put it down. In November about 1,000 foreigners were held as hostages in Stanleyville, made up of nineteen different nationalities but mostly Belgian and American. On the 21st of that month Belgium and the United States drew the Council's attention to the danger threatening them and later informed it that a rescue operation had been carried out by Belgian paratroops, transported by American aircraft, who had withdrawn by the 29th. The Congo government informed the Council that it had authorized the operation.

On 1 December twenty-one African and Asian states plus Yugoslavia requested a meeting of the Security Council to consider the situation created by this operation, which they looked upon as an intervention in African affairs and a threat to the peace and security of the continent. A few days later Tshombe also asked for a meeting of the Council to consider the flagrant intervention in Congolese domestic affairs by several states who were assisting the rebel government. The subsequent lengthy debates reached so low a level through racial emotion and lack of restraint that Adlai Stevenson remarked that never before in his seven years' service in the United Nations had he heard 'such irrational, irresponsible, insulting and repugnant language'.[81]

Fortunately several more moderate African states, led by Nigeria, defended the Congolese government's right to ask for outside help in such a case, and appealed both to African states and to the major powers to stop interfering in the Congo. The meetings ended with the unanimous approval, apart from France's abstention, of a draft resolution, sponsored by the Ivory Coast and Morocco, which called for an end to foreign intervention in the Congo, appealed for a cease-fire, and

[81] He pointed out that the United States had been accused, among other things of 'massive cannibalism'.

considered that the mercenaries should be withdrawn as a matter of urgency. It also encouraged the OAU to help the Congo government to achieve national conciliation and asked all states to assist the Organization in the attainment of this objective.

The Portuguese colonies

The retention by Portugal of its colonial territories, the bulk of which are in Africa, raises the whole question of the ethics of colonialism in the twentieth century. After the first World War the League Covenant's concern for the territorial integrity of its member states and for the inviolable character of matters within their domestic jurisdiction provided a most convenient international system for those countries which were already endowed with lands and colonial possessions. What you had you were allowed to keep. In the case of colonies and territories taken over by the victors from their defeated enemies, the wellbeing and development of their peoples were to 'form a sacred trust of civilization' under the Mandate system. But nothing was said about the wellbeing of the colonial subjects of the victors.

In its treatment of the colonial problem the UN Charter was an advance on the Covenant. It replaced the mandates by a system of trusteeship, which was a more carefully worked out arrangement, and in addition included a Declaration Regarding Non-Self-Governing Territories, which extended the 'sacred trust' principle to territories held by UN members, whose peoples have not attained a full measure of self-government. It required members to accept the obligation to promote to the utmost the wellbeing of the inhabitants of these territories, and to that end 'to develop self-government, to take due account of the political aspirations of the peoples, and to assist them in the progressive development of their free political institutions'. This trusteeship principle was both realized in, and then reinforced by the decision of Britain to leave India in 1947 and by the subsequent emergence as free states of the great majority of British, Dutch, and French colonies.

By 1970 Portugal was the main colonial power left in the world. Of the 28 million people still living in dependent status about a half were in the three Portuguese territories on the African mainland, Angola, Mozambique, and Portuguese Guinea. The Portuguese had started their colonizing ventures 500 years before, and, as Peter Calvocoressi has put it, their record in Africa and Asia is 'first in, last out: the first colonizers and the last imperialists'.[82] In contrast to Britain, France, and the Netherlands, Portugal is governed by a dictatorship, and its government has steadily maintained that it has no responsibilities under Chapter XI of the Charter on Non-Self-Governing Territories, and that historically Portugal is a unitary state, in which constitutionally the overseas provinces together with the European territory form a single nation. Its aim, according to the government, is to build a multi-racial society: there is no racial discrimination in its overseas provinces, and the Portuguese electoral law is exactly the same for all citizens. In Inis Claude's words, 'even Portugal is driven to *deny* rather than to *defend* its colonialism'.[83]

This legalistic attitude, of course, bears no relation to the prevailing political and humanitarian standards regarding colonies, and takes quite inadequate account of the broad principles laid down in the Charter on the subject of human rights, fundamental freedoms, and the political aspirations of peoples. The Portuguese colonies have been the subject of constant UN attention, both in the General Assembly and in the Security Council, for two reasons. In the first place, former colonial peoples in Latin America, Asia, and above all Africa feel very strongly about this surviving colonial anachronism, and the African states have taken advantage, though not always wisely, of every opportunity the UN offered to put Portugal in the dock. Secondly, anticolonialism is an area in which nearly all UN members have, to a large extent, been in agreement. The former colonies have been most ardent; the Western democracies have not been far behind, though among them former colonial powers are in a special category; and the super-powers, whether from motives of conviction or expediency, have not hesitated to proclaim themselves strong opponents of colonialism, though their practices have not fully conformed with their protests.

Condemnation of Portugal's colonial policy was not primarily a problem affecting peace and security, and the main indictment of the Portuguese system came from the General Assembly. Two actions taken by the Assembly formed the basis of the subsequent repeated protests made through the UN about Portuguese colonialism. The first was the Declaration on the Granting of Independence to Colonial Countries and Peoples, which was adopted on 14 December 1960, with no dissenting vote and only nine abstentions. It proclaimed 'the necessity of bringing to a speedy and unconditional end colonialism in all its forms and manifestations', declared that 'all peoples have the right to

---

[82] *International Politics Since 1945*, p. 415.
[83] *The Changing United Nations*, p. 59.

self-determination', and declared also that immediate steps should be taken in non-self-governing territories 'to transfer all powers to the peoples of those territories, without any conditions or reservations'. The next day, in response to Portugal's assertion that she did not administer any territories covered by Chapter XI of the Charter, the Assembly declared that Portuguese overseas territories were non-self-governing within the meaning of Chapter XI and that Portugal was under an obligation to transmit the information about them called for under Article 73 (e).

Henceforth the main issues before the Assembly were Portugal's response to the principles embodied in the Declaration and the question of her compliance or non-compliance with her obligations under Article 73. In dealing with these issues the Assembly has made use of three subsidiary organs. In April 1961, after the situation in Angola had been considered both by it and by the Security Council, it set up a Sub-Committee on Angola. During the same year a seven-member Special Committee on the Territories under Portuguese Administration was also established with the main task of collecting information on the territories to enable the Assembly to consider how far Portugal was complying with its obligations under Chapter XI. In 1961 also a more general body was created to accelerate the process of decolonization, the Special Committee on the Situation with regard to the Implementation of the Declaration on the Granting of Independence to Colonial Countries and Peoples. It began work in 1962 and came to be known as the Special Committee of Twenty-Four. Since then the General Assembly has kept the question of the Portuguese colonies under continuous review.

Consideration of the question by the Security Council on numerous occasions contributed to keeping up the pressure on the Portuguese government, inducing it to undertake some measures of reform within the African territories, and encouraging movements aimed at their liberation. But up to the spring of 1972 little tangible progress had been made towards solving the basic problem. Much more might have been achieved had the different elements in the Council agreed on a firm line of action which nevertheless took some account of Portuguese suscepti-bilities, though such agreement was perhaps too much to expect. As it was, the African and Asian states made repeated, strong, and sometimes exaggerated protests against Portuguese colonialism; the former colonial powers tolerated in their NATO ally a less enlightened policy than they had adopted themselves; the United States modified its anti-colonialism in return for defence facilities in the Azores; and the Soviet

Union supported and incited the African states. Nevertheless, in spite of the different attitudes of its members, the Council has in a number of cases taken specific and sometimes effective measures against Portuguese actions and policy.

In February 1961 riots took place in Luanda, the Angolan capital. They were suppressed, and Portugal subsequently imposed a censorship on outgoing messages and a ban on the entry of foreign journalists. The matter came before the Council, the main arguments put forward against Council action being first that it would contravene Article 2 (7) of the Charter concerning matters within the domestic jurisdiction of states, and secondly that no threat to international peace and security was involved. A draft resolution calling on Portugal to introduce reforms in Angola was rejected by five votes in favour and six abstentions. Much more serious disturbances soon followed, which, together with Portuguese repressive measures, involved many thousands of casualties and wholesale emigration from Angola to the Congo. When the Council considered the question again in May, at the request of forty-three mostly Asian and African states, the changed attitude of members was reflected in the approval of a stronger resolution in the same sense by nine votes in favour with two abstentions.

The Council took a still firmer line when it considered the general situation in the territories under Portuguese administration in 1963 and 1965. On each occasion it met at the request of thirty-two African states, and in 1963 also after the Committee of Twenty-Four had drawn its attention to the situation 'with a view to its taking appropriate measures, including sanctions', to secure Portuguese compliance with UN resolutions. In 1963 the Council passed a resolution in which it determined that the situation in the territories was seriously disturbing peace and security in Africa; called upon Portugal urgently to recognize the right of the peoples of the territories to self-determination and independence and to grant immediately thereafter independence to all the territories; and requested that all states should refrain from offering Portugal any assistance which would enable it to continue its repression in the territories, and take all measures to prevent the sale and supply of arms and equipment for this purpose to the Portuguese government. Another resolution in 1965 reaffirmed these clauses in stronger terms, and in addition called upon all states to take the necessary measures either separately or collectively to boycott all Portuguese imports and exports. Both resolutions were passed with no dissenting votes. Britain, France, and the United States abstained on each occasion, the Netherlands joining them in 1965.

The Security Council also dealt with many complaints about alleged frontier incidents, some of them of a trivial nature. In April 1961 Senegal asked for a meeting of the Council to consider 'repeated violations of Senegalese air space and territory' and complained that four Portuguese aircraft had dropped four grenades on a Senegalese village. Four years later Senegal complained of sixteen further violations. Portugal replied by suggesting the setting up of a three-man team of investigation, two members of which should be appointed by the parties and the third by the Secretary-General or President of the Security Council, but Senegal did not agree to the suggestion. Further complaints were made by Senegal in 1969 and 1971, after the second of which a mission was appointed by the Secretary-General and the President of the Security Council to carry out an investigation. In 1966 and 1967 the Congo complained that Portugal was allowing Angola to be used as a base for mercenaries plotting to overthrow the Congolese government. In 1969 there were complaints and counter-complaints by Zambia and Portugal about numerous violations of the frontiers between Zambia, on the one hand, and Angola and Mozambique on the other.

One of the most important cases that came before the Council related to a complaint made by the Republic of Guinea in November 1970. It was important because the episode giving rise to it was on a larger scale than the frontier incidents just mentioned, because it illustrated the intense emotionalism of African states in dealing with Portuguese colonialism, and because it revealed the limits of the Council's effectiveness in the face of diverse attitudes amongst its membership.

Guinea reported that its territory had been the object of an armed attack by Portuguese forces, requested a meeting of the Security Council as a matter of extreme urgency, and asked for immediate intervention by UN airborne troops to assist the Guinean army. Portugal denied the accusation and stated that it was 'not involved in the internal affairs of Guinea'. The Council passed a resolution demanding the immediate cessation of the armed attack against Guinea and the withdrawal of all external armed forces, and appointing a special mission to be formed after consultation between the President of the Council and the Secretary-General. The mission, which consisted of five members of the Council, was the first to be appointed in this way. It proceeded at once to Guinea.

By the time it arrived, the invaders had already withdrawn. The President of Guinea, Sékou Touré, expressed disappointment that the

Council had sent a mission of inquiry rather than the military assistance for which he had asked. The Guinean minister of finance later made a statement to the effect that the mission's judgment of the situation had very little importance for Guinea or for Africa and that he expected it to finish its work by noon the next day.[84] The mission then carried out a programme largely arranged by the Guinean government and heard many witnesses most of whom had been chosen by the authorities, including seven prisoners from the invading forces, who were interviewed in the presence of Guinean officials. The fact that the Chairman of the mission did not protest against these statements and this treatment reflected the mood of the mission and of the majority of UN members in relation to the colonial question, any victim of Portugal being the object of tolerant sympathy. But it did little for the prestige either of the Security Council or of the United Nations.

In its report to the Council the mission concluded that in its best judgment the invading force was assembled in Portuguese Guinea and that the invasion of the Republic of Guinea was carried out by naval and military units of the Portuguese armed forces, acting in conjunction with dissident Guinean elements from outside the Republic. The Council subsequently passed a resolution by eleven votes to nil, with four abstentions, endorsing the conclusions of the report; strongly condemning the Government of Portugal for the invasion; demanding that full compensation be paid by Portugal to Guinea for the damage to life and property caused by the invasion; reiterating its former exhortations, declarations, and requests regarding Portuguese colonialism, military aid to Portugal, and the rights of the peoples in Portuguese administered territories; and warning Portugal that in the event of any repetition of armed attacks against African states the Council would immediately consider appropriate effective measures in accordance with the provisions of the UN Charter. The diverse attitudes within the Council membership were revealed by the fact that Britain, France, Spain, and the United States abstained on the resolution, and by the more moderate element in the mission insisting that, as the evidence it had heard had been largely circumstantial, its conclusions should only take the form of an 'opinion' and a 'judgment'.

Sékou Touré weakened his own case against the Portuguese government by afterwards trying a large number of Guinean nationals for their part in the attack, ninety-one of whom were condemned to death,

[84] Report of the Security Council Special Mission to the Republic of Guinea Established under Resolution 289 (1970), Addendum, S/10009/Add. 1, 3 Dec. 1970, pp. 20 and 30.

though the number actually executed is doubtful. The most plausible explanation of what happened would appear to be that, while Portuguese involvement of some kind is certain, the invasion was not planned by the Portuguese government but was the result of the collaboration of Guinean opponents of Sékou Touré, from inside and outside of Guinea, with Portuguese colonists and former officers mostly coming from Portuguese Guinea.[85]

The problem of the Portuguese colonies has not been solved, because the opponents of colonialism in the UN, while in a large majority, have lacked either the strength or the will to take effective action, although by 1972 a substantial part of Portuguese Guinea was controlled by the liberation movement. Unless joint action is taken on the lines suggested (see p. 208), there seems no alternative to a solution by force with the liberation movements obtaining outside help. This being the case, the problem does constitute a 'dispute, the continuance of which is likely to endanger the maintenance of international peace and security', within the terms of Article 33.

The African and Asian states have turned to the Security Council as a body with the power in theory of enforcing its decisions, though only within the framework of Chapter VII, and the Council has added the weight of its authority to that of the Assembly in condemning Portuguese colonialism. But, in so doing, it has also diminished that authority, because the passing of repeated resolutions, which are not implemented, can only result in loss of prestige. Pre-conditions of the problem's solution are a stronger line towards Portugal on the part of the Western democracies and a spirit of greater realism on the part of the African and Asian states and of Portugal herself, to whom in the long run the use of force will do more serious damage than yielding to accepted international principles.

Racial discrimination in South Africa

In many ways the problems of racial discrimination in South Africa and Rhodesia are similar to the problem of Portuguese colonialism. In

[85] See *African Contemporary Record, 1970–71*, pp. 97 and 369–71. While the UN mission found that the invasion seemed 'to have been well planned and carried out with professional skill and precision', one of its chief witnesses, General Lansana Diané of the Guinean army, gave evidence that the invading troops who captured him were not only drinking whisky, until they shouted for joy, but also poured it on one another's heads, and washed with it—most unlikely behaviour in the case of members of the Portuguese regular army specially picked for a difficult operation (Report of the Special Mission, S/10009, 3 Dec. 1970, p. 13, and Addendum thereto, p. 44).

every case the emotions of the African peoples are deeply involved; in every case the attitudes of the Western democracies are ambivalent; and in every case the Security Council, when called upon to deal with the question, is faced with an intractable dilemma. Racial discrimination, however, is likely to prove a more stubborn problem than Portuguese colonialism, because the white minorities in South Africa and Rhodesia have a strong sense of national identity and independence, having been virtually self-governing for fifty or sixty years, because they have adequate and efficient armed forces at their disposal, and because their positions are strengthened by close economic or traditional ties with Britain, other European countries, and the United States.

The Union of South Africa

The racial policies of the South African government were repeatedly on the agenda of the General Assembly from 1946 onwards, when India complained that South Africa had passed legislation discriminating against South Africans of Indian origin. In 1952 the question of *apartheid* was also placed on the Assembly's agenda. In each case the South African government steadily maintained that the matter was essentially within its domestic jurisdiction and that, by the terms of Article 2 (7), the UN was not authorized to consider it. When the Assembly in 1952 set up a three-man commission to study the racial situation in South Africa, the South African government refused to recognize it or allow it to visit South Africa.

The question first came before the Security Council at the request of twenty-nine African and Asian states in March 1960 after the Sharpeville massacre, when eighty-three Africans were killed by the police and several hundred wounded during a peaceful demonstration against racial discrimination and segregation. The Council passed a resolution calling upon South Africa to abandon its policies of *apartheid* and racial discrimination and recognizing that the situation in the Union of South Africa, if continued, might endanger international peace and security.[86]

In 1962 the General Assembly, incensed by South Africa's disregard of previous UN action, passed a resolution requesting member states to break off diplomatic relations with South Africa; close all ports to vessels flying the South African flag and prohibit ships of each state from entering South African ports; boycott all South African goods and

[86] As a result of this resolution Hammarskjöld paid a brief visit to South Africa and had consultations with the Union government; see p. 219.

refrain from exporting goods, including arms and ammunition, to South Africa; and refuse landing and passage facilities to South African aircraft. It also requested the Security Council to take appropriate measures, including economic sanctions, to secure South Africa's compliance with the resolutions of the Assembly and the Council.

When the Council met the following August, it repeated some of its previous exhortations and in addition called upon all states to boycott all South African goods and to cease forthwith the sale and shipment of arms, ammunition, and military vehicles to South Africa. At another meeting in December it extended the arms embargo to include the sale and shipment of equipment and materials for the manufacture and maintenance of arms and ammunition in South Africa, and asked the Secretary-General to establish a small expert group to examine methods of resolving the situation in South Africa 'through full, peaceful and orderly application of human rights and fundamental freedoms' to all its inhabitants.

In its report of April 1964 the group recommended the establishment of a national convention fully representative of all the people of South Africa to decide the future of the country. The South African government, it said, should be invited to take part in discussions on the formation of the convention, and, if it refused to do so, the Security Council would be left with no effective peaceful means of helping to resolve the situation, except to apply economic sanctions. The group also stated that, for the convention to succeed, it should be accompanied by an amnesty to all opponents of *apartheid*, whether on trial, in prison, or in exile.

The following June the Security Council endorsed the group's main conclusions; urged the South African government to renounce the execution of persons sentenced to death for opposition to *apartheid*; decided to establish an Expert Committee, composed of representatives of all members of the Council for the year 1964, to undertake a technical study and report to the Council as to the feasibility, effectiveness, and implications of measures which could be taken by the Council under the Charter; and established an educational and training programme for South Africans to study and be trained abroad. South Africa rejected the relevant resolution as illegal and an invitation to 'abdicate its sovereignty to the UN'.

The Council's responsibilities were now left for a time in the hands of this broadly representative Expert Committee, which submitted a significant but noncommittal report in February 1965. Of four sets of draft conclusions which it considered, one was withdrawn and two were defeated. The fourth, which formed the basis of the report, was approved only by a majority of six votes to four, the United States, Britain, Norway, China, and two Latin American states supporting it, with the Soviet Union, Czechoslovakia, and two African states in opposition.

The report pointed out that South Africa's economic strength was such that it would not be readily susceptible to economic sanctions. The effectiveness of economic measures would depend on the universality of their application and on the manner and duration of their enforcement. South Africa's economy would be susceptible to the effects of a total trade blockade and to an interdiction of communications, while an embargo on petroleum and a cessation of emigration into South Africa would be particularly effective. An embargo on arms and ammunition could also make an important contribution. The Committee was concerned with the problem of adequate international machinery to prevent evasion of sanctions and believed that much would depend on the collective desire of the states imposing them to make the system work, especially of those maintaining close economic relations with South Africa. It would also be necessary to mitigate the hardships caused by the measures taken to the economies of certain states.

Members of the Committee differed as to which of two courses was preferable; a total blockade with the great cost it would involve or a partial blockade on vulnerable sections of the economy, which would affect the economy as a whole, as well as having political and psychological repercussions on the white minority. It was agreed that in applying measures against South Africa it would be essential to set up a coordinating committee, which would also have the task of mitigating the major hardships for individual states. Finally, it was emphasized that it was for the Security Council to evaluate the applicability and effectiveness of the measures outlined in the political and psychological context.

The conflicting views of members of the Committee, the emphasis on the difficulties of applying economic sanctions effectively, and the final passing of responsibility to the Security Council encouraged the South African government in its independent course and its defiance of the United Nations. It believed it had little to fear from the attempts of the Assembly and the Council to implement their resolutions.

During the next five years the General Assembly continued and strengthened its campaign against *apartheid*. In addition to resolutions directed towards the South African government, it urged all states to terminate diplomatic and consular relations with South Africa, to bring to an end all military, economic, and technical cooperation with that country, and to suspend cultural, educational, sporting, and other exchanges with it. It also continued to draw the Security Council's attention to the South African situation and recommended it to consider effective measures against South Africa under specific sections of the Charter.

In July 1970 the Security Council, at the request of forty states, resumed consideration of the question of racial conflict in South Africa resulting from the policies of *apartheid*, with a view to examining, in particular, the situation arising from the violations of the arms embargo called for by Council resolutions in 1963 and 1964. By twelve votes to nil, with three abstentions, the Council passed a resolution condemning violations of the embargo and calling on states to strengthen the existing embargo by ways enumerated in a series of much more detailed and comprehensive provisions than had been included in the earlier resolutions.

The question of South-West Africa (Namibia), although linked to the problem of *apartheid*, involves also the complex legal issue of the transfer of territories held under League of Nations' mandate to the UN trusteeship system. South-West Africa was a mandated territory, and the Charter made provision for the transfer of such territories to the new system. South Africa alone of the mandatory powers refused to enter into a trusteeship agreement with respect to its territory. It proposed to incorporate South-West Africa into South Africa, and, when the General Assembly refused to accept this solution, stated that it would maintain the *status quo*.

The Assembly later asked the International Court of Justice for an advisory opinion, which was delivered in 1950. The opinion was that South-West Africa remained a mandate and that South Africa was not competent to modify that status without the UN's consent, South Africa was not legally obliged to place the territory under the trusteeship system, but it continued to have international obligations under the mandate, including the obligation to submit annual reports to the General Assembly as the inheritor of the League's supervisory functions. The South African government did not accept the advisory opinion: it was unwilling to accept any form of UN supervision over South-West Africa, it refused to submit annual reports, and it proceeded step by step to introduce the principle of *apartheid* into its administration of the territory.

On the UN side the problem has been handled mainly by the General Assembly and the International Court of Justice, and it was not referred to the Security Council until 1968. The Assembly was aided by a succession of *ad hoc* committees until the end of 1962, when their functions were taken over by the Special Committee of Twenty-Four (see p. 208). Its first aim was to reach an agreement with South Africa on the implementation of the Court's advisory opinion. When this failed it began examining conditions in the territory through its committees, which found that South-West Africa was being administered on the basis of *apartheid*, and that this was contrary to the mandate, the Charter, the Universal Declaration of Human Rights, the International Court's Advisory Opinion, and the resolutions of the Assembly. In 1961 the Assembly proclaimed the inalienable right of the people of South-West Africa to independence and national sovereignty, and called for the repeal of *apartheid* and preparations for general elections based on universal suffrage under UN supervision.

In November 1960 Ethiopia and Liberia, two former members of the League, instituted proceedings against South Africa before the International Court, charging that South Africa had violated its obligations under the mandate. Under Article 94 of the Charter the judgment in such a case could be enforced by the Security Council. Not until July 1966 did the Court deliver an evasive judgment in which it declined to adjudicate on the merits of the case. By the narrowest possible margin (eight votes to seven), with the President using his casting vote, the Court found that Ethiopia and Liberia had not established any 'legal right or interest appertaining to them in the subject matter of the claims' and on these purely technical grounds decided to reject them.

This unexpected decision led to a sharpening of the conflict. In 1966 the General Assembly voted by an overwhelming majority to terminate the mandate and place the territory under direct UN responsibility. The following year it set up an eleven-member UN Council for South-West Africa to administer the territory until it achieved independence. It was, in fact, passing strong resolutions which it had no power to implement. The South African government, encouraged by the Court's judgment, accelerated its *apartheid* programme for South-West Africa and refused to admit the new UN Council to the territory.

The Assembly had repeatedly drawn the Security Council's attention to the threat or potential threat to international peace and security in South-West Africa, and in January 1968 the Council finally considered the question. The previous year guerilla activity in the territory had led to the arrest of thirty-seven freedom-fighters, who were taken to Pretoria for trial. The Council now approved unanimously a resolution calling on the South African government to discontinue forthwith the illegal trial and to release and repatriate the South-West Africans concerned. Two months later, again unanimously, it censured South Africa for its defiance of the previous resolution, demanded the immediate release and repatriation of the South-West Africans, and decided that, in the event of South Africa's failure to comply with its requirements, it would meet immediately to determine upon effective measures in conformity with the Charter. The Council was now following the Assembly's unfortunate example of passing strong resolutions which it would be unable to implement. Britain, France, and the United States made clear repeatedly that they were not prepared to support sanctions against South Africa under Chapter VII of the Charter. In 1969 the same procedure of resolution, repetition, and threat was followed, this time with the main emphasis on South Africa's withdrawal from the territory, but on this occasion a precise deadline was given for the withdrawal. After South Africa had failed to comply with this requirement, the Council's main reaction at a meeting early in 1970, apart from further repetitions, was merely to set up another *ad hoc* subcommittee to study ways and means of implementing its resolutions on South-West Africa.

In July 1970, after considering this subcommittee's report, the Security Council passed two resolutions. The first asked all states to refrain from any relations with South Africa that would imply recognition of its authority over South-West Africa; to ensure that companies owned or controlled by them cease all commercial dealings in the territory; to discourage their nationals and companies from investing there; and to discourage tourism and emigration to the territory. The second asked the International Court to give an advisory opinion on the legal consequences for states of the continued presence of South Africa in Namibia. In June 1971 the Court gave its opinion, which was that the General Assembly had properly exercised its power to terminate South Africa's mandate and that in consequence the continued South African presence in the territory was illegal. The opinion was not accepted by some UN members, who maintained that neither the League of Nations nor the United Nations had the power to terminate a mandate unilaterally, and that the powers of the General Assembly are, with certain clearly defined exceptions, recommendatory only and not binding.

In January 1972 the Security Council decided to hold meetings in Addis Ababa beginning on 28 January and ending not later than 4 February, which should be devoted to the 'consideration of questions relating to Africa with which the Security Council is currently seized and the implementation of the Council's relevant resolutions'. The decision was the result of a request from the OAU the previous July for a Council meeting in Africa to discuss African problems and of a report from a Security Council Committee set up on 11 January 1972 on 'Council Meetings away from Headquarters'. In the appropriate setting of the Ethiopian capital, the Council passed resolutions relating to the Portuguese colonies, *apartheid*, Namibia, and Rhodesia. Their provisions, for the most part, were similar to the provisions of previous Council resolutions. But, of two resolutions dealing with Namibia, one broke new ground by inviting the Secretary-General to initiate contacts with all parties concerned with a view to solving the problem of Namibia, calling on the South African government to cooperate fully with him, and requesting him to report the result of his efforts to the Council not later than the end of July 1972. This resulted in an invitation to the Secretary-General from the South African prime minister and a visit by Kurt Waldheim to the Union of South Africa and to Namibia. The development recalled a visit by Dag Hammarskjöld to South Africa in 1961, to discuss the question of *apartheid*, which the South African government had found 'useful and constructive'. It was a move also in the direction of contact rather than confrontation, which several members of the Council had been advocating as the most promising approach.

Rhodesia

The racial discrimination issue in Rhodesia, though on a smaller scale than in the Union, has presented the UN with a less clearcut and a more complex problem, the case of Rhodesia having been a tragic miscarriage in the otherwise largely successful history of British decolonization.

The whole of Rhodesia was governed by the British South Africa Company under Royal Charter from 1889 to 1923, and the regime the Company established was based on white supremacy. In 1923 Southern Rhodesia was taken over by the British government but was at the same time given internal self-government, subject only to certain reservations relating mainly to African interests and constitutional amendment. The following year, Northern Rhodesia became a British protectorate, and in 1930 Britain declared that in its protectorates native interests were paramount. In 1953 after lengthy negotiations the two Rhodesias and the neighbouring Nyasaland, which was also a protectorate, joined to form the Central African Federation. This could have led eventually to the victory of the racial ideas of the white minority in Southern Rhodesia or to the recognition of the political rights of the African majorities in all three colonies. The consciousness of these alternative possibilities and the resultant suspicions were the main reasons for the failure of the experiment. The Federation came to an end in 1963, and the next year Northern Rhodesia and Nyasaland became the independent states of Zambia and Malawi. Southern Rhodesia, henceforth to be known as Rhodesia, became an increasingly difficult problem for Britain, Africa, and the UN.

In Britain's relations with Rhodesia at this time two conflicting principles were involved: the right of colonies to self-government and non-discrimination with regard to political rights. In 1923, when Southern Rhodesia was given self-government, the colonial system in Africa was part of the accepted international order and the great majority of the African peoples had neither the education nor the political awareness to exercise democratic political rights. Moreover, when their political awareness developed rapidly after the second World War, there was at first no reason to assume that white Rhodesians, with preponderantly British traditions, would not support the progressive granting of political rights to Africans in Rhodesia, especially when the racially liberal Garfield Todd was prime minister from 1953 to 1958. It was only when the Federation broke up that the conflict of principles became serious. Even then it was at first difficult to justify the withdrawal of self-government at any given time from a country which had exercised it for forty years, on the grounds that the government at that time was racially illiberal. Any former British colony would have strenuously resisted such an attempt to put the clock back, in its progress to independence, on the grounds of infringement of human rights in its legislation or social structure.

Two sinister developments had occurred in Southern Rhodesia before the Federation dissolved. In 1960 security laws were passed which set up tight controls over public meetings, provided for the banning of any organization which was likely to prejudice the security of the country, and authorized emergency measures which included provisions for summary arrest and detention without trial. Under these laws all the African nationalist organizations were to be banned, and, as a protest against their arbitrary and repressive character, the chief justice of the Federation resigned. Also in 1961 a new constitution was introduced and approved by the British government. It guaranteed a slightly larger minority representation in parliament to Africans but at the same time ensured that the whites should have a majority and effective political control for the indefinite future, while Britain gave up its reserve powers relating to African interests and constitutional amendment. The British government sincerely wanted to safeguard African rights to political advancement, but they were misled by a Declaration of Rights and a statement that 'no written law shall contain any discriminatory provision', which were included in the constitution but subject to considerable qualifications. As things turned out, Britain's faith in white Rhodesian intentions and acceptance of a constitution which involved surrender of its reserve powers was an error with most serious consequences for the future.

Having now won full control over their internal affairs, the white minority in Rhodesia aimed at their country becoming an independent dominion, while the black majority, which, after some hesitation, had opposed the new constitution, did not wish to sever the British connection without some previous guarantee that they would achieve full political rights. When Rhodesia began negotiations with Britain about independence in 1963, the British Conservative government laid down five pre-conditions, including an end to racial discrimination, unimpeded progress towards majority rule, and guarantees against regressive amendments of the 1961 constitution. It also laid down that a settlement must be acceptable to the people of Rhodesia as a whole.

Shortly before this the United Nations had begun to concern itself with the Rhodesian question. The great tragedy of the situation from then on was that Britain and its supporters in the UN, on the one hand, and the majority of UN members led by the African states, on the other, could not usually cooperate effectively, though the aim of both was to bring an end to racial discrimination. Both sides were to blame for the failure. The British were too sensitive about their legal rights, too ready to trust the intentions of the White Rhodesians, and too often inclined to put expediency and economic interests before making sustained efforts in support of a principle. The Africans were highly emotional in their approach, unduly suspicious of British motives, and at times even resentful when Britain did take the initiative in measures against Rhodesia (see p. 223, n. 87).

The General Assembly was the first UN body to consider the Rhodesian question. In 1962 it asked the Committee of Twenty-Four to consider whether Southern Rhodesia had attained a full measure of self-government, and later, on the Committee's recommendation, affirmed that it was a non-self-governing territory. It also requested the United Kingdom to suspend the 1961 Constitution; to convene a fully representative constitutional conference for the purpose of formulating a constitution, which would ensure the rights of the majority of the people; to repeal all discriminatory legislation; and to release immediately all political prisoners. Britain's response to all UN action in the matter was that Southern Rhodesia had been self-governing since 1923 and Britain itself could not intervene in its internal affairs. Intervention by the UN would also be beyond the organization's competence.

The Security Council first dealt with the question in 1963, when it invited Britain not to transfer armed forces and aircraft to Southern Rhodesia and not to transfer power to its colony until a fully representative government had been established. The draft was vetoed by Britain for the reasons mentioned.

Successive British governments tried to come to an understanding with Rhodesia without success, and the issue now became whether the Rhodesian government would resort to a unilateral declaration of independence (UDI) or not. The advent of a Labour government to power in Britain in October 1964 increased Rhodesia's desire for independence, while negotiations were intensified and became more acrimonious. Shortly after taking office the new British Prime Minister, Harold Wilson, warned Rhodesia that UDI would be 'an open act of defiance and rebellion'. A year later the Rhodesian Prime Minister, Ian Smith, and Wilson exchanged visits in London and Salisbury, and between the visits Wilson appealed to Smith by letter to pause before taking an irrevocable step, 'for the sake of your country, for the sake of Africa, and for the sake of future generations of all races'. A final suggestion from London that a royal commission should be appointed under the Rhodesian Chief Justice was rejected by Smith.

Meanwhile the United Nations continued to concern itself with Rhodesia. The Committee of Twenty-Four made repeated protests against the way things were developing and called the Security Council's attention to the question. In May 1965 the Council passed a resolution by seven votes to nil with four abstentions, asking all member states not to accept UDI, requesting Britain to take all necessary action to prevent it and not to transfer to Rhodesia, as at present governed, any of the powers or attributes of sovereignty, and repeating the General Assembly's request for the convening of a fully representative constitutional conference. However, in November the Smith government declared Rhodesia independent. It was formally dismissed by the Governor of Rhodesia but remained the effective government of the country.

During his negotiations Harold Wilson had made clear, as he informed Parliament, that Britain would not use military force to solve the problem. The British government therefore had two possible courses open to it: further negotiations or economic sanctions. It at first tried both, but, when negotiations failed, strong economic action was the only alternative to surrender and the betrayal of long and firmly held principles.

On the day Rhodesia declared its independence Britain announced its own extensive programme of economic and financial sanctions against it, the General Assembly condemned UDI at an emergency meeting by 107 votes to two with one abstention, and Britain and thirty-five African states requested an urgent meeting of the Security Council, which met the following day. As Rhodesia's action conflicted with the UN Charter, was opposed almost unanimously by UN members on political and ethical grounds, and could only be countered effectively by some form of enforcement action, it clearly concerned the Security Council, and the Rhodesian question was in fact henceforth handled mainly by the Council. The Council's first action was to condemn UDI and call on all states not to recognize the illegal minority regime in Rhodesia. Eight days later it passed another resolution calling upon states to desist from providing Rhodesia with arms, equipment, and military material, to break all economic relations with it, and to impose an embargo on oil and petroleum products.

The following April a British frigate intercepted a tanker on its way to the Mozambique port of Beira, one of the main sea outlets for Rhodesia, for which its oil cargo was intended. The captain was asked to alter his plans for unloading at Beira but refused to change course. Britain thereupon, on 7 April, requested an emergency meeting of the Council the same day in order to deal with the situation, though the President, who was the representative of Mali, did not call a meeting for two days, in spite of a strong protest from Lord Caradon on the 8th and the fact that a majority of members supported the request.[87] When it did meet, it approved a draft resolution submitted by Britain stating that the situation constituted a threat to the peace, calling on the British government to prevent, by force if necessary, the arrival at Beira of vessels believed to be carrying oil for Rhodesia, and calling on Portugal not to receive at Beira oil destined for Rhodesia.

In December 1966, after the failure of talks between Wilson and Smith on HMS *Tiger*, Britain decided that the time had come to ask the Council to impose selective mandatory sanctions. The Council met and approved, with certain amendments, a draft resolution submitted by Britain which, after citing Articles 39 and 41 of the Charter, determined

[87] The president's conduct made nonsense of the Charter's provision that the Council 'shall be so organized as to be able to function continuously'. Mali was very critical of Britain's policy towards Rhodesia at this time, and the most probable, though depressing, explanation is that its representative was piqued by the promptness with which she was taking the right action on this occasion.

that the situation constituted a threat to international peace and security, *decided that* (as opposed to *calling on* or *requesting*) all member states of the UN should impose certain specified economic sanctions against Rhodesia, and reminded them that failure to implement the resolution would constitute a violation of Article 25 of the Charter. For the first time the Council was acting decisively in the economic field within the framework of Chapter VII. In May 1968 it made the selective mandatory sanctions comprehensive and *decided* that all UN members should prevent the import into their territories of 'all commodities and products originating in Southern Rhodesia'. In March 1970 it went one stage further and, following the proclamation of a republic in Rhodesia, *decided* that Members should sever immediately all diplomatic, trade, military and other relations with the illegal regime and interrupt any existing means of transportation to and from Rhodesia.

From UDI until June 1970 the British Labour government actively participated in the UN's progressively severe programme of economic sanctions against Rhodesia. Lord Caradon, its representative in the Security Council, was a passionate opponent of racial discrimination and had been the effective rapporteur of the group of experts appointed by the Council in 1963 to examine the situation in the Union of South Africa. During this period the main difference between the African states and Britain regarding Rhodesia was on the use of military force against the Smith regime. A series of draft resolutions, calling on Britain to use force, were submitted to the Council. They were not adopted, first owing to lack of the necessary nine votes, and later owing to Britain's use of the veto. A draft calling for the use of force, which was put forward in March 1970, was vetoed by both Britain and the United States. Max Jakobson, the wise representative of Finland, then made a strong plea for the restoration of Council unity on the policy of economic sanctions, and the resolution referred to in the last paragraph was approved.

The successful implementation of the sanctions programme is the main hope of defeating racism in Rhodesia without bloodshed and would be of immeasurable value in strengthening the prestige and influence of the United Nations. So far the programme has had a significant effect on the Rhodesian economy, but has been unsuccessful in its main purpose. During the first year or two after UDI Rhodesian imports and exports dropped by about a third but then recovered as the economy adjusted itself to the new conditions.[88] An official British

[88] See the article by Margaret Doxey, 'The Rhodesian sanctions experiment', in *The Year Book of World Affairs*, 1971, pp. 154–6.

report to the UN, published in June 1970, stated that there had been no growth in the Rhodesian economy since UDI and that *per capita* income in real terms was virtually the same as in 1965.[89] This seemed to indicate that the Rhodesian economy was surviving, though under difficulties. The main infringements of the sanctions programme were due to the refusal of South Africa and Portugal to comply with the Security Council's directives, and it was South Africa and Mozambique that provided the channels through which Rhodesia continued its trade with the outside world. But many UN Members were lukewarm and lax in their compliance,[90] and such important countries as France, Japan, West Germany, and Communist China are considered to have been halfhearted in their application of sanctions, the last not altogether surprisingly owing to its exclusion from the UN. Even some African states have taken up a cynical and halfhearted attitude towards an international experiment in which they have so big a stake. Until October 1971 Britain and the United States were, of all UN Members, the most conscientious in carrying out the system, Britain, as requested by the Council, giving maximum assistance to its Sanctions Committee in the form of thorough economic intelligence reports, and in addition prosecuting successfully a number of firms and individuals for breaking sanctions.[91]

In October 1971 the United States Senate, on the initiative of Senator Byrd and under pressure from the 'chrome lobby', removed chrome and some other less important strategic materials from the Rhodesian sanctions list. As a Member of the United Nations, the United States was bound by a solemn international obligation under Article 25 of the Charter to carry out the Security Council's decision of December 1966, imposing economic sanctions on Rhodesia, and President Johnson had, within three weeks of the decision, signed an Executive Order implementing it so far as the United States was concerned. The Senate's action was taken in face of a formal protest from the State Department but with no effective discouragement from the White House. The strategic arguments put forward in its defence were invalid, because the country had at the time a stockpile of over 5 million tons of chrome, and the Office of Emergency Preparedness had declared that 2·2 million tons were in excess of foreseeable strategic needs. The United States was thus in deliberate breach of sanctions in company with Portugal and

[89] *Ibid.*, p. 153.

[90] The Security Council's Sanctions Committee stated in June 1969 that thirty-three states had failed to reply to the Secretary-General's requests for information on measures taken to carry out sanctions.

[91] See Doxey, p. 155.

H

South Africa, but it was alone in defying by legislation its obligations under the Charter. This ominous break with the United States' great traditions recalls a passage in Dag Hammarskjöld's last annual report as Secretary-General:

> Were the respect for the obligations flowing from Article 25 of the Charter to be allowed to diminish, this would spell the end of the possibilities of the Organization to grow into what the Charter indicates as the clear intention of the founders, as also of all hopes to see the Organization grow into an increasingly effective institution.

In face of this bad example from the UN's most powerful member, much depends on whether other members treat the setback as a challenge or are influenced by President Nixon's cynicism.

The British Conservative administration of Edward Heath, which replaced the Labour government in June 1970, decided to make one more attempt at a Rhodesian settlement, in spite of the deterioration in the situation since they had last tried. After long preparatory negotiations the foreign secretary, Sir Alec Douglas-Home, and Ian Smith agreed on proposals for a settlement in November 1971. They were an improvement on the retrograde constitution adopted by Rhodesia in 1969 shortly before it became a republic, and they were a small step in the right direction. But they involved unsatisfactory modifications in the spirit of the preconditions laid down by the previous Conservative government in 1963, the majority of UN members opposed them strongly, and during the winter of 1971–72 two draft resolutions were submitted to the Security Council urging Britain to change her policy. These were vetoed by the British representative.

However, the precondition that a settlement must be acceptable to the people of Rhodesia as a whole was not modified. A strong commission carried out a thorough investigation of the people's reactions, and for the first time in Rhodesian history the African majority had a fair opportunity of expressing their views, which they did very clearly. The commission reported in May 1972 that the proposals were not acceptable, the constitution remained unmodified, and sanctions continued. The cost was high, but the majority of Rhodesians had spoken and the situation in their country would never be the same again. Ironically, they could not have so spoken had the opposition to the negotiations been successful.

The regimes in South Africa and Rhodesia have defied human rights. The problem of racial discrimination is primarily a moral, rather than a political, or an international one, except in so far as moral standards are held to be absolute and therefore universal, though this is not quite the same as international. The record of the United Nations in dealing with it has not so far been successful. Its critics have sometimes expected the impossible or at any rate oversimplified the issues. It is not irrelevant to compare the evils of discrimination and *apartheid* with the wholesale massacres in other parts of Africa, which have already been mentioned, or in other parts of the world, such as Indonesia and Pakistan, or with racial discrimination in the United States, Ceylon, and even Canada, with its unsolved Indian problem. The comparisons once made, it must remain a matter of opinion as to which evils are the worst. But the open and unashamed denial of human rights in South Africa and Rhodesia is unique and highly provocative.

It was decided at the San Francisco Conference that the Security Council should not be empowered to enforce settlements under Chapter VI of the Charter (see p. 63). The use of force is only provided for within the framework of Chapter VII, and it will always be difficult to decide whether grave social injustice constitutes a threat to the peace and justifies forceful measures. In recent years there has been a growing trend of opinion, in which U Thant has concurred, against the collective use of military force to solve international problems. There is understandably less reluctance to use economic sanctions. But they have in practice had the effect of strengthening the resistance and solidarity of those against whom they were directed, for example, Italy in 1935–36, South Africa, and Rhodesia.[92] It is arguable that, in the long term and as a general rule, voluntary action and methods of persuasion have a better prospect than organized collective measures of modifying the conduct of governments and societies.[93] But this approach requires patience, faith, and sustained effort; in particular, more patience than can reasonably be expected of the African victims of *apartheid* and discrimination and of their supporters throughout the world. Apart from Portugal and South Africa, there is general support for economic sanctions against Rhodesia. In this case, therefore, the right policy would appear to be a serious, sustained, and truly cooperative effort to make sanctions effective. Such an effort has not yet been made, but, if successful, it would be an important step also towards solving the still more intractable problem of *apartheid* in the Union of South Africa.

[92] See Doxey, pp. 157–62.
[93] See Leland M. Goodrich, 'Peace enforcement in perspective', *International Journal*, Autumn, 1969, p. 672.

THE UNITED STATES AND LATIN AMERICA

Chapter VIII of the Charter took account of the part that might be played by 'regional arrangements or agencies' in the international order. The Organization of American States (OAS), which came into existence in 1948 with an elaborate institutional structure, became the most important of the regional organizations. It was a new form of the old Pan-American Union, which dated back to 1889, so organized as to fit in with the requirements of the UN Charter for regional arrangements. The relations of the United States with other members of the OAS provide the most revealing example of the relationship between a great power and the states in its region and of the interaction of that relationship with their common membership of the United Nations. The Soviet Union was the most alert critic of US intervention in Latin American affairs. It was a case of the pot calling the kettle black, because Moscow interfered, when it thought necessary, with the members of its own regional organization in Eastern Europe, and states belonging to the Warsaw Treaty group had owed their Communist political complexion in the first place mainly to Soviet military and political pressure. However, US policy in Latin America did sometimes recall Soviet methods in its own sphere of influence.

Guatemala, 1954

Guatemala appealed to the Security Council on 19 June 1954 to put a stop to the aggression in progress against its territory from Honduras and Nicaragua. Its reformist government, which was led by Arbenz Guzmán, was considered by the United States to be largely Communist controlled. Washington was particularly concerned about a radical land reform of the Arbenz government which had expropriated a large amount of land belonging to the American United Fruit Company. A few days before, the secretary of state, John Foster Dulles, had stated publicly that he hoped the OAS would be able 'to help the people of Guatemala to rid themselves of the malignant force' which had 'seized on them'.[94] The previous March, with Guatemala in mind, at an Inter-American Conference in Caracas he had secured the passage of a resolution which declared that 'the domination or con-

---

[94] See Inis L. Claude, Jr, 'The OAS, the U.N. and the United States', *International Conciliation*, Mar. 1964, p. 29.

trol of the political institutions of any American State by the international communist movement . . . would constitute a threat to the Sovereignty and political independence of the American States', which would call for 'appropriate action'.

When the Council met on 20 June, in response to the appeal, Guatemala complained that the United States had been encouraging a campaign against it and referred to the US role at the Caracas Conference. Its appeal to the Council had been accompanied by another to the Inter-American Peace Committee, an OAS agency. But when Honduras, Nicaragua, and the United States in turn all stated before the Council that the case should be dealt with by the OAS, Guatemala suspected the Organization's impartiality and withdrew its appeal to the Committee.

The main point discussed in the Council was the relative roles that should be played in this case by the Security Council and the OAS. A draft resolution submitted by Brazil and Colombia would have referred the Guatemalan complaint to the OAS, as desired by Honduras, Nicaragua and the United States. Guatemala maintained that it had 'an unchallengeable right of appeal to the Council' and no obligation to submit the question to the OAS. According to Article 103 of the Charter, in case of a conflict between the obligations of UN members under the Charter and under any other international agreement, their obligations under the Charter must prevail. It considered that the Council should send a warning to Honduras and Nicaragua calling on them to apprehend the exiles and mercenaries who were carrying out the invasion, and requested that an observation commission should be sent to verify that the countries accused by Guatemala had connived at it. Guatemala was strongly supported by the Soviet Union, whose representative stated that the OAS was dominated by the United States, which was using it in support of its plan to replace the Arbenz government. Britain, France, and New Zealand took the middle line of supporting reference of the case to the OAS, while at the same time asserting the ultimate authority of the Security Council.

The Brazilian–Colombian draft resolution was supported by ten members of the Council but vetoed by the Soviet Union. Thereupon a French amendment to the draft, which had been accepted, calling for the immediate termination of the invasion and abstention by UN members from lending it support, was submitted as a separate resolution and adopted unanimously. This also was incidentally a unanimous vindication of the Security Council's right to act in the matter.

On 22 June Guatemala stated that this resolution had not been complied with and requested another meeting of the Council. Henry Cabot

Lodge, the American President of the Council, was in no hurry to call a meeting and, in spite of Guatemala's request being supported by the Soviet Union, delayed doing so until 25 June. This enabled the invasion to continue without further challenge for another three days. When the Council did finally meet, it discussed whether the question should be put on its agenda, the Inter-American Peace Committee having meanwhile taken up the matter. But this, in fact, involved a reopening of the debate of 20 June in sharper terms. Denmark, Lebanon, New Zealand, and the Soviet Union were all in favour of adopting the agenda, in order to vindicate the Council's authority. Britain and France affirmed their confidence in the OAS but considered that the Council could not divest itself of ultimate responsibility: they therefore abstained. Lodge gave an arbitrary, subjective and inaccurate interpretation of Article 52 of the Charter, dealing with regional arrangements, adding that the Guatemalan and Soviet proposal was an effort to promote international anarchy rather than international order and that, if the rights of the OAS to achieve a settlement in this case were not respected the result would be a catastrophe of such dimensions as gravely to impair the future effectiveness of both the UN and regional organizations. He succeeded in mustering five votes against the adoption of the agenda, which was therefore not approved.

At the beginning of July the leader of the invading forces, Colonel Castillo Armas, an exiled Guatemalan officer, replaced Arbenz as head of the Guatemalan government. On 2 July Honduras, Nicaragua and the new Guatemalan regime informed the Inter-American Peace Committee that the dispute between them was over, and this message was passed on to the Security Council three days later.

Article 15 of the OAS Charter lays down that: 'No state or group of states has the right to intervene, directly or indirectly, for any reason whatever, in the internal or external affairs of any other state'. During the Security Council's first meeting on the Guatemalan case Lodge stated that the reports the United States was receiving were incomplete and fragmentary, that the information available strongly suggested that the situation did not involve aggression, and that the United States had no connection whatever with what was taking place. In 1960 James Reston wrote in the *New York Times*: 'Every official who knows anything about the fall of the Arbenz government . . . knows that the United States government, through the Central Intelligence Agency, worked actively with, and financed, and made available the arms, with which the anti-Arbenz forces finally "threw him out".'[95] After leaving

[95] *Ibid.*, p. 32.

office Eisenhower admitted supplying arms to Nicaragua and Honduras in May 1954 and providing two fighter-bombers, which played a key role, to Castillo Armas.[96]

Security Council action succeeded neither in stopping the invasion of Guatemala nor preventing the overthrow of the Arbenz government. But it did draw attention to a case of intervention which infringed both the UN Charter and the Charter of the OAS.

The United States and Cuba: the missile crisis, 1962

At the beginning of 1959 the Cuban revolutionary movement led by Fidel Castro was successful. During his first year in office Castro came to an understanding with the Cuban communists and made an alliance with the Soviet Union. Relations between Cuba and the United States in consequence deteriorated, and between the summer of 1960 and the spring of 1962 Cuba complained to the Security Council three times about the United States' actions or intentions.

On the first two occasions, in July and December 1960, Cuba charged the States with harbouring aggressive designs against her. The first time, as in the case of Guatemala, Council discussions centred round whether the OAS or the UN was the right body to handle the question. The second time Cuba asserted that aggression was to be perpetrated 'within a few hours', and, when this forecast failed to materialize, even a mild draft resolution calling upon the parties to settle their dispute peacefully was not pressed by its sponsors. Thirdly, in January 1962 a meeting of OAS Ministers of Foreign Affairs decided that adherence by any OAS member to Marxism-Leninism was incompatible with the Inter-American system; that incompatibility on this ground excluded the present Cuban government from participation in the system; and that members of the OAS should immediately suspend trade in arms with Cuba and study the feasibility and desirability of extending the suspension of trade to other items, especially those of strategic importance. Cuba complained to the Security Council that the decisions amounted to illegal enforcement measures, but the item was not accepted for the agenda. In March, however, the Council did consider a Cuban request that it should seek the advisory opinion of the International Court of Justice on a number of points relating to the OAS decisions. The question of the interpretation of Article 53 (1) of the UN Charter dealing with regional enforcement actions was a point of some subtlety,

[96] Dwight D. Eisenhower, *Mandate for Change*, pp. 425-6.

on which a Court ruling would have been useful. But under US leadership the proposed reference to the Court was rejected by two votes to seven with one abstention.

A serious dispute between Cuba and the United States, which would normally have been referred to the Security Council, was in fact considered by the General Assembly. In April 1961 a force of Cuban refugees, with United States' logistic and other support, landed in the Bay of Pigs on the Cuban coast in the hope of touching off risings against the Castro government. The Assembly happened to be meeting at the time, and the question was brought before it by Cuba, which thus had an opportunity of denouncing the United States at the UN. As the invaders were quickly defeated by Cuban action, there was no need to request a meeting of the Council.

Friction between Cuba and the United States culminated in the missile crisis of October 1962, which quickly developed into the most serious international dispute since the second World War and involved a major confrontation between the two super-powers. During the summer of 1963 Khrushchev decided to make Cuba into a Soviet base which would be a nuclear threat to the United States and other countries in Central and South America. Defensive surface-to-air missiles were sent first; they were followed by Soviet fighters and nuclear bombers; and finally, in mid-October, Washington became aware that ground-to-ground missiles were being installed with a formidable capacity for striking at many of the main cities and bases in the United States. This development was all the more sinister, because responsible Russians had repeatedly denied that they were doing anything more than strengthening Cuban defences.

President Kennedy decided that Soviet nuclear weapons must be removed from Cuba, and the problem was how to produce this result with a minimum risk of nuclear war. The matter was urgent, because once the missiles were operational the difficulty of removing them would be far greater. Kennedy gathered round him a strong group of advisers, who worked in complete secrecy and with great thoroughness to decide on the best policy. Fortunately he and his advisers combined firmness with understanding of Khrushchev's sensitivity as leader of a world power.

On 22 October the President explained in a televised speech the situation in Cuba and the United States' reaction to it, the essential points of which were a demand for the removal of the missiles from Cuba and a naval blockade of the island to prevent any more Soviet weapons from reaching it. At the same time the United States called for an emergency meeting of the Security Council[97] and a meeting of the OAS Council. Both bodies met the following day.

The meeting of the Security Council gave the United States an opportunity to make clear to the world the gravity of the crisis, the attitude of the United States to the setting up of the missile sites, and the fact that it had the full backing of the OAS. It also enabled the US representative, Adlai Stevenson, on 25 October, to confront the Soviet representative and other members of the Council with photographic evidence of the existence of the sites. The Council passed no resolution and after the meeting on 25 October did not meet again until the crisis was over. But its meetings brought home vividly the UN's opportunity to play a conciliatory role, and the Secretary-General took over where the Security Council left off.

Three draft resolutions were submitted to the Council, though none of them was even voted on. Two were sponsored by the United States and the Soviet Union, and a third by Ghana and the UAR after consultation with a large number of UN members. This last resolution requested the Acting Secretary-General to confer promptly with the parties directly concerned on immediate steps to remove the threat to world peace and to normalize the situation in the Caribbean. U Thant acted in this sense on 24 October by sending identical letters to Kennedy and Khrushchev urging the need to refrain from action which might aggravate the situation, emphasizing the importance of gaining time, and suggesting the mandatory suspension for two or three weeks, on the one hand, of all arms shipments to Cuba and, on the other, of the quarantine measures involving the search of ships bound for Cuba.

This intervention was somewhat embarrassing to Kennedy, who was determined to stop the build-up of missile sites. But it facilitated concessions on both sides. Khrushchev first diverted some of the Soviet ships which were en route for Cuba and then ordered the return to Russia of all those carrying weapons, while Kennedy instructed the intercepting American warships to exercise the greatest restraint and tact in carrying out their task. It was much easier for each superpower to respond to UN conciliation than to yield to threats from the other side. The Secretary-General also agreed to a suggestion in the American draft resolution that the UN should 'assure and report on' the dismantling and withdrawal from Cuba of all missiles and other offensive weapons, and went to Cuba himself to discuss the matter. The proposal was rejected by Castro, but the UN's readiness to help contributed to the reduction of tension between Moscow and Washing-

[97] The Soviet Union also did so the next day.

H*

ton. During the many conversations in New York, which took place at this time between the American and Soviet representatives, U Thant was usually present, and his calm self-effacing personality, combined with his determined advocacy of peace, made him ideally suited to the part which he was called upon to play. Referring to the Secretary-General's letters of 24 October to Kennedy and Khrushchev, Adlai Stevenson later wrote: 'The mere existence of an impartial office which could perform such a service . . . at such a time is no small asset to the human race.'[98]

During the weekend of 26 to 28 October an exchange of letters between Khrushchev and Kennedy led to a final settlement. Khrushchev undertook to dismantle and remove the offensive weapons from Cuba, while Kennedy agreed to end promptly the quarantine measures then in effect and to ensure that there would be no invasion of Cuba either by the United States or by other nations of the Western hemisphere. On 7 January 1963 in a joint letter to the Secretary-General, Mr Kuznetsov, first deputy foreign minister of the Soviet Union, and Mr Stevenson, permanent representative of the United States at the United Nations, expressed their appreciation to U Thant for his efforts in assisting the two governments to avert the serious threat to the peace which had recently arisen in the Caribbean area and added that it was not necessary for the item to occupy further the attention of the Security Council.

Panama, 1964

In January 1964 a provocative flag incident at an American school in the Panama Canal Zone led to hostile reactions amongst citizens of Panama.[99] Some disorder followed during which the American police and armed forces in the Zone finally opened fire, resulting in the death of about twenty people and the wounding of several hundred others. The episode caused the Panamanian government with some justification to accuse the United States of what amounted to a colonialist attitude, and the governments of Panama and the United States jointly requested the Inter-American Peace Committee to look into the events which had occurred. Although the Committee decided at once to investigate the

[98] Adlai S. Stevenson, *Looking Outward*, p. 126.

[99] The United States' protectorate over the Zone had been ended by treaty in 1939, but Panama's titular sovereignty did not include the right to fly the Panamanian flag in the Zone. Progressive but limited concessions over the flag question satisfied neither side, and the flag issue had become a symbol of tension between the two parties.

case on the spot, Panama also requested a meeting of the Security Council to consider the grave situation which existed between Panama and the United States as a result of the Canal enclave in Panamanian territory. It was in the interests of the United States to keep the matter within the narrower context of the OAS and avoid the additional publicity of a Council meeting. But the Council put the item on its agenda and, in contrast to the case of Guatemala, adopted a compromise solution proposed by Brazil. On the basis of a consensus the President stated at the end of the discussion that he was authorized to appeal to the governments of the United States and Panama to end the bloodshed, bring about a cease-fire, and impose the utmost restraint on the military forces under their command.

The Dominican Republic, 1965

After the assassination of the dictator, Trujillo, in 1961, the Dominican Republic had been unable to settle down politically. The left-wing leader, Juan Bosch, had been elected president by democratic process in December 1962, but turned out by a military coup the following September and sent into exile. In April 1965 another military uprising took place under Colonel Caamano, who seized power with the intention of restoring Bosch, but his authority was challenged by a rival group set up by the navy and air force, first under General Wessin and later under General Imbert, and the country lapsed into civil war. On 28 April the United States government sent in a force of marines and paratroops, ostensibly with the humanitarian motive of protecting the lives of Americans and other foreigners in the Republic.

Two days later President Johnson announced in a radio talk to the people of the United States that, with the help of this force, over 2,400 Americans and other nationals had been evacuated from the Dominican Republic, and then added that there were signs that 'people trained outside the Dominican Republic' were seeking to gain control of the country.[100] On 2 May he stated that the Dominican uprising which 'began as a popular democratic revolution' had been seized by 'a band of Communist conspirators' and that he had ordered another 4,500 US troops to the Dominican Republic, bringing the total to about 14,000. The next day he defended the military landings by saying: 'We don't

[100] See *Background Information Relating to the Dominican Republic*, printed for Committee on Foreign Relations, US Senate, p. 53.

propose to sit here in our rocking chair with our hands folded and let the Communists set up any government in the Western Hemisphere'.[101] Within a few days the US forces involved totalled 22,000. The action of the United States, which began as a rescue operation, had quickly become military intervention with a primarily political purpose, and there is good reason to believe that the political motive was present from the beginning.[102]

The United States intervention violated the Charters of both the UN and the OAS. After the event Washington informed both the Council of the OAS and the Security Council of the action it had taken. But the majority of Latin American states resented the procedure that had been adopted, partly because it was a slight to the OAS but chiefly because it revived their old fears of Yankee imperialism. The Costa Rican delegate to the OAS expressed a widely held view when he criticized 'the mental laxity that confuses social reform with Communism'. Many people in the United States believed that the OAS should have been consulted first, and their government quickly tried to make amends for the mistake, first, by suggesting the despatch of a five-man OAS peace committee to help bring about a cease-fire and restore order in the Dominican Republic, and secondly, by trying to camouflage US forces as part of an inter-American force under OAS authority. However, the newly constituted force consisted of the US contingent of 22,000 together with about 25 Costa Rican policemen and some 1,600 troops from three military dictatorships, Brazil, Honduras, and Nicaragua, of which three-quarters were provided by Brazil. The appointment of a Brazilian General to be Commander of the force was more than offset by the fact that the deputy commander was an American, who announced that he would retain tactical command of the force.[103]

On 1 May the Soviet Union requested an urgent meeting of the Security Council to consider the question of the armed intervention by the United States in the internal affairs of the Dominican Republic. Two days later the Council included the item in its agenda, and between 3 and 25 May the question was considered at sixteen Council meetings. At the first of these the Soviet Union stated that while the United States had intervened under the pretext of saving American lives, its action was really designed to maintain in power a reactionary regime which suited its interests, and that it had again raised the bogy of anti-

---

[101] *Ibid.*, pp. 20, 21
[102] See the passage in Philip Geyelin's articles in the *Wall Street Journal* of 28 April, 4 May, and 11 May 1965.
[103] See Alan James, *Politics of Peacekeeping*, p. 240.

Communism to justify what it had done. During the first two days of the discussions no member of the Council spoke in support of the anti-Communist aspect of the US action, and only Britain and France expressed understanding of the humanitarian aspects of rescuing foreigners. France, however, together with Uruguay, was also strongly critical of American intervention in other respects. The United States made clear that it wanted the Council to leave the question to the OAS. But in the end two resolutions were approved on 14 and 22 May. The first, which was passed unanimously, called for a cease-fire and invited the Secretary-General to send, as an urgent measure, a representative to the Dominican Republic for the purpose of reporting on the situation to the Council. The second asked that the suspension of hostilities in the Dominican Republic be transformed into a permanent cease-fire and invited the Secretary-General to submit a report on the implementation of this request. It was passed without a dissenting vote, though the United States abstained, because the resolution was the result of a report from the Secretary-General's representative, strongly implying that the American force was, in effect, aiding General Imbert's faction.

Detached observers noticed this partiality from the early days of the American intervention. On 8 May the London *Economist* reported that the US administration 'only ostensibly' remained neutral between the Dominican factions, the real situation being indicated by the convention which labels the forces of General Wessin as 'loyalists' and those of Colonel Caamano as 'rebels'.[104] On 21 May *The Times* reported that nobody supposed 'that General Imbert could control the capital if the American forces were not there'. The situation changed when the Secretary-General appointed his personal representative on 17 May, and this appointment, which provided a counterweight to American influence, was one of the Security Council's main contributions to a Dominican settlement. U Thant's choice was J. A. Mayobre, a Venezuelan from the UN Economic Commission for Latin America, who was not biased against Caamano's constitutionalists and in his reports to the Secretary-General gave both factions' versions of what had taken place. His presence was resented by the United States, and during a conference soon after his arrival in the Dominican Republic he was browbeaten by a three-man US delegation, headed by the presidential assistant, McGeorge Bundy, most improper reference being made to what his own country, Venezuela, owed to the United

---

[104] Quoted in *Background Information Relating to the Dominican Republic*, p. 21: see note on p. 235.

States.[105] But he was not intimidated and he persevered steadily, with interrupted success, to bring about a real cease-fire in accordance with the Security Council's resolutions. He worked also behind the scenes to achieve a provisional political settlement acceptable to the Dominican constitutionalists and the majority of Latin American states.

The Security Council considered the question on a number of occasions during June and July but could not maintain the measure of agreement that it had achieved in May. The main differences of opinion were on the relative roles of the UN and the OAS and on the legality or illegality of the United States' intervention. At the last meeting in which the Council considered the question, on 26 July, the President gave a rather noncommittal summary of points on which members were agreed. They were that reports from the Dominican Republic indicated that there had been violations of the cease-fire and gross violations of human rights, which the Council condemned; that members desired that the violations should cease; and that they considered it necessary that the Council should continue to watch the situation closely and that the Secretary-General should continue to report on it. This at least resulted in developments in the Republic remaining under international observation, until elections took place the following June.

Throughout the whole operation support for the anti-Communist aspect of US intervention was very limited and was virtually confined to a few Latin American dictatorships, the more democratic states in the hemisphere making clear that they did not intend to be associated with the restoration of a dictatorship in the Dominican Republic. From about the middle of May onwards Washington appeared to be doubting the accuracy of the early reports it had received from its diplomatic representatives in the Republic; to be realizing that the constitutionalists had in fact wide support in the country and that the role of the Communists had been greatly exaggerated; and to be thinking in terms of a solution based on compromise rather than on the victory of the so-called 'loyalist' group. After the Brazilian contingent had joined the Inter-American force, the United States withdrew 6,000 of its troops and before the end of June the force had been reduced altogether by about 15,000.[106] Early in September Dr Garcia Godoy was made provisional president for a nine-month period, and on 1 June 1966 fair elections led to the defeat of Bosch by the politically more skilful Dr Balaguer.

The intervention in the Dominican Republic was the first occasion

[105] This was told to me by someone who was present at the conference.
[106] *Report of the Security Council to the General Assembly, 1956–66*, p. 16.

since the early 1930s on which the United States indulged overtly in the policy of the 'big stick' towards a Latin American country, that is to say, military intervention on a substantial scale. It is estimated that the crisis resulted in 3,000 Dominican deaths, most of which occurred after the intervention, some in clashes between the constitutionalists and US troops, but the majority due to operations by the Imbert faction, which received protection and support from the US force. The episode did much damage to the reputation of the United States in Latin America. But American journalists played an honourable part in it, such influential newspapers as the *Christian Science Monitor, New York Times, New York Herald Tribune, Wall Street Journal*, and *Washington Post* having published frank and critical reports and editorials on the subject.[107] A number of leading Americans were strongly critical of their government's policy, and it was mainly over this affair that President Johnson lost the support of Senator Fulbright, chairman of the Senate Foreign Relations Committee.

CYPRUS

In the process of decolonization after the second World War Cyprus presented a difficult case. On the one hand, four-fifths of its mixed Greek and Turkish population were Greeks, and, if the principle of self-determinaiton had been applied, the vote would certainly have gone in favour of Greece. On the other hand, the Greeks were the hereditary enemies of the Turks, and Cyprus was only forty miles from the coast of Turkey, whose population was three times that of Greece. Moreover, when Turkey handed Cyprus over to Britain in 1878, the island had been part of the Ottoman Empire for over three hundred years. Although the Turks only made up eighteen per cent of the population, therefore, there were strong geographical, strategic, and historical reasons why Turkey should participate in the government of Cyprus, if it ceased to be British. Against this complex background the British began to attach more importance to Cyprus as a base, owing to their withdrawal from Palestine in 1948 and from the Suez Canal Zone in 1954–55, and announced on several occasions that they had no intention of leaving the island.

In the end a settlement was reached in 1959 after some ten years of controversy, during which negotiations had alternated with violence

---

[107] See Abraham F. Lowenthal, 'The Dominican intervention in retrospect' *Public Policy*, Fall 1969, p. 133.

and the Greeks had aimed at the union of Cyprus with Greece, while the Turks had tended to favour partition. The terms were agreed at a meeting of the Greek and Turkish foreign ministers in Zurich and at a later conference in London, and they went into effect in 1960. They provided for an independent Cyprus with special rights for the Turkish minority. There was to be a Greek president and a Turkish vice-president, with a cabinet of seven Greeks and three Turks and the same proportions at the lower administrative levels. Britain was to retain sovereignty over two areas, which were to be maintained as military bases, while Britain, Greece, and Turkey were to guarantee the independence and territorial integrity of the island and the state of affairs established by the constitution, with the right to intervene jointly or separately, if there were a breach of the constitution. Greece and Turkey were also to maintain small national contingents in Cyprus.

The Greek Cypriot president, Archbishop Makarios, had accepted the settlement with reluctance, and a constitution, which was difficult to implement in practice, was made much more difficult by the fact that the head of state had described it as unworkable. In November 1963 Makarios put forward to the Turkish vice-president proposals for revising the constitution, which Turkey rejected. Tension grew, and in December serious intercommunal fighting broke out. On 26 December Makarios accepted an offer from Britain, Greece and Turkey to make available a joint peace-keeping force, and on the same day Cyprus requested an urgent meeting of the Security Council to consider its complaint against Turkey on account of acts of aggression and the threat and use of force against Cyprus. When the Council met, Turkey denied the charges and made counter-charges, while the Cypriot representative stated that the Turkish ships making for Cyprus had turned in another direction, and that he attributed this to his application to the Council. On 13 January the Secretary-General informed the Council that Britain, Cyprus, Greece and Turkey had asked him to appoint a personal representative to look into the situation on the island, and four days later he announced an appointment.

Meanwhile the British element in the peace-keeping force, which was under British overall command, had inevitably borne the main burden of the force's responsibility, because Greece and Turkey were parties to the dispute. Other attempts at a settlement having failed, including a proposal for a peace-keeping force provided by NATO members, which was rejected by Makarios, Britain, on 15 February, requested an urgent meeting of the Security Council to resolve the dangerous and deteriorating situation on the island. Cyprus requested a meeting of the

Council on the same day to consider 'the increasing threat from war preparations' of the Turkish government, which had made the danger of an invasion imminent.

The Council considered the Cyprus problem at a series of meetings starting on 17 February, and on 4 March approved a resolution unanimously recommending the creation of a United Nations peace-keeping force in Cyprus (UNFICYP). Its composition and size was to be established by the Secretary-General in consultation with the governments of Cyprus, Greece, Turkey, and the United Kingdom. Its commander was to be appointed by the Secretary-General and to report to him. The Secretary-General in turn was to report periodically to the Security Council on its operation. On 27 March the force became operational under the command of an Indian general. In the same resolution the Council also recommended that the Secretary-General should designate a mediator, in agreement with the four governments, to promote a peaceful solution to the Cyprus problem.

On 2 May 1964 the Secretary-General reported to the Council that at the end of April the military strength of UNFICYP was 6,341 men with an additional police contingent of 28, which was later increased to 173. It had originally been recommended that the force should be stationed in Cyprus for three months. But its existence was repeatedly extended by periods of three, or more often six months, the normal procedure being for the Security Council to approve unanimously a resolution presented by the President after consultations with members. Between June 1964, when the initial three-month period ended, and December 1971 extensions were approved twenty times, but by the end of 1970 the force had been reduced to a total of 3,182 men. It was made up of personnel from Austria, Canada, Denmark, Finland, Ireland, Sweden and the United Kingdom and was the only UN peace-keeping force for which a permanent member of the Council provided a major military contingent.

The Council resolution of 4 March 1964 laid down that all costs pertaining to UNFICYP should be met by the governments providing the contingents and by the government of Cyprus, but that the Secretary-General might also accept voluntary contributions for the purpose. Substantial voluntary contributions have been made by the United States and Britain, and contributions have also come from Greece, Turkey, and, mostly on a modest scale, from many other countries. The cost of the initial period was fully met, but since then the operation has normally been run under the shadow of a deficit, and U Thant has frequently criticized the method of financing, describing it on one occasion as 'inadequate, inequitable, and insecure'.[108] Several states also made clear that their voluntary contributions were not to be understood as a rejection of the International Court's advisory opinion of 1962 that UN peace-keeping costs are part of the organization's normal expenses.

The UNFICYP operation was carried out under the Security Council's authority. But the resolution initiating it gave the Secretary-General considerable powers, and France and the Soviet Union had strong reservations on this point. Both of them abstained in a separate vote on the financial paragraph of the resolution, and neither of them has made any financial contribution to the force.

The presence of UNFICYP in Cyprus has without question had a salutary influence. It has been reassuring for the civilian population; it has reduced the amount of violence; and, when hostilities have broken out, it has prevented them from developing into full-scale war, of which on several occasions there has been a serious danger. Deep suspicion and tension between the two communities has remained, and during the first four years until 1968 there were serious outbreaks of fighting; for example, in August 1964, when the Security Council had to call for a cease-fire, and in November 1967, when the Council, the Secretary-General, NATO, and the United States all added their influence to UNFICYP's in order to relieve the tension. However, during the first half of 1968, with the help of U Thant's special representative, two leaders of the Greek Cypriot and Turkish Cypriot communities began a series of talks on the basic problem, and at the end of the year the Secretary-General was able to report that at last the emphasis seemed to be shifting from military confrontation to negotiation. During the previous six months, he wrote, there had been no bloodshed or serious inter-communal incident. Two years later he reported that there was still no real prospect of a long-term settlement but that the talks remained the sole means of achieving agreement and avoiding a return to violence. During the first half of 1972 there was a marked improvement in relations between the Greek and Turkish governments, though the problems to be solved in Cyprus still remained formidable.

It has often been suggested that the very success of UNFICYP, by preventing a full-scale conflict and reducing the sense of urgency, has delayed a final settlement. But this suggestion, in so far as it is valid, involves a strong element of cynicism. Without UNIFICYP an earlier solution could no doubt have been reached, but it would have been

[108] *Secretary-General's Annual Report to the General Assembly, 1965–66*, p. 7.

based on force and would have left behind a legacy of bitterness, not to mention a breach in the NATO alliance. UNFICYP had made possible an accommodation based on agreement and common sense, though by the spring of 1972 such a settlement had not yet been achieved.

ALLEGED ACTS OF AGGRESSION

A number of complaints were made to the Security Council, mostly against a super-power, about alleged acts of aggression, which were usually on a minor scale. They had the advantage of enabling a state to give vent to its feeling of resentment before an international body, as an alternative to retaliatory action, which might have had serious consequences. They also led, on one occasion, to an admission of error and, on another, to a change of policy, in each case by the United States.

On 28 and 30 August 1950 the Chinese People's Republic complained to the Secretary-General that United States military aircraft from Korea had flown over Chinese territory and caused material damage and loss of life. It asked that the Security Council should take action, and the Council considered the question at four meetings between 31 August and 12 September. The US representative first stated that American aircraft in Korea were under strict instructions not to cross the Korean frontier into adjacent territory. But, following a further complaint from China on 24 September, he informed the Council that one American plane in the UN service might inadvertently have violated Chinese territory and dropped bombs on 22 September. The United States government, he said, deeply regretted any violations of Chinese territory and any damage which might have occurred and was willing, in the case of all charges against it, to pay compensation through the UN for damages which an impartial on-the-spot investigation might show to have been caused by US planes. In fact, two weeks before the Soviet Union had vetoed an American proposal to set up a commission of investigation. However, the frank US admission did vindicate the usefulness of referring such cases to the Council.

On 8 September 1954 the United States informed the Security Council that a US Navy aircraft on a peaceful mission over international high seas had been attacked without warning by two Soviet aircraft and destroyed. The Council considered the question at two meetings. The United States representative pointed out that the attack was one of a series, that his government considered the International Court of

Justice to be the correct forum for the settlement of such incidents, but that the Soviet Union had refused to submit a similar previous case to the Court. The Soviet Union challenged the American account of the incident and made a number of counter-charges.

On three occasions the Soviet Union complained to the Security Council about flights by United States military aircraft. In April 1958 it requested an urgent Council meeting to consider 'measures to put an end to flights by US military aircraft armed with atomic and hydrogen bombs in the direction of the frontiers of the Soviet Union'. The United States representative made clear that the flights were of a routine operational character and part of his country's defence system against surprise attack. The Council could agree on no course of action, a Soviet draft resolution blaming the United States being defeated by ten votes to one, and an American draft recommending the establishment of a northern zone of international inspection against surprise attack, on lines already considered by the UN Disarmament Sub-Committee, being vetoed by the Soviet Union. But the debate, during which the Secretary-General spoke, did underline the importance of some progress being made towards strengthening security by agreement. In May 1960 the Soviet Union requested a meeting of the Council to examine the question of repeated encroachments upon Soviet air-space by US military aircraft, which had culminated on 1 May in the shooting down by Soviet rockets of a U-2 type aircraft that had penetrated over 2,000 kilometres into the Soviet Union. When the Council met, the Soviet representative stated that the United States government, instead of halting its policy of sending aircraft over the territory of other states, had declared such incursions to be its official policy, personally approved by the President. The Council could not agree on any course of action, but the United States representative announced during the debate that the flights over the Soviet Union had been suspended after the recent incident and were not to be resumed. On 13 July 1960 the Soviet Union asked for an urgent meeting of the Council to consider the question of 'new aggressive acts' by the US Air Force against the Soviet Union. During the subsequent Council meeting the Soviet representative complained that a US reconnaissance aircraft of the RB-47 type had penetrated into Soviet air-space before being shot down over Soviet territorial waters. The debate centred round whether or not the aircraft had been trespassing and how the surviving aircrew should be treated. But the Council could not agree to adopt any of the three draft resolutions submitted to it.

In three communications to the Security Council during April 1964,

Britain charged Yemen with carrying out air raids against the Federation of South Arabia and stated that on 28 March British aircraft had carried out a counterattack on a fort near Harib just inside the Yemeni frontier, after a preliminary warning to minimize the risk of casualties. On 1 April Yemen requested an urgent meeting of the Council to consider the situation resulting from continuous British acts of aggression against peaceful Yemeni citizens, culminating in the attack on the fort. The Council considered the question at six meetings between 2 and 9 April, a substantial part in the discussion being taken by Arab states, Iraq, Syria and the UAR all having asked to participate. Britain and Yemen accused each other of aggression against South Arabia and Yemen respectively, Britain pointing out that it had proposed a demilitarized zone on the frontier the previous year. In the end the Council adopted a resolution by nine votes to nil, with Britain and the United States abstaining, which condemned reprisals as incompatible with the purposes and principles of the UN; deplored the British military action near Harib; deplored all attacks and incidents which had occurred in the area: and called upon Yemen and Britain to exercise the maximum restraint in order to avoid further incidents and to restore peace in the area. The anticolonial issue played a large part in the Council discussions, Britain's concern for South Arabia being the result of her occupation of Aden. But the publicity given through the Council to the disturbed conditions on the frontier was salutary for both sides.

TWO UNUSUAL CASES

Complaint by Argentina: the Eichmann Case, 1960

During the spring of 1960 Jewish volunteer groups, including Israeli citizens, captured on Argentine territory the notorious Nazi war criminal, Adolph Eichmann, and transferred him to Israel. The Argentine government protested to Israel against this illegal act as a violation of Argentine territory and demanded reparations in the form of Eichmann's return and the punishment of those guilty of the violation. The prime minister of Israel expressed his regret about any violation of Argentine laws which might have been committed but made clear that Israel intended to retain Eichmann and bring him to trial. On 15 June, therefore, Argentina requested an urgent meeting of the Security Council to consider 'the violation of the sovereign rights of the Argentine

Republic resulting from the illicit and clandestine transfer of Adolph Eichmann' from Argentina to Israel. The Council included the item in its agenda and considered the question at four meetings on 22 and 23 June.

In presenting its case to the Council Argentina maintained that, by its decision to detain and try Eichmann, Israel had *ipso facto* become an accessory to, and ultimately responsible for, the violation of Argentine territory. At the same time it submitted a draft resolution declaring that acts which affect the sovereignty of a member state and therefore cause international friction, 'may, if repeated, endanger international peace and security', and requesting Israel to 'make appropriate reparation' in accordance with the Charter and the rules of international law. The Israeli representative pointed out that his government had already apologized, that it believed that the 'isolated violation' must be seen in the light of the 'exceptional and unique character of the crimes attributed to Eichmann', and that in its view its expression of regret constituted adequate reparation. The United States representative proposed two amendments to the draft, which were accepted by Argentina, referring to the universal condemnation of the Nazi persecution of the Jews and to the concern of people in all countires that Eichmann should be brought to justice, and expressing the hope that 'the traditionally friendly relations between Argentina and Israel will be advanced'. All members of the Council were concerned about the violation of sovereignty that had occurred. The United States and Britain shared the view that the adoption of the draft resolution together with Israel's expression of regret would constitute adequate reparation to Argentina, while other members considered that the adoption of the draft would be a satisfactory solution of the question. The draft was finally approved without a dissenting vote, but with Poland and the Soviet Union abstaining, and Argentina not participating.

The Council's handling of the problem facilitated a formal international protest against the violation of Argentine sovereignty; it acted as a safety valve for Argentina's resentment; and it gave some respectability to treating an illegal act as exceptional. The act itself did not really endanger international peace and security, though it was dangerous because the repetition of such incidents, as the Argentine representative told the Council, would strike at the roots of international order. This being the case, it was not altogether fortunate that the Security Council became the vehicle for such a compromise.

The Council's record   247

Northern Ireland, 1969

On 17 August 1969 the Irish government requested an urgent meeting of the Security Council to consider the situation in Northern Ireland, resulting from a Protestant parade in Londonderry, which the Royal Ulster Constabulary had been unable to control and which had led to the intervention of British military forces. The Irish representative pointed out that his government's proposals to the United Kingdom for the despatch of a United Nations or a joint British-Irish peace-keeping force had been rejected. The Council met on 20 August to deal with the matter and discussed only whether or not the proposed item should be included in the agenda, though some speakers in fact referred to the substance of the question.

The British representative maintained that the situation in Northern Ireland was an internal matter for the United Kingdom and that, by the terms of Article 2(7) of the Charter, the UN was not authorized to intervene in matters which were essentially within the domestic jurisdiction of a state. He added that the situation was under control and that there was no threat to international peace and security. Furthermore, a public debate on the matter would inflame feelings in Northern Ireland still further. But he did not object to a Finnish proposal that, as a matter of courtesy, the Irish foreign minister should be allowed to address the Council, although there was no precedent for a non-member doing so before the agenda had been adopted. Most Council members were highly sensitive about their rights under Article 2(7), and only four out of fifteen took part in the debate. A Zambian proposal was then adopted without objection, adjourning the meeting and postponing a decision as to whether or not to adopt the provisional agenda.

The Council's handling of this question provided an unusual example of wisdom and restraint. U Thant used his good offices behind the scenes; the British representative, Lord Caradon, and the Irish foreign minister, Dr Hillery, met in New York before the Council session; their statements during the session were reasonable and restrained; and the suggestion of Max Jakobson, the Finnish representative, was a wise conciliatory gesture. The Council thus again acted as a safety valve, this time as an outlet for Irish feelings.

During the first twenty-seven years of its existence the Security Council, hampered by the attitudes of its members, has not fully carried out its main responsibility: it has not maintained international peace and it has not given UN members a real sense of security. But, if its objective is redefined in more modest terms, appropriate to an adolescent organization, as to contribute to a more peaceful world, its record shows that it has done this on many occasions and in a great variety of ways. Its biggest successes have been during the Suez and Congo crises and, with certain reservations, during the Korean action, while its achievements in the Cuban missile crisis and in Cyprus have been considerable. Moreover, even limited results are of great value in the fields of peace-keeping and peace-making, and the Council's most modest successes have been innovations in world history. No state can now make war without knowing that its actions will be watched and discussed by an international body of great potential influence, while major powers or super-powers, which interfere in the affairs of smaller states, are aware that they cannot escape the attention and criticisms of the participants in a world forum.

6
The Security Council as a forum and a rendezvous

The Security Council has played important roles as a forum and as a natural rendezvous for the representatives of states. In addition to passing resolutions and taking appropriate action in fulfilment of its primary responsibility to maintain peace and security, the Council has provided a forum for the expression and development of world opinion and for the presentation by states before the international community of their points of view on disputes and controversial matters. It has provided also a meeting place where statesmen and diplomatists, in addition to carrying out their official public duties, can exchange views and discuss common problems on an informal or semiformal basis.

The part played by public opinion and publicity in furthering international cooperation and the establishment of an international system was appreciated, as has been seen, by President Wilson and Lord Cecil. Wilson once said of the League of Nations' Assembly that it 'was created in order that anybody that purposed anything wrong should be subjected to the awkward circumstance that anybody could talk about it.'[1] Gilbert Murray wrote in 1921: 'The League's true weapon is not force but publicity.'[2] More recently President Johnson said at the twentieth anniversary celebration of the United Nations in 1965 at San Francisco: 'By persuading nations to justify their own conduct before all countries, it [the UN] has helped, at many times and in many places, to soften the harshness of man to his fellow men.'[3] Louis Henkin has summed up the UN's present influence in the following words:

> Today a nation can initiate the use of force only with full awareness that it will have to answer in this world forum, a prospect which few nations

[1] Quoted by M. Zafrulla Khan in *The General Assembly in U.N. and World Affairs*, p. 169.
[2] *The Problem of Foreign Policy*, p. 118.
[3] Quoted in the Letter of Transmittal accompanying the *President's Annual Report to Congress* on *U.S. Participation in the U.N.* for 1964.

can face with equanimity. Even if a proceeding produces nothing more than condemnatory addresses and resolutions and hostile headlines in the world press, the prospect of being accused is a significant cost of violation that all governments take into account.[4]

The Security Council acts as a world forum in three ways. The first is negative in its results and hinders rather than furthers the fulfilment of the Council's main responsibility. The Council provides opportunities for states to present partisan points of view before a world audience, and to make points in a diplomatic dual with another state or in a confrontation between groups of states. Examples of this negative function have been frequent in the Arab–Israel conflict, in the Kashmir dispute between India and Pakistan, and most of all during the height of the Cold War. But they have diminished in frequency and still more in gravity, since relations between the super-powers have improved. Moreover, the climate of opinion in the UN, at least among the more experienced members, has turned increasingly against this misuse of the Council for interstate polemics.

The other two ways are both positive from an international standpoint. The Council, in its second role as a forum, provides a place where a state can express its point of view on a controversial issue with the moderation and carefully prepared arguments which are most likely to impress and influence an international body. It may thus facilitate a fair settlement and reduce the elements of power and chance which too often play a decisive part in interstate disputes. The stronger the case and the better presented it is, the more likelihood that a settlement will be reached. In addition the very act of giving the controversy a public airing at the UN is likely at least to reduce tension and act as a safety-valve for enflamed public opinion. The role of the Security Council as a safety-valve or a decompression chamber deserves wider recognition than it has had.

Thirdly, the Council's most important role as a forum is to provide opportunity for the expression and development of world opinion on international issues and to put in the dock states, even the most powerful states, which infringe accepted international standards. By its successful insistence on cease-fires in Indonesia, the Middle East, Kashmir, and Cyprus, it has contributed to the renunciation of war in practice, as well as in theory. It has contributed also to the widespread acceptance of the anticolonial principle and to the condemnation of racial discrimination. Furthermore, it has encouraged representatives of states to think of their national problems with a much greater consciousness

[4] *How Nations Behave*, p. 156.

of the world background and the wider interests of humanity as a whole. In more particular terms, the Council action has at times exercised an immediate or long-term influence on individual states, which have pursued their national interests without regard for the principles of the Charter. Among states put in the dock have been Britain and France at the time of Suez and the two super-powers during their interventions in Eastern Europe and Latin America.

In exercising its influence in these ways the Security Council has no monopoly. The General Assembly plays a somewhat similar role. But of the two bodies the Council is more important as a forum. Its special responsibility for peace and security and its mandatory powers under Chapter VII, though rarely used, give it greater weight. Its membership includes the two super-powers, Communist China, and always several of the most powerful and influential states after this trio. Moreover, there is an element of uncertainty and the unexpected about its meetings. It can be called urgently at a time of crisis, whereas the Assembly's annual sessions last for months and tend to be taken for granted. Television has greatly increased the UN's impact on the general public, especially in the United States, and the Council's TV coverage is, on the whole, more pointed and dramatic than that given to the Assembly. During the Korean, Suez, and Cuban crises its meetings were watched by millions of people throughout the world.

In two of the earliest cases which the Council considered its influence was exerted more through the force of international opinion expressed at its meetings than through resolutions. On the Iranian question the two resolutions it adopted were deliberately restrained, one requesting a report on the results of the negotiations, and the other deferring further Council proceedings on the matter until the date announced for the completion of the Soviet withdrawal. The Council's contribution to the settlement was made, therefore, through the publicity it gave to the Iranian complaint and through the support Iran received in consequence from UN members. In the case of Syria and Lebanon the Council's two draft resolutions were both defeated, one by a majority and the other by a veto, but Britain and France responded voluntarily to the views of most members of the Council.

The Council's handling of the Indonesian problem was not primarily an example of its function as a forum. It passed a series of strong resolutions and set up three subsidiary organs with the purpose of ending hostilities and bringing about a settlement. But the pressure of international opinion also played a part in achieving a relatively speedy solution. Portugal, a less powerful country than the Netherlands and without their long democratic traditions, has for years resisted sustained UN pressure without relinquishing its African colonies. The Dutch government and people considered that they were unfairly treated at the UN over Indonesia, but they were nevertheless sensitive about their country's reputation in the world, and, in Alastair Taylor's words, 'it came as a heavy blow to Dutch pride . . . to be treated—in their eyes at least—at the Security Council like a prisoner in the dock'.[5] This sensitivity contributed to the final settlement.

Before a number of cases are considered in which the Council's role as a forum has been of considerable significance, two instances may be mentioned for the sake of balance in which it had virtually no influence. In the Kashmir dispute the attitudes of India and Pakistan were so charged with emotion and their conflicting views so strongly held that both parties were largely impervious to international opinion and scarcely responsive at all to the most earnest attempts at conciliation. The United Nations in general and the Security Council in particular were the objects of harsh criticism from both sides. India complained frequently that she was the victim of power politics, especially on the part of 'the Atlantic powers', and Pakistan considered that her just cause was not receiving the support it deserved. A study of the daily and periodic press of the two countries reveals not only that the strong lines taken by their two governments were widely supported by public opinion but that such criticisms as were expressed almost all took the form of favouring still stronger policies. In the Arab-Israel conflict a similar obsession with the rightness of their own causes and a similar insensitivity to world opinion have on the whole been shown by both parties.

In contrast to these two cases the British reaction to the Suez crisis was a striking example of the influence that could be exerted both by the Security Council and the General Assembly as channels for the expression of world opinion. On the whole, the policy of Eden's government was supported in parliament by the Conservatives and opposed by the Labour and Liberal parties. But in the country as a whole the division of opinion cut across party lines. Many members of the working class, who usually voted Labour, supported Eden's policy, while a considerable number of Conservatives, who believed in the United Nations and international cooperation, were deeply disturbed by the government's action. They, together with likeminded members of the Labour and Liberal parties, were particularly shocked by the British veto in October 1956 of the two draft resolutions submitted to

[5] *Indonesian Independence and the United Nations*, pp. 303–4.

the Security Council, calling for a cease-fire and the withdrawal of forces, and by the subsequent adoption by the General Assembly, with an overwhelming majority, of a similar resolution directed against the intervention of British and French forces in Egypt.

A small but influential group of Conservative members of parliament were actually opposed to the government's policy, though not all of them made a public issue of it; while Anthony Nutting, Minister of State in the Foreign Office, has pointed out that a small group of senior Foreign Office officials were deeply troubled by the government's policy and seriously thought of resigning.[6] A member of the foreign affairs department in the Conservative party organization resigned at this time and gave his reasons in a letter to the press as follows: 'I resigned on principle. As a nation we had broken our pledge to the UN—the most sacred pledge of a modern state . . . Today our moral position is hopelessly compromised.'[7]

The public adverse reaction to Eden's Suez policy was due more to Britain's arraignment at the United Nations, which could be watched on television, and to the disapproval of members of the Commonwealth than to Soviet threats,[8] or to United States' financial pressure, which was too involved a subject for the average citizen to understand. The strength of the reaction, both public and official, was a main reason for the government's change of policy and contributed to Eden's resignation two months later. Britain's vetoes and defiance of UN opinion resulted finally in the resignation of Nutting and Sir Edward Boyle, two of the ablest and most promising younger members of the government, and aroused serious misgivings in the minds of more senior ministers, including the Foreign Secretary. The Suez crisis was an episode which no future British government could wisely ignore.[9]

The Congo crisis combined features of the Kashmir and Suez examples and was in some ways comparable to the Indonesian case. On the one hand, the Belgian people felt very strongly about their former colony, which they had relinquished so recently, and their government's intervention, when the lives of many Belgians was at stake, had more justification than the British and French action against Egypt. The great majority of Belgians, therefore, supported unhesitatingly their

[6] See his *No End of a Lesson*, p. 138.

[7] Tom Houston in a letter to the *Daily Herald*, 13 Nov. 1956.

[8] At the height of the Suez crisis the Soviet Union sent threatening notes to Britain, France, and Israel, which referred to Soviet atomic power and to the possibility of sending Russian 'volunteers' to help Egypt.

[9] I owe to Mr Richard Coldwell the research for this section on British opinion during the Suez crisis, and to Mr Richard Stanton and Monsieur J. G. Rozenberg that for the following section on Belgian opinion during the Congo crisis.

country's policy in the Congo and regarded the actions of the Security Council and the attitude of most UN members as unfair and ill-informed. On the other hand a small minority, who could be described as their country's intellectual and political *élite* and included influential politicians, had a rather different point of view. They were conscious and proud of Belgium's democratic traditions, aware that a small industrialized country was dependent on its good relations with other countries, and sensitive to the importance of Belgium's membership of such international organizations as the European Common Market, NATO, and the UN.

The Belgian government's handling of the Congo crisis falls naturally into three phases: first, July–August 1960, from the beginning of UN involvement until Brussels had had time to react to the first three Security Council resolutions; secondly, from September 1960 to April 1961, when the Liberal-Social Christian administration of Eyskens and Wigny gave way to the Social Christian-Socialist coalition of Lefèvre and Spaak; and finally, from April 1961 onwards, when Spaak, as foreign minister, was the dominant figure. From the point of view of the Council's role as a forum the first of these phases was the most important.

Belgium, as opposed to Britain during the Suez crisis, had no power of veto. So the Council, during the first phase, passed three resolutions between 14 July and 9 August, by which it called upon Belgium to withdraw its troops, in the first two, from the Congo, and, in the third, from the province of Katanga. But, as has been seen, Portugal and Rhodesia had both defied resolutions of the Council successfully, and Belgium's acquiescence in that body's requirements on this occasion was due partly to the pressure of international opinion expressed during the Council's meeting. The three resolutions were passed with no dissenting votes and only few abstentions, while the attitude of the UN membership, as a whole, was convincingly revealed in September, when an Assembly resolution approving the Council's action was passed also without dissent (see p. 197).

The Belgian government reacted appropriately to this impressive display of opinion. The foreign minister, M. Wigny, had given his support to the despatch of UN military assistance to the Congo on 12 July, the day the Congolese government asked for it and before the relevant Council resolution was passed,[10] and was thus able to say

[10] See his statement before the Belgian parliament on 17 August: Annales Parlementaires: Chambre des Représentants: Session 1959–60, vol. 11, 17 August 1960.

later that the UN intervened at the request of Belgium as well as of the Congo.[11] There were indications also that the Belgian government came to realize that it ought to have sent its troops in with international approval, instead of acting unilaterally, and Wigny pointed out repeatedly the need for Belgium to cooperate with the UN, whose force, he said, was to take over the Belgian troops' duty of protecting lives. Belgium's most significant concession to international opinion was the difficult decision to withdraw their troops from Katanga, to which they had been invited by Tshombe himself.

During the second phase, which lasted until the spring of 1961, the official Belgian attitude hardened considerably, due to differences of opinion with ONUC over Katanga and over the role played by the Belgian experts and technicians who had been invited to the Congo by the Leopoldville government. Such influence as was exerted on Belgium by world opinion, channelled via the UN, found expression mainly through the Socialist opposition, which criticized the government from time to time for its equivocal policy in Katanga and its failure to appreciate ONUC's achievements. During the third phase Spaak's respect for the UN as an institution, his desire to work with it, and to lead Belgium out of its diplomatic isolation, made any additional international influence unnecessary. On taking office he announced that Belgium recognized the Leopoldville government as the sole legal government in the Congo and did not recognize Katanga's secession. Together with the US State Department he even helped to draw up the Thant Plan for National Reconciliation which led to the final solution.[12]

As regards the Council's role as a forum, the examples of Soviet intervention in Eastern Europe and United States' intervention in Latin America are of special interest and importance, because in the case of the super-powers international opinion is virtually the only sanction that can be brought to bear. Its influence as a forum has never been decisive in the short term and in the long run its effects are difficult to assess, but over the years evidence has accumulated that they are far from negligible.

Soviet interventions in Eastern Europe were brought before the Council on three occasions, twice in relation to Czechoslovakia in 1948 and 1968, and once in the case of Hungary in 1956. In 1948 there was no military intervention, but a skilfully engineered Communist political *coup*, in which control over the police and the left-wing social democrats played the decisive part. As the Communist party was already

[11] Interview with *Le Soir*, 27 July 1960.
[12] P. H. Spaak: *Combats Inachevés*, vol. II, 243 and 256–57.

the largest in the country and President Beneš remained in office the whole time, the Czech government did not appeal to the Council, but a complaint was made about the Soviet threat to Czechoslovakia by Jan Papanek, the Czech representative to the UN, who broke with his government at the time, and it was later followed up by the representative of Chile.

The Chilean representative submitted a draft resolution which provided for the appointment of a subcommittee to study the situation in Czechoslovakia. The Soviet representative voted against the Council's decision on the draft being considered a matter of procedure, and his 'double veto' was upheld by the President. So he then proceeded to veto the draft itself, and the Council was powerless to take any effective action. However, the Soviet government, through its agents, had been carrying out a series of political manoeuvres in East European countries with the object of establishing Communist control, and the Council's debates on Czechoslovakia, which were spread over ten meetings between 17 March and 26 May, provided the first major opportunity for public international protests against Soviet methods. In the two votes on the establishment of a subcommittee the only dissenting voices had been Communist, those of the Soviet Union and the Ukrainian SSR.

In Hungary Soviet military forces intervened twice between 22 October and 3 November 1956, in order to put down a reformist movement which aimed at liberalizing the Communist regime. On 27 October, Britain, France, and the United States requested a meeting of the Security Council to consider the situation in Hungary, where 'foreign military forces' were 'violently repressing the rights of the Hungarian people'. The following day Hungary protested against the Council's considering the Hungarian situation, and was strongly supported by the Soviet Union. But on 2 November Imre Nagy, the new and more liberal Marxist prime minister, having temporarily established his authority over the government, appealed himself to the United Nations. He pointed out that large Soviet military units had crossed the Hungarian border, and requested the Secretary-General, first to call on the Great Powers to recognize the neutrality of Hungary, and secondly to ask the Security Council to instruct the Soviet and Hungarian governments to start negotiations immediately.

The Council considered the Hungarian question at four meetings between 28 October and 4 November. The United States submitted a draft resolution calling on the Soviet Union to desist forthwith from any form of intervention, particularly armed intervention, in the internal affairs of Hungary and to withdraw all its forces from Hungarian territory. At the last meeting on 4 November this draft was approved by nine votes but vetoed by the Soviet Union, Yugoslavia not participating in the voting.

This was not the end of UN action on the matter. On 4 November the Council also passed a resolution by ten votes to one (Soviet Union), invoking the 'Uniting for Peace' resolution and calling a special emergency session of the General Assembly to consider the situation in Hungary. The Assembly met the same day and passed a resolution condemning the action of the Soviet Union and calling on it to withdraw its forces without delay. The voting was fifty votes in favour to eight against (the Soviet bloc) with fifteen abstentions. In this case, therefore, the two main UN organs shared the forum role. The Assembly continued its emergency session until 10 November and passed further resolutions, calling for amongst other things the withdrawal of Soviet forces, free elections in Hungary, the admission of UN observers, and the halting of deportations to the Soviet Union. In January 1957 it set up a Special Committee on the Problem of Hungary which produced an impressive report the following June. This found that the Nagy government had been overthrown by force and that the Hungarians under Nagy had shown clearly, so long as they were free to, their desire for genuine independence.[13] The Assembly approved the report and then appointed a special representative on Hungary,[14] who in turn submitted a series of reports, while the Assembly itself discussed the Hungarian question every year until 1962 and deplored repeatedly the Hungarian and Soviet disregard of its decisions. The Soviet intervention was thus given maximum publicity on an international level.

The UN's handling of the Hungarian question, which started in the Security Council, while failing in its main purpose owing to the Soviet veto and Soviet power, had nevertheless a considerable effect both on Moscow and on the situation in Hungary. The Soviet Union under Stalin's successors was not altogether insensitive to world opinion, and was no doubt concerned by the fact that fifteen Afro-Asian states had approved the first Assembly resolution condemning Soviet action, while none had opposed it, at a time when Moscow was doing its utmost to win their support. This at least partly explains why the regime of Janos Kadar, who was installed by the Soviet Union as Hungarian prime minister after Nagy, pursued a much more moderate

---

[13] *Report of the Special Committee on Hungary*, paras. 366–68, UN, New York, 1957.
[14] The office was held successively by Prince Wan of Thailand, 1957–58, and Sir Leslie Munro of New Zealand, 1958–62.

policy than had been expected of it in 1956, and within a few years had become one of the most liberal in Eastern Europe.

The Soviet intervention in Czechoslovakia in 1968 was in one important respect more significant that the Hungarian case. The Dubcek regime, which the Soviet Union and its associates decided to overthrow, had been trying since the beginning of the year with a good deal of success to liberalize Czech Communism, to give 'socialism' in their country 'a human face'. It did not withdraw from the Warsaw Pact or defy the Soviet Union diplomatically, as Nagy, with Soviet troops on his doorstep, had unwisely decided to do, when he appealed to the United Nations and declared Hungary neutral. On the contrary, Dubček and most of his colleagues made every effort to keep on good terms with the Soviet Union, while developing their own version of Marxism at home, which was not very different from Gomulka's version in Poland in the autumn of 1956. The intervention therefore meant that the Soviet government claimed the right to decide the acceptable limit of socialist deviation amongst members of the Warsaw Pact, a claim which was later to be formulated in the Brezhnev doctrine.

On the night of 20–21 August, troops of the Soviet Union and four other Warsaw Pact countries invaded Czechoslovakia, and Dubček and other Czech political leaders were arrested. The following day six UN members requested an urgent meeting of the Security Council to consider the serious situation in Czechoslovakia. In face of strong Soviet opposition the item was accepted for the agenda, and the Council considered the question at five meetings between 21 and 24 August. The debates, on the whole, were of a high level, with members showing deep consciousness of the importance of the issue, although the Soviet Union and some of its allies filibustered to gain time. The Soviet representative at first maintained that the troops had entered Czechoslovakia at the Czech government's request but later stated that the appeal had come from 'a group of members' of the Czech Communist party, government, and National Assembly. The Czech representative, who had been invited to participate, denied the Soviet version, described the occupation as illegal, and made a moving speech on his country's behalf, which was all the more impressive for being calmly and factually expressed. A draft resolution, sponsored by eight states, condemning the intervention and calling on the invaders to withdraw their forces forthwith, was vetoed by the Soviet Union on 23 August.

The Council then concerned itself with the safety of the arrested Czech leaders, some of whom were known to be in Moscow. The same eight states submitted a second draft resolution, which asked the Secretary-General to send a special representative to Prague to seek the release and ensure the personal safety of the Czech leaders. It was not pressed to a vote, though the Council debates may well have helped to bring about the release of the leaders. On 24 August the Czech foreign minister addressed the Council, demanding the withdrawal of the foreign troops but expressing the hope that the negotiations going on in Moscow might lead to a solution. At his request the Council's consideration of the question was suspended and, following an agreement in Moscow, it was not resumed, though the matter remained on the list of matters of which the Council was seized.

The Moscow agreement was based on insincerity and not honoured by the Soviet Union.[15] The Dubček government was gradually replaced and Soviet power prevailed. But the armed intervention in Czechoslovakia has permanently damaged the Soviet image in the world, and the international publicity given to it in the Security Council contributed substantially to this result. During the debates the natural comparison was made between Hitler's treatment of Czechoslovakia in 1938–39 and the Soviet treatment in 1968. After Communist China joined the Council in the autumn of 1971 its representative referred more than once to the Soviet intervention. On 5 December 1971 he said: 'The Soviet social imperialists are carrying out aggression, control, subversion and expansion everywhere. Everyone will recall the Soviet military aggression and armed occupation of Czechoslovakia in 1968.' And no Soviet action better justified the Chinese description of them as 'social imperialists' than the invasion of Czechoslovakia in 1968.

The Soviet invasions of Hungary and Czechoslovakia in 1956 and 1968 were larger in scale and more overt in execution than the United States' interventions in Guatemala and the Dominican Republic. Nevertheless a valid parallel may be drawn between the two pairs of cases, even as regards the deliberate misrepresentation indulged in by the two super-powers (see pp. 230–1 and 236–9). The legacy of Europe's past persists, and the world as a whole is more interested in what happens in Central Europe than in the fate of small Central American and Caribbean states. Yet United States' policy towards Latin America has international significance in an age when mankind is trying to evolve universal standards in interstate relations.

The Security Council's handling of the cases of Guatemala and the Dominican Republic did not have much influence on United States'

---

[15] The text can be found in *The Czechoslovak Crisis 1968*, Appendix 4, edited by Robert Rhodes James.

opinion, for three reasons. First, American journalists in both cases sent reports back to the American press at once, and the Council's later discussions therefore had little news value. Secondly, both interventions occurred before 1966, when US influence in the Council was still dominant and that body's role in both cases was correspondingly limited; for example, Lodge was able to prevent the substance of Guatemala's second appeal from being considered at all. Thirdly, the Monroe doctrine tradition caused the Council's role to be resented. A liberal-minded élite in American political and academic circles did however feel a good deal of concern about their country's record in both cases, and the Council's airing of the disputes no doubt contributed to their concern, though only to a limited extent.

Yet outside the United States the Council's consideration of the items drew international attention to questions which would otherwise have remained local in character, aroused misgivings in the allies of the United States, and gave the Soviet Union grounds for strong criticism of American policy. On 14 July 1954, in the British House of Commons, Clement Attlee, leader of the opposition, said with regard to Guatemala:

> The fact is that this was a plain act of aggression, and one cannot take one line on aggression in Asia and another line in Central America. I confess that I was rather shocked at the joy and approval of the American Secretary of State on the success of this *putsch* . . . it seems in some instances that the acceptance of the principles of the UN is subordinated to a hatred of communism.[16]

It is unlikely that the Guatemalan question would have been mentioned in the House of Commons had it not come before the Security Council. The case of the Dominican Republic had wider international repercussions, because sending 22,000 troops into a foreign country is a more serious matter than covertly fomenting a civil war. Although the Council's role had limited influence on opinion in the United States, it had a considerable impact on Latin America and on informed circles throughout the world and thus played a part in making Washington reconsider its Dominican policy. The whole affair was a considerable setback to the prestige of the United States, especially in the Western hemisphere.

The Council's role as a forum was a feature in its handling of a number of relatively minor questions including some of the alleged acts of aggression dealt with at the end of the last chapter. It then acted either as a safety valve for reducing tension and assuaging public opinion

---

[16] Quoted by Philip B. Taylor, Jr., in 'The Guatemalan affair: a critique of US Foreign Policy', *American Political Science Review*, September 1956.

or as a channel for the expression of international opinion. In one such instance its function was confined entirely to its roles as a forum and a rendezvous, because the East–West element in the case and the possible use of the veto precluded any effective action.

On 23 January 1968 a small American naval vessel, the USS *Pueblo*, was seized by armed North Korean vessels and forcibly detained with its crew in a North Korean port. American public opinion was naturally incensed by this action, and on 25 January the United States requested an urgent meeting of the Security Council to consider the grave threat to the peace brought about by a series of increasingly dangerous and aggressive actions by North Korean authorities, including the seizure of the *Pueblo*. In spite of Soviet opposition the Council considered the question at two meetings on 26 and 27 January.

Charges and countercharges were exchanged between the American and the Soviet representatives, Ambassador Goldberg pointing out on behalf of the United States that the seizure had taken place in international waters and that Soviet intelligence ships frequently operated close to the shores of other states. But a suggestion by Ethiopia that the Council should carry out an investigation was not taken up, and no draft resolution was submitted to the Council. It was realized that North Korea, after the UN intervention in 1950, would be particularly sensitive to any action by the UN, and that any proposals to condemn North Korea would be vetoed by the Soviet Union. Washington also was aware that any attempt to recover the *Pueblo* and its crew by force might have the most serious consequences.

A Canadian suggestion, however, was adopted. This was that private consultations might be more fruitful than public debates. North Korea turned down a proposal for UN mediation through five Asian and African states but agreed to the problem being discussed by the armistice Commission at Panmunjom, which had been set up at the end of the Korean War. The following December the crew of the *Pueblo* were released. Thus the Security Council did not itself settle the dispute, but it reduced the tension, acted as a safety-valve for American public opinion, and set in train negotiations through which a settlement was reached.

The Council has served as a rendezvous for national representatives in a variety of ways. One of the purposes of the United Nations, as laid down in Article 1 of the Charter, is to be a centre for harmonizing the actions of nations. It has contributed to the fulfilment of this purpose by providing a meeting-place where diplomatists and statesmen can get to know one another in a way that had never previously been possible, except in a more restricted sense at Geneva during the lifetime of the League. This function of the UN has been facilitated by the provision of Article 28 that the Security Council should be so organized as to be able to function continuously, which has made it essential that all permanent members of the Council should have permanent missions in New York. In fact, with the exception of one or two very small states,[17] all UN members have established such missions, in order to have qualified personnel available to attend meetings of the UN's many subsidiary organs and committees, and to provide for the possibility of their being elected to the Security Council.

The General Assembly and the Security Council both participate in the role of a rendezvous, as to a less extent do all the UN's principal and subsidiary organs. The meetings of the General Assembly are usually attended by a number of heads of state and by a majority of the foreign ministers of member states and provide many opportunities for private and semiformal discussions. Dean Rusk has stated that during the autumn of 1963, as Secretary of State, he conferred during the Assembly meeting, in a period of eleven days, with the foreign ministers or heads of government of fifty-four nations.[18] The Security Council's role as a rendezvous is more concentrated, more continuous, and therefore more fruitful. Within its framework diplomatists can get to know and understand one another to an extent which comes closer to the fellowship that can be attained by members of a cabinet or a committee than to the more diluted association between members of a parliament or a large conference, although the sense of common purpose in the Council is still limited and uneven. In general, UN headquarters provides opportunities for quiet and informal diplomacy, which are already very useful and potentially of great value. As Dag Hammarskjöld once said:

> Over the years the diplomatic representatives accredited to the UN have developed a co-operation and built mutual contacts in dealing with the problems they have in common, which in reality make them members of a kind of continuous diplomatic conference, in which they are informally following and able to discuss, on a personal basis, all political questions which are important for the work of the Organization.[19]

The UN's role as a rendezvous is of special significance in the case of the smaller member states. Most of these states cannot afford to maintain embassies or legations in more than a few, perhaps a dozen,

---

[17] For example, Gambia and the Maldives.
[18] See his Dag Hamarskjöld memorial lecture at Columbia University on 10 Jan. 1964, published in Cordier and Foote, *op. cit.*
[19] Address to both Houses of Parliament, London, April 1958.

countries with which their relations are particularly important. For them the UN has become the diplomatic capital of the world or, as Dean Rusk said of the General Assembly, the 'greatest switchboard for bilateral diplomacy'.[20] Their missions in New York have many duties besides representation in the UN, and for this reason their staffs are often larger than would otherwise be expected. In fact the term rendezvous, with its implication of fulfilling a special purpose, is not quite appropriate for this particular service performed by UN headquarters for the small states. For them the UN is rather a permanent and vitally important centre for maintaining international contacts with countries with which they have not exchanged ambassadors or ministers. It is the UN as a whole rather than the Security Council in particular which fulfils this function, though it is also true that the smaller states which are elected to the Council tend to develop a special interest in international problems and have, through their contacts in the Council, special opportunities for cultivating it.

The meeting-place role is also particularly useful in facilitating contacts between states in cases where relations are either severely strained or have been formally suspended. When diplomatic relations between two states have been broken off, some contact is usually maintained through the embassies of friendly countries, but this attenuated official relationship can now be supplemented by informal talks between representatives of the states in New York. This is what happened after diplomatic relations had been broken between the United States and the UAR in 1967 during the Six-Day War. In the case of the much worse relations between Israel and the Arab states, between whom no peace has been made since 1948 and direct negotiations have been impossible even on an informal basis, some form of communication has taken place through the mediation of third parties at the UN. Most important of all, the UN is the natural centre for conciliation between the Communist and non-Communist worlds with representatives of each working side by side in many UN bodies, and it has on a number of occasions proved its value as such a centre.

The best-known and most productive occasion was in February 1949 during the Soviet blockade of Berlin. The previous October the Berlin situation had come before the Security Council, but the Soviet Union had questioned the Council's competence in the matter, refused to take part in the discussion, and finally vetoed a conciliatory draft resolution sponsored by the six relatively non-engaged members. The main result of the Council's handling of the question was to bring home its gravity

[20] *Op. cit.*

to UN members. By February there were some signs that Stalin might have become slightly less intransigent, and Dr Philip Jessup, the Deputy US Representative to the UN, was told by Washington to seek a casual talk with Mr Malik, the Deputy Soviet Representative, and inquire about Stalin's intention on an apparently small point.[21] The talk took place in the delegates' lounge during a Security Council session. Jessup had to wait a month for an answer. But the contact led to further informal conversations, and early in May an agreement was reached under which the blockade was lifted. This result was of the greatest importance. The dispute had hitherto been very stubborn and without the opportunity for an informal conversation provided by the Council session it is difficult to envisage how negotiations could have been started so soon as they were.

There were other occasions when the UN acted as a contact point with useful results, though the Security Council did not always play the main part. During the Korean War, for example, Soviet and United States diplomatists could meet at the UN, and on one occasion Andrew Cordier of the Secretariat brought Dean Rusk and Malik together at his house in New York. Also the Council considered the Cuban missile crisis at an early stage, and the UN then proved the place where Soviet and US negotiators were most easily able to meet. The super-powers' common membership of the Council again greatly facilitated their cooperation on the non-proliferation treaty of 1968. While, after the Six-Day War, President Johnson took advantage of Kosygin's presence at the emergency session of the Assembly to invite him to a meeting in New Jersey, which in the circumstances could hardly have been arranged had Kosygin not been at the UN.

Finally, after the *Pueblo* incident, the Security Council acted as a valuable rendezvous as well as a forum. Relations between the two sides in the dispute were so tense that, without contacts through the UN, negotiations would have been very difficult to initiate. As it was, George Ignatiev, the Canadian representative on the Council, found out that his Hungarian colleague, Csatorday, was representing the interests of North Korea and that the captured crew of the *Pueblo* were all alive. This led to a meeting between Csatorday and Goldberg, the United States representative, and to the beginning of the ultimately successful negotiations in the armistice commission at Panmunjom.

---

[21] The point, which had important implications, was whether Stalin's omission to mention the Berlin currency issue in a recent interview with a journalist was intentional.

7
Problems of peace-keeping

Several of the plans put forward during the seventeenth and eighteenth centuries for a better ordering of Europe included the creation of an international army or at least military collaboration in the common cause by European states. In 1910, stimulated by Theodore Roosevelt, the United States Congress unanimously approved a joint resolution proposing, among other things, that the combined navies of the world should constitute 'an international force for the preservation of peace' and requested President Taft to sound out the European powers on the subject. The European reaction was mixed, and by the outbreak of war in 1914 the commission suggested by Congress to look into the matter had not yet been appointed by the President. Article 16 of the League of Nations' Covenant provided for the use of armed forces against covenant-breaking states, though the provision was never implemented (see Chapter 2, esp. p. 35).

An international force was actually used or at least organized on a number of occasions before 1945 to prevent minor disputes from developing into more serious conflicts. From 1897 to 1909 a force was stationed in Crete by the European powers most interested in the Eastern Question, in order to ensure the island's autonomy and to prevent its union with Greece. In 1920, when a plebiscite was proposed in Vilna, the League of Nations planned that it should be supervised by a force provided by nine countries not immediately concerned with the dispute, and the preparations reached an advanced stage, though the plebiscite was cancelled, and the force never went to Vilna. The Saar plebiscite in 1935 was the occasion for the most important of the early examples of international peace-keeping. A force of 3,300 troops, made up of contingents from Britain, Italy, the Netherlands, and Sweden, was stationed in the territory and, despite a delicate diplomatic situation between Germany and France, voting was carried out in a fair and orderly manner. In 1933 and 1934 also, during the last stage of the

I*

dispute between Peru and Colombia over Leticia, the disputed territory was administered by a League Commission with the help of a small force which, though composed only of Colombian troops, was under the Commission's command and was regarded as an international body.

The UN Charter envisaged the organization of armed forces under international control for the purpose of maintaining international peace and security. But, as the Security Council never fulfilled its intended role under Article 43, the UN's peace-keeping forces had to be improvised within the framework of certain agreed principles, in accordance with the requirements of each international crisis as it occurred. The first improvisations were the observer groups which were formed in Indonesia, the Balkans, the Middle East, and Kashmir between 1947 and 1949 (see pp. 126, 130, 136, and 172–3). They were only peace-keeping forces in an embryonic form: they were not known as peace-keeping forces; their duties were only to observe and report; and, apart from the group in Indonesia, they were not even armed. The first real UN force with a peace-keeping purpose did not come into existence until UNEF was set up in 1956.[1]

By September 1948 it had become clear that the Security Council could not agree on how to carry out its duties under Article 43, and the Military Staff Committee had announced that it could make no further progress until the Council came to some agreement in principle. It was clear also that the UN's missions and observer groups in different countries had been performing useful service, and the assassination of Count Bernadotte in that month brought home the need for giving these bodies some protection. Moreover, the Council's duty to negotiate agreements governing the UN's peace-keeping forces under Article 43 (3) was mandatory and not dependent on agreed recommendations from the Military Staff Committee.[2] It was therefore arguable that, if the duty could not be fulfilled on the lines suggested in the Charter, some other solution of the basic problem should be found.

Moved by these considerations, the Secretary-General, Trygve Lie, made alternative proposals 'for further strengthening of the United Nations' in his annual report to the General Assembly for 1947–48, and submitted a detailed report to the Assembly on 28 September 1948 on the need for a United Nations guard force. He proposed the creation of a small UN guard force of 1,000 to 5,000 men which would be recruited by the Secretary-General and placed at the disposal of the Security

---

[1] The UN forces in Korea were, as has been seen, a special case and were not under UN command.

[2] See Bentwich and Martin, pp. 98–99.

Council and the General Assembly. He emphasized that it would be no substitute for the forces envisaged in Articles 42 and 43 of the Charter, that it should consist at first of a nucleus of 800 men, and that its equipment would be limited to personal defence weapons. It would not be used to resist an aggressor but would be a peace-keeping force, which could be employed for such duties as supervising plebiscites, patrolling cease-fire zones, and protecting the property and personnel of UN missions.

The report was referred to the General Assembly, to its *Ad hoc* Political Committee, and, at the Secretary-General's suggestion, to a special committee of fourteen created to consider it. The plan met with a good deal of opposition on grounds of cost and difficulty of organization, and because it was to be internationally recruited. The Soviet bloc, in particular, objected to any force which would not be controlled by the Security Council. Before the report was considered by the special committee in June 1949 the Secretary-General had revised it radically.

His new proposal was for the establishment of two units, a UN Field Service and a Field Reserve Panel, later to be renamed the UN Panel of Field Observers. The Field Service was to consist of a maximum of 300 men, who were to ensure the security of UN field missions and provide them with technical and administrative support. It was to comprise security guards, vehicle mechanics, radio operators and technicians, and male secretaries. They were to be recruited either directly by the Secretary-General or through secondment from member governments. They would be part of the Secretariat, and the cost of the Service would be borne by the UN budget. As the functions to be performed were already being carried out by the Secretariat staff, the Field Service was officially described as amounting to 'a systematization of the regular functions of the Secretariat'. The Panel of Field Observers was to consist of the names of up to 2,000 men in the national service of governments, who could, when required, assist UN missions in the functions of observation and supervision. The Panel, in fact, has hardly been utilized.

In November 1949, in face of Soviet opposition, the establishment of both units was approved by the General Assembly. UN members showed little enthusiasm for what they were doing, and the Field Service, in the light of its subsequent record, deserved a better send-off. The Service has provided technical and administrative personnel for most of the UN's peace-keeping operations. When UNEF was set up under emergency conditions in 1956, the Field Service, among other contributions, provided its commander with a chief administrative officer and a complete staff. More than three-quarters of the personnel have permanent appointments. So, when the Service helped in the creation of later peace-keeping forces, for example in the Congo, their experience and expertise were of great value. In the spring of 1972 the total strength was nearly 340, of whom 85 were security officers and 120 communications experts. The largest contingent of 200 was with UNTSO in the Middle East; 31 were with UNMOGIP on the Indo-Pakistani border; 25 with UNFICYP in Cyprus; and 35 with the UN Relief Organization in Bangladesh. The rest were serving in smaller groups with various UN missions, organizations, radio stations, and depots.

Trygve Lie's initiative in 1948 has not been fully appreciated. The contribution of the Field Service to the UN's work has been valuable and essential, though on a limited scale, while the early proposal for a Guard Force was an idea which had influence on the development of the UN's later peace-keeping role.

The 'Uniting for Peace' resolution, which was passed by the General Assembly in November 1950, recommended amongst other things that each UN member should 'maintain within its national forces elements so trained, organized and equipped that they could be promptly made available . . . for service as a UN unit or units, upon recommendation by the Security Council or the General Assembly'. It also set up a Collective Measures Committee to study and report on measures which could be used collectively to maintain and strengthen international peace and security. The following spring the Committee asked all UN members what they intended to do to implement the recommendation to earmark forces. Of the sixty UN members at that time only four, Denmark, Greece, Norway and Thailand, made relatively unconditional offers of national contingents, amounting to a total of 6,000 men, while Uruguay offered two destroyers to act as escorts. Even the United States, which sponsored the resolution, gave a cautious and evasive reply, referring to its existing commitments in Korea and NATO.

Little progress had, in fact, been made in the organization of standby forces, when in 1956 the first serious emergency arose, which called for the creation of a peace-keeping force. UNEF, as has been seen, was followed by other peace-keeping forces, each of which had to be improvised as the need arose. The UN's main peace-keeping problems, therefore, centred at first round the assembly, control, and administration of improvised forces rather than round the organization in advance of permanent forces adequate to cope with any emergencies that might arise.

The unusual circumstances in which UNEF was created were due to the Suez crisis being referred, following the British and French vetoes, to an emergency session of the General Assembly. The UN's first major peace-keeping force, therefore, was brought into existence on the authority of the Assembly. The two subsequent forces of comparable size and importance, in the Congo and Cyprus, were both created by resolutions of the Security Council. The General Assembly set the example, in the case of UNEF, of asking the Secretary-General to draw up a plan for the establishment of the force and of authorizing him to issue all regulations and instructions which might be essential to its effective functioning and to take all other necessary administrative action. The Security Council also, in the Congo and Cyprus, made the Secretary-General responsible for making the peace-keeping forces operational and for conducting the resulting operations.

The Assembly resolution, which set up UNEF, debarred from membership of the force the nationals of states that were permanent members of the Council.[3] This principle was adhered to in the Congo force, although, for the sake of convenience, it was not followed in the case of Britain's membership of UNFICYP, because the British had already been carrying out peace-keeping duties in Cyprus with the government's approval and were well acquanted with conditions in the island. Some permanent members also, particularly the United States, gave vital support to the UN's peace-keeping operations by providing aircraft and other forms of transport to convey troops and supplies to the troubled areas. But most of the military contingents came from the middle and smaller powers. In the case of UNEF, there were twenty-four offers of assistance of which ten were accepted, the only two major powers involved being Brazil and India; in the Congo, the majority of military contributions came from African states; while in Cyprus, apart from Britain, Australia, Canada, and New Zealand, all the contributors were small European countries.

The ban on the permanent members minimized the cold war element in the operations. It also had the very considerable advantage of diversifying participation in a vitally important aspect of the UN's activities and thus increasing the sense of international responsibility in the middle and smaller powers that were involved.

The Charter had given the Security Council primary responsibility within the UN for the maintenance of international peace and security. Yet the Council had failed to implement Article 43 and the Assembly

[3] It did so, not explicitly, but by approving the guiding principles proposed in the Secretary-General's report of 6 Nov. 1956, of which this was one.

and Council between them had authorized the Secretary-General to play the key role in the UN's three main peace-keeping operations. It was this contradiction between what the Charter intended and what UN members decided through their organization's two principal organs that gave rise to the UN's main peace-keeping problem and to a stubborn controversy on the subject between the two super-powers as to how peace-keeping by the UN was to be controlled and financed.

Hammarskjöld, with his high conception of his office and his devotion to the UN, exercised to the full the authority he had been given. U Thant, with Hammarsjöld's example before him and with most of Hammarskjöld's advisers and staff to assist him, carried on the tradition, though in his own more subdued style. In the case of UNEF, the General Assembly actually appointed the commander, but the Secretary-General suggested his name. He also decided which offers of contributions should be accepted, and he negotiated with the governments concerned about their contributions; with Egypt about the admission of the force, and with Britain, France, and Israel about the withdrawal of their invading armies. In the case of ONUC, Hammarskjöld himself recommended the creation of the force, the Security Council gave him even wider powers and discretion than he had received in 1956, and he personally appointed the commander. The failure of the Council to give him sufficiently explicit directives also strengthened his authority (see p. 201). In the case of UNFICYP, U Thant was empowered to decide on the size and composition of the force and to appoint its commander, who was to be responsible to him.

As head of the Secretariat the Secretary-General's position was strengthened by having at his disposal a staff, including the Field Service, with a unique and growing experience of observer and peace-keeping operations. The appointment of advisory groups was an added advantage, because they protected him against the accusation of too arbitrary and personal an interpretation of his duties. To help him administer the UNEF operation the General Assembly created an advisory committee made up of the representatives of seven states the majority of which were contributors to the force (see p. 145). In the Congo Hammarskjöld himself proposed and appointed an advisory committee of fifteen, later nineteen, contributor states. In each case the Secretary-General was chairman of the committee.

The Soviet Union protested formally against the power given to the Secretary-General in questions of peace and security on the ground that it contravened the Charter. When UNEF was created in 1956 the United States still had a strong position both in the Assembly and the Council, and the Soviet Union defended jealously the Council's authority, because it was the one body whose decisions on substantive questions it could control through its veto. It did not oppose the Assembly's resolutions setting up UNEF, as Egypt was prepared to accept the force on its territory, but it abstained in the voting, because it considered that only the Council could create an international armed force according to the Charter, and later refused to pay its assessed contributions to the cost. It supported the Council's first three resolutions on the Congo, as a gesture of solidarity with the new African states against Belgium, but subsequently disapproved the conduct of the operation, joined with France in refusing it financial support, and violently attacked Hammarskjöld. In the case of Cyprus, the Soviet Union, like France, voted for the resolution setting up UNFICYP, because the government of Cyprus considered it would be useful and it was only to be sent to the island for three months. But both countries abstained in a separate vote on the paragraph empowering U Thant to determine the size and composition of the force and to appoint its commander. The Soviet Union also insisted that the Security Council should meet and authorize the creation of the UN Observation Mission in Yemen, although Yemen and Saudi Arabia, the two parties concerned, after negotiations with the Secretary-General, had both expressed a desire for the mission and undertaken to defray its cost (see p. 159).[4, 5]

The controversy as to who should control the UN's peace-keeping operations, the Secretary-General and his staff or the Security Council with its divided views and its proved shortcomings in practice, was reflected in the subsidiary problem of the Secretary-General's military advisers and its brief history.

A heavy responsibility was placed on the Secretary-General when UNEF was created. In particular, the duties given him of drawing up within forty-eight hours a plan for establishing the force and of issuing all regulations and instructions essential to its effective functioning required of him and his staff military understanding and experience. In Hammarskjöld's own words:

> In the administration of UNEF at Headquarters, certain special arrangements were made on an *ad hoc* basis to provide expert military guidance.

[4] See also Higgins, i, pp. 613–14.

[5] An exception to the Soviet Union's championship of the Security Council's authority was its approval in September 1963 of the General Assembly resolution providing for a UN observer group and security force in West Irian and giving the Secretary-General considerable powers. The reasons were probably political, as in the case of its support for the Security Council's first resolutions during the Congo crisis: see pp. 131–2 and 199 and Higgins, vol. II, pp. 110–22.

Thus, a Senior Military Adviser and three officer assistants were attached to the Executive Office as consultants. The Military Adviser, and the Under-Secretary representing the Secretary-General on current matters relating to the Force, were assisted by a group of military representatives from the countries providing contingents, sitting as an informal military advisory committee.

These arrangements, he added, proved in the initial stage to be 'of great value organizationally', though once the operation was firmly established they were 'reduced and simplified'.[6]

In the introduction to his Fifteenth Annual Report to the General Assembly, dated 31 August 1960, that is, six weeks after the establishment of ONUC, Hammarskjöld wrote: 'It is . . . a considerable weakness that the Secretariat has not in its ranks a highly qualified military expertise which is able, on a current basis, to maintain a state of preparedness for the kind of situation which the Organization has suddenly had to face'. Hammarskjöld sought to remedy this weakness by appointing as military adviser, Brigadier, later Major-General, Indar Rikhye, an Indian, who remained with the UN for eight years and, with a small group of officers, constituted the Secretary-General's military staff.

The United States, in contrast to the Soviet Union, supported the authority given to the Secretary-General in the peace-keeping field and approved the strengthening of his military staff. Informed opinion within the UN membership was also, on the whole, in favour of more expert advice on peace-keeping being available in the Secretariat. This view was held very strongly by officers and political advisers who had seen at first hand the immense difficulties involved in improvising urgently UNEF and the Congo force. Each operation, it is true, presented special and unforeseen problems, but a group of experts with UN experience would have been best fitted to deal with them.

In spite of these considerations, the Secretary-General's military staff was almost dispensed with in 1968. Major-General Rikhye and all but one of his staff were withdrawn, leaving only a single Finnish officer, whose appointment was terminable at one month's notice and who combined his duties in the Secretary-General's office with another sometimes exacting post.[7] There were three quite different reasons

---

[6] See *Summary Study of the experience derived from the establishment and operation of the Force (UNEF): report of the Secretary-General,* 9 October 1958 (A/3943). Reproduced in full in Higgins, vol. I, 483–521.

[7] Colonel Koho, the officer concerned, was military liaison officer in the Secretary-General's Executive Office and also adviser to Ambassador Jarring, the Secretary-General's special representative in the Middle East.

for this development. In the first place, the Soviet Union opposed both the strengthening of the Secretary-General's peace-keeping authority and the military staff which it required. Secondly, the different attitudes of the super-powers towards the control of peace-keeping made it impossible for a group of military advisers in the Secretariat to be truly international and include Soviet and US personnel and at the same time work towards a common purpose. Lastly, in February 1965 the General Assembly set up a Special Committee on Peace-keeping Operations, which has been considering the problem ever since: it was logical, therefore, to postpone settling the Secretariat aspect of the question, until the Committee had reached some general conclusions.

The Special Committee on Peace-keeping Operations, which came to be known as the Committee of Thirty-Three, was instructed by the Assembly to undertake a comprehensive review of the peace-keeping operations, including ways of overcoming the financial difficulties of the Organization. The reason for the special mention of finance was that the Soviet and French attitudes towards this aspect of peace-keeping had caused the UN great financial embarrassment and led to a deadlock between the Soviet Union and the United States regarding the applicability of Article 19.[8]

Peace-keeping operations were financed in a variety of ways. The Korean action was exceptional in character: it was on so large a scale and was so strongly opposed by the Communist bloc that there could be no question of its being defrayed under the UN's regular budget. Its full cost was therefore borne by the participating states. The military observers in Indonesia also were first paid for by the Dutch government and the participating states and later, when UNCI was established, by the UN on its regular budget. The cost of the observer groups in the Middle East and Kashmir, UNTSO and UNMOGIP, was defrayed by the UN through its regular budget. The financing of UNEF was more complex and on a much larger scale, the UN itself paying about $213 million for it during the ten and a half years of the operation. The basic pay and equipment costs for the national contingents were covered by the participating states, while a UN special account was set up to meet all other expenses. Funds for it were to come from voluntary contributions and assessments on all UN members. These arrangements were approved by the General Assembly, although individual members

[8] The Article provides that a UN Member, 'which is in arrears in the payment of its financial contributions to the Organization shall have no vote in the General Assembly if the amount of its arrears equals or exceeds the amount of the contributions due from it for the preceding two full years'.

made alternative suggestions. The Soviet Union, in particular, maintained that the total cost should be borne by Britain, France, and Israel, the 'aggressors' against Egypt, and refused to make any contributions, voluntary or assessed. The expenses of the Congo force were defrayed on similar lines, and the Soviet Union and France both declined to contribute. In the cases of UNTEA and UNYOM the costs were borne by the parties concerned, that is, Holland and Indonesia, Saudi Arabia and Yemen. The financing of UNFICYP was different again, and was very complex (see pp. 241–2). It avoided some of the difficulties encountered over UNEF and the Congo, but its unsatisfactory and uncertain nature provided an additional reason for seeking a better solution to the problem of how to finance peace-keeping.

The refusal by France and the Soviet Union to make certain financial contributions resulted in a dual crisis in December 1961. In the first place, the UN faced a deficit of $92 million on UNEF and the Congo force, and the Assembly authorized the sale of $200 million worth of UN bonds for a period of twenty-five years. Secondly, UN members decided that they needed guidance as to whether the French and Soviet conduct ought to be tolerated and therefore asked the International Court of Justice for an Advisory Opinion on whether the peace-keeping costs incurred for UNEF and the Congo force were 'expenses of the Organization' within the meaning of Article 17 (2) of the Charter.[9] The Court answered in the affirmative, and the Assembly accepted its opinion by a large majority.

A serious clash between the super-powers ensued. The Soviet Union and France were not prepared to yield either to the Court's opinion or to its endorsement by the Assembly. By the summer of 1964 they were both so much in arrears with their payments that they were liable under Article 19 to forfeit their votes in the General Assembly and the United States was disposed to demand this penalty. Most members wished to avoid the issue, the Soviet Union having made clear that it would leave the UN if deprived of its vote, and the General Assembly in its nineteenth session was reduced to near impotence by a tacit agreement to avoid discussing any issue on which a vote might be required. The crisis was ended in August 1965, when, after the formation of the Special Committee on Peace-keeping, the United States announced that it would not 'frustrate' the consensus of opinion in the Assembly by seeking to apply Article 19 but reserved its own right to make exceptions to the principle of collective financial responsibility within the UN,

[9] The paragraph provides that 'the expenses of the Organization shall be borne by the Members as apportioned by the General Assembly'.

if there were compelling reasons to do so. The Committee had been instructed to review ways of overcoming the financial difficulties, and the Soviet Union has since conceded, in general terms, that it will contribute to the cost of peace-keeping, if the Security Council both establishes the forces and decides how they are to be financed.[10]

In his Annual Report to the General Assembly's fifteenth session in 1960 Hammarskjöld dealt, not only with the need for military expertise in the Secretariat, but with the whole problem of how, in the existing circumstances, the UN's peace-keeping forces should be raised. The relevant passage was the following:

> It should, however, be stressed that the Congo experience has strengthened my conviction that the organization of a standing United Nations force would represent an unnecessary and impractical measure, especially in view of the fact that every new situation and crisis which the Organization will have to face is likely to represent new problems as to the best adjustment of the composition of a force, its equipment, its training and its organization.
>
> It is an entirely different matter if governments, in a position and willing to do so, would maintain a state of preparedness, so as to be able to meet possible demands from the United Nations. And it is also an entirely different matter, for the Organization itself, to have a state of preparedness with considerable flexibility and in the hands of a qualified staff which quickly and smoothly can adjust their plans to new situations and assist the Secretary-General in the crucially important first stages of the execution of a decision . . . to set up a United Nations force, whatever its type or task.

Hammarskjöld went on to point out that the value of such preparedness could be seen from the fact that the Organization of the UN force in the Congo had been considerably facilitated by the UNEF experience and that the Congo operation itself was likely to lead to a new series of valuable experiences which the UN should utilize. With regard to the preparedness of member states, the Secretary-General had the year before, in 1959, already inquired of the twenty-three states which had supplied peace-keeping personnel in the Middle East, whether, in their national military planning, they were willing to take into account the possibility that they might be asked to provide such personnel again.[11] As regards preparedness within the UN organization, shortly before his death in 1961 he approved an internal training programme for

---

[10] See Rosalyn Higgins, 'United Nations peace-keeping—political and financial problems', *The World Today*, Aug. 1965, p. 332.
[11] See Larry L. Fabian, *Soldiers without Enemies*, p. 85.

military and civilian peace-keeping personnel, though it was not in the end implemented.[12]

In June 1963 U Thant, speaking at Harvard, expressed views similar to Hammarskjöld's on two basic points. While making clear his conviction that the world should eventually have an international police force which would be accepted as an integral and essential part of life, he expressed the opinion that a permanent UN force was not a practical proposition at the time and doubted whether many governments would be prepared to accept the political and financial implications of such an institution. He then said:

> I believe there are a number of measures which could be taken even now to improve on our present capacity for meeting dangerous situations. It would be extremely desirable, for example, if countries would in their national military planning make provision for suitable units which could be made available at short notice for United Nations service and thereby decrease the degree of improvisation necessary in an emergency.[13]

With two respected Secretaries-General in succession expressing such views, it was natural that efforts to strengthen the UN's peace-keeping potential should centre round the contributions of individual states rather than attempts to organize a permanent international force, as suggested by Trygvie Lie. In fact, it was the support of several UN members for this approach which encouraged Hammarskjöld and U Thant to take up the attitudes they did. This method of solving, or helping to solve the peace-keeping problem had the great advantage of imposing no financial burden on the UN and avoiding the political conflicts, which the alternative method would have involved. Canada and the Scandinavian countries took the lead in it.

Canadians first carried out peace-keeping duties in 1949 as observers in Kashmir. Since then they have taken part in nearly all the UN's peace-keeping forces and observer groups, a duty which by 1968 had involved more than 46,000 men.[14] A Canadian brigade served in Korea

---

[12] *Ibid.*, pp. 96, 207 and 208.

[13] U Thant's address to the Harvard Alumni Association, 13 June 1963, reproduced in Lincoln P. Bloomfield, *International Military Forces.*

[14] This included duty under the 'UN flag or under other international peace-keeping arrangements'. See the commentary submitted by Canada in June 1968 to the UN Special Committee on Peace-Keeping Operations, Part I, entitled 'Canadian Armed Forces Participation in Peace-Keeping Operations and Observer Missions'. The text is published in *Proceedings of the Canadian House of Commons*, 2nd Session, 1969–70, No. 31, 21 May 1970, Standing Committee on External Affairs and Nations Defence, p. 64 ff. Fabian, pp. 132–3, gives the figure as 'some 25,000 men', while Arthur M. Cox, in his *Prospects for peacekeeping* writes 'more than 30,000'.

in 1950, and the Canadian government then announced that the brigade was earmarked for service either with the UN, in Korea, or with NATO, or with the UN elsewhere.

Lester Pearson, while Canadian minister for external affairs, not only played a key role in the creation of UNEF but subsequently identified himself, in the eyes of his fellow-countrymen and of the world, with support for the UN's peace-keeping role and for Canada's national contribution to it. He emphasized repeatedly that Canada was holding standby forces in a state of readiness for service with the UN, and, in an address to the General Assembly in 1963, added the proposal that interested governments should examine the problems and techniques of peace-keeping operations, which 'could lead to a pooling of available resources and development in a co-ordinated way of trained and equipped forces for UN service'. This led on in turn the following year to a government-sponsored conference in Ottawa of military experts from twenty-three governments, which considered the technical aspects of UN peace-keeping.

Canada has for years maintained a standby battalion group, able to respond within seven days to a peace-keeping commitment. As she informed the UN Special Committee on Peace-Keeping Operations in 1968,[15] this can be modified to form an air-transportable unit; she also has available for peace-keeping service, reconnaissance, signals, and headquarters elements and an air transport unit, such as have already all been provided for service with UNEF, ONUC, or UNFICYP. The Canadian forces have special advantages for peace-keeping work: like the Scandinavians, they are free from the stigmas that may be attached to super-powers or former colonial powers, and also their signals units are bilingual in English and French.

Preparation for peace-keeping plays an important part in the training of the Canadian defence forces. Special programmes are organized for the various standby units, emphasis being placed on the qualities of character required, when a soldier is called upon to perform 'a mediatory rather than a normal military function'. Courses on UN peace-keeping are given at the Military Staff College, and special courses are arranged to prepare officers for observer duty. But UN peace-keeping is also an integral part of normal military training, as indicated in the statement: 'Canadian forces will be trained and equipped in a way which will permit immediate and effective response to United Nations require-

---

[15] See preceding footnote: Canada's standby battalion is part of her regular army and is not, like the Scandinavian standby units, raised on a voluntary basis.

ments'.[16] Such response is, of course, greatly facilitated by the practical experience of peace-keeping, which so many Canadian soldiers have gathered over the years.

The contributions of the Scandinavian countries have been of comparable value. Their joint approach to the problems of peace-keeping was productive in itself and potentially stimulating as an example. In their very positive response to the idea that states should train their own units, they were influenced by Hammarskjöld's report on UNEF (see p. 272, n. 6), by his inquiry of 1959 (see p. 275), and no doubt also by the fact that the UN's first two Secretaries-General were both Scandinavians. In September 1960 the Defence Ministers of Denmark, Norway, and Sweden discussed plans for a Scandinavian standby force. They have since met regularly twice a year to coordinate their preparations, and in 1963 were joined by Finland. By that year a plan was ready for a Scandinavian force of about 4,000 men.[17]

In March 1968 the Danish, Finnish, Norwegian, and Swedish governments, in response to an invitation from the Chairman of the UN Special Committee on Peace-Keeping Operations, sent memoranda to the Secretary-General giving details of their standby forces for service with the United Nations.[18] The figures they gave for the forces were: Denmark, 936; Finland, 601; Norway, 1,330; and Sweden, 1,582. They added that the numbers who had already served in UN peace-keeping operations, including observer groups, were respectively 18,000, 5,239, 13,000, and 27,153. The standby forces included infantry battalions, military observers, military police, medical units, technical units including amongst others engineering and communications sections, movement control units, and small naval and air-force elements, including air transport and helicopter units. Their personnel had all received special training for service with the UN. They were all volunteers, although the regular armed forces had in each case given assistance with such things as organization and training and through the secondment of officers and non-commissioned officers.

The unique and most important aspects of the Scandinavian contribution were the joint planning and the joint training programmes it involved. When the project for internal training of peace-keeping

---

[16] From the commentary of June 1968, *ibid.*, p. 66.

[17] Per Haekkerup: 'Scandinavia's peace-keeping forces for UN', *Foreign Affairs*, July 1964. For convenience, though not quite accurately, I have continued to refer to a Scandinavian force or group after Finland joined the three Scandinavian countries.

[18] UN General Assembly documents A/AC.121/11–14, of 20, 28 and 29 March 1968.

personnel within the UN came to nothing, the task of coordinating training was left with individual states, and it was this task which the Scandinavian countries took the lead in assuming. The first regional training session was held in Sweden in 1965, when officers from the four states came together for a course in UN observer duties. Later courses or seminars were also arranged for staff officers, military police, and technicians; they were held in all four countries, the language used most often being English. In this way some progress was made in sharing experiences and in a joint approach to peace-keeping problems.

Five other offers of standby forces were made by the Netherlands, Austria, Italy, Iran, and New Zealand. Of these the most substantial came from the Netherlands and Austria and were described in memoranda sent by these two states to the Secretary-General in 1968.[19] The Netherlands government had already in 1963 put a contingent of 300 marines at the UN's disposal. It now offered in addition another similar contingent of marines, if required, several naval vessels, a mechanized infantry battalion, a medical company, and a small airforce element, including a transport aircraft and three helicopters. The Austrian offer included a standby battalion, which would take several weeks to mobilize, a small group of officers for staff and observer duties, and civilian police not exceeding in numbers the contingent of forty-five which was already serving with success in Cyprus. Italy promised to have available twenty-two officers for staff or observer duties, while Iran and New Zealand made general offers, which were neither accompanied nor followed by specific commitments, though Iran sent representatives to the conference in Ottawa on peace-keeping in 1964.

Britain and the United States, who as permanent members of the Security Council would not normally have been eligible to provide contingents for peace-keeping forces, promised logistic support. In February 1965 the British foreign secretary said that Britain would help to provide logistic backing for a UN force of up to six infantry battalions, which could include engineering and signals personnel, ambulance and motor transport units, and troop-carrying aircraft. In 1960 President Eisenhower, in the General Assembly, made an offer of logistic facilities, particularly transport. It was repeated by the Secretary of State at the end of the year and confirmed by a memorandum to the Secretary-General in 1968.[20] The offer was in general terms, but the US

[19] UN General Assembly documents A/AC.121/18 and 19, of 26 June and 9 July 1968.
[20] UN General Assembly document A/AC.121/15 of 21 May 1968.

contribution to the UN in this field in the past had been so substantial that it was of great potential value.

Two other countries have made contributions to peace-keeping which were impressive, though not on a standby basis. India has provided altogether about 45,000 troops, approximately one-third for UNEF and two thirds for ONUC.[21] Ireland, whose regular army is usually well below its authorized strength of 12,000, had by 1967 already contributed 5,300 men to ONUC and nearly 5,000 to UNFICYP, as well as providing more than 100 observers to five UN missions.[22] Up to 1965 she even declined to accept from the UN the money it normally paid to participating states to cover expenses over and above basic pay and equipment costs.[23] Irish peace-keeping contingents are all made up of volunteers, and their personnel have gained the reputation of being amongst the most experienced and professional UN soldiers.

In default of a permanent international force and a strong military element in the UN Secretariat, the existence of national contingents earmarked for peace-keeping duties had the great advantages of building up traditions of service with the UN, stimulating experiments in specialized training, and, in the case of the Scandinavian group of likeminded and peaceloving states, encouraging cooperation in an international task. It was unfortunate that the controversy between the super-powers as to how peace-keeping should be controlled had the effect of limiting these creative trends. The United States welcomed the setting up of standby national contingents, because it was a helpful improvisation in face of the failure to implement Article 43. The Soviet Union opposed this development, as it did not want a successful alternative to Security Council control. From 1965 onwards the Committee of Thirty-Three's failure to reach an agreed solution of the problem of control took the enthusiasm out of the individual efforts of Canada, the Scandinavian group, and the other states which had earmarked forces for UN service.

The Committee's financial task, as has been seen, had been eased by a compromise six months after it was set up (see pp. 274–5). But there were strong reasons, apart from finance, why 'a comprehensive review of peace-keeping operations' was needed and why the Committee was established in 1965. The UN's peace-keeping forces had proved to be

[21] Fabian, p. 161.
[22] These figures are total and cumulative: the Irish contingent in ONUC exceeded 700 only for a short time, and its contribution to UNFICYP, though over a thousand in 1964 and 1965, varied afterwards between 400 and 500.
[23] *Ibid.*, pp. 158–60.

of great value, and dependence on improvisation for setting them up was clearly unsatisfactory. UNEF and ONUC had been organized rapidly and efficiently, thanks to Hammarskjöld's energy and resource, but Hammarskjöld was now dead, and his small group of expert and experienced advisers would not be available to his successors indefinitely. Moreover, in the case of UNFICYP, there was for political rather than administrative reasons a dangerous three-weeks delay. It would therefore clearly be preferable to make preparations in advance and agree on a procedure for setting up a peace-keeping force promptly, when need arose, instead of having to improvise after a crisis had arisen.

Within the framework provided by the Committee of Thirty-Three, the United States spent several years working for a solution of the peace-keeping problem on the lines suggested by Hammarskjöld and U Thant and approved by the majority of UN members. The Soviet Union strongly opposed this approach, because it believed that it would undermine the Security Council's authority. As a result the middle and smaller powers eventually indicated that they were not willing to get involved with the United States in a head-on collision with the Soviet Union and made clear that the two super-powers should attempt to reach some positive understanding with each other on the subject.[24] In April 1968 the Committee appointed a working group of eight to make a study, on its behalf, of peace-keeping operations and their financing for submission to the General Assembly: it consisted of the permanent members of the Security Council, apart from China, together with Canada, Czechoslovakia, Mexico, and the United Arab Republic. From the winter of 1968–69 onwards the most important negotiations have taken the form of bilateral discussions between the Soviet Union and the United States.[25]

The working group tried to reach agreement on two models, which would indicate the normal way in which the UN would send, in the one case, military observers and, in the other, a military force on a peace-keeping operation. But the basic controversy between the Soviet Union and the United States as regards peace-keeping had to be settled by some form of compromise before recommendations on either of these two subjects could be agreed. The controversy centred round the problem

---

[24] See the statement by Ambassador S. M. Finger before the Sub-Committee on International Organizations and Movements of the House Foreign Affairs Committee, Washington, D.C., 24 Feb. 1970 (press release of US Mission to the UN, USUN—19 (70), 20 Feb. 1970).
[25] *Ibid.*

of control; how far peace-keeping operations should be controlled by the Security Council and what should be the role of the Secretary-General and the Secretariat.[26]

The sharpness of the contrast between the Soviet and United States' views on the subject was partly a legacy of the Cold War. In 1968 the Soviet government still remembered Hammarskjöld's 'Congo Club' and the virtual exclusion of Communist officials in the Secretariat from any influence over the Congo operation, and in 1968 the chief experts in the Secretariat on peace-keeping forces were still American, British, or at least Western orientated. The Soviet Union was to some extent responsible for this state of affairs. Its failure to attend the Security Council during the Korean crisis led to the bypassing of the Russian Under-Secretary-General for Political and Security Council Affairs and to the appointment later first of one, then of a second Under-Secretary-General for Special Political Affairs, on whom the Secretary-General was largely to depend in the conduct of peace-keeping operations. Moreover, when Hammarskjöld took with him to the Congo a Soviet member of the Secretariat, things were made so difficult for this member by his unofficial Soviet supervisor in New York that the Secretary-General sent him back to Headquarters. In the circumstances the Soviet Union took its stand firmly on Article 24 of the Charter, which gave the Security Council primary responsibility for maintaining peace and security. In fact, Article 24 supported the Soviet view in the controversy, while the United States' standpoint was based rather on UN precedent in Egypt, the Congo, and Cyprus.

The United States' view, which was supported by most other Western powers, was justified partly by this precedent of successful peace-keeping operations. It could also be supported by two other strong arguments. First, the Soviet alternative of full Security Council control would not have worked under cold war conditions. For example, the Congo operation would have broken down after the first few weeks had it been under the continuous direction of the Security Council. Secondly, even under more favourable conditions, without serious ideological rivalry in the Council to contend with, it would not have been reasonable to expect rapid action on relatively small matters from such a body or even from a committee responsible to it. It was much more practicable to delegate day-to-day decisions to politically detached officials like the Secretary-General and his senior advisers.

---

[26] A subsidiary controversy centred round the relative responsibilities of the Council and the Assembly, with the middle and smaller powers supporting a role in peace-keeping for the Assembly.

A good case could therefore be made for the standpoints of both super-powers. France sympathized with the Soviet emphasis on the Security Council's responsibility, and most Western powers, including the United States, now realized the need for some concessions, while the Soviet Union saw the advantage of the Secretary-General playing some administrative role and handling the negotiations with the implicated states. As the cold war tension diminished, therefore, there was some hope of a compromise settlement, but the rigid attitudes and prejudices of the protagonists, based on past experiences and present suspicions, were difficult to break down.

The suggestion was made during the negotiations that the Military Staff Committee should be revitalized, not with the broad tasks envisaged for it in Chapter VII of the Charter but for the specific purpose of planning and directing peace-keeping operations authorized by the Security Council. The advocates of this course mostly agreed that the Committee should be enlarged by the addition of states participating in the peace-keeping. It was also proposed that the Chairman should hold office for anything from six months to two years, in order to ensure a degree of continuity and experience in the direction. Opponents of the idea pointed out that such a body would be subject to the veto, with all the inconvenience that implies; that it would lack continuity and expertise in direction, unless the Chairman were appointed for a longish period, as suggested; and that a committee of military experts would be quite unsuited to take over from the Secretary-General such political or diplomatic tasks as selecting contingents for a peace-keeping force and negotiating with the host state.

The Soviet Union and the United States came nearer to a settlement in 1969, thanks mainly to the efforts of their two negotiators L. I. Mendelevich and S. M. Finger, and the good personal relations established between them. But hopes were disappointed owing to the failure of the two governments to reach a compromise on the basic difference between them. In 1970 it seemed possible that a Middle East settlement would require the presence of a UN peace-keeping force; that in this case Soviet and US participation would be necessary; and that an *ad hoc* procedure decided upon by the super-powers for this eventuality might then be used as a precedent for a general agreement. However, this hope also came to nothing at the time, with the failure of Dr Jarring's attempt to reach a settlement.

The main obstacle to a settlement thus remained the problem of how peace-keeping should be controlled. Since 1969 no apparent progress was made in the Committee of Thirty-Three, its working group, or the bilateral discussions, until two communications were sent to the Secretary-General by the Soviet Union and the United States in March 1972 and subsequently published as UN documents.[27] By the end of April 1972 a final solution of the main problem had still not been reached, but the communications showed that fruitful, if slow-moving bilateral discussions had, in fact, taken place during the previous two years and that each side was prepared to make helpful concessions in stating its case.

The United States' communication included a copy of some proposals which had been submitted to the Soviet Union in February 1970, together with certain clarifications which had been made during the ensuing bilateral discussions. As an alternative to the reactivation of the Military Staff Committee with its disadvantages for peace-keeping purposes, Canada had suggested, in the working group, the setting up of a special subsidiary organ of the Security Council under the terms of Article 29. The United States incorporated this idea into its proposals by suggesting the establishment by the Security Council of a sub-committee 'to hold a "watching brief" over the conduct of the (peace-keeping) operation, advise the Secretary-General and receive his reports between Council meetings'. Representatives of contributing nations were to be included on the subcommittee. Delegations could include military experts, who, in the case of permanent members, could be their Military Staff Committee representatives.

The composition of a peace-keeping force would be determined by the Secretary-General, who would name the force commander and compile a roster of potential commanders. The Secretary-General would also keep records of troop offers by member governments and undertake specific arrangements under which such personnel or services could be made available. Yet the United States announced as a 'clarification' that there was no dispute about the Council's primary responsibility for maintaining peace and security and consequently for authorizing UN peace-keeping operations. It added in explicit and therefore conciliatory terms, so far as the Soviet Union was concerned, that the Council would normally indicate the means for financing an operation and the approximate size of a force. The Secretary-General should be given some latitude to adapt the size to changing circumstances but would be expected to consult the committee or perhaps even the Council about a substantial increase or decrease. One point in the proposals, which the Soviet Union was most unlikely to accept,

[27] UN General Assembly documents A/8669 of 20 March 1972 and A/8676 of 3 April 1972.

concerned the Council's power to disapprove the Secretary-General's decisions: the vote in such cases was to be procedural, that is, not subject to the veto. But, on the whole, the proposals were conciliatory both in substance and in style.

The Soviet communication consisted mainly of a document on the Basic Guiding Principles for the Conduct of UN Peace-Keeping Operations, which had been sent to the United States in July 1971, in response to the American proposals of February 1970. The document opened with forthright statements that all decisions of the Security Council on UN peace-keeping operations should be subject to the veto and that the Council, having authorized an operation, should continue to exercise supreme control over all aspects of its establishment and of its subsequent direction. It went on to refer to the Military Staff Committee's role in all questions relating to the Council's 'military requirements for the maintenance of international peace and security', but added that the Council might find it useful to set up, as a special subsidiary organ, a committee directly responsible to it for advice and assistance with regard to an operation. Its nucleus would be the permanent members of the Council, each of whom would have the power of veto, but other UN members could be invited to join it, epecially non-permanent members of the Council and contributing states. No UN member was to be excluded from participation in an operation because of its 'political social and economic system or because of its belonging to a certain geographical region', but, in choosing the participants, the consent of the host country would be needed, and the necessity of ensuring good working relations should be borne in mind.

The document subsequently dealt with the role of the Secretary-General, referred to 'his capacity as determined by Articles 97 and 98' and stated that he should 'assist by all means at his disposal in the implementation of the resolutions or other forms of authorization by the Security Council with regard to the operation'. The Council should request member states for advance information on the number of contingents and facilities they could make available for peace-keeping operations, but the Secretary-General should maintain an open roster of information on the resultant offers. Acting in contact with the advisory committee he should also, when an operation had been authorized, enter into preliminary consultations with the host country and with interested states as to their readiness to participate. The Secretary-General would request governments to suggest the names of potential force commanders; a list would be approved by the Council; and, when an operation was authorized, he would consult the host country 'confidentially and informally' regarding the suitability of several candidates selected by the advisory committee.

The Soviet Union's statement was wary in the extreme. But it was conciliatory and positive in tone, and in its description of the respective roles of the Council and Secretary-General it represented an advance towards common ground. By the spring of 1972, therefore, the two parties in the main peace-keeping controversy were moving towards an understanding, though the differences were still manifest.

The UN's main peace-keeping achievements hitherto have been the result of improvisations at times of crisis. It is possible that another serious emergency will be needed, perhaps in the Middle East, to bridge the remaining gap in viewpoints between the Soviet Union and the United States. The arrival of Communist China in the Security Council may well have increased the will on both sides to find a settlement, but it may also add to the difficulty of their doing so.

8

The Security Council and the General Assembly

Although the Charter made a clear division between the responsibilities of the Security Council, the Economic and Social Council, and the Trusteeship Council, it did not distinguish with precision between the responsibilities of the Security Council and the General Assembly. This omission left a good deal of flexibility in the relationship between the two bodies and resulted in changes of emphasis in the attitudes of UN members towards them.

As a small body containing five influential permanent members the Council was given by Article 24 primary responsibility for the maintenance of international peace and security, 'in order to ensure prompt and effective action'. But the Charter also gave wide powers to the Assembly in the same field. Article 10 provided that it could discuss any matters within the scope of the Charter and, except as provided in Article 12, make recommendations on them to UN members or to the Council. The first three paragraphs of Article 11 dealt specifically and fully with its authority in matters of peace and security and have already been quoted, as have the relevant passages of Articles 14, 15, and 35. The main difference between the powers of the Council and the Assembly as regards the maintenance of peace and security was that the Council, in addition to recommending, could make decisions which were binding on all UN members, whereas the Assembly, according to the Charter, could do no more than consider, discuss, and make recommendations, which members were morally obliged to pay attention to but not bound to carry out (see pp. 55, 56 and 58).

The indefiniteness and consequent flexibility in the relationship between the Council and the Assembly arose out of the lack of clarity in the wording of Articles 24, 11, and 12. The 'primary responsibility' conferred on the Council by Article 24 does not imply that the responsibility is exclusive, while Articles 11 and 12 indicate the nature of the Assembly's residual responsibility but leave a number of points open to doubt. According to Article 11, paragraph 2, the Assembly must refer to the Council any question on which action is necessary, but it does not make clear whether 'action' in this case refers to action under Chapter VII or whether it also includes exhorting parties to a dispute, under Article 33, to seek a solution by negotiation, enquiry, conciliation, or other peaceful means. Article 12 provides in its first paragraph that, while the Council is exercising its functions in respect of any dispute or situation, the Assembly shall not make any recommendation with regard to that dispute or situation, but it does not indicate whether 'exercising' means actively dealing with the matter or retaining it on a list of matters of which the Council is seized. Each interpretation was supported by Council members in connection with the Spanish question in 1946. In any case this restriction applies only to disputes and situations and not to every matter being considered by the Council.[1] On the whole, UN members over the years have tended to take a broad rather than a restricted view of the Assembly's authority in questions of peace and security, but there has been plenty of scope for conflicting viewpoints.

During the UN's early years the Security Council's position was unrivalled. Its permanent members included the United States, the Soviet Union, and Britain, all of whom had emerged from the war with enhanced prestige; its potential power under Chapter VII was formidable and its decisions were binding upon the whole UN membership. But the realization of its promise was dependent on two conditions; the cooperation of the permanent members in maintaining and restoring international peace and security and the organization of the military forces necessary for the achievement of these purposes; and neither of the conditions was fulfilled.

It took some time for the resulting situation to become clear, and for about five years the Council retained most of its original aura. But the tension between the Soviet Union and the West, the repeated use of the veto, and the failure of the Military Staff Committee to achieve its main purpose led to increasing frustration and disillusionment. In consequence, a number of questions were referred to the General Assembly which might in more favourable circumstances have been handled by the Council.

The position of the United States and the West in the Assembly was strong at the time, and most of the cases which were transferred to that body or submitted to it rather than to the Council found their way

[1] See the commentary on Article 12 in Goodrich, Hambro, and Simons, pp. 130–31.

there as a result of Western initiative. In September 1947, after numerous Council meetings on the Greek question and two Soviet vetoes, the matter was removed from the list of matters of which the Council was seized and taken up the following month by the Assembly. During the same session the Assembly was asked by the United States to consider the Korean question, after the failure of negotiations on the subject between the United States and the Soviet Union had made clear that no solution could be reached in the Council. In April 1948 the Council requested the Secretary-General to convene a special session of the Assembly on Palestine, having failed itself to implement a plan for that country drawn up and referred to it by the Assembly the previous autumn. In the case of the Spanish question, the Council, after a series of frustrating meetings on the subject, decided unanimously in November 1946 to take it off the list of matters of which the Council was seized, all members apparently hoping that there would be a better chance of a satisfactory solution in the Assembly.

Nevertheless there were two strong reasons why references to the Assembly were limited. Other things being equal the permanent members of the Council preferred matters to be dealt with in the Council, where they had the veto. Also the Council was 'so organized as to be able to function continuously', whereas the Assembly normally had only one long session a year, and a special session involved considerable trouble and expense.

In 1947 the United States devised a method of overcoming this last difficulty. At the opening of the Assembly the secretary of state, General Marshall, proposed that the Assembly should set up an Interim Committee for a period of one year. The suggestion was approved in November, and the body came to be known as the Little Assembly. Its life was renewed in 1948 for a further year and in 1949 indefinitely. All UN members were to be represented on the Committee. It was intended, according to its terms of reference, to assist the Assembly between sessions in discharging its functions in the field of peace and security; more particularly to make studies and recommendations for international cooperation, in accordance with the Assembly's responsibilities under Articles 11(1) and 13(1a), and to consider matters specifically referred to it by the Assembly and disputes and situations proposed for inclusion in the agenda of the Assembly's next session. But the main, if formally unstated, purpose behind its creation was to provide an organ which could investigate serious situations and, if necessary, call a special Assembly session, in the event of the Security Council being paralysed by the veto.

K

The Interim Committee never fulfilled its chief purpose: it was opposed by the Soviet bloc as an illegal attempt to circumvent the Charter, and bloc members never attended its meetings. Without being formally abolished, it ceased to meet after March 1951. It did make two useful suggestions for improving conciliation procedure,[2] but its main significance was as the first of two attempts to develop an alternative to an ineffective Security Council, the second of which had, for a time, a good deal more success.

The second attempt was the General Assembly's 'Uniting for Peace' resolution of 3 November 1950, to which reference has already been made. There were two reasons why the United States sponsored this resolution (see p. 166). The UN operation in Korea had been made possible by the Soviet Union's absence from the Security Council the previous June. After the Soviet representative returned to the Council to take up the presidency at the beginning of August any further positive action by the Council in relation to Korea was made impossible by the Soviet veto, and the main aim of the Assembly resolution was to provide an alternative method by which the UN could continue to exercise its responsibilities in a major operation which it had initiated. Also, in a more general sense, in spite of official statements to the contrary,[3] the United States had reached the conclusion during the postwar years that there was no real basis for positive cooperation with the Soviet Union, and that the UN was most useful as a means of furthering its own interests and those of the West as a whole. In 1950 it still had a dominant position in the General Assembly, and it would therefore be to its advantage if the Assembly's influence in matters of peace and security could be strengthened.

The main provision of the resolution ran as follows:

> If the Security Council, because of lack of unanimity of the permanent members, fails to exercise its primary responsibility for the maintenance of international peace and security in any case where there appears to be a threat to the peace, breach of the peace, or act of aggression, the General Assembly shall consider the matter immediately with a view to making appropriate recommendations to Members for collective measures, including in the case of a breach of the peace or act of aggression the use of armed force when necessary.

Provision was also made for the calling of emergency special sessions of the Assembly on twenty-four hours' notice, either by the vote of any

[2] It proposed the setting up of a panel for inquiry and conciliation to be available to states involved in controversies and the use by the Security Council of rapporteurs or conciliators. Soon after this second suggestion was made General McNaughton was appointed as conciliator in the Kashmir dispute: see p. 96.

[3] See Weiler and Simons, *The United States and the United Nations*, pp. 553–57.

seven embers of the Council or by a majority of UN members; that is, reference of a matter to the Assembly by the Council was not subject to the veto. The resolution set up in addition a Peace Observation Commission, to observe and report on the situation in areas where peace was threatened, and the Collective Measures Committee described in the last chapter. The Peace Observation Commission was only used once, when it set up its Balkan Sub-Commission in 1951, a formal request for its services by Thailand in 1954 being allowed to lapse following a Soviet veto.

The Soviet Union opposed the resolution on the grounds that it conflicted with the Council's 'primary responsibility for the maintenance of international peace and security', and that the procedural vote, which was all that was required for calling an emergency session of the Assembly, violated the principle of great power unanimity. The supporters of the resolution pointed out that a matter would only be referred to the Assembly after the Council had had an opportunity of exercising its responsibility and had failed to do so, and the great majority of members clearly felt that 'Uniting for Peace' was a common-sense method of fostering the UN's primary purpose, as stated in Article 1 of the Charter, 'to maintain international peace and security'. Their attitude was reflected in the voting on the resolution which was fifty-two in favour, five against, and two abstentions. After this vote even the Soviet Union, which wanted to make use of the Assembly's anti-colonial majority for its own purposes, was not, on the whole, inclined to call that body's authority in question. During the Suez crisis in 1956 it actually supported the resolution calling for an emergency meeting of the Assembly under the terms of 'Uniting for Peace'.[4]

The bulk of the UN membership believed that these measures did not alter the terms of the Charter but merely facilitated the Assembly's use of the general and residual authority in matters of peace and security, which the Charter had already given it. The 'Uniting for Peace' resolution emphasized the Assembly's power to *recommend* but did not and could not transfer to it the Council's power of *decision*, which was binding. Nor did most members call in question the Assembly's right to convene an emergency meeting at short notice, though this was one of the points in the resolution to which the Soviet Union objected. It could be argued with a good deal of force that the resolution conflicted with the spirit of the Charter, which had envisaged the

---

[4] In June 1967 also, as has been seen (p. 152), the Soviet Union requested an emergency special session of the General Assembly to consider the Middle East, although it avoided reference to 'Uniting for Peace'.

Security Council making and enforcing decisions in matters of peace and security, but then the Charter itself had in practice not worked out as had been intended, and this was the basic reason why the resolution was needed.

'Uniting for Peace' amounted to a formal expression of disillusionment with the Security Council. It marked the culmination of a process that had been going on for several years and also the beginning of a decade during which the authority of the General Assembly in matters of peace and security reached its height. The Council's intended role was to a large extent assumed by the Assembly. The shift in the centre of gravity had two other results. The Assembly passed resolutions, some of which had very important results, but it was too large and cumbersome a body to deal with the administrative consequences, and some of its new authority came into the able and willing hands of the new Secretary-General, Dag Hammarskjöld. So the decade which saw an increase in the influence of the General Assembly saw also a strengthening of the Secretary-General's authority.[5] Furthermore, the failure to establish a general system of collective security through the Security Council led to the development of regional security systems such as NATO and the Warsaw Pact.

An indication of the reduced importance of the Council during the 1950s was the marked decline in the number of its meetings. Up to 1949 it had averaged over a hundred meetings a year, while from 1951 to 1958 the average fell to forty, and in 1959 it met only five times.

From 1950 to 1960 on five occasions the General Assembly dealt with matters relating to peace and security after the Security Council had failed to exercise its 'primary responsibility', in each case with important consequences. On three of the occasions the Council, citing the 'Uniting for Peace' resolution, called an emergency special session of the Assembly, in order that it could 'make appropriate recommendations'. The three cases were the Suez crisis in October 1956, the situation in Hungary in November 1956, and the moment during the Congo crisis in September 1960 when a Soviet veto called the whole UN policy in question. In the other two cases the procedure was not exactly that laid down in the 'Uniting for Peace' resolution, but the net result was much the same as if it had been. The first took place during the Korean operation in February 1951. The Council simply voted to remove from its agenda the alleged aggression of Communist China against South Korea, an item on which its permanent members would certainly not

[5] See the Fifteenth Annual Report of the Secretary-General to the General Assembly, 31 Aug. 1960.

agree. The Assembly, being in regular session at the time, took up the matter and declared Communist China guilty of aggression. The second case concerned the dispute between Lebanon and Jordan and the UAR in 1958. Both the Soviet Union and the United States, not being able to agree in the Security Council, wanted to refer the matter to the General Assembly, and the Council decided to call an emergency special session of the Assembly, without, however, actually citing the 'Uniting for Peace' resolution, out of deference to Soviet susceptibilities.

Apart from these specific instances the 'Uniting for Peace' resolution exerted an important influence on permanent members of the Council, because they had to face the fact that, if they used the veto, an emergency session of the Assembly might follow. The extent of this influence cannot be judged precisely. But it is of some significance that in 1951, the year after the resolution was approved, no veto was cast; after the Suez and Hungarian cases in October and November 1956 there was no veto until February 1957; and after the Lebanon-Jordan case in August 1958 there was none for nearly two years, apart from two cast by the Soviet Union on applications for membership against which the Assembly was powerless.[6]

About 1960 the trend of the 1950s was reversed and, in relation to the General Assembly, the influence and prestige of the Security Council began to revive. There were three main reasons for this development.

First, during the ten years from 1950 to 1959 UN membership had increased from fifty-nine to seventy-three, the twenty-four new members comprising ten European states, Japan, and thirteen former colonies and dependent territories in Asia and Africa, an expansion which on the whole added authority and interest to the General Assembly. But in 1960 alone sixteen new African states joined the UN, while during the six years from 1960 to 1965 the number of new members totalled thirty-six, of which all were diplomatically inexperienced, some very small, and all but four new states in Africa and Asia. As a result the United States lost its controlling position in the Assembly, and neither the United States nor other Western powers were as ready as they had been in 1950 to transfer the consideration of important questions to a body containing representatives of so many untried, non-aligned, and diplomatically uncertain countries. The Soviet Union, while gratified by the decline of American influence in the Assembly, still preferred the Security Council, in which it had a veto.

Secondly, during the Khrushchev era from 1955 to 1964 there was on

[6] According to Article 4 of the Charter admission to membership was dependent upon the Security Council's recommendation.

the whole, despite surprises and setbacks, a progressive improvement in relations between the Soviet Union and the West, in which three landmarks were the Camp David meeting between Eisenhower and Khrushchev in 1959, the culmination of the Sino-Soviet dispute in 1960, which strengthened the Soviet desire for a *détente* with the United States, and the establishment in 1963 of the 'hot-line' for direct communication between Washington and Moscow, following the Cuban missile crisis. This improvement was reflected in a marked drop in the number of Soviet vetoes cast in the Security Council, which averaged only one a year in the four years from 1962 to 1965, and a renewed preference, on the part of the major powers, for the Council as compared with the Assembly. Although the Council met only five times in 1959, it held 104 meetings in 1964 and 81 in 1965.

Lastly, the 'Uniting for Peace' procedure had been usefully employed on a number of occasions and was to be so used again, but as a device for virtually amending the Charter it had been largely discredited. The Charter did not intend enforcement action to be taken against a permanent member of the Council, and it was quite clear, when a matter had been transferred to the Assembly, that it would be highly dangerous to attempt to do so. UN members had no intention of supporting the United States in a show-down with the Soviet Union, while the United States itself during the Hungarian crisis of 1956, having called an emergency meeting of the Assembly, showed no inclination to make an experiment in collective security.

In fact, from 1960 onwards the Security Council resumed its role as the UN's main organ in matters of peace and security, as the Secretary-General pointed out in his annual report for 1959–60. Hammarskjöld also explained that the reason for 'this return to the Security Council from the General Assembly' was that two main questions with which the Council had dealt during the year, the Congo and South Africa, had both been 'of a nature which has to a degree placed them outside the conflicts . . . between the main power blocs'. After their experiences of transferring matters to the Assembly and of the financial crisis over peace-keeping which largely arose from it, the United States and the Soviet Union had come to realize the advantages of cooperation over confrontation in the Council. In the Congo, where the Council gave the main directives for the operation, the Soviet Union supported the first three Council resolutions and later used its veto with restraint, abstaining on the two key resolutions in 1961. In Cyprus the two superpowers cooperated in setting up UNFICYP in 1964 and in retaining control of it in succeeding years, and they worked together to bring about a cease-fire in Kashmir in 1965. Between 1962 and 1965 the Council was also the operative UN body in the Cuban missile crisis, Yemen, and the Dominican Republic, though in each case its role was limited.

In 1966 the increase in the Security Council's size made it a more representative and balanced body and brought an end to the built-in advantage the United States had enjoyed in the Council since its creation. It did not alter fundamentally the trend in the Council's favour, which started in 1960, but it introduced certain new and complex elements into its relations with the Assembly, which were not yet ripe for final assessment by the spring of 1972.

On the one hand, two changes associated with the expansion were unfortunate in their consequences. In the first place, for reasons that have already been explained (see pp. 99–100 and 189–190), African representatives in the Council, and sometimes Asian representatives as well, were often inexperienced and chosen rather to further African or Asian interests in international causes of their choice than to promote the Security Council's main purpose. Secondly, and partly as a result of the first change, group or regional politics began to play an important part in the Security Council and interfered as much with its primary task as the Cold War had in the past. The Council, in fact, took on some of the characteristics of the General Assembly on a small scale, thus sacrificing partially the executive qualities appropriate to itself without matching the Assembly as a vehicle for parliamentary diplomacy.

On the other hand the Council still retained its primary responsibility for peace and security; it still had the power to make decisions binding on the whole UN membership; it still had the prestige associated with its permanent members, who were greatly reinforced in the autumn of 1971 by the arrival of Communist China; and it had the additional advantage of being organized so that it could function continuously. The Assembly, on the other hand, with a total of 132 members in the spring of 1972, had become increasingly cumbersome, while its membership had been depreciated by an influx of so-called mini-states. Of the sixteen new members which joined between 1965 and 1971 all but three had a population of under a million; two had no permanent missions in New York; and one (the Maldive Islands) during seven years of membership only sent a representative to an Assembly session on a single occasion.

In a survey of the relationship between the Council and the Assembly the problem of disarmament must be considered, because the Charter gives each body a separate responsibility in relation to it, without indicating how their duties should be coordinated. Article 11 provides that 'the General Assembly may consider the general principles of co-operation in the maintenance of international peace and security, including the principles governing disarmament and the regulation of armaments'; Article 26 states that 'the Security Council shall be responsible for formulating, with the assistance of the Military Staff Committee' plans for 'the establishment of a system for the regulation of armaments'; and Article 47 includes in the questions on which the Committee shall advise and assist the Council 'the regulation of armaments and possible disarmament'. Three points in these provisions are noteworthy. First, the Assembly's competence is general and permissive, while the Council's is specific and mandatory. Secondly, Article 11 refers to disarmament, Article 47 to 'possible disarmament,' and Article 26 does not mention disarmament at all. This inconsistency appears to have been due to differences of opinion when the Charter was drafted.[7] Thirdly, Article 11 includes the Assembly's responsibility for disarmament under 'the maintenance of international peace and security'. So the Council's 'primary responsibility' mentioned in Article 24 covers disarmament and the regulation of armaments, though the point has not been stressed in practice.

The Charter's references to the armaments problem are briefer and more restrained than those of the League Covenant, Article 8 of which dealt with the reduction of national armaments at some length and in strong terms as the *sine qua non* for the maintenance of peace. The main reasons for this change in emphasis were the failure of the League's disarmament efforts and the widespread feeling that a principal cause of the second World War was the military weakness of the Western democracies.

In the disarmament negotiations that have taken place since the second World War, the main cleavage has been not so much between the Council and the Assembly. It has been rather between, on the one hand, the United Nations as a whole and its three principal organs concerned, the Assembly, the Council, and the Secretariat, and on the other hand the various *ad hoc* bodies that have been set up outside the UN and the less formal, though often very important discussion groups that have come into existence beside them. The Council and the Assembly have lacked both expertise in their membership for technical and highly complex discussions and sufficient time to devote to so demanding and time-consuming a subject. The Council has also suffered from the veto and from being the focal point of cold war dissension, while the

[7] On these two points see Goodrich, Hambro, and Simons, pp. 119 and 118.

Assembly has had the disadvantage of a perennially overcrowded agenda. The most effective negotiations have, therefore, on the whole been between major powers, between the super-powers meeting bilaterally, or between groups of states with a regional or other common interest.

Of the bewildering number of bodies that were used in the negotiations the early ones were set up on the UN's initiative and were subsidiary organs of the bodies establishing them. The very first resolution of the General Assembly, which was passed in January 1946, set up the Atomic Energy Commission to deal with the problems arising out of the discovery of atomic energy and atomic weapons. It was composed of the members of the Security Council and Canada. It was to submit its reports and recommendations to the Security Council and to be accountable to the Council in matters affecting security. In February 1947 the Council itself established the Commission for Conventional Armaments, which had the same composition as its parent body and was charged with preparing proposals for the general regulation and reduction of armaments. During the same month the Council considered the first report of the Atomic Energy Commission. But by this time relations between the Soviet Union and the Western powers were rapidly deteriorating. Before the end of 1949 the Council had considered two more reports of the Atomic Energy Commission and two from the Commission for Conventional Armaments, and the Soviet Union had used its veto four times on resolutions arising out of the reports. During the summer of 1949, therefore, the Atomic Energy Commission decided that it could serve no useful purpose by meeting again, and the following April the Soviet Union withdrew from the Commission for Conventional Armaments, thus virtually bringing its work to an end. The Security Council since then has played no further part in the main UN discussions on disarmament.

In January 1952 the General Assembly established 'under the Security Council' a Disarmament Commission, with the same membership as the Atomic Energy Commission, which was to combine the functions of the two previous Commissions. At the same time it dissolved the Atomic Energy Commission, and the following month the Security Council, on the Assembly's recommendation, dissolved the Commission for Conventional Armaments. In 1957 the Assembly increased the new Commission's size by the addition of fourteen members and in 1958, on Soviet urging and with reluctant Western consent, enlarged it to include all UN members. Since then it has held only two sessions—in 1960 and 1965.

K*

From 1959 onwards the most important discussions and negotiations on disarmament have taken place not in principal or subsidiary UN organs, but in *ad hoc* bodies, set up to consider problems of disarmament and outside the formal framework of the United Nations but receiving its blessing and support. In 1959, as a result of discussions between the foreign ministers of the United States, the Soviet Union, France, and Britain, the first of these bodies was created, consisting of five NATO and five Warsaw Pact countries, and known as the Ten-Nation Disarmament Committee. In 1961, following an agreement between the United States and the Soviet Union in Washington, which was endorsed by the General Assembly, this Committee was expanded into the Eighteen-Nation Disarmament Committee by the addition of eight non-aligned countries. France decided not to participate, but the other seventeen members have been meeting in almost continuous sessions in Geneva since 1962. In 1969 the Committee was enlarged to include eight more countries, and its name was changed to the Conference of the Committee on Disarmament.

Until 1959, when tension between the West and the Communist bloc was at its height and disarmament negotiations were carried on formally within the UN organs, the record was one of almost complete failure. But since then the diplomatic climate has improved and there has been a series of encouraging achievements. They have not been due to the Security Council, but they have been within its field of responsibility, and in one or two cases the Council has been marginally involved.

The breakthrough came in 1959 with the Antarctic Treaty, by which the twelve countries most interested in Antarctica, including the United States, the Soviet Union, France, and Britain, agreed to the freezing of territorial claims in the area, its demilitarization, the prohibition of nuclear explosions, and the encouragement of its use for peaceful purposes only and for scientific investigation, under a system of supervision. This was followed by the Test-Ban Treaty of 1963, by which the United States, the Soviet Union, and Britain agreed not to undertake nuclear tests in the atmosphere, in outer space, or under water. It was signed or acceded to by the great majority of UN members, though France and China have not signed and have since carried out tests in the atmosphere. The same year the Soviet Union and the United States agreed to set up the 'hot line' between Moscow and Washington, and similar arrangements have since been made with the Soviet Union by Britain and France.

In 1964 through 'the policy of mutual example' the Soviet Union and the United States both undertook unilaterally to reduce their military expenditure and, together with Britain, to cut back their production of fissionable material for nuclear weapons. The year 1967 saw two steps forward in the control of nuclear armaments. The Outer Space Treaty, which was signed by the United States, the Soviet Union, Britain, and the majority of UN members, provided that outer space was to be used exclusively for peaceful purposes and that nuclear weapons or any other weapons of mass destruction were not to be placed in orbit round the earth or installed on celestial bodies. Also the Treaty for the Prohibition of Nuclear Weapons in Latin America was signed by twenty-one Latin American states and went into force two years later. It prohibited the use and manufacture of nuclear weapons of all kinds in Latin America, provided for an effective system of supervision and control, and was accompanied by a protocol, which has been signed by Britain and the United States, by which nuclear powers pledge themselves to respect the area as a nuclear-free zone.

In 1968 the United States and the Soviet Union agreed on the terms of a Treaty on the Non-Proliferation of Nuclear Weapons, which U Thant, after its signature, described as 'a major success for the cause of peace'. Under its first two articles the nuclear powers undertook not to transfer, or give access to nuclear weapons to any non-nuclear-weapon states, and non-nuclear states undertook not to receive or manufacture nuclear weapons. The Treaty went into force in March 1970, after it had been signed by ninety countries, including such potential nuclear powers as Canada, West and East Germany, Italy, and Japan, and been ratified by forty-seven, including the United States, the Soviet Union, and Britain. In 1970 the two super-powers also agreed on the terms of a draft Sea-Bed Treaty, prohibiting the use of the sea-bed for nuclear weapons, which was approved by the Conference of the Committee on Disarmament and by the General Assembly. It was signed by the United States, the Soviet Union, Britain, and sixty-four other states in February 1971 and went into force in May 1972 after the required number of ratifications. The terms of a draft Convention on Bacteriological (Biological) Weapons were also commended by the Assembly in December 1971, and the Convention was signed in April 1972 by the United States, the Soviet Union, Britain, and some seventy other countries. The signatories undertook not to produce or stockpile biological weapons and to destroy existing stocks within nine months of the Convention coming into force. They undertook at the same time to continue negotiations with a view to reaching a similar ban on the development, production, and stockpiling of chemical weapons. Finally, the United States and the Soviet Union, following their agreement on the Non-Proliferation

Treaty, decided to start talks on the limitation of strategic arms.[8] They began in the autumn of 1969 and bore their first fruits in May 1972 during President Nixon's visit to Moscow, when a formal treaty was signed, limiting anti-ballistic missile systems, and an interim agreement was reached on the limitation for up to five years of offensive strategic missiles.

Although these impressive achievements were not reached in UN organs, the United Nations played an important supporting role. For the many conferences that took place at Geneva the UN provided the accommodation and the servicing. Under the Secretary-General's direction the Secretariat prepared reports with expert assistance on the economic and social consequences of disarmament, the effects and implications of nuclear weapons, and chemical and biological warfare. U Thant himself, in simple and deeply sincere terms, has expressed human aspirations for peace and the control of armaments; in particular, he has emphasized the imperative need to control the nuclear arms race and has thus strongly supported the negotiations for a nuclear test ban and the Non-Proliferation Treaty.

Since 1959 the General Assembly has exerted a much greater influence on the disarmament negotiations than has the Security Council. During its annual sessions it has devoted a considerable amount of time to debating and passing resolutions on various aspects of the disarmament problem, to exhorting the *ad hoc* bodies to greater efforts, and commending them for their achievements. In general it has been the main forum for the expression of world opinion on the subject and the natural channel through which the middle and smaller powers can give expression to their views and from time to time bring effective pressure to bear on the major powers. More specifically it has requested the *ad hoc* bodies, in particular the Eighteen-Nation Disarmament Committee and its successor, to submit reports to the UN, which it has then discussed. It has passed resolutions, which have often been influential, relating to the following amongst other subjects: the Test Ban and Outer Space Treaties, the Treaty for the Prohibition of Nuclear Weapons in Latin America, the Non-Proliferation and Sea-Bed Treaties, and the Convention on Bacteriological and Other Weapons.

The Security Council can claim very little credit for the successes in the limitation of armaments, but its responsibility for peace and security was not forgotten, least of all by the Soviet Union. In the various abortive proposals put forward by the Soviet Union for the reduction of armaments or general disarmament a supervisory or peace-

[8] They came to be known as SALT (Strategic Arms Limitation Talks).

keeping role was quite often given to the Council.[9] In some of the treaties that were successfully concluded it was also given certain responsibilities. Under the Sea-Bed Treaty it was to supervise the fulfilment of obligations. Under the Non-Proliferation Treaty it was given a vital role: the nuclear powers undertook to provide immediate assistance to any non-nuclear-weapon state that was a party to the Treaty, should it be the victim of nuclear aggression, and this undertaking was confirmed by the passing of a resolution in the Council itself, accepting its own responsibility in such a case.

The increase in the non-permanent members of the Council in 1966 has made it even less likely than before that the Council will play an effective part in disarmament negotiations. But the improvement in relations between the super-powers has made it more probable that it will in future be given further responsibilities for ensuring the fulfilment of treaty obligations in the disarmament field.

[9] See *The United Nations and Disarmament 1945–1970*, UN, New York, 1970, Ch. III and IV.

9
Future prospects

Since the United Nations came into existence in 1945 the world has changed at a speed and on a scale that no one could foresee at the time. The change that is most relevant to the Security Council is in the nature of war that man now has it in his power to wage. The ordinary individual cannot fully comprehend the facts that are available to him about nuclear energy. But he must accept the statement of experts that one large hydrogen bomb has a destructive power greater than all the conventional explosives that have so far ever been used in warfare and realize the terrible implications of this fact: that all the great and beautiful creations of mankind over the millenia would be in danger of destruction in an hour or two, if nuclear war broke out.

However, other changes that have taken place, involving progress in the scientific, economic, and medical fields, have also had direct or indirect effects on the relations between nations and on the problems of international peace and security.

Developments in jet engines, rocketry, and computers have had their bad as well as their good aspects. During the quarter-century following the second World War economic progress took place at an unprecedented rate. Between 1948 and 1970 world production of primary commodities, that is agricultural products and minerals, rose by 74 per cent and world industrial production by more than 215 per cent.[1] During the same twenty-five years there was an immense advance in the conquest of disease, due partly to medical progress and partly to the work of the World Health Organization. The most dramatic achievement was against malaria. By the end of 1970 seventy-four per cent of the 1,800 million people living in malarious areas were protected against the disease by eradication programmes which were either complete or making effective progress. The world total of reported smallpox cases fell from 332,224 in 1950 to 52,770 in 1971.[2] The drive against the

---

[1] These figures are based on tables published in the UN *Statistical Yearbooks*.

[2] Figures provided by WHO, which estimates that the drop in the total of *actual* cases was much greater owing to a substantial increase over the period in the proportion of cases reported.

tropical disease, yaws, was almost completely successful after 38 million people had received penicillin treatment in some forty different countries. Yet these results had their accompanying dangers. Higher production led to better standards of living but resulted in an increase rather than a reduction of the differences between developed and developing, between the have and the have-not countries. Better living standards and medical progress led to a more rapid growth in population, so that world population rose from an estimated 2,517 million in 1950 to an estimated 3,632 million in 1970 and is likely to exceed 6,500 million by the year 2000. Scientific and economic progress and the greater exploitation of the world's natural resources have resulted in environmental problems in the form of waste, pollution, imbalance, and overcrowding, of which mankind is only in process of becoming adequately conscious.

The development of radio throughout the world and of television in many parts of it has increased terrestrial self-knowledge and made people more sensitive about conditions and recent changes in countries other than their own. The speeding up of all forms of communication has made the earth in temporal terms a smaller place, and the developments in method of travel on land, in the air, and under water have reduced the inaccessible and mysterious qualities of the great deserts and made journeys over or under the polar ice-caps a matter of routine for air-liners and nuclear submarines. The sea-bed has become a major source of petroleum and natural gas, and its vast potentialities as a source of minerals and food have come to be realized. These changes have given man a new sense both of the greatness and of the limits of his earthly heritage, while spatial and lunar exploration have opened new perspectives and unlimited possibilities of scientific inquiry and adventure. Photographs of the earth taken from and on the way to the moon have brought home as never before the natural unity of our planet and the littleness of human divisions and conflicts.

The social and political changes of the last quarter-century, though less significant in their long-term implications than the scientific advances, have also been great. The emphasis given in the UN Charter to the social aspect of international relations, together with the social consequences of the scientific and economic developments that have just been described, have resulted in social problems being recognized as worldwide for the first time. The Universal Declaration of Human Rights, which was approved by the General Assembly in December 1948, has remained an ideal, a signpost for human endeavour, rather than a programme for immediate implementation. Yet it has contributed greatly to the realization that racial and other forms of discrimination, religious intolerance, and slavery, overt or disguised, are universal problems.

The political changes have transformed the whole pattern of inter-state relationships in ways which, with one exception, could not be anticipated in 1945. The one exception was the rise of the United States and the Soviet Union to dominant positions on the international scene. At the end of the war it was already clear that these two states had emerged from the crisis with such increased power and prestige that they would be without rivals in the world, apart from each other. But even in this case no one could have foreseen the speed with which nuclear weapons were to be developed, the astonishing progress of the Soviet Union in nuclear research and spatial exploration, and the resulting 'bipolar' diplomatic alignment. Britain, and still more France, had clearly suffered greatly from the war, but the dissolution of their empires was not expected so soon: if it had been, they could hardly have been put in the same category as the United States and the Soviet Union in the Security Council. Nor was the rapid recovery and surge forward of Germany and Japan anticipated. The most momentous surprise of all was the emergence in 1949 of a unified China under an efficient Communist government which commanded the loyalty of the great majority of the Chinese people.

The end of two great colonial empires resulted in an increase in UN membership from 83 to 132 during the twelve years, 1960 to 1971, and, after Communist China had taken over the Chinese seat from Taiwan in 1971, the UN included almost the whole world apart from Taiwan, Switzerland, and the three divided countries, Germany, Vietnam, and Korea. The increase in numbers meant greater variety of membership, and the price of near universality for the organization was much greater complexity. 'Foreign affairs', wrote an authority on international history in 1961, 'are now more complicated than at any other period in history',[3] and this was still more true a few years later. Lester Pearson remarked in 1963: 'The UN has had to develop during a period of acute difficulty in international affairs. It did not cause this difficulty, but it is bound to reflect it.'[4]

In spite of the complexity and the difficulty, there has been a growing realization of the need for closer international cooperation in the political, economic, and scientific fields. Apart from the existence of

[3] C. K. Webster, 'The Machinery of British foreign policy in the 19th and 20th Centuries', in *The Art and Practice of Diplomacy*, p. 53.
[4] In an address to the UNA Montreal: see his *The Four Faces of Peace*, p. 127.

nuclear weapons, closer contacts between states may lead to friction as well as to understanding, and a conscious effort to conteract the one and encourage the other has become necessary. Economically the contrast in standards is so great and now so well known that the have-not states are becoming increasingly impatient about their position. In 1966 the *per capita* income of the United States was $3,175 and of the European Economic Community, $1,412, compared to an average in Asia of $170 and in Africa of $140.[5] The need for a world approach to such problems as population control, use of the sea-bed, waste, and pollution has also become clear.

A good start has been made with international cooperation on problems of environment and the sea-bed, as both these questions are relatively new ones, untrammelled by traditional approaches and past disputes. The General Assembly set up in 1968 a Committee on the Peaceful Uses of the Sea-Bed and the Ocean Floor beyond the Limits of National Jurisdiction, and in 1970 the Committee submitted its report to the Assembly. In the spring of 1972 the treaty limiting the military use of the sea-bed went into force. In 1968 also the Assembly called for the convening of a conference on the human environment, to be held in Stockholm in 1972. The conference took place successfully in June of that year and approved by acclamation a Declaration on the Human Environment which was included in its report to the General Assembly.

But in the economic and political fields the response has scarcely begun to meet the need. The institutional framework exists on the economic side. ECOSOC, its four regional commissions, and the relevant specialized agencies, particularly the World Bank and the Food and Agriculture Organization, have provided useful channels for economic cooperation and aid. Compared with pre-UN days the extent of economic cooperation has also been considerable. But since the war the need for it has become more evident, the obligation stronger, and the power of the wealthier countries to help the poorer greater. So much more has naturally been expected. If the United States has at times made gestures of great generosity, it has scarcely suffered in so doing, and it has chosen, on the whole, to give assistance bilaterally rather than through the appropriate international organizations, its motives having frequently been to further its national interests in the Cold War. Other developed countries have also, in their aid programmes, often been moved by motives of national self-interest. Moreover, most of them have accepted the target of devoting to their official aid programmes

---

[5] These figures, taken from the UN *Statistical Yearbook*, 1971, are the latest comparative figures available.

0·7 per cent of their gross national product by 1975 at the latest, though by 1971 only one[6] had reached this target and the average percentage of all OECD countries was 0·35.[7] Not surprisingly, therefore, the discrepancy in living standards between the have and the have-not countries has grown rather than receded.

The developing countries can scarcely be reproached for giving priority to raising their living standards and sometimes appearing lukewarm to environmental problems, but they themselves have often been to blame for inefficient handling of the money, the equipment, and the other facilities which have been provided. The failure of many of their governments to prevent corruption, waste, and misuse has understandably irritated the donor countries and thus contributed to the cessation or shrinkage of aid programmes.

Political cooperation has also been disappointing. Nationalism amongst the UN's original members has shown few signs of receding, and to it has been added the nationalism of the newly emerged states. African members have complained of the artificial frontiers and divisions imposed on their continent during the colonial era, but they have shown no urge to rectify past mistakes by sacrificing the independence of small, scarcely viable states. The two most terrible African conflicts of the last decade, in the Sudan and Nigeria, have been the result not of movements for integration but of action by central governments to prevent further separation due to racial, tribal, and religious intolerance. Barbara Ward and René Dubos in *Only One Earth* described the present age in 1972 as 'dominated as never before by separate nationalist aspirations and pretensions', and, if nationalism is to be assessed by the number of its practitioners, they were unquestionably right.

The Test Ban Treaty still does not cover underground tests and has not been adhered to by two of the five nuclear powers, while the Non-Proliferation Treaty has not been signed by a number of potential nuclear powers, including India and Israel. National antagonisms have been accentuated by ideological conflict reminiscent in its doctrinaire bitterness of religious wars in the past, and, as the cold war tension declined, it was replaced as the world's most ominous controversy by Sino-Soviet rivalry based on old-fashioned nationalism and Marxist schism. The Arab–Israel dispute, also, through its international ramifications, has presented a threat to world peace out of all proportion to the size and strength of the countries involved.

---

[6] Portugal, an exceptional case owing to its colonies.
[7] See *Development Co-operation: 1972 Review*, OECD, 1972, Table IX, p. 225.

In Western Europe alone there has been hopeful progress in the limitation of nationalism and in conscious improvement on the past. Latin America and South-East Asia have given indications of interest in the European example, but in no other region has there been any achievement comparable to the European Economic Community.

The problem of international security, therefore, was as important in 1971 as it had been in 1946, and the conditions under which it had to be solved were much more complex. The United Nations as an institution was needed as much as ever, and its task had become more difficult. Moreover, after twenty-five years its position and reputation were still a matter of controversy. On the positive side, it had many varied achievements to its credit; it was performing useful functions as a matter of day-to-day routine; and there was a growing body of people in the world with experience and knowledge of international institutions. On the other hand, there was disillusionment with its failures and cynicism about its future.

There were several basic reasons for the disenchantment. It is the fate of great institutions to raise high expectations. The euphoria following the San Francisco Conference was bound to have its anticlimax. Article 1 of the Charter, describing the purposes of the United Nations, contained a programme which would require many decades, if not centuries, for its fulfilment. Yet every subsequent failure to solve a problem or dispute seemed to fall short of these high intentions. Furthermore, it was mainly the tough problems which were brought to the UN after they had proved insoluble by normal diplomatic methods. Cynicism about the future was due partly to the contrast between the UN's aspirations and its achievements, but it was due also to the trend of opinion in the twentieth century, when two world wars, totalitarian ruthlessness, and nuclear weapons have produced a sharp reaction to Victorian optimism.

The failure of the UN, in so far as it has failed, has had two main causes: the lack of will and ability in men throughout the world to give it effective support and the deliberate choice of member states to use it as an instrument of national policy, rather than to make the sustained effort necessary to built it into the great instrument of international cooperation it was intended to be.

Illogically the UN as an institution has been made a scapegoat, as if it had an existence independent of the governments and peoples of its member states. In a speech to the General Assembly, a few months before his death, Adlai Stevenson expressed a more rational point of view in the following words: 'We have learned how heavy are the chains of inherited tradition that inhibit man's journey towards wider community. We have learned that the United Nations will be no less—and can be no better—than its membership makes it in the context of its times.'[8] A few years later U Thant said: 'The failure of the UN is the failure of the human community. The explanation is as simple as that. The UN will be as strong or as weak as its member states wish it to be.'[9]

An international organization made up of sovereign states will inevitably and rightly be used by its members for furthering their national interests. Yet the signatories of the Charter not only recognized the sovereign equality of the member states but gave their support to the great purposes and principles laid down in the Preamble and Articles 1 and 2. They therefore repudiated diplomacy in the classical sense of pursuing national self-interest by negotiation and the exercise of power, in favour of a new diplomacy based on the recognition of certain common ends and the renunciation of force except when used in the common interest. There is no necessary incompatibility between the purposes and principles of the Charter and the furtherance of national interests: in fact, few would deny that in a nuclear age peace and international cooperation to promote peace are the greatest of national interests. But there may be certain cases in which the two appear incompatible, and governments then tend to put their national interests before their obligations under the Charter, just as selfish individuals put their own interests before those of the community in which they live. Or some governments may even fail to realize that peace is of primary importance. Most member states make use of the United Nations as a convenient organization to further their own ends and help them out of difficulties, when other means fail, and this applies to strong and weak powers alike, although the need of the smaller powers to do so is, on the whole, greater. Unfortunately the small states have great interest in a strong UN but little or no power to make it strong, while the superpowers and major powers could do much by their influence and example to strengthen the UN but see little present advantage in so doing, restricting their sights in most cases to short-term and selfish considerations.

The United States government and people supported the UN with enthusiasm when it was founded. The American people are attracted by general ideals, the UN embodied their postwar hopes, and they were pleased that its headquarters were to be in their country. Furthermore,

[8] At the end of the General Debate on 26 Jan. 1965.
[9] In an informal address at the UN Association headquarters in London in April 1969.

as Inis Claude has written, it became the symbol of America's repentance for not having supported the League of Nations and of 'its determination to undertake the responsibility that it had previously spurned'.[10] For some twenty years the United States was the most powerful, and, on the whole, a consistent supporter of the UN. But its support was not based only on ideals. Its position both in the General Assembly and the Security Council being very strong during the early years, it was able to use the UN to good effect as an instrument of American policy in the Cold War, not, unfortunately, to improve its relations with the Soviet Union but to gain support in its confrontation with the Communist bloc. Moreover, the emphasis in American policy was to further national interests rather than to strengthen the UN or to promote international understanding. Truman brought the UN in, when he considered it appropriate in the case of Korea, but his successors preferred to keep it at a distance so far as Latin America was concerned, as also during the crucial early years of US involvement in Vietnam.

Starting about 1960, when the UN membership increased by seventeen, the attitude of the United States towards the organization began to change and to become less positive, the process being accelerated by the deaths of President Kennedy in 1963 and of Adlai Stevenson in 1965. Stevenson was the most distinguished Head of Mission ever sent to New York. He was succeeded by Arthur Goldberg, an able and sincere man, with a national reputation as former Judge of the Supreme Court. On Goldberg's resignation in 1968 came three representatives in quick succession, who were scarcely known to the general public. The process culminated in 1971 with President Nixon's appointment of George Bush, who was no better known than his immediate predecessors and did not share the diplomatic qualifications of two of them. This decline in the standard of representation was symptomatic of a diminishing interest and belief in the UN on the part of the American people and administration. After their initial optimism and goodwill the American people's support of the UN was sustained by their country's leading role in its activities and by the benefits which accrued to US diplomacy. But when, with the increase in membership, the United States lost its assured majority in the Assembly their attitude began to change. The change would have been less marked had the support from the beginning been for the UN as an international organization rather than as an instrument of national policy, and it is this no doubt that Adlai

[10] See his article, 'The symbolic significance of the United Nations', *The Virginia Quarterly Review*, autumn 1971, pp. 490–91.

Stevenson had in mind when he said in 1962: 'The crisis of our loyalty to the United Nations is still ahead of us.' For more than twenty years nearly all public opinion polls had revealed a positive attitude towards the UN on the part of the American people. But in a 1967 Gallup poll only 49 per cent of those interviewed said that they thought the UN was doing a good job. The percentage fell to 40 in 1970 and to 35 in November 1971.

The changed attitude of the American administration has been even more serious. In the light of the UN's record in Korea, the Suez crisis, the Congo, and to a smaller extent, in the Cuban missile crisis and Cyprus, successive American Presidents were, and could hardly fail to be, appreciative. But subsequent disappointments in the Middle East, especially in 1967, and Vietnam caused the UN too often to be made a scapegoat for American deficiencies.[11] President Nixon, no doubt influenced by his adviser, Henry Kissinger, has proved to be the most negative and cynical of all American Presidents towards the UN. In his speech to the Twenty-Fifth Anniversary Session of the General Assembly in 1970 he gave the impression of being interested only in the economic, social, and technological aspects of UN activity. In 1971 he did not attend the Assembly at all, and it was during that year's session that the United States broke its obligation under the Charter by the decision to allow chrome imports from Rhodesia. The President in his Report to Congress on US Foreign Policy in 1970 made the following statements: 'Skeptics do not build societies: the idealists are the builders', and 'We cannot expect it [the UN] to be a more telling force for peace than its members make it.' Two years later he said in his corresponding Report: 'A pervasive skepticism concerning the UN is widespread' and 'The UN is on the verge of bankruptcy. . . . It is the policy of this administration to bring down the level of US contributions to the UN and its Specialized Agencies from 31·52 per cent to 25 per cent.'

The President's personal record was partly offset by the work of his Commission for the observance of the twenty-fifth anniversary of the United Nations, which was set up in July 1970 and reported in April 1971, and for which he, of course, deserves some credit. It was chaired by Ambassador Henry Cabot Lodge and had an impressive membership, including four Senators and four Congressmen. Its report combined realism with a positive and constructive attitude. It recommended the reduction in the US contribution to the United Nations,

---

[11] The withdrawal of UNEF in May 1967 was the one case in which it can be argued that there was some justification for blaming the UN itself (see pp. 147–9).

referred to by the President, but in the contribution to the UN's *assessed regular budget*, and emphasized that it was 'in no way proposing any diminution of the overall commitment of US resources to the UN system', adding that 'each reduction in the US share of the regular budget must be clearly marked by at least a corresponding increase in US contributions to one or more of the voluntary budgets or funds in the UN system'. A member of the Commission, in a Supplementary Comment to the Report, pointed out that, if the United States were assessed on the same ability-to-pay basis as other member states, its share would amount to nearly 40 per cent of the regular UN budget and and that the cost to the United States of the 1970 regular budget was less than 25 cents per person. The Commission's Report, probably gave a balanced impression of enlightened American opinion towards the UN and of the way in which it was likely to develop under a regime with a more positive approach to international cooperation: it did not reflect so accurately the attitude of the Nixon administration itself.

There were two main differences between the attitude of the United States towards the UN and the attitude of the other super-power. The Soviet Union was unable at first to use the UN as an effective instrument of national policy owing to its minority position both in the Security Council and the General Assembly. Secondly, the Soviet government and the Soviet peoples under Stalin did not combine with their UN membership even a tincture of broad international idealism,[12] because they were adherents of a rationalist doctrine, which in the UN's early years divided the world into Marxian sheep and non-Marxian goats and grudgingly accepted only a minimum degree of coexistence as a temporary expedient.

Tsarist Russia had not fully outgrown the sense of inferiority to Western Europe which had been responsible for Peter the Great's furious modernization. Between the two World Wars this traditional cleavage was greatly increased by the Bolshevik victory, and the Soviet Union was isolated by the mutual suspicion of its leaders and its neighbours. After 1945 the suspicion was accentuated by the assertive megalomania of Stalin and the country's greatly increased power. Soviet leaders and ambassadors were as a rule crude and inexperienced, though not always inexpert practitioners of the old diplomacy, little interested in furthering the purposes and principles of the UN Charter

---

[12] The small liberal-minded minority, mostly scientists, writers, and artists, which has always existed in the Soviet Union, had no influence on official policy under Stalin, nor even the very limited opportunities to express their views, which they have seized rather than been given more recently.

or in building up the UN itself as an instrument for interstate cooperation. Later, when the US built-in majorities in the Council and Assembly disappeared, it began to use the UN to further its national interests, and, in the face of nuclear reality, to see some advantages in international understanding. But its attitude to the institution remained hardheaded, pragmatic, and somewhat cynical.

So with its own quite different background and political beliefs the Soviet Union did much less than the United States to strengthen the United Nations as an institution, though its attitude towards it was more consistent. As a state working for human salvation through the class war the line it took was understandable. Responsibility for the UN's success rested largely, apart from the United States, on the established European democracies with their experience of the disasters of uncurbed international rivalry, their knowledge and experience of democratic institutions, and their social and political ideals which were embodied in the Charter.

Britain and France were two member states which could be expected to take a positive attitude towards the UN, both as an instrument of national policy and as an international institution: their experience of the League of Nations during its good and bad periods and their contribution to its administrative structure as well as to the International Labour Organization gave them advantages compared with the two super-powers. But their will to do so and their effectiveness were diminished by the UN's anti-colonialism and by their own disingenuous and disastrous defiance of the Charter during the Suez crisis. In the case of France there were the additional disadvantages of extreme sensitivity about the country's wartime record, which was personified in de Gaulle especially during his two periods in power, and resentment of the UN's attitude on Algieria. After de Gaulle's retirement in 1969, and to some extent even earlier, a more tolerant, rational, and positive attitude towards the UN asserted itself. Apart from Suez and decolonization, Britain has always been well disposed and positive towards the UN. Yet in the colonial question she has, in a sense, avenged herself for what she considered unduly harsh criticism by handing over to the Organization a series of problems arising out of her imperial past, among others Palestine, Kuwait, Cyprus, Southern Rhodesia, and Bahrein, though her actions were also a sign of confidence in the UN's potential usefulness. During the immediate post-war years, in return for American help and understanding of her economic and diplomatic burdens, she acquiesced too readily in the United States' use of the UN as an instrument in her cold war policy instead of working actively to strengthen the organization as a force for reconciliation and peace.

India was another power which disappointed hopes that she would prove a firm and consistent supporter of the United Nations. Under the influence of Gandhi and of his disciple, Nehru, India seemed a natural champion of international cooperation and peaceful diplomacy. Nehru's remark in January 1951 that one cannot 'talk of peace and think and act in terms of war. . . . If we desire peace, we must develop the temper of peace' seemed characteristic.[13] But by then India had already used force in Junagadh and Hyderabad, and she was to do so again in Goa ten years later. In Kashmir her attitude towards UN action became increasingly critical, and her policy over East Pakistan and the Bangladesh War was reminiscent of nineteenth-century *Realpolitik* in Europe. India's voting at the UN during the Hungarian and Czech crises of 1956 and 1968 and over the Soviet Union's default in its payments has been reasonably interpreted as repayment for Soviet support on Kashmir.[14] The culmination of her change in attitude was her refusal to sign the Treaty on the Non-Proliferation of Nuclear Weapons, which was in complete contrast to Gandhi's philosophy and the so-called Panch Shila principles, according to which India and China undertook in 1964 to base their relations on mutual respect and peaceful coexistence. The refusal was largely due to China's claims on Indian territory, which led to military action in 1962, and to her subsequent acquisition of nuclear weapons. The result of these various events and developments was to deprive the UN of a strong potential backer in the Asian continent.

The new African states also have as yet done disappointingly little to strengthen the United Nations as an institution. Originally, as Francis Wilcox has written, the UN was largely 'a creation of the Western world . . . it was deeply rooted in the values and cultural patterns of the West. It was based upon Western legal concepts and Western parliamentary principles, and led largely by diplomats and members of the Secretariat from Western countries.' The sudden and considerable increase in African members, which started in 1960, was therefore a 'profound transformation'.[15] But it was a necessary and desirable transformation, if the UN was to become the truly world organization that it

[13] In a broadcast from London: see Jawaharlal Nehru, *India's Foreign Policy: Selected Speeches Sept. 1946–April 1961*, Indian Ministry of Information and Broadcasting, 1961, p. 185.

[14] See Swadesh Rana, 'The changing Indian diplomacy at the United Nations', *International Organization*, winter 1970, p. 65.

[15] *The United Nations and the Nonaligned Nations*, p. 3.

was intended to be. The new African states joined the UN with enthusiasm, because they believed in what it stood for and because it strengthened their identity as independent countries. Yet, as has been seen, they worked mainly to promote African interests, held together as a bloc, and were strongly influenced by the Organization of African Unity. This had its advantages. It helped the forty-one African members, many of them small and the great majority of them inexperienced, to gain confidence, learn the techniques of UN membership, and exert an influence in the organization earlier than would otherwise have been the case. But it restricted their usefulness as members: in fact, they employed the UN as an instrument of bloc policy just as the United States and other powers have used it as an instrument of national policy. Furthermore, there is a danger, which has already revealed itself, that failure to achieve bloc objectives, for example, on the apartheid question, will lead to disillusionment and a loss of interest in the other great purposes for which the organization stands.

These negative or at least ambiguous attitudes towards the United Nations, on the part of its most influential members and of the largest bloc of states within the organization, have been reflected in its financial position, which has been a continuous cause of concern in recent years to successive Secretaries-General and to UN supporters. The human race and its rulers have so far been extraordinarily niggardly in providing money for international purposes. In 1784 Kant wrote, in connection with his belief in the need for a 'universal *Cosmopolitan Institution*': 'Our rulers at present have no money to spend on public educational institutions, or in general on all that concerns the highest good of the world—because all their resources are already placed to the account of the next war'.[16] At the League of Nations' Assembly meeting in 1933 the British government made a strong attack on League expenditure, which resulted in a saving of some £6,000 of which the British share was £600.[17] Figures given by Quincy Wright show that during the period 1956 to 1964 the annual *per capita* cost of international organization in the world was $0·17 and of armaments $40·00, so that the *per capita* cost of armaments was 235 times the greater. According to Richard Gardner the 'total US contributions to the UN system in 1969, including the Specialized Agencies and the voluntary programs, amounted to $250 million—less than the cost of the New York City Fire Department',[18]

---

[16] *The Idea of a Universal History*, pp. 23–24.
[17] Viscount Cecil, *A Great Experiment*, p. 179.
[18] See his article, 'Can the United Nations be revived?', *Foreign Affairs*, July 1970, p. 673.

and U Thant pointed out in 1970 that the money being spent on the Vietnam War for one year would be sufficient to operate the UN for another 185 years.[19] It is clear, therefore, that in the United Nations there is no true financial crisis but rather a crisis of will amongst its members. The sacrifice of a few atomic submarines or large military transport planes would wipe out the organization's entire debt.

The future of the Security Council will depend mainly on the future of the United Nations as a whole. It will be influenced by the changes in the world scene that have just been considered and the way they work themselves out in relation to international institutions, by the attitude of UN members to the Organization, the extent to which they are ready to improve on their past record, and the extent to which they are negative and cynical or positive and imaginative in their approach. But it will depend also on how far the Council is able to solve its own special problems.

One of its main problems relates to the Council's membership in the broadest sense and has three aspects: whether provisions of the Charter dealing with the Council's composition should be revised; in what ways the membership under the present provisions could be improved; and how far the standard of member states' representatives could be raised.

The present composition of the Security Council must be considered unsatisfactory, when Britain and France have the same privileged position as China, the Soviet Union, and the United States, while India, Japan, and Brazil have no special privileges. Two proposals for radical reform have been made: the introduction of a new category of semi-permanent members, following the example of the League of Nations, by allowing immediate re-election in the case of a limited number of non-permanent members; and, secondly, a more thoroughgoing revision of the Charter involving a reallocation of the permanent seats and the possible restriction of the veto to the super-powers.

The first plan has the advantage of being less drastic and less likely to arouse the insuperable opposition of the present permanent members. But it has the great disadvantage of introducing an intermediate category for which there would be too many claimants. If India and Japan became semi-permanent members, why not Indonesia? Would a semi-permanent seat for Brazil satisfy Latin America? How would the aspirations of Africa and the Middle East be met? and what about Italy, Pakistan, Bangladesh, and ultimately Western Germany? The strongest

[19] *Remarks at a reception given by Speakers Research Committee of United Nations, New York, 10 May 1967* (Press Release SG/SM/707).

candidates, India and Japan, would probably not be satisfied with semi-permanent status. Furthermore, the semi-permanent category would reduce frequency of representation for ordinary members, and there is a strong and justified feeling that an increase in the Council's size to meet this point would change its character and reduce its effectiveness.

This plan, therefore, would be very difficult to carry out, although the alteration involved in the Charter would be small and would not necessarily go beyond the sentence in Article 23 (2) dealing with the re-election of members. Yet some arrangement along these lines might be made informally by the UN's geographical groups. The Latin Americans have wisely seen to it that for three-fifths of the time either Brazil or Argentina, their two largest and most influential states, has been a member of the Council. It might be possible for the Asian members to arrange that India, Japan, and Indonesia should be more frequently represented on the Council than other Asian countries, and for the West Europeans to agree that Italy should more often be a member than smaller states. The equivalent arrangement in Africa would be for preference to be given to Nigeria, the UAR, and Ethiopia, although African members appear to be wedded to the principle of the sovereign equality of states, not modified, as the Charter intends, by the specific terms of Article 23 (1).

The alternative proposal for a reallocation of the permanent seats and a reconsideration of the veto would involve a much more controversial change in the Charter. Apart from the anomalies already mentioned, it is obviously illogical and wrong that three of the five permanent seats in the Council should be held by North Atlantic powers with much in common culturally, politically, and economically. Also Lord Cecil pointed out in 1949 that the binding authority of the Security Council under Articles 24 and 25 had made the veto necessary, because the great powers were not prepared to allow the Council to order them about to the extent of using their military forces in a cause of which they might disapprove'.[20] As the provisions of Article 43 regarding military forces have never been implemented, some fresh thinking about the veto would be appropriate. On the other hand, the Soviet Union is strongly opposed to Charter revision, especially to a reconsideration of the veto, and a revision conference in the near future would probably do more harm than good by stimulating controversy over problems that are at present insoluble. It is arguable, therefore, that, until the international climate has been improved, a better course would be to concentrate on

[20] See his comment following an address by Kathleen D. Courtney, 'The United Nations in a divided world', *International Affairs*, April 1949, p. 174.

progress within the framework of the existing Charter, which has proved itself to be flexible and capable of organic growth.

In the long term the solution of the problem may be a Security Council based on regional representation. If the European Economic Community develops well politically after the accession of Britain, Denmark, and Ireland, the neatest answer to the problems of the growing anachronism of British and French permanent membership and of the claims of Italy and probably of Western Germany would be one permanent seat for Western Europe. At present no other regional organization compares with the EEC in cohesion and effectiveness, but the OAS, the OAU, and South-East Asia may be stimulated by Europe's example, and the way would then be prepared for a broader transformation of the Council system of representation on the lines suggested by Churchill in 1943.[21] One advantage of the regional system is that it would facilitate a reduction in the Council's present size.

Meanwhile more needs to be done to raise the standard of Council membership under the present provisions of the Charter. This can be achieved by paying greater attention to the provision of Article 23(1), stating that, in the election of non-permanent members, due regard should be specially paid to the contribution of members to the maintenance of international peace and security. The enlargement of the Council in 1966 has led to a lowering of standards. The Afro-Asian beneficiaries of the change did not all fully realize the difference between the Assembly, where they had gained their first UN experience, and the Council with its great responsibilities and its need on occasions to make big decisions at short notice. The three African members in 1970, as has been pointed out (p. 100), represented countries with an aggregate population of only about 10 million: the corresponding figure for the two Asian members, Nepal and Syria, was about 15 million. It was not surprising, therefore, that when Japan succeeded Nepal the following year the new Asian representative was listened to with more attention, and the Council seemed to have gained in importance. Such a judgment is not derogatory to Nepal. The UN body, which reflects the sovereign equality of states, is the General Assembly, and in the Security Council other criteria should prevail. It is not derogatory to the state of Nevada that it sends fewer Congressmen to Washington than New York: in the Senate both states have two representatives.

[21] An interesting proposal for Security Council reform based on regional representation has been put forward by Arthur Lall in *The Security Council in a Universal United Nations*, pp. 33–34.

The practice of the African group, in selecting its representatives for the Security Council, of putting bloc loyalty before actual or potential contribution to peace and security also must ultimately be modified. During the fifteenth session of the Assembly in 1959 Nehru said: 'We are against the formation of isolated blocs in the UN, because it means that this Assembly has no capacity to decide in freedom; that decisions are reached elsewhere beforehand and that all that happens is degrees of master-minding.'[22] A Council member, whose individuality is absorbed by the bloc and who has no higher loyalty to the UN itself, like the member of parliament despised by Edmund Burke, sacrifices to the coercive authority of instructions both his judgment and his conscience.

There is reason to suppose that the group-centredness of African members will in time give way to a broader allegiance. An encouraging phenomenon at UN headquarters is that members of missions from all parts of the world, who arrive in New York with a critical and cynical attitude towards the organization, more often than not acquire a more positive standpoint as the months and years go by. They develop a loyalty towards the UN, an understanding of its administrative problems, and an appreciation of its broad political purposes and of its potential value to the world.[23] In the case of African members this process should become easier as economic difficulties are overcome and the legacies of colonialism disappear. It should be accompanied also by a greater readiness within the group to choose candidates for Council membership who are best suited to handle the broad problems affecting international peace and security with which that body has to deal.

Further the calibre of the heads of missions has a considerable effect upon the Council's influence and prestige. The tape-recordings of some of the Council's big debates, when good and bad representatives are speaking, provide good evidence on this point. At their worst the Council's proceedings are a parody of what they should be; at their best they are dignified and momentous occasions, worthy of a great international body. A member state ought at least to appoint to New York one of the best of its professional diplomatists, with a personality suited to the special requirements of the UN. In September 1970 U

[22] G. A. Official Records (15th session) 906th meeting, 17 Oct. 1959, p. 752.

[23] This view is based partly on the writer's judgment, as a frequent visitor to the UN and as an occasional participant in UN proceedings over a period of ten years, but also on the views of experienced and hard-headed members of the Secretariat. Experience at the UN may also result in serious disillusionment, but this most often happens when early hopes have been pitched too high.

Thant commended the action of a few governments in making their representatives in New York members of their Cabinets.[24] President Eisenhower made Henry Cabot Lodge a member of his Cabinet, when he appointed him Head of the US Mission in 1953, and, notwithstanding the decline in American representation at the UN following Stevenson's death, the US Head of Mission still attends Cabinet meetings concerned with foreign policy. The British Labour government wisely made Lord Caradon, their choice as head of mission, a member of the government, but the new Conservative government in 1970 reverted to the appointment of a professional diplomat. Adlai Stevenson and Caradon, each in his different way, did a great deal for the United Nations during their terms of office in New York, and such well-chosen representatives and loyal supporters of the organization as Max Jakobson of Finland and Davidson Nicol of Sierra Leone exerted an influence for good disproportionate to the size and importance of their countries.

The Council's membership was strengthened and its prestige raised, when in November 1971 the People's Republic of China replaced Taiwan as the official representative of China at the United Nations. This long overdue change brought an end to the absurd anomaly, much more absurd than any inappropriate choice of African members and the result of sustained efforts by the United States, by which for over twenty years Taiwan, with about 14 million inhabitants, occupied a permanent seat in the Security Council with power of veto, when it was openly opposed to the political system supported by the great majority of the Chinese people, numbering over 700 million. The arrival of the new representative made the Council a more realistic and interesting body and brought the UN as a world organization much nearer to completeness.

By the spring of 1972 it was possible to form only a provisional impression of Communist China's attitude and policy as a UN member. But this impression was favourable. Chinese contributions to the debates were well prepared, dignified, and refreshingly relevant and concise. China had had virtually no experience of UN affairs before 1971, and, due to her long period of relative isolation and the interruption of higher education during the Cultural Revolution, she was short of diplomatists and of qualified candidates for the diplomatic service. Soon after her admission by General Assembly vote Premier Chou En-lai expressed surprise at the result and said that China would be very cautious in its approach to UN problems. Vice-foreign minister Chiao

[24] In a speech at the Waldorf Astoria, New York (Press Release SG/SM/1335, 18 Sept. 1970).

Kuan-hua, head of the Chinese delegation, admitted that his country was short of qualified diplomatists.[25] China's wise and restrained reaction to this situation was that she did not at first participate in the work of some UN committees and of a number of specialized agencies. In those bodies in which she did participate her attitude was, on the whole, modest and cooperative.

China expressed her disapproval of the UN Force in Cyprus, was against negotiations about the Middle East on the basis of Resolution 242, and was opposed to the use of UN observers. But she showed no desire to sabotage constructive UN operations that had been initiated and approved before her arrival on the scene. She refused an invitation to join the four-power talks on the Middle East and in the case of a resolution on UNFICYP neither voted for or against nor abstained but chose rather 'not to participate', a procedure, which suited her unique position as a permanent member of the Council who had only just arrived. During the five-power meetings in December 1971 on the election of the Secretary-General her attitude was unexceptionable, and she showed respect for the international status of the Secretariat by making no fuss about members from Nationalist China.

As regards broad international alignments the Chinese have emerged as bitter rivals of the Soviet Union, opponents of super-power pretensions, and champions of the Third World, of which she claimed membership. In reply to speeches of welcome in November 1971 Chiao Kuan-hua made the following characteristic statements in the General Assembly:

> China is still an economically backward country as well as a developing country. Like the overwhelming majority of the Asian, African, and Latin American countries, China belongs to the Third World. . . .
> With a population of 700 million, China ought to make a greater contribution to human progress. And we hope that this situation of our ability falling short of this wish of ours will be gradually changed.[26]

The *détente* between the United States and the Soviet Union may to some extent be impeded by China, which takes every opportunity of accentuating the differences between them. On the other hand, her presence in the Council has produced an interesting triangular situation in which the unrestricted rivalry between two super-powers of the early Cold War is not likely to recur.

[25] Chou En-lai's statements were reported in the press: Chiao Kuan-hua's remark was made to a head of mission at the UN.
[26] G.A. Official Records, 1,983rd meeting, 15 Nov. 1971.

Experts on China are less disposed than many others to prophesy about that country's future, and it would be unwise to generalize on her future role in the United Nations on the basis of impressions formed in a few months. But her emergence from relative isolation and her participation at New York and elsewhere in the many activities of the UN and its specialized agencies can only be advantageous. Contacts through the United Nations have unquestionably contributed to the East–West *détente*. And the admission of the Chinese People's Republic to the organization, within a few years of its acquisition of nuclear weapons, will no doubt, in direct and indirect ways, further the maintenance of international peace and security.

Comparable in importance to the question of the Council's membership is the problem of its procedure, which has many aspects; some on a high level such as the use of the veto on important issues, others of less significance like the polite or overpolite conventions of speakers in the Council. Taken together, they have had great influence on the Council's past record and reputation and will play a major part in moulding its future.

Over the years there have been some positive and encouraging procedural developments. The veto, during the last decade, has been used much less frequently and with more discretion than during the Council's first fifteen years. The double veto, after being successfully evaded, has fallen into disuse. The development of the consensual approach, despite some disadvantages, has resulted in a more constructive and cooperative attitude towards the problems considered, which has great possibilities for the future, and in this connection the sense of responsibility, the initiative, and the authority of Council presidents have noticeably increased.[27] On the other hand, bad habits have grown up and much remains to be done.

The growing number of states and individuals who have been invited to participate in Council discussions is an ominous development, which culminated at the Addis Ababa meeting. Many thoughtful and responsible UN members and supporters believe that it should be checked, by paying more attention to the wording of Article 31. If the Council is allowed to become a small version of the General Assembly and a sounding-board for propaganda, it cannot at the same time be an effective body for grappling, through constructive and cooperative discussion, with major problems of peace and security. The vigilance,

---

[27] For example, during the four-power talks on the Middle East after 1967, the President acted as a liaison between the permanent and non-permanent members, keeping the latter informed about the progress of the talks.

L

which is the price to be paid for the successful running of democratic institutions—and the UN, apart from the veto, is essentially democratic in conception and structure—demands sustained effort and courage from those who must be vigilant. The courage includes a readiness to put the furtherance of great purposes before temporary popularity with fellow members.

Again the Council's efficiency could be increased and much time saved, if its procedure were improved in many points of detail, which have been dictated by custom. Small improvements that have recently been made support the belief that more could be done. The practice since 1969 of members waiving the right to consecutive translation was followed in 1971 by sensible statements from two American representatives in succession that they waived the right for all their interventions, unless they made specific statements to the contrary in advance. A habit has grown up by which after a new President has assumed office at the beginning of each month every member thanks the last President and congratulates his successor. In February 1971 a brave request was made by Ambassador Yost and Sir Colin Crowe of the United Kingdom that these formalities should be dispensed with. It was supported by France and Italy and by Yost's successor but had only limited success, the representative of one very small state, after relinquishing the presidency, even going so far as to reproach the United States Mission with not having bestowed on him the accolade of American appreciation. Members also from time to time offer fourteen separate congratulations to a colleague on his promotion or fourteen condolences on the death of a countryman. The simple solution of this problem, which would contribute to the Council's efficiency, would be for members to agree that their present or past President should perform these public acts of courtesy on behalf of the whole Council.

Two suggestions have been made to help the Council to deal quickly, and yet thoroughly, with the questions referred to it. The first was that the provision made in procedural Rule 28 for the appointment of a rapporteur should be implemented. In cases where the issues are political the argument against a rapporteur is usually decisive (see p. 96). But in minor or relatively uncontroversial matters the experiment might be tried, and, if successful, might prove capable of development.[28]

The second suggestion was the Brazilian proposal, to which reference

[28] The suggestion has been revived from time to time, since it was approved by the General Assembly in 1949, because rapporteurs were widely employed by the League of Nations, because they have been successfully used by committees of the UN Assembly, and because they can be appointed and can work more quickly than a commission or a committee.

has already been made (p. 111), for setting up *ad hoc* committees of the Council to deal with particular disputes. It was contained in a memorandum of the government of Brazil, which was sent to the Secretary-General and the President of the Security Council in the spring of 1970.[29] The memorandum pointed out that the consensus procedure had been accompanied by a trend to more unanimous Council decisions but that they had often been achieved by the deliberate evasion of underlying disagreements. Furthermore, the resulting resolutions were not always observed. The proposed *ad hoc* committees would ensure 'the substantive examination of the fundamental issues involved' by enabling the parties to each situation to participate in the process of consultation. They would also 'provide a suitable framework for the discussion of some important international issues and problems from which the United Nations has been excluded, not for want of competence, but possibly for lack of a more flexible machinery'. Brazil gave high priority to the need for Charter revision but recognized the difficulties involved, and Ambassador Castro, the Brazilian representative, pointed out to the General Assembly that his government's proposal would not require any revision of the Charter nor any change in the provisional rules of procedure.[30] The proposal has aroused the interest and support of many delegations but has not yet received the careful consideration by the Council itself which it deserves.

The passing of Council resolutions which cannot be, or are unlikely to be, observed has been a phenomenon of growing frequency during recent years. As an alternative to this mainly fruitless procedure a former President of the Council has suggested that it should sometimes discuss and give advice on a question without attempting to pass a resolution. The advice might take the form of a presidential statement of consensus, in which case it would fit in with existing practice. At all events the adoption of resolutions which are not implemented, for some propaganda or other purpose, is severely damaging in its cumulative effect to the prestige and authority of the Council, and it is the duty of all Council members to weigh up more carefully than many of them have done in the past the advantages of a largely impotent gesture against the disadvantage of permanent damage to the Council's effectiveness.

With regard to the timing of Council meetings three points deserve careful consideration. First, the suggestion has been made and supported by a number of non-permanent members that there should be at least one meeting a month, when the new President assumes office, to

[29] See UN Document S/9786 of 8 May 1970.
[30] UN Document A/C.1/PV.1725.

survey and, if necessary, discuss matters of which the Council is seized. In the spring of 1972 there were eighty-eight such matters, some of them going back to the Council's early years. This innovation would demand restraint on the part of members, but it should also encourage a sense of responsibility, and it would make it possible for some problems and situations to be discussed without waiting for them to reach the critical state, which would make consideration of them imperative. Secondly, the position with regard to periodic meetings is fundamentally unsatisfactory. It is laid down in the Charter that they shall be held twice a year, and successive Secretaries-General have urged that the obligation be honoured. Yet it was left to the initiative of a small state to propose the one periodic meeting that has been held. That meeting was badly prepared and casually handled, and the venture has not been repeated. To allow sleeping dogs to lie is conducive to a quiet life but will not contribute to the success of a great institutional experiment. Thirdly, failure to call meetings of the Council in good time—for example, over the admission of Communist China in the spring of 1950, over the Arab–Israel dispute in April 1967, and over East Pakistan in 1971—has had most serious and incalculable implications (see pp. 69, 148 and 182). Careful consideration and discussion of the reasons for these failures and of how to avoid a repetition of them would, after careful preparation at a lower level, be an appropriate item for a periodic meeting.

The Security Council's future will be strongly influenced by the extent to which it solves its own problems of membership and procedure. But it will depend also, as will the future of the United Nations as a whole, on much broader considerations. Human institutions are a response to the needs of the societies which they serve: they do not beget those societies. The prerequisite for flourishing international institutions is a well-developed international society, and as yet that is only in the making. The harsh fact is that the United Nations with its acknowledged limitations is probably all that the world is at present ready for. Side by side, therefore, with the endeavour to improve the UN and its organs a major effort is required to develop a greater sense of interdependence and community amongst peoples.

The obstacles to doing so are formidable. In the first place, the two super-powers and China, with their immense influence and resources, have traditions of isolationism or near isolationism. China has, it is true, recently emerged from almost complete detachment, with consequences that cannot as yet be foreseen, and the Soviet Union has in the past decade been rather more positive towards the UN. But the United States, on whose example and openhandedness international undertakings have depended so much since 1945, has appeared to revert to former habits of mind as a result of political disappointment and economic uncertainty. Secondly, the emotions, the traditions, and the prejudices of nationalism die very hard, even in the second half of the twentieth century and in countries who have suffered greatly from them. Lastly, the development of international consciousness has been most marked in the past during wars and their aftermath. It requires apparently the pressure and incentive generated by disaster to bring home the need for progress in this direction, and the relative stabilization of relations between the major powers and the super-powers since the second World War has reduced the sense of urgency.

In material things nations are in a high degree interdependent, and, from an economic point of view only, an international society already exists. But more is required to form the foundations of a true international community. Economic contacts may produce friction as well as friendship, and to these contacts must be added political understanding, cultural tolerance, and that sense of belonging together and common destiny on the international plane which, on a more restricted scale, is the essence of nationalism. They alone can provide the basis for a really satisfactory international organization. U Thant once said, after referring to human achievements in art, science, literature, and religion: 'Is all this to end because so few are able to think of man rather than this or that group of men?'[31]

To strengthen the United Nations as a whole and the Security Council in particular the second main need is that more member states, their governments, their statesmen, and their representatives in New York, should support and work to improve it as an object worthwhile in itself. The present tendency is to take it as it is, lament its shortcomings with more or less cynicism, and use it for the furtherance of national policies. To treat the UN as an end in itself is not just an altruistic exercise: if peace is the greatest national interest, to strengthen the main institution working for peace will also be nationally advantageous, just as Kant's categorical imperative, in the form quoted in the first chapter, is both ethnically unexceptionable and an excellent recipe for good industrial relations. Also the world's newly discovered ecological interdependence reinforces the need for international order. In the case of the Security Council, which acts on behalf of all UN members in matters of peace and security and whose decisions are binding, its members have a clear moral obligation to act not merely as the representatives of their own country but on behalf of the UN as a whole. By implication also they

[31] In an address in New York in 1963, reproduced in *Portfolio for Peace*, pp. 25–26.

have a duty, in the terminology of Rousseau, to discover and follow the general will of the organization and to do all that they can to strengthen the Council as an institution for implementing the UN's general will.

Amongst heads of missions a minority only—though a significant one and from all regional groups—have conceived their duty, towards the UN in general and the Security Council in particular, in this way. But as regards statesmen of high rank the United Nations has been even less well served than the League of Nations, none having made contributions comparable to those of Briand, Cecil, and Smuts. Britain, France, and the United States have produced no outstanding UN supporter at this level, although Truman, Kennedy, and Harold Wilson have shown real understanding of its importance, the last two in particular by their choice of representatives in New York. The record of middle and smaller powers has been better: as foreign minister and prime minister of Canada, Lester Pearson made a greater contribution than any other political leader of the first rank, and a number of Scandanavian statesmen also have worked wholeheartedly to strengthen the UN as an institution.

The United Nations has been well served by its first three Secretaries-General, and the contribution of Hammarskjöld was outstanding. He gave to the UN an imaginative purpose and made work in the Secretariat, for those who could appreciate his intentions, interesting and adventurous. No one has done more for the education of the Security Council as an institution than Hammarskjöld did during the Congo crisis, when he first called on it to take action and then challenged it to give him clearer directives. As Barbara Ward has said, he 'was a man of the next generation. He truly belonged to the whole world', and 'he was pointing the way forward for all humanity'.[32] Almost equally remarkable in a different way was Ralph Bunche, who served the UN with devotion for twenty-five years, won the confidence of nearly everyone with whom he negotiated, and did not hesitate, when he thought it right, to side with the Secretary-General in discussion against the American Secretary of State.

But the support the UN has received, however distinguished in a few cases, has been quite insufficient. None of the permanent members of the Security Council has been working consistently to build up the UN's authority. The United States has been best situated to do so effectively,

---

[32] In her Dag Hammarskjöld Memorial Lecture, 'The UN and the decade of development', published in *The Quest for Peace*, ed. A. W. Cordier and W. Foote, p. 201.

and two American authorities have summed up the position pessi-
mistically. Benjamin Cohen wrote in 1966: 'Most national statesmen,
while paying lip-service to the UN . . . and professing to wish to see it
strengthened, have done precious little to develop and dramatize the
great potentialities of the U.N. under the present Charter in the field
of peace-keeping and pacific settlement.'[33] And Richard Gardner, in
1970, after referring to the 'low profile' of the Nixon Administration in
the United Nations, added: 'In both the US Mission and in the State
Department's Bureau of International Organization Affairs the emphasis is on damage-limitation rather than institution building.'[34]

Three further considerations will have a decisive influence on the
UN's future and its work for peace. It has in the past thriven on crises
successfully surmounted, in which it has played a constructive part.
Its reputation has never been higher than after the decision to resist
aggression in Korea and after the settlement of the Suez crisis in 1956.
In the more complex cases of the Congo and the Cuban missile crisis,
and after its smaller-scale achievement in Cyprus, it gained in prestige
in the eyes of more knowledgeable observers. More recently it has been
in increasing need of some further proof of its capacity for useful action,
and it would be greatly strengthened in the unlikely but not impossible
event of its contributing to a Middle East settlement.

Secondly, a great deal will depend on a sizeable number of statesmen
and other influential people making a constructive, imaginative, and
confident approach to UN problems. We live in a cynical era overshadowed by conscious and subconscious fears of nuclear catastrophe.
Some years ago Bertrand Russell wrote of 'the sombre fears that rob
our age of hopefulness'. Matters are made worse by the depressing but
undoubted fact that bad news has greater 'news value' than good news.
The failures of the Security Council are given full publicity, while its
successes are either not mentioned at all or are quickly forgotten. What
is wanted in the UN's supporters is not airy idealism, the twin brother
of disillusion, but restrained optimism based on the rational assumption that great effort, intelligently applied, produces positive results.

Lastly, there is the challenging and Herculean task of educating
peoples throughout the world to appreciate the need for international
organization, to study the difficulties in the way of making it effective
and the methods by which they might be overcome; in fact, to create
'the organized opinion of mankind', which President Wilson proposed

[33] See his article, 'The United Nations in its twentieth year', *International
Organization*, Spring 1966, p. 196.
[34] 'Can the United Nations be Revived?', *Foreign Affairs*, July 1970, p. 672.

to use before it existed. This work of public education needs to be done in the developed as well as in the developing countries; at the levels of statesmen as well as of the simplest voters; and among the young as well as the old. The education of youth is the most important task and should be the easiest of all. But the present younger generation presents a special problem. While more sensitive than any that preceded it to the need for tolerance and for fulfilling international obligations, it has deep-lying suspicion of institutions, without which no international order can be achieved.

Against the background of world history the United Nations is at an early stage of a great international experiment being carried out during a time of bewilderingly rapid change. Within the UN organization the Security Council has been given the greatest responsibility. It has never been able to carry out the main task for which it was intended by the Charter, the enforcement of a limited system of collective security through a continuation of the wartime alliance of the permanent members. Instead it has handled, with varying success, a whole range of tasks in the fields of peace-making and peace-keeping, most of them arising out of the dissolution of the European colonial empires.

Many of the difficulties which the Council has encountered have been in the nature of adolescent ailments, which, it may be hoped, will gradually be outgrown and in any case cannot recur. Decolonization in Africa and Asia is almost complete. The rapid increase in UN membership cannot go much further, because membership now covers most of the earth. The many problems that have accompanied the increase may with reason be considered temporary, although the time required for their solution will vary: diplomatic inexperience is being quickly overcome; neo-nationalism will prove more stubborn; and preoccupation with group and regional interests, linked as it is with economic difficulties and problems of human rights, will need the cooperation of all UN members for its solution.

The adolescent aspects of the United Nations' problem, however, are by no means confined to its newer members. In fact, the development of a truly international approach to the UN's tasks may well come more easily to newly created states, which are less bound by tradition and less self-reliant than many older members. The UN has been experiencing institutional adolescence. Unlike the political institutions of the more successful democracies it is not the result of organic growth: its Charter was drawn up round the conference table by representatives of states with varied characteristics and traditions. They had different aspirations, different interests, and different methods of work. The document which resulted, therefore, was both a great human achievement and a diplomatic *tour de force*, but no final solution. The sustained effort of member states over a long period will be needed to evolve satisfactory procedures and to give the United Nations and its Security Council the authority that is appropriate to them.

Bibliography

The bibliography is confined to primary and secondary sources which have been useful in the preparation of this book or are referred to in the text or footnotes. It is divided into two parts, general and sectional, and in each part three subheadings, Documents, Books and monographs, and Articles and speeches, are used. No item appears twice, and the reader may therefore have to refer to both main parts before finding the entry he is seeking. Items which have special relevance to one section of the book may be included in the general part because their relevance is not confined to that section.

General

Documents

(*a*) Basic UN Documents

Annual Reports of the Secretary-General on the Work of the Organisation. United Nations, New York, 1946–. General Assembly, Official Records: Supplement no. 1.

Reports of the Security Council to the General Assembly. United Nations, New York, 1946–. General Assembly, Official Records: Supplement no. 2.

Security Council Official Records (S/PV). United Nations, New York, 1946–. (English abbreviation—SCOR)

Repertoire of the Practice of the Security Council 1946–1951; Supplements 1952–55, 1956–58, 1959–63, 1964–65, and 1966–68. New York, United Nations Department of Political and Security Council Affairs, 1954, 1957, 1959, 1965, 1968 and 1971.

Repertory of Practice of United Nations Organs, vol. II, *Articles 23–54 of the Charter*; Supplement no. 1, vol. I.
Articles 1–54 of the Charter; Supplement no. 2, vol. II,
Articles 9–54 of the Charter; Supplement no. 3, vol. II,
Articles 23–72 of the Charter; United Nations, New York, 1955, 1958, 1964, and 1971.

(*b*) Other documents

CORDIER, ANDREW W. and FOOTE, WILDER, eds. *Public Papers of the Secretaries-General of the United Nations,* Vol. I: '*Trygve Lie 1946–1953*'. Columbia University Press, 1969.

FOOTE, WILDER. *The Secret of Peace, A Selection of Statements and Speeches of Dag Hammarskjöld.* London, Bodley Head, 1962.

HAMMARSKJÖLD, DAG. *The International Civil Servant in Law and in Fact*, address at Oxford University, 30 May 1961. UN Office of Public Information, New York Release SG/1045 of 29 May 1961.

HAMMARSKJÖLD, DAG. 'The vital role of the United Nations in the diplomacy of reconciliation' (address to both Houses of Parliament, London), *U.N. Review*, May 1958, vol. IV, no. 11.

ISRAEL, FRED L., ed. *The State of the Union Messages of the Presidents, 1790–1966*, 3 vol. New York, Chelsea House-Robert Hector, 1966.

NEHRU, JAWAHARLAL. *India's Foreign Policy: selected speeches, Sept. 1946—April 1961*. New Delhi, Indian Ministry of Information and Broadcasting, 1961.

Report of the Secretary-General on the withdrawal of the United Nations Emergency Force, 26 June 1967. UN General Assembly. Official Records, A/6730 and Add. 1–3.

Statement by Y. A. Malik, Permanent Representative of the USSR to the UN at a UNITAR Seminar on the Role of the UN Secretariat, 19 May 1972. Press Release of the USSR Mission to the UN, 18 May 1972.

US Department of State, *Dumbarton Oaks Documents on International Organization*, Publication 2257 (1954).

Report of the Security Council Committee on Council Meetings away from Headquarters. UN Security Council document S/10514, 18 Jan. 1972.

US Foreign Policy for the 1970s: a new strategy for peace. A Report to the Congress by Richard Nixon, President of the United States, 18 February 1970. US Government Printing Office, Washington, DC.

US Foreign Policy for the 1970s: the emerging structure of peace. A Report to the Congress by Richard Nixon, President of the United States, 9 February 1972. US Government Printing Office, Washington, DC.

US Participation in the UN: Reports (annual) by the President to the Congress. US Government Printing Office, Washington, D.C.

U THANT. *Portfolio for Peace: Excerpts from the writings and speeches of U Thant, Secretary-General of the United Nations, on major world issues 1961–70*. New York, United Nations, 1970.

Books and monographs

ACHESON, DEAN. *Present at the Creation: my years in the State Department*. New York, Norton, 1969.

ALMOND, GABRIEL A. *The American People and Foreign Policy*. Harvard University Press, 1963.

ARMSTRONG, HAMILTON FISH. *The Calculated Risk*. New York, Macmillan Company, 1947.

BAILEY, SYDNEY D. *Peaceful Settlement of International Disputes: some proposals for research*, third (rev.) edn. New York, United Nations Institute for Training and Research, 1971.

BENTWICH, NORMAN and MARTIN, ANDREW. *A Commentary on the Charter of the United Nations*. London, Kegan Paul, 1950.

BHUTTO, Z. A. *Peace Keeping by the U.N.* Karachi, Pakistan Publishing Company House, 1967.

BLOOMFIELD, LINCOLN P. and others. *International Military Forces*. Boston, Little, Brown, 1964.

BLOOMFIELD, LINCOLN P. *The United Nations and United States Foreign Policy.* Boston, Little Brown, 1960.

BLOOMFIELD, LINCOLN P. and LEISS, AMELIA C. *Controlling Small Wars: the strategy for the 1970s.* London, Allen Lane, the Penguin Press, 1970.

BOWETT, A. W. *United Nations Forces.* London, Stevens and Sons, 1964.

BOYD, ANDREW. *Fifteen Men on a Powder Keg: a history of the U.N. Security Council.* London, Methuen, 1971.

BOYD, ANDREW. *United Nations—Piety, Myth, and Truth,* rev. edn. Harmondsworth, Penguin Books, 1964.

BRIERLEY, J. L. *The Basis of Obligation in International Law and Other Papers,* selected and edited by Sir Hersch Lauterpacht and C. H. M. Waldeck. Oxford, Clarendon Press, 1958.

BRIERLEY, J. L. *The Law of Nations,* sixth edn. Oxford, Clarendon Press, 1963.

BRITISH INFORMATION SERVICE. *Britain and the United Nations.* London, Central Office of Information, 1969.

BUCHAN, ALASTAIR. *War in Modern Society.* London, Collins (Fontana Library), 1966.

BURNS, ARTHUR LEE and HEATHCOTE, NINA. *Peace Keeping by United Nations Forces.* London, Pall Mall Press, 1963.

BUTTERFIELD, HERBERT. *International Conflict in the Twentieth Century: a Christian view.* London, Routledge & Kegan Paul, 1960.

BUTTERFIELD, HERBERT and WIGHT, MARTIN, eds. *Diplomatic Investigations.* London, Allen & Unwin, 1966.

BYRNES, JAMES F. *Speaking Frankly.* New York and London, Harper, 1947.

CALVOCORESSI, PETER. *World Order and New States.* London, Chatto &Windus, 1962.

CALVOCORESSI, PETER. *World Politics since 1945.* London, Longmans, 1968.

CARR, E. H. *Nationalism and After.* London, Macmillan, 1945.

CHURCHILL, WINSTON S. *The Second World War,* vol. IV, *The Hinge of Fate.* London, Cassell, 1951.

CLARK, GRENVILLE and SOHN, LOUIS B. *World Peace Through World Law.* Harvard University Press, 1966.

CLAUDE, JR, INIS L. *The Changing United Nations.* New York, Random House, 1967.

CLAUDE, JR, INIS L. *The Impact of Public Opinion Upon Foreign Policy and Diplomacy: open diplomacy revisited.* The University of Michigan Press, 1965.

CLAUDE, JR, INIS L. *Power and International Relations.* New York, Random House, 1962.

CLAUDE, JR, INIS L. *Swords Into Plowshares,* second edn. New York, Random House, 1959.

CLAUSEWITZ, CARL VON. *On War,* trans. J. J. Graham. 3 vols. London, Kegan Paul, 1940.

A Commentary on the Charter of the United Nations, Cmd 6666. HMSO, Miscellaneous no. 9, 1945.

CORBETT, PERCY E. *The Growth of World Law.* Princeton University Press, 1971.

CORDIER, A. W. and FOOTE, W. *The Quest for Peace: the Dag Hammarskjöld Memorial Lectures.* Columbia University Press, 1968.

CORDIER, ANDREW W. and MAXWELL, KENNETH L. *Paths to World Order.* Columbia University Press, 1967.

COX, ARTHUR M. *Prospects for Peacekeeping.* Washington, Brookings Institute, 1967.

DALLIN, ALEXANDER. *The Soviet Union at the United Nations.* New York, Praeger, 1962.

EGGE, BJORN and others, eds. *Peace Keeping, Experience and Evaluation: the Oslo Papers.* Oslo, Norwegian Institute of International Affairs, 1964.

EICHELBERGER, CLARK M. *New Dimensions for the U.N.: the problems of the next decade.* N.Y., Dobbs Ferry, Oceana, 1966.

EICHELBERGER, CLARK M. *United Nations: the first twenty years.* New York, Harper & Row, 1965.

EVATT, HERBERT VERE. *The United Nations.* Harvard University Press, 1948.

FABIAN, LARRY L. *Soldiers without Enemies—preparing the United Nations for peacekeeping.* Washington, DC, Brookings Institution, 1971.

FALK, RICHARD A. and MENDLOVITZ, SAUL H. *The Strategy of World Order,* vol. III. New York, The United Nations, World Law Fund, 1966.

FINKELSTEIN, LAWRENCE S. *The United States and International Organization.* Massachusetts Institute of Technology, 1969.

FULBRIGHT, J. WILLIAM. *The Arrogance of Power.* New York, Random House, 1966.

GARDNER, RICHARD N., ed. *Blue Print for Peace, being the proposal of prominent Americans to the White House Conference on International Co-operation.* New York, McGraw-Hill, 1966.

GARDNER, RICHARD N. *In Pursuit of World Order: United States policy and international organizations,* rev. edn. New York, Praeger, 1966.

GORDENKER, LEON. *The U.N. Secretary-General and the Maintenance of Peace.* Columbia University Press, 1967.

GOODRICH, LELAND M. *The United Nations.* New York, Crowell, 1959.

GOODRICH, LELAND M., HAMBRO, EDVARD, and SIMONS, ANNE PATRICIA. *Charter of the United Nations: commentary and documents.* Columbia University Press, 1969.

GOODRICH, LELAND M. and SIMONS, ANNE P. *The United Nations and the Maintenance of International Peace and Security.* Washington, DC, Brookings Institution, 1955.

GOODWIN, GEOFFREY L. *Britain and the United Nations.* Oxford University Press, 1957.

GROSS, ERNEST A. *The United Nations: structure for peace.* Published for the Council on Foreign Relations, New York, Harper & Row, 1962.

GROSS, FRANZ B. *The United States and the United Nations.* University of Oklahoma Press, 1964.

HAAS, ERNEST B. *Collective Security and the Future of the International System. System.* University of Denver Press, 1968.

HALLE, LOUIS. *The Cold War as History.* New York, Harper & Row, 1967.

HARBOTTLE, MICHAEL. *The Blue Berets.* London, Leo Cooper, 1971.

HARBOTTLE, MICHAEL. *The Impartial Soldier.* Oxford University Press, 1970.

HASLUCK, PAUL. *Workshop of Security.* Melbourne and London, Cheshire, 1948.

HEMLEBEN, SYLVESTER J. *Plans for World Peace through Six Centuries.* University of Chicago Press, 1945.

HENKIN, LOUIS. *How Nations Behave: law and foreign policy.* New York, Praeger, 1968.

HIGGINS, ROSALYN. *The Administration of the United Kingdom Foreign Policy Through the United Nations.* New York, Maxwell School of Citizenship and Public Affairs, Syracuse University, 1966.

HIGGINS, ROSALYN. *The Development of International Law Through the Political Organ of the United Nations.* Oxford University Press, 1963.

HIGGINS, ROSALYN. *United Nations Peace Keeping 1946–1967, Documents and Commentary:* vol. I, *The Middle East,* vol. II, *Asia.* Oxford University Press, 1969, 1970.

HINSLEY, F. H. *Power and the Pursuit of Peace.* Cambridge University Press, 1963.

VAN HORN, CARL. *Soldiering for Peace.* London, Cassell, 1966.

HOVET, TH. *Bloc Politics in the United Nations.* Harvard University Press, 1960.

JACOB, PHILIP E. and ATHERTON, ALWINA L. *The Dynamics of International Organizations: the making of world order.* Homewood, Ill., Dorey Press, 1965.

JAMES, ALAN. *The Politics of Peacekeeping.* London, Chatto & Windus for ISS, 1969.

JAMES, ALAN. *The Role of Force in International Order and U.N. Peace-Keeping,* Ditchley Paper no. 20. The Ditchley Foundation, 1969.

JAMES, ROBERT RHODES. *Britain's Role in the United Nations.* United Nations Association of Great Britain and Northern Ireland, 1970.

JESSUP, PHILIP C. *The International Problem of Governing Mankind.* Claremont, California, 1947.

JOHNSON, LYNDON BAINES. *The Vantage Point: perspectives of the presidency 1963–1969.* New York, Holt, Rinehart & Winston, 1971.

KAHNG, TAE JIN. *Law, Politics and the Security Council.* The Hague, Martinus Nijhoff, 1964.

KENNAN, GEORGE F. *Russia, the Atom and the West.* New York, Oxford University Press, 1958.

KHAN, M. ZAFRULLA. *The General Assembly in U.N. and World Affairs* in Cordier and Foote, *The Quest for Peace.*

LALL, ARTHUR. *Modern International Negotiations: principles and practice.* Columbia University Press, 1966.

LALL, ARTHUR. *The Security Council in a Universal United Nations,* New York, Carnegie Endowment for International Peace, Occasional Paper no. 11. 1971.

LASH, JOSEPH P. *Dag Hammarskjöld.* London, Cassell, 1962.

LIE, TRYGVE. *In the Cause of Peace, Seven Years With the United Nations.* New York, The Macmillan Company, 1954.

LIPPMAN, WALTER. *Public Opinion and Foreign Policy in the United States.* London, Allen & Unwin, 1952.

LIPPMAN, WALTER. *The Public Philosophy.* London, Hamish Hamilton, 1955.

LUARD, EVAN, ed. *The Evolution of International Organizations.* London, Thames & Hudson, 1966.

MCIVER, R. M. *The Nations and the United Nations*. New York, Manhattan Publishing Co., 1959.

MCLAURIA, JOHN. *The United Nations and Power Politics*. London, Allen & Unwin, 1951.

MARTIN, ANDREW. *Collective Security*. Paris, UNESCO, 1952.

MARTIN, ANDREW and EDWARDS, JOHN B. S. *The Changing Charter: a study in the reform of the United Nations*. London, Sylvan Press, 1955.

MARTIN, PAUL. *Canada and the Quest for Peace*. Columbia University Press, 1967.

MURRAY, GILBERT. *From the League to U.N.* Oxford University Press, 1948.

MURRAY, GILBERT. *The Problem of Foreign Policy*. London, Allen & Unwin, 1921.

MURRAY, GILBERT. *An Unfinished Autobiography*, ed. Jean Smith and Arnold Toynbee. London, Allen & Unwin, 1960.

NEF, JOHN U. *War and Human Progress: An Essay on the Rise of Industrial Civilization*. Harvard University Press, 1950.

NICHOLAS, H. G. *The United Nations as a Political Institution*, fourth edn. Oxford University Press, 1971.

NORTHEDGE, F. S. *The Settlement of International Disputes*. David Davies Annual Memorial Lecture, 1969. London, The David Davies Memorial Institute of International Studies,.

NORTHEDGE, F. S. and DONELAN, M. D. *International Disputes—the Political Aspects*. London, Europa Publications, 1971.

O'BRIEN, CONOR CRUISE. *Conflicting Concepts of the United Nations*. Leeds University Press, 1964.

O'BRIEN, CONOR CRUISE and TOPOLSKI, FELIKS, *United Nations: Sacred Drama*. London, Hutchinson, 1968.

OSGOOD, ROBERT E. and TUCKER, ROBERT W. *Force, Order and Justice.*Baltimore, Johns Hopkins Press, 1967.

PEARSON, LESTER B. *Democracy in World Politics*. Princeton University Press, 1955.

PEARSON, LESTER B. *Diplomacy in the Nuclear Age*. Harvard University Press, 1959.

PEARSON, LESTER B. *The Four Faces of Peace and the International Outlook*. New York, Dodd, Mead, 1964.

PEARSON, LESTER B. *Peace in the Family of Man*. The Reith Lectures, 1968, London, BBC, 1969.

PEARSON, LESTER B., GROSS, ERNEST A. and DEAN, SIR PATRICK. *A Critical Evaluation of the United Nations*. University of British Columbia Press, 1961.

PECHOTA, VRATISLAV. *Complementary Structures of Third-Party Settlement of International Disputes*. New York, United Nations Institute for Training and Research, 1971.

REUTER, PAUL. *International Institutions*, trans. J. M. Chapman. London, Allen & Unwin, 1958.

RUBINSTEIN, ALVIN Z. *The Soviets in International Organizations: changing policy toward developing countries: 1953–1963*. Princeton University Press, 1964.

RUSSELL, BERTRAND. *Common Sense and Nuclear Warfare*. London, Allen & Unwin, 1959.

RUSSELL, RUTH B. *A History of the United Nations Charter: the role of the United States, 1940–1945*. Washington, DC, Brookings Institution, 1958.

RUSSELL, RUTH B. *The United Nations and United States Security Policy*. Washington, DC, Brookings Institution, 1968.

SCOTT, WILLIAM A. and WITHEY, STEPHEN B. *The United States and the United Nations: The Public View 1945–1955*. New York, Manhattan Publishing Company, 1958.

SCHEINMAN, LAWRENCE. 'Nuclear safeguards, the peaceful atom, and the IAEA', *International Conciliation*, March 1969. New York, The Carnegie Endowment for International Peace.

SHULMAN, MARSHAL D. *Stalin's Foreign Policy Reappraised*. Harvard University Press, 1963.

SPAAK, PAUL HENRI. *Combats Inachevés*. 2 vols. Paris, Fayard, 1969.

STAWELL, F. M. *The Growth of International Thought*. London, Butterworth, 1929.

STEVENSON, ADLAI S. *Looking Outward: years of crisis at the United Nations*. Collection of speeches and papers, ed. Robert L. and Selma Schiffer. New York, Harper & Row, 1964.

STOESSINGER, JOHN G. *Nations in Darkness: China, Russia, and America*. New York, Random House, 1971.

STOESSINGER, JOHN G. *The United Nations and the Super Powers*. New York, Random House, 1965.

TAVARES DE SA, HERNANE. *The Play Within the Play*. New York, Knopf, 1966.

TAYLOR, ALASTAIR M. *Indonesian Independence and the United Nations*. London, Stevens, 1960.

TOWNLEY, RALPH. *The United Nations: a view from within*. New York, Scribner's Sons, 1968.

TRUMAN, HARRY S. *Memoirs*. 2 vols. New York, Doubleday, 1955–56.

VANDENBERG, JR., ARTHUR H. *The Private Papers of Senator Vandenberg*. Boston, Houghton Mifflin, 1952.

WARD, BARBARA, *Nationalism and Ideology*. London, Hamish Hamilton, 1967.

WARD, BARBARA and DUBOS, RENÉ. *Only One Earth*. New York, Norton 1972.

WEBSTER, C. K. *The Art and Practice of Diplomacy*. London, Chatto & Windus, 1961.

WEILER, LAWRENCE B. and SIMONS, ANNE PATRICIA. *The United States and the United Nations: a search for international peace and security*. Prepared for the Carnegie Endowment for International Peace. New York, Manhattan Publishing Company, 1967.

WILCOX, FRANCIS O. and HAVILAND, JR., H. FIELD. *The United States and the United Nations*. Baltimore, Johns Hopkins Press, 1961.

WILCOX, FRANCIS O. and MARCY, CARL M. *Proposals for Change in the U.N.* Washington, DC, Brookings Institution, 1955.

WINT, GUY. *What Happened in Korea? A study in collective security*. London, Batchworth Press, 1954.

WOLFERS, ARNOLD, ed. *Alliance Policy in the Cold War*. Baltimore, Johns Hopkins Press, 1959.

WRIGHT, QUINCY. *International Law and the United Nations*. Bombay, London, New York, Asia Publishing House, 1960.

WRIGHT, QUINCY. *On Predicting International Relations, the Year 2000*. University of Denver, 1969.

WRIGHT, QUINCY. *A Study of War*, second edn, with a Commentary on War since 1942. University of Chicago Press, 1965.

YOST, CHARLES. *The Insecurity of Nations: International Relations in the 20th Century*. Published for the Council on Foreign Relations, New York, Praeger, 1968.

YOUNG, ORAN R. *Trends in International Peacekeeping*. Research Monograph no. 22. Center of International Studies, Princeton University, 1966.

Articles and speeches

BEATON, LEONARD. 'The Great Powers abdicate', *International Journal*, Winter 1967–68.

BLOOMFIELD, LINCOLN P. 'Toward the U.N. and some bureaucratic reflections', *International Organization*, Winter 1958.

BLOOMFIELD, LINCOLN P. 'Peace keeping and peace making', *Foreign Affairs*, July 1966.

BLOOMFIELD, LINCOLN P. 'United Nations and national security', *Foreign Affairs*, July 1958.

BLOOMFIELD, LINCOLN P. 'The United States, the Soviet Union, and the prospects for peacekeeping', *International Organization*, Summer 1970.

BULL, HEDLEY. 'World opinion and international organization', *International Relations*, April 1958.

CHEEVER, DANIEL S. 'The role of the United Nations in the conduct of US foreign policy', *World Politics*, 1950.

CLAUDE, JR., INIS L. 'The management of power in the changing U.N.', *International Organization*, Spring 1961.

CLAUDE, JR., INIS L. 'Multilateralism—diplomatic and otherwise', *International Organization*, Winter 1958.

CLAUDE, JR., INIS L. 'The symbolic significance of the United Nations', *The Virginia Quarterly Review*, Autumn 1971, no. 4.

CLAUDE, JR., INIS L. 'The United Nations and the use of force', *International Conciliation*, March 1961.

COHEN, BENJAMIN V. 'The impact of the U.N. on U.S. foreign policy', *International Organization*, May 1951.

COHEN, BENJAMIN V. 'The United Nations in its 20th year', *International Organization*, Spring 1966.

COURTNEY, KATHLEEN D. 'The United Nations in a divided world', *International Affairs*, April 1949.

DIXON, SIR PIERSON. 'Diplomacy and the U.N.,' *International Relations*, October 1958.

EMERSON, ROBERT. 'Reflections on the Indonesian case', *World Politics*, October 1948.

EMERSON, RUPERT and CLAUDE, JR., INIS L. 'The Soviet Union and the United Nations: an essay and interpretation', *International Organization*, February 1952.

FRIEDMANN, WOLFGANG. 'The role of international law and the conduct of international affairs', *International Journal*, Spring 1965.

FRYE, WILLIAM R. 'Press coverage of the U.N.', *International Organization*, May 1956.

FULBRIGHT, J. WILLIAM. 'For a concert of free nations', *Foreign Affairs*, October 1961.

GAGNON, MONA HARRINGTON, 'Peace forces and the veto: the relevance of consent', *International Organization*, Autumn 1967.

GOODRICH, LELAND M. 'The maintenance of international peace and security', *International Organization*, Summer 1965.

GOODRICH, LELAND M. 'Peace enforcement in perspective', *International Journal*, Autumn 1969.

GOODRICH, LELAND M. 'The U.N. Security Council', *International Organization*, Summer 1958.

GOODWIN, GEOFFREY. 'The expanding United Nations, I. Voting patterns', *International Affairs*, April 1960.

GOODWIN, GEOFFREY. 'The political role of the United Nations: some British views', *International Organization*, Autumn 1961.

GOODWIN, GEOFFREY. 'The role of the United Nations in world affairs', *International Affairs*, January 1958.

GOODWIN, G. L. 'The United Nations: expectations and experience', *International Relations*, November 1970.

GORDENKER, LEON. 'U Thant and the office of the U.N. Secretary-General', *International Journal*, Winter 1966–67.

HAAS, ERNEST B. 'Regionalism, functionalism and universal international organization', *World Politics*, January 1956.

HOFFMANN, STANLEY. 'Erewhon or Lilliput—a critical view of the problem', *International Organization*, Spring 1963.

HOFFMANN, STANLEY. 'International organization: limits and possibilities', *International Organization*, August 1956.

HOFFMANN, STANLEY. 'National attitudes and international order: the national studies on international organization', *International Organization*, Spring 1959.

HOLMES, JOHN W. 'Canada's role in the United Nations', *Air University Review* (Department of the Air Force, Washington), May–June 1967.

HOLMES, JOHN W. 'The political and philosophical aspects of U.N. security forces', *International Journal*, Summer 1964.

HYDE, JAMES M. 'U.S. participation in the U.N.', *International Organization*, February 1956.

International Affairs. A special issue to mark the fiftieth anniversary of Chatham House. Includes the following relevant articles: H. G. NICHOLAS, 'From League to United Nations'; L. W. MARTIN, 'The changed role of military power'; J. E. S. FAWCETT, 'The development of international law'; Oxford University Press for the Royal Institute of International Affairs, 1970.

JAMES, ALAN. 'U.N. action for peace, I. Barrier forces. II. Law and other forces', *The World Today*, November and December 1962.

JEBB, SIR GLADWYN. 'The free world and the United Nations', *Foreign Affairs*, April 1953.

JACKSON, ELMORE. 'The developing role of the Secretary-General', *International Organization*, Summer 1957.

JOHNSON, HOWARD C. and NIEMEYER, GERHARD. 'Collective security: the validity of an ideal', *International Organization*, February 1954.

JOHNSON, JOSEPH E. 'The Soviet Union, the United States and international security', *International Organization*, February 1949.

KIRK, GRAYSON. 'The Atlantic Pact and international security', *International Organization*, May 1949.

KIRK, GRAYSON: 'The United Nations Charter: development and text. The Security Council,' *International Conciliation*, November 1953.

LASH, JOSEPH P. 'Dag Hammarskjöld's conception of his office', *International Organization*, Summer 1962.

LERNER, DANIEL and KRAMER, MARGUERITE N. 'French elite perspectives on the United Nations', *International Organization*, Winter 1963.

MCNAUGHT, KENNETH. 'Ottawa and Washington look at the U.N.', *Foreign Affairs*, July 1955.

MILLER, THOMAS B. 'The Commonwealth and the United Nations', *International Organization*, Autumn 1962.

MITRANY, DAVID. 'The United Nations in historical perspective', *International Relations*, November 1970.

MURRAY, G. S. 'United Nations peace-keeping and problems of political control', *International Journal*, Autumn 1963.

NICHOLAS, HERBERT. 'U.N. peace forces and the changing globe: the lessons of Suez and Congo', *International Organization*, Spring 1963.

NICHOLAS, H. G. 'The United Nations in crisis', *International Affairs*, July 1965.

NORTHEDGE, F. S. 'Law and politics between nations', *International Relations*, April 1957.

PADDLEFORD, NORMAN J. 'Financial crisis and the future of the United Nations', *World Politics*, July 1963.

PADDLEFORD, NORMAN J. 'Politics and change in the Security Council', *International Organization*, Summer 1960.

PADDLEFORD, NORMAN J. 'Regional organization and the United Nations', *International Organization*, May 1954.

PEARSON, LESTER B. 'The present position of the United Nations', *International Relations*, October 1957.

RANA, SWADESH. 'The changing Indian diplomacy at the United Nations', *International Organization*, Winter 1970.

RUDZINSKI, ALEXANDER W. 'The influence of the U.N. on Soviet policy', *International Organization*, May 1951.

SCHWARZ, URS. 'Great power intervention in the modern world', *Adelphi Paper* no. 55, London, Institute of Strategic Studies, 1969.

SOHN, LOUIS B. 'The authority of the U.N. to establish and maintain a permanent U.N. force', *American Journal of International Law*, vol. 52, 1958.

SALTER, SIR ARTHUR. 'The U.N. and the atomic bombs', *International Conciliation*, January 1946.

TANDON, Y. 'The peaceful settlement of international disputes', *International Relations*, April 1964.

URQUHART, BRIAN E. 'U.N. peace forces and the changing United Nations: an institutional perspective', *International Organization*, Spring 1963.

U THANT. Towards a second United Nations era: statement at Annual Dinner of 'U.N. We Believe', 18 September 1970. Press Release SG/SM/1335, 18 September 1970.

U THANT. 'U.N. Peace Force', Address to the Harvard Alumni Association, Cambridge, Mass., 13 June 1963, in L. P. Bloomfield, *International Military Forces*.

VALLETT, F. A. 'The General Assembly and the Security Council of the United Nations'. in *The British Year Book of International Law 1952*. Oxford University Press, 1953.

WILCOX, FRANCIS O. 'The Atlantic Community and the United Nations', *International Organization*, Summer 1963.

WILCOX, FRANCIS O. 'Regionalism and the United Nations', *International Organization*, Summer 1965.

WRIGHT, QUINCY. 'International conflict and the United Nations', *World Politics*, October 1957.

YOST, CHARLES W. 'The United Nations: crisis of confidence and will', *Foreign Affairs*, October 1966.

YOST, CHARLES W. 'World order and American responsibility', *Foreign Affairs*, October 1968.

Sectional

CHAPTER 1: INTRODUCTION

Books and monographs

AQUINAS. *Selected Political Writings*, ed. A. P. D'Entreves, trans. J. G. Dawson. Oxford, Blackwell, 1948.

KANT, IMMANUEL. *Perpetual Peace*, ed. L. W. Beck. The Library of Liberal Arts, New York, Bobbs-Merrill, 1957.

KANT, IMMANUEL. *Principles of Politics*, ed. and trans. W. Hastie. Edinburgh, T. and T. Clark, 1891. Containing: *The Idea of a Universal History from a Cosmopolitan Point of View;* and *The Principles of Progress, considered in connection with the Relation of Theory to Practice in International Law*.

Articles and speeches

Bourke, John. 'Kant's doctrine of perpetual peace', *Philosophy*, 1942, p. 330·

DRAPER, GERALD. 'The Idea of the Just War', *The Listener*, 14 August 1955.

CHAPTER 2: BACKGROUND

Books and monographs

Albrecht-Carrié, René. *The Concert of Europe*. New York and London, Harper & Row (Torch Books), 1968.

ANGELL, NORMAN. *After All*. London, Hamish Hamilton, 1951.

ANGELL, NORMAN. *Defence and the English-Speaking World*. London, Pall Mall Press, 1958.

342   Bibliography

ANGELL, NORMAN. *The Great Illusion*. London, Heinemann, 1910.

BASSETT, REGINALD G. *Democracy and Foreign Policy: a case history, the Sino-Japanese dispute 1931–33*. London, Longmans, 1952.

BEALES, A. C. F. *The History of Peace*. New York, Dial Press, 1931.

CECIL, VISCOUNT, OF CHELWOOD. *All the Way*. London, Hodder & Stoughton, 1949.

CECIL, VISCOUNT, OF CHELWOOD. *A Great Experiment: an autobiography*. London, Cape, 1941.

CONWELL-EVANS, T. P. *The League Council in Action*. Oxford University Press, 1929.

CRUTWELL, C. R. M. E. *History of Peaceful Change in the Modern World*. Oxford University Press, 1937.

DARBY, W. EVANS. *International Tribunals*, fourth ed. London, Dent, 1904.

DICKINSON, G. LOWES. *The International Anarchy, 1904–1914*. London, Allen & Unwin, 1926.

FLEMING, D. F. *The United States and the League of Nations 1918–20*. New York, Putnam, 1932.

HOLBRAAD, CARSTEN. *The Concept of Europe: a study in German and British international theory, 1815–1914*. New York, Barnes & Noble, 1971.

MCCALLUM, R. B. *Public Opinion and the Last Peace*. Oxford University Press, 1944.

MANTOUX, M. PAUL. 'Action of the Council of the League of Nations in International Disputes', in *The Problems of Peace*. Published for the Committee of the Geneva Institute of International Relations by Oxford University Press, 1927.

MOWATT, R. B. *The Concert of Europe*. London, Macmillan, 1930.

MURRAY, GILBERT. *The League of Nations Movement: some recollections of the early days*. London, David Davies memorial, Institute of International Studies, 1955.

MURRAY, GILBERT. 'A survey of recent world affairs', in *Problems of Peace: eighth series*. Published for the Committee of the Geneva Institute of International Relations by Oxford University Press, New York, 1934.

PHILLIPS, W. A. *The Confederation of Europe*, second edn. London, Longmans, 1920.

POLITIS, N. *La Justice Internationale*. Paris, Librairie Hachette, 1924.

POLLOCK, SIR FREDERICK. *The League of Nations*. London, Stevens, 1920.

RALSTON, JACKSON H. *International Arbitration from Athens to Locarno*. Stanford University Press, 1929.

RAPPARD, WILLIAM E. 'Nationalism and the League of Nations today' in *Problems of Peace: eighth series*. Published for the Committee of the Geneva Institute of International Relations by Oxford University Press, New York, 1934.

RAPPARD, WILLIAM E. *The Quest for Peace*. Harvard University Press, 1940.

ROOSEVELT, THEODORE. *America and the World War*. New York, Scribner's Sons, 1915.

ROOSEVELT, THEODORE. 'Utopia and Hell', *The Independent*, 4 January 1915.

SALTER, SIR ARTHUR. *Security: Can We Retrieve It?* London, Macmillan, 1939.

SHOTWELL, JAMES T. and SALVIN, MARINA. *Lessons on Security and Disarmament from the History of the League of Nations.* New York, Carnegie Endowment for International Peace, 1949.

WALTERS, F. P. *A History of the League of Nations.* Oxford University Press, 1952.

WOOLF, L. S. *International Government.* London, Allen & Unwin, 1916.

ZIMMERN, ALFRED. *The League of Nations and the Rule of Law, 1918–1935,* second edn. London, Macmillan, 1939.

Articles and Speeches

LODGE, SIR OLIVER. 'The irrationality of war', *International Conciliation,* 1912.

RAPPARD, WILLIAM E. 'What is the League of Nations?', *International Conciliation,* 1938.

CHAPTER 3: THE COUNCIL IN THEORY AND PRACTICE

Document

Postwar Foreign Policy Preparation 1939–45. Department of State Publication 3580. Washington, Government Printing Office, 1949.

Books and monographs

The Charter of the United Nations and the Covenant of the League of Nations. UN Department of Information, Research Section, 23 June 1947.

Articles and speeches

GOODRICH, LELAND M. 'From the League of Nations to the United Nations', *International Organization,* February 1947.

CHAPTER 4: PROCEDURE

Books and monographs

BAILEY, SYDNEY D. *Voting in the Security Council.* Indiana University Press, 1969.

CHAI, F. Y. *Consultation and Consensus in the Security Council.* New York, UNITAR, 1971.

Articles and speeches

PADDLEFORD, NORMAN J. 'The use of the veto', *International Organization,* June 1948.

RESTON, JAMES B. 'Votes and vetos', *Foreign Affairs,* October 1946.

TEJA, JASKARAN S. 'Expansion of the Security Council and its consensus procedure', *Netherlands International Law Review* (Leiden). vol. XVI, no. 4, 1969.

CHAPTER 5: THE COUNCIL'S RECORD

THE COLD WAR: THE EARLY STAGES

Books and monographs

FATEMI, NASROLLAH SAIFPOUR. *Oil Diplomacy—Powderkeg in Iran.* New York, Whittier, 1954.

SMITH, M. H. 'Indonesian independence: an example of United Nations peacemaking' (unpublished M.A. dissertation, University of Sussex, 1970).

VAN WAGENEN, RICHARD W. *The Iranian Case 1946.* New York, Carnegie Endowment for International Peace, 1952.

Articles and Speeches

VAN DER VEUR, PAUL W. 'The United Nations in West Iran', *International Organization,* Winter 1964.

THE MIDDLE EAST

Documents

Report by the Secretary-General on the Activities of the Special Representative to the Middle East. UN Security Council, S/10074, 4 Jan. 1971.

Books and monographs

BAR ZOHAR, MICHAEL. *The Armed Prophet: a biography of Ben Gurion,* Trans. Len Ortzen. London, Arthur Barker, 1967.

BURNS, LT. GEN. E. L. M. *Between Arab and Israel.* New York, Ivan Obolenski, 1962.

NUTTING, ANTHONY. *No End of a Lesson: the story of Suez.* London, Constable, 1967.

Articles and speeches

BURNS, E. L. M. 'The withdrawal of UNEF and the future of peacekeeping', *International Journal,* Winter 1967–68.

CURTIS, GERALD L. 'The UN observation group in Lebanon', *International Organization,* Autumn 1964.

GOODRICH, LELAND M. and ROSNER, GABRIELLA C. 'The United Nations Emergency Force', *International Organization,* Summer 1957.

HOWARD, MICHAEL, and HUNTER, ROBERT. *Israel and the Arab World: the crisis of 1967.* Adelphi Papers, no. 41. London, Institute for Strategic Studies, 1967.

MURPHY, JOHN F., HARGROVE, JOHN LAWRENCE., BASSIOUNI, M. CHERIF, and MOORE, JOHN NORTON. Symposium: 'The Middle East Crisis', *Kansas Law Review,* vol. XIX, no. 3, Spring 1971.

ROOSEVELT, KERMIT. 'The Partition of Palestine: a lesson in pressure politics', *Middle East Journal.* Jan. 1948.

KOREA

Books and monographs

GOODRICH, LELAND M. *Korea: A study of US policy in the United Nations.* New York, Council on Foreign Relations, 1956.

Articles and speeches

GOODRICH, LELAND M. 'Korea: collective measures against aggression', *International Conciliation,* October 1953.

INDIA AND PAKISTAN

Documents

Report of the Secretary-General on East Pakistan and the Indian sub-continent. UN Security Council, S/10410 of 3 December 1971.

Books and monographs

KORBEL, JOSEF. *Danger in Kashmir*, revised edn. Princeton University Press, 1966.

Articles and speeches

KORBEL, JOSEPH. 'The Kashmir dispute after six years', *International Organization*, November 1953.
LYON, PETER. 'Kashmir', *International Relations*, October 1966.
SCHARNBERG, SYDNEY H. 'Pakistan divided', *Foreign Affairs*, October 1971.
'UN's failure in Kashmir: a factual survey', *The Economic Weekly*, 2 October 1965, Bombay.

VIETNAM

Books and monographs

BLOOMFIELD, LINCOLN P. *The UN and Vietnam*. New York, Carnegie Endowment for International Peace, 1968.

AFRICA

Documents

LEGUM, COLIN, ed. *Africa Contemporary Record*. Annual Survey of Documents, 1970–71. London, Rex Collings, 1971.
Report of the Security Council Special Mission to the Republic of Guinea Established under Resolution 289 (1970). UN Security Council, S/10009 of 3 December 1970.

Books and monographs

GÉRARD-LIBOIS, J. *Avant le voyage royal: dix ans de relations Belgique-Congo*. Courrier Hebdomedain du CRISP, Brussels, Centre de Recherche et d'Information Socio-Politique, 1970.
GÉRARD-LIBOIS, JULES. *Katanga Secession*, trans. Rebecca Young. University of Wisconsin Press, 1966.
GÉRARD-LIBOIS, J. *Le Rôle de La Belgique dans l'operation des Nations Unies au Congo* (1960–1964). Brussels, Travaux Africains—Etudes de CRISP, 1971.
GÉRARD-LIBOIS, J. *UN Peacekeeping in the Congo*. Washington, D.C., Brookings Institution, 1965.
GORDON, KING. *The United Nations in the Congo: A Quest for Peace*. Carnegie Endowment for International Peace, 1962.
LEFEVER, ERNEST W. *Uncertain Mandate: politics of the United Nations Congo operation*. Baltimore, John Hopkins Press, 1967.

LEGUM, COLIN. *The United Nations and Southern Africa*, ISIO monographs, first series, no. 3. Institute for the Study of International Organization, University of Sussex, 1970.

LEISS, AMELIA C. *Apartheid and the United Nations Collective Measures: an analysis*. New York, Carnegie Endowment for International Peace, 1965.

O'BRIEN, CONOR CRUISE. *To Katanga and Back: a UN case history*. London, Hutchinson, 1962.

A Principle in Torment. I. *The United Nations in Southern Rhodesia*; II. *The United Nations and Portuguese Administered Territories*. New York, United Nations, 1969 and 1970.

TONDEL, JR., LYMAN M. (Editor). *The Legal Aspects of the United Nations in the Congo*. New York, Oceana Publications, 1963.

YOUNG, CRAWFORD. *Politics in the Congo: decolonisation and independence*. Princeton University Press, 1965.

Articles and speeches

VAN BILSEN, A. A. J. 'Some aspects of the Congo problem', *International Affairs*, January 1962.

DOXEY, MARGARET. 'The Rhodesian sanctions experiment' in *The Year Book of World Affairs, 1971*. vol. xxv. London, Stevens 1971.

HIGGINS, ROSALYN. 'The advisory opinion on Namibia: Which UN resolutions are Binding under Article 25 of the Charter?', *International and Comparative Law Quarterly*, April 1972.

HIGGINS, ROSALYN. 'The International Court and South West Africa: the implications of the judgment', *International Affairs*, October 1966.

HOLMES, JOHN W. 'United Nations and the Congo', *International Journal*, Winter 1960–61.

KAREFA-SMART, JOHN. 'Africa and the United Nations', *International Organization*, Summer 1965.

KAY, DAVID A. 'The impact of African states on the United Nations', *International Organization*, Winter 1969.

MARTELLI, GEORGE. 'Portugal and the United Nations', *International Affairs*, July 1964.

MAZRUI, ALI A. 'United Nations and some African political attitudes', *International Organization*, Summer 1964.

SPENCER, JOHN H. 'Africa and the United Nations: some resolutions', *International Organization*, Spring 1962.

WIGNY, PIERRE. 'Belgium and the Congo', *International Affairs*, July 1961.

THE UNITED STATES AND LATIN AMERICA

Documents

Background Information Relating to the Dominican Republic, printed for Committee on Foreign Relations, US Senate. Washington, D.C., US Government Printing Office, 1965.

Books and monographs

ABEL, ELIE. *The Missile Crisis*. Lippincott, Philadelphia, 1966.

CAREY, JOHN, ed. *The Dominican Republic Crisis 1965*. New York, Oceana Publications, 1967.

CONNELL-SMITH, GORDON. The Inter-American system: problems of peace and security in the western hemisphere', in Robert W. Gregg, ed., *International Organizations in the Western Hemisphere*. Syracuse University Press, 1968.

EISENHOWER, DWIGHT D. *Mandate for Change 1953–1956*. New York, Doubleday, 1963.

GREGG, R. W. ed. *International Organizations in the Western Hemisphere*. Syracuse University Press, 1968.

KENNEDY, ROBERT F. *Thirteen Days—A Memoir of the Cuban Missile Crisis*. New York, Norton, 1969.

MATTHEWS, HERBERT. *The United States and Latin America*. Headline Series, no. 100, New York, Foreign Policy Association, July-August, 1953.

PACHTER, HENRY M. *Collision Course, The Cuban Missile Crisis and Co-existence*. London, Pall Mall Press, 1963.

PORTER, CHARLES O. and ALEXANDER, ROBERT J. *The Struggle for Democracy in Latin America*. New York, The Macmillan Company, 1961.

SLATER, JEROME. *Intervention and Negotiation: the United States and the Dominican revolution*. London, Harper & Row, 1970.

SLATER, JEROME. *The OAS and United States Foreign Policy*. Ohio State University Press, 1967.

SZULC, TED. *Dominican Diary*. New York, Delacorte Press, 1965.

SZULC, TED, ed. *The United States and the Caribbean* (The American Assembly, Columbia University), Englewood Cliffs, NJ, Prentice-Hall, 1971.

SZULC, TED and MEYER, KARL E. *The Cuban Invasion: the chronicle of disaster*. New York, Ballantine Books, 1962.

WHITTACKER, ARTHUR P. 'Guatemala, O.A.S. and U.S.', *Foreign Policy Bulletin*, vol. XXXIII, no. 24, September 1964.

WIARDA, HOWARD J. *The Dominican Republic: nation in transition*. New York, Praeger, 1969.

Articles and speeches

CLAUDE, jr., INIS L. 'The O.A.S., the U.N. and the United States', *International Conciliation*, March 1964; New York, Carnegie Endowment for International Peace.

DRAPER, THEODORE. 'A case of defamation: US intelligence versus Juan Bosch', *The New Republic*, 19 and 26 February 1966.

DRAPER, THEODORE. 'The Dominican crisis: a case in American policy', *Commentary*, December 1965.

LOWENTHAL, ABRAHAM F. 'The Dominican intervention in retrospect', *Public Policy*, Fall 1969.

OGLESBY, J. C. M. 'The prospects for democracy in the Dominican Republic', *International Journal*, Spring 1966.

SLATER, JEROME. 'The limits of legitimization in international organizations: the organization of American States and the Dominican crisis; *International Organization*, Winter 1969.

TAYLOR, jr., PHILLIP B. 'The Guatemalan affair: a critique of U.S. foreign policy', *American Political Science Review*, September 1956.

CYPRUS

Documents

Report by the Secretary-General on the United Nations Operations in Cyprus (for the period 2 June 1970 to 1 December 1970). UN, Security Council, S/10005, 2 December 1970.

Articles and speeches

GORDON, J. KING. 'The UN in Cyprus'. *International Journal*, Summer 1964.
HIGGINS, ROSALYN. 'Basic facts on the UN force in Cyprus', *The World Today* August 1964.

CHAPTER 6: THE SECURITY COUNCIL AS A FORUM AND A RENDEZVOUS

Documents

Report of the Special Committee on the Problem of Hungary. UN General Assembly, Official Records, Eleventh Session. Supplement no. 18 (A/3592), United Nations, New York, 1957.

Books and monographs

ARMBRISTER, TREVOR. *The Matter of Accountability: a true story of the 'Pueblo, affair*, London, Barrie & Jenkins, 1971.
DAVISON, W. PHILLIPS. *The Berlin Blockade*. Princeton University Press 1958.
JAMES, ROBERT RHODES, ed. *The Czechoslovak Crisis 1968*. Institute for the Study of International Organization, University of Sussex, London, Weidenfeld & Nicolson, 1969.
KORBEL, JOSEPH. *The Communist Subversion of Czechoslovakia: the failure of coexistence*. Princeton University Press, 1959.

CHAPTER 7: PROBLEMS OF PEACE-KEEPING

Documents

Letter and Document entitled 'Basic guiding principles for the conduct of United Nations peace-keeping operations including United Nations Observer Missions', submitted by the USSR to the Secretary-General, 17 March 1972. UN General Assembly document A/8669 of 20 May 1972.
Letter and Memorandum on Establishment and Conduct of United Nations Peace-keeping Operations which are Authorized by the Security Council, submitted by the USA to the Secretary-General, 30 March 1972. UN General Assembly document A/8676 of 3 April 1972.

Books and monographs

FRYE, W. R. *A U.N. Peace Force*. New York, Oceana Publications, 1957.
SCHWARZENBERGER, GEORG. *Report on Problems of a United Nations Force*. International Law Association. Hamburg Conference, 1960.

Articles and speeches

EASTMAN, S. MACK. 'The United Nations Guard: historical background', *International Journal*, Spring 1949.

HAEKKERUP, PER. 'Scandinavia's peace-keeping forces for UN, *Foreign Affairs*, July 1964.

HIGGINS, ROSALYN. 'United Nations peace-keeping—political and financial problems', *The World Today*, August 1965.

RIKHYE, MAJOR-GENERAL I. J. *Preparation and Training of United Nations Peace-keeping Forces*, Adelphi Paper no. 9. London, Institute for Strategic Studies, 1964.

TACKABERRY, R. B. 'Organizing and training peace-keeping forces: the Canadian view', *International Journal*, Spring 1967.

CHAPTER 8: THE SECURITY COUNCIL AND THE GENERAL ASSEMBLY

Books and monographs

EPSTEIN, WIDIAN. *Disarmament: twenty-five years of effort*. Toronto, Canadian Institute of International Affairs, 1971.

TACKABERRY, R. B. *Keeping the Peace: a Canadian military viewpoint on peace-keeping operations*. Toronto, Canadian Institute of International Affairs, 1966.

The United Nations and Disarmament, 1945–1970. New York, United Nations, 1970.

Articles and speeches

PETERSEN, KEITH S. 'The use of the Uniting for Peace Resolution since 1950', *International Organization*, Spring 1959.

VALLET, F. A. 'The General Assembly and the Security Council of the United Nations', in *The British Yearbook of International Law*, 1952, Oxford University Press, 1953.

CHAPTER 9: FUTURE PROSPECTS

Documents

Development Co-operation: 1972 Review, OECD, 1972

Memorandum of the Government of Brazil on the strengthening of international security. UN Security Council document S/9786 of 8 May 1970.

Books and monographs

JOHNSON, BRIAN. *The United Nations System and the Human Environment*. ISIO monographs, first series, no. 5. University of Sussex, Institute for the Study of International Organization, 1971.

Articles and Speeches

GARDNER, RICHARD N. 'Can the United Nations be revived?', *Foreign Affairs*, July 1970.

Index

Headquarters of UN, 78, 99, 262, 263, 264
Heath, Edward, 226
Henkin, Louis, *cited*, 142n., 249–50
Higgins, Dr Rosalyn, *cited*, 113n., 115n., 138n., 139n., 147n., 148n., 165, 175n., 271n., 272n., 275n.
Hijacking, case of, 107
Hillery, Dr Patrick John, 247
Hitler, Adolf, 44, 47, 48, 51, 67, 100, 136, 140, 170n., 259
Hoare, Sir Samuel, 47, 48
Hoare-Laval plan, 48
Holy Alliance, Declaration of the, 25
Honduras, 229, 230, 236
'Hot line', 150, 151, 294, 298
House, Col. Edward M., 32
Houston, Tom, 253n.
Howard, Michael and Hunter, Robert, *cited*, 147n.
Human rights, 54, 190–1, 214, 227, 238, 328; Universal Declaration of, 191, 217, 303–4. *See also* Apartheid, Racial discrimination
Hungarian question, 255, 256–8, 259, 292, 293, 294, 313; Special Committee on the Problem of Hungary, 257; Gen. Assembly's Special Representative on the Hungarian Question, 257
Hyderabad, *see* India

Ignatiev, George, 69n., 264
Ileo, Joseph, 202, 204
Imbert Barrera, Gen. Antonio, 235, 237, 239
India, 69, 97, 101, 129, 144, 168, 189n., 206, 306, 313, 316; Goa, 182–3, 313; Hyderabad, 168, 169–70, 171, 172, 183, 313; Junagadh, 168–9, 171, 172, 183, 313; peace-keeping operations, 145n., 147, 204n., 241, 269, 280; SC, part in, 111, 124, 125, 126, 315, 316. *See also* Bangladesh, Kashmir.
Indo-China, 125, 131, 184. *See also* Cambodia, Laos, Vietnam
Indonesia, 131, 200, 204n., 227, 315, 316: British troops in,

complaint of, 68, 119, 122; Netherlands, dispute with, 69, 96, 123–31, 226, 274 – Dutch attitude to, 123, 130, 252 – Dutch 'police action' and public reaction to, 124, 127, 128–9, 131, 170 – Hague Round-Table Conference, 130 – Linggadjati Agreement, 124, 127, 128 – Renville Agreement, 127–8 – Security Council consideration, 87, 93, 124, 125, 128, 129–30, 131, 250, 251 – SC members positions 125 – UN efforts for settlement, 125, 129, 130–1 – US pressure on Netherlands, 127, 128, 131; Malaysia, dispute with, 88, 188; West Irian (West New Guinea) 131–2. *See also* Consular Commission (Batavia), Security Council Committee of Good Offices for Indonesia (GOC), United Nations Commission for Indonesia (UNCI)
Indo-Pakistan hostilities, *see* Bangladesh, Kashmir
Inter-American System: conferences, 65n., 228, 229; treaties 64, 65n., 76. *See also* Organization of American States (OAS).
Interim Committee of the General Assembly (Little Assembly), 91, 289, 290
International Bank for Reconstruction and Development (World Bank), 140, 305
International Committee of the Red Cross, 88
International Court of Justice, 58, 66, 97, 170, 243–4: Advisory opinions, 66, 170, 216–17, 218, 231–2, 242, 274; Judgements, 122, 160–1, 217
International Labour Organization (ILO), 312
International Monetary Fund, 144
Inverchapel, Lord, 123
Investigations, *see* Enquiry
Iran, 279: Anglo-Iranian oil dispute, 160–1; Bahrein, 161–3; Soviet troops in, complaint of, 68, 116–18, 119, 122, 251
Iraq, 43, 138, 156, 158–9, 245

Printed in the United States
By Bookmasters